Mussolini,
Mustard Gas, and the
Fascist Way of War

Mussolini, Mustard Gas, and the Fascist Way of War

Ethiopia, 1935–1936

Charles Stephenson

Pen & Sword
MILITARY

AN IMPRINT OF PEN & SWORD BOOKS LTD
YORKSHIRE – PHILADELPHIA

First published in Great Britain in 2023 by
PEN & SWORD MILITARY
an imprint of Pen & Sword Books Ltd
Yorkshire – Philadelphia

Copyright © Charles Stephenson, 2023

ISBN 978-1-39905-166-8

The right of Charles Stephenson to be identified as the author of this work has been asserted by him in accordance with the Copyright, Designs and Patents Act 1988.

A CIP catalogue record for this book is available from the British Library.

All rights reserved. No part of this book may be reproduced or transmitted in any form or by any means, electronic or mechanical including photocopying, recording or by any information storage and retrieval system, without permission from the Publisher in writing.

Typeset by Concept, Huddersfield, West Yorkshire, HD4 5JL.
Printed and bound in England by CPI Group (UK) Ltd, Croydon, CR0 4YY.

Pen & Sword Books Ltd incorporates the imprints of Aviation, Atlas, Family History, Fiction, Maritime, Military, Discovery, Politics, History, Archaeology, Select, Wharncliffe Local History, Wharncliffe True Crime, Military Classics, Wharncliffe Transport, Leo Cooper, The Praetorian Press, Remember When, White Owl, Seaforth Publishing and Frontline Books.

For a complete list of Pen & Sword titles please contact
PEN & SWORD BOOKS LTD
47 Church Street, Barnsley, South Yorkshire, S70 2AS, England
E-mail: enquiries@pen-and-sword.co.uk
Website: www.pen-and-sword.co.uk
or
PEN & SWORD BOOKS
1950 Lawrence Rd, Havertown, PA 19083, USA
E-mail: uspen-and-sword@casematepublishers.com
Website: www.penandswordbooks.com

Contents

List of Plates vi
List of Maps viii
Introduction ix
  1. Del Boca and the 'irreducible Montanelli' 1
  2. The Sawdust Caesar 13
  3. 'a terrain of crag and precipice' 23
  4. 'Fascism believes neither in the possibility nor the utility of perpetual peace' 33
  5. War in the 'Old-Style' 41
  6. Graziani 53
  7. 'a small masterpiece' 63
  8. 'The Awful Warning' 71
  9. Keeping Mussolini awake at night 83
10. An 'African Thermopylae' 93
11. Amba Aradam 103
12. The Second Battle of Tembien and the Battle of Shire 113
13. Serdo and Gondar 123
14. The Emperor's Army 131
15. Totalitarian Motorisation 141
16. 'The March of the Iron Will' 157
17. 'a policy of terror and extermination' 167
Notes 183
Bibliography 231
Index 251

List of Plates

Mussolini on 5 May 1936.
Mussolini and Badoglio.
Emilio de Bono.
Badoglio in April 1936.
Badoglio observing the Battle of Amba Aradam.
Badoglio in 1943 with Allied war correspondents.
Graziani addressing his officers in Somalia-Ogaden.
Graziani as defence minister of the RSI.
Graziani at his trial.
Galeazzo Ciano in 1939.
Victor Emmanuel III pictured next to Hitler and Mussolini in 1938.
Vittorio Mussolini.
Colonel Vittorio Ruggero and Sergeant Major Francesco de Martini at Beilul.
Haile Selassie.
Haile Selassie in 1935, manning an anti-aircraft gun.
Ras Desta Damtew.
Ras Getachew Abate.
Ras Imru Haile Selassie.
Ras Kassa Hailu.
Ras Mulugeta Yeggazu.
Ras Nasibu Zeamanuel.
Ras Seyoum Mengesha.
Italian troops in front of Amba Aradam in 1936.
Amba Aradam.
Amba Alagi.
Amba Alagi: an Italian column passing the mountain.
Amba Uork.

List of Plates   vii

Road building.

A 'rosary of trucks'.

A postcard advertising the *82° Battaglione CC.NN. 'Benito Mussolini'*.

Types of aircraft used in East Africa.

The *bomba C.500.T*, developed in early 1935 for the conquest of Ethiopia.

A pair of C.500.T bombs slung under a Caproni Ca.101.

An aeroplane over Amba Alagi.

The airfield constructed near Makalle.

* * *

The British Red Cross Field Hospital near Korem.

Gorrahei, on the southern front.

The L3/35 (or Carro Veloce CV-35) light tank.

Infantry using a Fiat-Revelli Modello 1914 medium machine gun.

Strafing. Sergeant Bacio Gallini, aircraft machine-gunner.

Lorry-mounted *dubats* in the Ogaden.

Mountain guns deployed by Alpine troops and transported by pack animals . . . and the African equivalent.

A Pavesi P4 towing what appears to be a *Cannone da 105/28*.

The Pavesi artillery tractor.

A Caterpillar train.

Each unit in the train consisted of one tractor and two (sometimes three) trailers.

Mastodontici autotreni (mammoth road trains).

'The Fascist Revolution is not only Italy's privilege and effort, but the watchword and hope of the world.'

A highly stylised rendition by Achille Beltrame of Blackshirts of the '28 October' Division defending the Uarieu (Worsege) Pass.

Ethiopian troops literally taking shelter under the Red Cross during the bombing of the British Field Hospital.

Members of the '23 March' Blackshirt Division planting the flag atop Amba Aradam.

Prince Filiberto of Savoy, Duke of Genoa and Duke of Pistoia.

List of Maps

Italian military operations during the Italo-Ethiopian War xii
East Africa showing Ethiopia and Eritrea: the northern front 25
Somalia and Ethiopia: the southern front 27
Key points on the northern front 42
The initial Italian advance from Eritrea 44
Key points on the southern front 55
Key points on the northern front 73
Key points pertaining to the Ethiopian counter-offensive 85
Key points relating to the First Battle of Tembien 95
Military movements during the First Battle of Tembien 96
The Battle of Amba Aradam 106
The Second Battle of Tembien and the Battle of Shire 116
Lieutenant Gianfranco Litta Modignani's advance across the Danakil to Serdo, and Achille Starace's fast column to Gondar 128
Key locations pertaining to the Battle of Maychew 134
The Battle of Maychew 137
Key locations related to Graziani's advance from Somalia 143
The Italian advance in three columns. 147
The Battle of Gianagobo. 149
'The March of the Iron Will' 164
Africa Orientale Italiana, 1936 173

Introduction

> To initiate a war of aggression ... is not only an international crime; it is the supreme international crime differing only from other war crimes in that it contains within itself the accumulated evil of the whole.
> [*Nuremberg Trial Proceedings*, Vol. 22: Monday, 30 September 1946][1]

* * *

The invasion of Ethiopia by Fascist Italy in October 1935 was an operation entirely of choice, a choice made by the leader, *Il Duce*, of Fascism, Benito Mussolini. The resultant conflict is often described as a colonial war. Whilst it was certainly launched with the intention of turning Ethiopia into an Italian possession, it was in fact a war of aggression against an independent, sovereign, state with membership of the League of Nations, a state that had, according to one of its nineteenth-century rulers, been 'for fourteen centuries a Christian island in a sea of pagans'.[2] This cut no ice with *Il Duce*; as he phrased it: 'Ethiopia is the last strip of Africa that has no European master.'[3] He intended to change that, and indeed to become that master. In order to do so he launched the first large-scale international conflict where air-power was a decisive factor.

It was then a war of aggression and annexation which, viewed from that perspective, is arguably comparable with the German invasion of Poland in 1939. In any event, it was the first large-scale act of that nature involving a European state since the end of the First World War in 1918. The British prime minister during the second half of that conflict, David Lloyd George, had once argued that 'a war of annexation ... against a proud people must be a war of extermination.'[4] That Ethiopians were a proud people seems beyond argument, as the British medical man Dr John Macfie noted:

> Since returning to Europe I have been asked again and again if I thought our efforts to assist the Ethiopian wounded and sick were appreciated. I must say I doubt it ... We were to them foreigners and perhaps they only dimly distinguished between us who were trying to help them, and those who were fighting against them.[5]

Thus, those Ethiopians who refused to accept Italian rule were subjected to a policy of, in Mussolini's words of July 1936, 'terror and extermination against rebels and accomplice populations'.[6]

The swiftness of the Italian victory resulted from their possession and ruthless use of technology that had either seen first use during, or come of age in, the First

World War; most particularly aircraft, mustard gas and motorisation. Since the Italians were fighting an enemy who possessed none of these things, then they were able to wage, indeed inaugurate, what the prominent military theorist J.F.C. Fuller, a self-described 'full-blooded Fascist', dubbed 'totalitarian warfare'. This, he opined, was the Fascist, the scientific, way of making war. In his considered view, the Fascist Army that waged it was 'a scientific military instrument'.

This work deals primarily with that campaign of military conquest, scientific or not, which was complete in May 1936. It also looks at the political context within which it occurred, the ominous backdrop being of course concern over a resurgent, and rearming, Germany under Hitler. Also discussed is Italian domestic 'amnesia', a condition which descended in respect of Ethiopia following Italy's traumatic participation in the Second World War and events thereof.

It is, though, not meant to be, and does not aspire to be, an academic work. There are no theoretical frameworks within which the tale is constructed, nor any new or startling conclusions or theses. It is then targeted at the general reader, rather than the specialist or professional historian, and seeks to advance a narrative on the course of the war, mainly from the Italian perspective.[7] It is not, however, a military treatise, and it does not attempt to offer blow-by-blow accounts of every battle, nor comprehensive lists of each and every unit engaged. Those who desire that level of detail will find all they could wish for and more in Luigi Emilio Longo's two-volume opus, *La Campagna Italo-Etiopica (1935–1936)*.[8]

Neither is this book grounded in original research based upon the careful scrutiny of archival sources; or rather it is, but none of this study is mine. Rather it draws upon, or perhaps ruthlessly plunders would be a more apt description, the original work of many, mainly Italian, scholars of eminence and attempts to weave their threads into a narrative. Chief amongst these scholars is that doyen of the subject, Angelo Del Boca, as well as Roberto Gentilli, Nicola Labanca, the aforementioned Longo, Ferdinando Pedriali, Giorgio Rochat and several others. Whatever the source, I have, in every case, taken care to attribute it correctly.

Many of these sources, unfortunately for those who don't read Italian, have yet to be translated into English. Where there is an English version of any given work, I have tended to use it. Otherwise, all translations are mine. One other point in terms of language: the country now universally known as Ethiopia was until fairly recently also called Abyssinia. Whilst I have adopted the modern form, I have not altered any quotations which differ so both versions will be encountered and can be taken as synonymous.

Finally, it remains for me to thank those who have been of great assistance in putting this work together. I am once again immensely grateful to Charles Blackwood for providing the excellent maps, for deploying his graphic skills with respect to the pictures, and for his good sense and advice on the work as a whole. I am similarly indebted to Michael Perratt, who allowed me to use him as a 'sounding board' as the text progressed, and for his suggestions regarding improvements. He provided what I consider the acid test to a volume of this sort: is it intelligible and accessible to the interested lay reader? Happily, he thought so. I am also, yet again, deeply grateful to Sarah Cook for deploying her superlative copy-editing skills on my behalf and thus greatly enhancing my draft text. Last, but by no means least, I am obligated to Isabel Axon for designing and producing the front-cover graphic.

As ever, though, any errors or defects that may be perceived in the work are my responsibility, and mine alone.

Charles Stephenson
November 2023

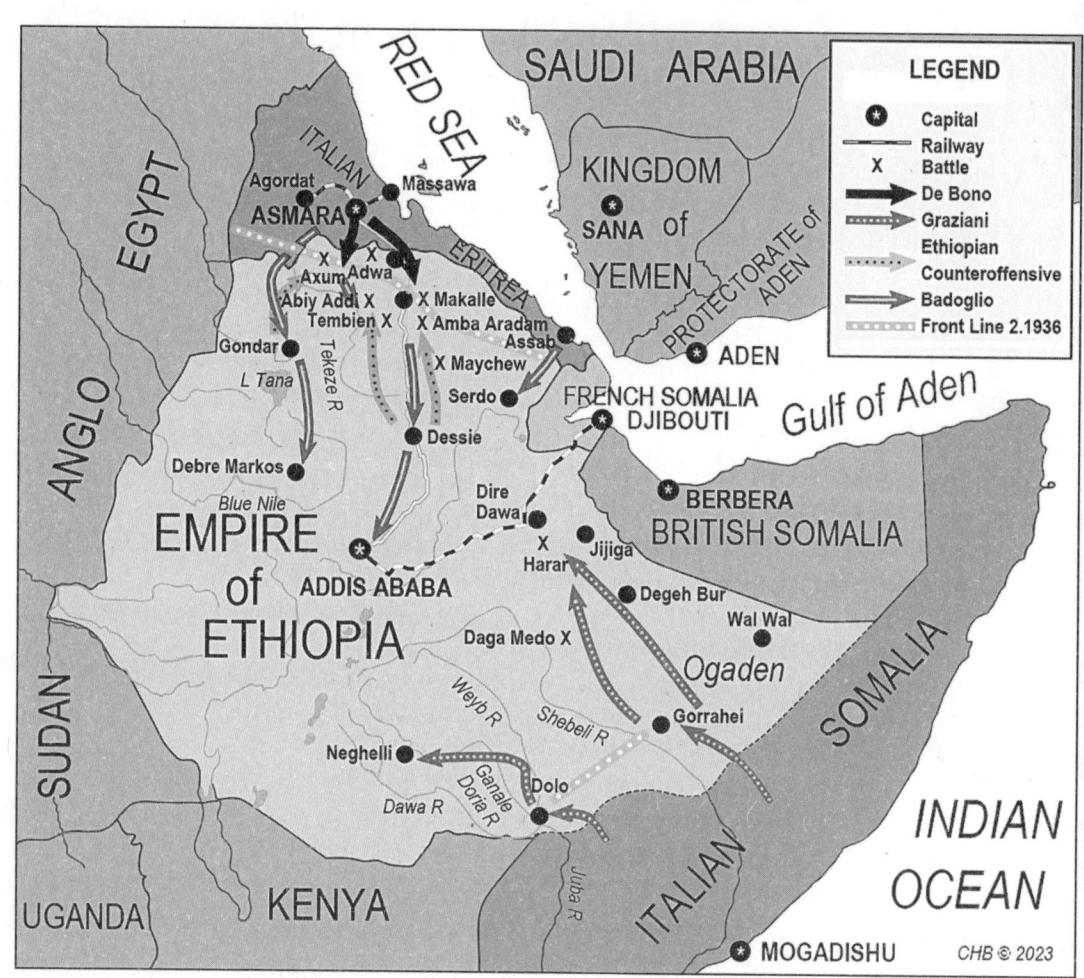

Italian military operations during the Italo-Ethiopian War. (© *Charles Blackwood*)

Chapter One

Del Boca and the 'Irreducible Montanelli'

It had taken thirty years and government intervention to break the irreducible Montanelli.[1]

* * *

The Black Lives Matter (BLM) protests which erupted in 2020 famously led to several statues and monuments, those which the protestors associated with racial injustice, being defaced or toppled. Though the majority of these were located in the United States, there were similar actions in Europe, notably the removal of the statues of Edward Colston at Bristol, England, on 7 June 2020 and of Leopold II at Ekeren, Belgium, two days later.[2] Less well known was the defacing of the statue of Indro Montanelli in Milan, Italy.[3] Unlike Colston and Leopold II, however, Montanelli was not a long-dead historical figure. Indeed, the bronze monument which, in the words of the authors of one of his biographies, 'embalmed him in imitation gold', had been inaugurated on 22 April 2006, the date of the subject's 97th birthday (albeit on his part the celebration was posthumous, since he had passed away five years earlier). This metallic *memoriale* sits in the *Giardini Indro Montanelli*, a public space renamed in his honour.[4]

Montanelli's fame came from his writing: 'his seventy years of activity left a lasting imprint on a large part of Italian public opinion, and on Italian journalistic nostrums. In republican Italy, Montanelli's pen remains unique.'[5] These 'seventy years' included a period when he acted as a young envoy, or correspondent, for *Civiltà fascista* (Fascist Civilization) in Italian East Africa and also commanded the XX *Battaglione eritreo* of *ascari* (locally recruited Eritrean soldiers).[6] *Civiltà fascista* was, as the oxymoronic title suggests, a Fascist propaganda journal, and its January 1936 edition included a piece by the young Montanelli:

> Racism, this is a catechism that, if we do not know it, we must hurry to learn and adopt it. We will never be rulers, if we do not have the exact awareness of our fatal superiority. You don't fraternize with blacks. It cannot be done. It should not be done. At least until they are given a civilization ... the White commands.[7]

This was written at a time when Italy was engaged in a war of conquest, an unashamedly imperial conflict waged by Mussolini's Fascist regime against Ethiopia, and such sentiments were no doubt widely, and certainly became officially, held.[8]

It must be said that Montanelli was in no way responsible for the way in which that war was waged. Further, he had broken with Fascism decisively, been captured by the Germans and sentenced to death in early 1944, and then escaped.[9] This version of events, largely based on Montanelli's account, is, however, contested.[10] Be that as it may, there can be no doubt that, in his post-war incarnation, Montanelli became one of the foremost defenders of the Italian colonialism he had been a part of, and written about, and its methods. He argued in 1949 that: 'I am convinced that our colonialism was, of all [European colonialism], the most human and the least inhumane: this is evidenced by the memory that the Ethiopians themselves, not to mention the Eritreans, retain for Italians.'[11]

That view, that Italians are decent people (*Italiani brava gente*), was propagated and widely accepted at that time and remained, and remains, so among large sections of the population. It is indeed a 'myth that dies hard'[12] and one with a lengthy pedigree: the military periodical *La Preparazione* had opined in 1909 that 'Italians never leave hateful memories behind them ... because of all the superior races ours is the least rapacious, the least overbearing, the most equal towards the inferior or subject races.'[13]

In fact most former colonial powers, or at least as gauged by press coverage, seem to consider that 'their' imperialism was the most enlightened.[14] Much more controversial was the admission, if that is the correct term, that Montanelli made on an Italian TV programme in 1969. This was to the effect that, whilst serving in Italian East Africa (*Africa Orientale Italiana*), he violated his own stricture concerning fraternisation by purchasing a 12-year-old girl, named Destà (or Fatima), whom he kept as his 'wife' for around two years before gifting her to an *ascaro* NCO.[15] This led to a confrontation with an audience member, the Eritrean-Italian feminist Elvira Banotti, who accused him of rape and pointed out that if he had performed such actions in Italy, he would have faced severe punishment. She noted that the only distinctions were that Destà was black and that she lived in a state of colonial, and racial, subjugation.[16] The controversy endured, and indeed endures still. It is then perhaps unsurprising that those who defaced Montanelli's statue, the erection of which was itself subject to much disagreement, spray-painted the words *razzista* (racist) and *stupratore* (rapist) onto its base.[17]

What is arguably rather more surprising is that amongst the ranks of those who condemned this act of vandalism, as they saw it, was Angelo Del Boca. A historian, journalist and essayist, Del Boca was a pioneer of studies on Italian colonialism and is considered the first Italian scholar to deal with the critical and systematic reconstruction of the political-military history of Italian conquest and expansion in East Africa and Libya. He was the first to denounce the numerous war crimes committed by Italian troops during the colonial wars, and the Fascists, in particular, for their use of poison gas.[18]

It is also the case that Del Boca and Montanelli had been two of the most notable protagonists in respect of the former's attempt to dismantle the mythology behind *Italiani brava gente*. One particular facet of this long-running 'culture war' revolved around Italy's use, or 'alleged use' from the Montanelli perspective, of chemical weaponry by Italy in Ethiopia. This claim had been widely reported at the time, in non-Italian newspapers,[19] and was, both contemporaneously and subsequently, extensively written about.[20] It was, though, an accusation that was vehemently and officially denied in Italy, even after Del Boca revealed its use in his 1965 work on the Ethiopian War.[21] This met with a furious backlash. As he later phrased it:

> My revelations, in fact, initially aroused incredulity and indignation, so much so that my sources and my objectivity as a historian were doubted. Then, with the passing of the years, when the neo-fascist and nostalgic-conservative newspapers began to address the problem, then the smear campaign against me no longer knew limits or pauses and turned into an authentic lynching.[22]

Foremost amongst the critics, as might be expected, were the military veterans embodied in *L'Associazione Nazionale Reduci d'Africa* (ANRA), which had been formed in 1961.[23] The monthly journal *Il reduce d'Africa* ('The African Veteran') dedicated space to a lengthy article by *Italicus* which attacked both the book and its author. Del Boca, it was claimed, was 'foolish and servile' and featured 'among the champions of our defeatism'. His work was aimed at 'devaluing every national enterprise' and destroying 'the heritage and traditions of our homeland'. *Italicus* concluded that: 'The fact remains, however, that our intervention in Abyssinia really represented the hand of God and was indeed a work of civilization.' Angelo Del Boca was then 'spitting on the truth'.[24] Attacks in a similar vein continued for several months.[25]

Further books published by Del Boca and others, such as Giorgio Rochat, Ferdinando Pedriali and Roberto Gentilli, which revealed unwelcome truths concerning Italian colonialism, were similarly demonised. The weight of evidence began to tell as archival sources were unearthed. One noteworthy example of this occurred on 3 October 1985 during the showing on *Radiotelevisione italiana* (RAI), Italy's national public broadcasting company, of a production entitled *L'impero: un'avventura africana* ('The Empire: an African adventure'). Presented by Del Boca, who stood alongside, and placed his paperwork on, a 205-litre oil-drum upon which was conspicuously stencilled the word 'IPRITE' – the Italian term for mustard gas[26] – it featured an appearance by Alessandro Lessona. Then aged 94, and the last surviving senior member of Mussolini's regime, Lessona had held various ministerial posts with responsibility for colonial matters, particularly in relation to East Africa, from 1929 to 1937.[27]

He had also, in a book published in 1973, admitted that chemical weaponry had indeed been used in Ethiopia but, he claimed, only minimally and in retaliation for the torture and murder of two Italian airmen who had fallen into enemy hands.[28] After railing against the 'calumny' directed at Italy around the alleged use of gas, the explanation given was thus:

> It is true that General Graziani, commander of the Somali sector, asked for authorization to use [gas] in cases of extreme gravity and that the Duce

granted it only for those cases, but it is equally true that the gases were used only once ... Graziani ... had three gas bombs dropped in retaliation. These, and no others, were the only gas bombs used ... .[29]

This position was later modified, but only slightly, with Lessona arguing in 1980 that it was possible that the military men on the spot might have gone further than Mussolini wanted. He also claimed that Italian chemical warfare agents were only sent to Africa in the first place in case the enemy used them first.[30] Del Boca said that he expected Lessona to reiterate this position on the 1985 TV programme but to his surprise the former minister effectively withdrew these earlier 'confessions'. He no longer seemed willing to admit that they had occurred, pleading lapses of memory whilst floundering in 'a sea of reticence and contradictions'.[31]

Lessona was, of course, a very old man, so may perhaps be excused memory lapses and confusion. Del Boca, however, did not spare him: 'I therefore decided, as host of the broadcast, to resort to the hard way, as if we had moved into a courtroom.' Atop his *iprite* drum was a 'voluminous folder' which 'bore the name of Lessona'.[32] It had been removed from the Rome offices of the Ministry of Italian Africa (*ministero dell' Africa italiana*)[33] during September 1943. Thence it went to the short-lived German puppet state in northern Italy, the *Repubblica Sociale Italiana* (RSI) or Italian Social Republic, also known as the Republic of Salò (*Repubblica di Salò*), from where it subsequently disappeared following the collapse of German resistance in April 1945.[34] An anonymous donor had sent it to Del Boca in 1969, and he had authenticated its contents: 120 telegrams that Mussolini and the military commanders in East Africa, Marshals Pietro Badoglio and Rodolfo Graziani, had exchanged during the Italo-Ethiopian conflict. A selection of these were then published in November 1969 in *Il Giorno*, the national daily newspaper based in Milan. Many of the messages concerned the use of chemical weaponry and, as historian Giorgio Rochat and journalist Lamberti Sorrentino looked on, Del Boca 'began to read them in dead silence ... I continued to read the telegrams for a good five minutes, beyond the time foreseen by the script, in an increasingly loud and categorical tone of voice.'[35] One example will suffice: 'Rome, March 29, 1936. (To Badoglio, Macallè). Secret ... Given the enemy's methods of warfare, I renew the authorization to use gas of any kind and on any scale. Mussolini.' Del Boca continued to read aloud similar documents until, as he put it:

> the former Minister of Italian Africa raised his arms, he waved them, as if to say that he was surrendering to the evidence of the documents. Then I was silent, and there was no need to comment on Lessona's surrender. We moved on to another scene.[36]

The evidence presented to Lessona and the wider TV audience, taken from official files, did not, however, succeed in convincing Montanelli. Indeed, he continued to traduce Del Boca via his column, *La stanza di Montanelli* (Montanelli's

Room), which appeared over the years in various, wide-circulation newspapers such as *Il Giornale, La Voce* and *Corriere della Sera*:

> His [Montanelli's] language, already habitually pungent, was acrimonious towards me when it was not brutally offensive. On several occasions I tried to reply by indicating the archival location of the most significant documents on the use of chemical weapons. But it was all in vain.[37]

Eventually Del Boca gave up and, as he stated it, 'disinterested' himself in attempting to counter such smear campaigns and, as regards Montanelli, he filed him as being amongst those 'desperate, incorrigible cases'.[38] However, this mutual antipathy and estrangement was to soften somewhat in 1995. This followed the publication of Del Boca's biography of the last Emperor of Ethiopia, Haile Selassie.[39] When Montanelli reviewed the book in the pages of *Corriere della Sera* on 11 August 1995 he was highly complimentary, claiming that the portrayal of Haile Selassie was 'the most complete and convincing of those which had appeared in any language'.[40] He would not, though, concede the point about chemical weapons, arguing that the documents cited by Del Boca all originated with the Ethiopians or those who were pro-Ethiopian. He spoke from the point of view of a witness, rather than that of a historian, pointing out that he had been present shortly after one mountain peak had, allegedly, been sown with mustard gas:

> A battalion of Alpine troops and the ascaris of the Dalmazzo brigade, of which I was a part, were the first to reach the summit. There was no one there, but there was also no mustard gas, which we would certainly have been warned against.[41]

Del Boca's response was published in *Corriere della Sera* the following day, stating that he had used documents from the Italian archives. These showed that the Italian air force had in fact dropped over 2,500 bombs loaded with mustard gas over the course of the campaign. He also proposed a solution to the ongoing dispute. Would Montanelli accept the arbitration of the Foreign and Defence Ministries in the matter? They were the custodians of the archives, and could publish an 'official note' which would, once and for all, untie this 'knot in our national history that has caused so much argument'.[42] Montanelli agreed, though perhaps hedged his bets somewhat:

> I have no doubts about the seriousness of the documents that ... have [been] cited. I only doubt, as an eyewitness, their correspondence to the facts. So I add ... my invitation to the ministries concerned so that they can finally tell us if the order to launch the gases was actually given (which is probable); and if it was actually carried out: which seems difficult to me, not to say impossible due to the absolute lack of targets against which to use them ... But if from the archives of the so-called competent ministries it turns out that we ... were thrown into the counter-offensive without being warned that we

were advancing into a hell of mustard gas; if all of this turns out to be true, I won't just apologize ... I will demand a trial to the memory of our commanders with them being burned in effigy as the final sentence.[43]

One positive outcome of this exchange, and agreement as to settling it, was that it provoked a debate in the press pertaining to Italian colonialism. Between August and October 1995 about a hundred articles, letters and the like appeared on the subject in newspapers and weekly journals. This was in the main a constructive affair, though Del Boca was still subjected to partisan attacks,[44] and it produced benefits in the shape of unpublished testimonies on the Italo-Ethiopian conflict. It also reawakened public interest in 'a forgotten page of history', albeit, as Del Boca said, 'half a century late'.[45] The whole thing was, at least in journalist Gianni Riotta's analysis, 'a civil dispute between two professions, the historian who swears by the archives, the envoy who swears by his eyes'.[46]

Persuading the government departments in question to provide a definitive answer was, however, another matter entirely. They had hitherto adopted a policy of *omertà*. Del Boca remarked upon this in his autobiography: 'What disturbed me, above all, was the silence of the military authorities, who knew perfectly well what had happened in Africa, because they were the custodians of documents that proved the use of gas.'[47]

The Italian political system is well known for producing frequent changes of government. Silvio Berlusconi had become prime minister in May 1994 but was forced to resign 225 days later, his replacement being Lamberto Dini, who headed a so-called technical, or technocratic, government. Dini's minister of defence was General Domenico Corcione, the first military man to hold the position in Republican Italy.[48] Whether the fact that the defence minister was not a politician made the difference is not known,[49] but in response to pressure from several elected politicians for the government to end the long-standing quarrel over the use of chemical weapons in Ethiopia, the tectonic plates appeared to shift.

This was indicated in an article by General Alberto Rovighi which appeared in the newspaper *Il Messaggero* on 1 November 1995. Rovighi[50] had access to the documentation at both the Ministry of Defence and the Ministry of Foreign Affairs. This was a facility that had been denied to Del Boca, who complained:

> between 1965 and 1975, I asked in vain to access the very rich archives of the Foreign Ministry. They did not refuse, but simply did not respond to my requests [. . .] In 1976 ... access to the archives became easier and research was facilitated. However, restrictions reappeared in the second half of the 1980s under obscure, indecipherable, pretexts. Only after much insistence did I gain access to documents, but under the very restrictive condition that I did not mention the archival location.

Del Boca's experience in respect to obtaining documentation in the military archives was worse. As the then head of the Army General Staff Historical Office,

General Pier Luigi Bertinaria, informed him in the 1980s, this was because he was perceived as being 'an enemy of Italy and of the army', and of 'siding with the Ethiopians'. Accordingly: 'my stay in the military archives was short-lived. Every time I asked for documents, the difficulties and vetoes increased. Eventually I realized that the task was to tire me out. Then I threw in the towel.'[51]

That the ire of the military authorities was directed at Del Boca personally is evidenced by the fact that other scholars, such as Giorgio Rochat, were allowed greater freedom to conduct research.[52]

In any event, the officially sanctioned Rovighi was able to state authoritatively that chemical weaponry had indeed been used in Ethiopia, and on a systematic basis. This was qualified inasmuch as this usage, given the dispersion of enemy forces and the high ambient temperature, was not decisive and that Italian victory was more to do with better armament and a huge logistical effort.[53]

Rovighi's article, which was much discussed, was not an official government response and did not settle the matter. It did, though, change the nature of the debate. For example, the deputy minister of defence, Professor Carlo Maria Santoro, was interviewed on 10 November and admitted that Rovighi had been accurate but that the matter did not upset him; the war with Japan had ended with the dropping of two atomic weapons. The Italian air force had, he said, dropped '1,020 500-kilo bombs loaded with mustard gas on the northern front, ninrety-five mustard gas bombs and 271 phosgene bombs on the southern front ... with very modest effects on the military level'. As for Del Boca, he was:

> together with Giorgio Rochat, one of our best Africanists, but his historiographical slant does not convince me. He is extremely hostile and prejudicial to us. On the one hand the Negus [Haile Selassie] is magnified as Saint Francis [of Assisi]; on the other the Italians are treated worse than Babau ...[54]

Santoro repeated these claims two days later, arguing that the theses Del Boca promoted were 'too one-sided'.[55] The December edition of *Il reduce d'Africa* was rather more blunt: Del Boca's was 'undoubtedly the most poisonous pen in Italy'.[56] The victim of these barbs recorded:

> A new scenario was thus opening up. For years the right-wing had accused me of creating fake stories and that I was an enemy of the country. Then this changed; my sources were Ethiopian and therefore partial. When, finally, the examination of our archives, carried out at the highest level by the defence officials, confirmed what I had been writing since 1965, then my objectivity as a historian was questioned and my historiographical slant was criticized. In other words, the accusation of forgery having been dropped, that of my anti-patriotism remained.[57]

Complete absolution from accusations of anti-patriotism was probably too much to ask, but on 7 February 1996 what Del Boca termed 'the last act of the gas affair' was finally reached. The written reply to the parliamentary requests for clarification appeared. It was signed by the minister of defence, General Domenico

Corcione, who also spoke on behalf of the minister of foreign affairs. Though couched in pure bureaucratese – 'even if it essentially admits the facts, it is a minor masterpiece of ambiguity'[58] – the operative section stated:

> From those [documents] available in the archives – some of which are attached – it appears ... that in the Italo-Ethiopian War aircraft bombs and artillery shells loaded with mustard gas and arsine were used and that the use of these gases was known to Marshal Badoglio, who signed reports and communications on the subject in his own hand.[59]

There were two attached documents, neither previously known, which were deemed by Del Boca to be of 'extraordinary importance'. Both related to the Battle of Enderta, or Amba Aradam, which had taken place over the period 10–19 February 1936, resulting in an Italian victory. The first was a message sent to the Colonial Ministry, dated 29 February 1936 and signed by Marshal Badoglio:

> A total of 196 aircraft were used to launch approximately 60 tonnes of mustard gas on the mountain passes and on the routes and paths the [retreating] enemy columns were obliged to use ... thus completing, in good time, an offensive that initial information unanimously affirms has had great moral and material effect.[60]

The second document was taken from the January–February 1936 diary of the Artillery High Command (*Comando superiore Artiglieria*), and bore the signature of Brigadier General (*generale di brigata*) Emilio Garavelli, General Officer Commanding Artillery, Italian East Africa General Headquarters. It gave a detailed description of the manoeuvres carried out by the artillery before and during the Battle of Enderta. On 11 February 1936 Garavelli reported that:

> this Command has since early this morning used two groups of 105s [105/14 Howitzers (Obice da 105/14 modello 18)] to discharge concentrations of arsine grenades into areas where major agglomerations and enemy activities had occurred in recent days, and especially towards the Amba Aradam where shelters are believed to exist and from where outlets for Abyssinian counter-attacks are foreseen.[61]

Del Boca considered these documents vitally important because the first detailed the massive use of air-delivered mustard gas, whilst the second confirmed a claim he had already made: that at the beginning of the battle in question the Italian artillery had employed large quantities of arsine-loaded ordnance. They thus served to demonstrate that the use of chemical weaponry was not accidental or minor, and nor was it used in retaliation. Rather it was a calculated tactic intended to inflict maximum harm. Further, and in relation to the aerial bombardment, an attached map detailed twenty-two objectives over an area of 10,000 sq. km. This demonstrated great knowledge of the terrain with its passes and caravan routes, but given the multiplicity of targets it also showed that the civil population would be in harm's way just as much as the retreating Ethiopian troops.[62]

The official admission by the government led to much comment in the press, though this reporting, predictably, tended towards the partisan. For example, the left-wing *l'Unità* gave a full page to a report penned by the socialist writer Vittorio Emiliani, headlining it: 'For the first time the government and the army admit bombing with mustard gas: fascist shame kept secret.'[63] On the other hand, the more conservative *Corrierre della Sera*, the paper for which Montanelli wrote, confined its coverage to a fourteen-line article on page 13. This provoked Del Boca into writing to Paolo Mieli, the editor:

> I was fully convinced that today (9 February), after the clear admission of the Defence Minister ... the Corriere della Sera would have given due importance to the news ... As you know, I never demanded Indro Montanelli's apologies ... because I believe that Montanelli has always denied, but in good faith, the use of prohibited weapons. I have no desire for revenge, therefore. But I was hoping that the dispute would end in a different way, above all out of respect for the readers, and for that completeness of information which everyone invokes but few exercise.[64]

Montanelli remained silent until 13 February, when his column *Stanza di Montanelli* appeared. It published Del Boca's letter and his reply to it, the title of which was 'Gas in Ethiopia: the documents prove me wrong'.[65] Montanelli beat a dignified retreat:

> Mieli has passed me your letter which ... I hasten to publish in this 'room' of mine to show you, if you ever suspected it, that it was not I who asked him to silence the communiqué from General Corcione, who proves me wrong on the issue of Italian gases in Ethiopia ... you remind me of the commitment I had made in our friendly polemic to apologize to the readers in the event that the documents showed that the gases were actually used, here I am ready to acquit it by acknowledging that the documents actually do prove me wrong.

Montanelli acknowledged that Del Boca's 'historical reconstruction' of the Ethiopian campaign had indeed been proven correct by the release of the documents, and addressed the point about having denied that fact in good faith:

> I denied the use of gases simply because, on the spot, I had neither seen nor heard of them. And the curious fact is that, among the veterans of that distant and wrong enterprise, now reduced – I imagine – to a few dozen, I have never found one that remembered the gases ... Would that mean the documents are therefore false? Not a chance. Those documents are undoubtedly authentic.

He did, though, insert a caveat, arguing that in the Italian wars the 'fact' does not always, indeed almost never, correspond to the 'document'. He concluded by apologising to 'you and the readers' for his 'blunder', but pointing out that the truth in Italy always has 'many faces, among which it is easy to be mistaken'.[66]

Despite this caveat Del Boca accepted the answer as being 'comprehensive, loyal and generous' and, of itself, 'no small gesture' given Montanelli's 'authority and temperament' and that he had 'chivalrously admitted his mistake', indeed his 'blunder' to use his own words. 'It had', he stated, 'taken thirty years and government intervention to break the irreducible Montanelli' and that even if he were a loser he deserved the honours of war.[67]

It wasn't quite the end of the matter for Montanelli, however, although this was only revealed nine years after his death. In 2010 the Milan publishing house Rizzoli decided to reprint Montanelli's 1936 book about his time with the XX Eritrean Battalion.[68] This new edition was 'enriched by a photographic section and by ... unpublished correspondence'. It also featured an Introduction by Angelo Del Boca, in which he publicised the fact that his erstwhile opponent had changed his mind and continued to cleave to his 'ancient certainties':

> A few months after the conclusion of the dispute ... Montanelli and I were invited to participate in a debate at Bocconi [Bocconi University, a private university in Milan]. Just before the debate began, Indro almost pressed me against a wall and excitedly said to me: 'I was too hasty in acknowledging my faults. I was there and I can assure you that gases were never used.' Using all my patience, I tried to explain to him that the first mustard gas bombs ... had been dropped ... when he was no longer on the front line but in hospital. All to no avail. He would accept no explanation. Luckily they called us back to the stage and the argument ended. I hadn't known how unyielding Indro was up to that point.[69]

Despite knowing that Montanelli was indeed still privately 'irreducible', Del Boca remained magnanimous. Indeed, he defended Montanelli and his memory, and as noted previously condemned in no uncertain terms the defacing of his memorial.[70]

The thirty-year battle between Del Boca and Montanelli was, of course, merely a microcosmic representation of the effort to, as Nicholas Doumanis put it, bridge the 'gap between academic history and popular opinion'.[71] Dispelling the myth of *Italiani brava gente* was never going to be 'popular', though. As a recent newspaper article, *vis-à-vis* another context altogether but with universal applicability, phrased it: 'History helps people feel they belong. This is why people can feel angry when history is reinterpreted or retold in ways that make them feel uncomfortable.'[72]

Indeed so, but even contemporaneously the essential nature of the Italian campaign in Ethiopia was clearly seen by some commentators. J.F.C. Fuller wrote, whilst the conflict was still ongoing, of mountain heights being 'sprayed with mustard gas rendering them unoccupiable by the enemy, save at the gravest risk'. Such tactics he considered to be 'an exceedingly cunning use of this chemical'.[73] A German account of the war, completed shortly after its conclusion, also mentions the use of mustard gas, but it is perhaps its title, or rather part of its subtitle, that is most revealing. According to Rudolf Ritter und Edler von Xylander it was 'the first modern war of annihilation'.[74] The sub-title added 'on colonial soil' (*auf kolonialem Boden*) but Ethiopia wasn't an Italian colony, or at least not until the conclusion of the Italian campaign to make it so. Rather it was an independent, sovereign, state and one of only two African nations to avoid European domination during the period characterised as 'the Scramble for Africa'.[75] In fact the king, or emperor, of Ethiopia, Menelik II, had addressed the governments of Britain, France, Germany, Italy and Russia in 1891, stating his conception of 'the boundaries of Ethiopia'. As he told them: 'Ethiopia has been for fourteen centuries a Christian island in a sea of pagans. If powers at a distance come forward to partition Africa between them, I do not intend to be an indifferent spectator.'[76]

As it turned out, Menelik was just a few years later to play a part very far from that of a spectator indifferent or otherwise when Italy, under the bellicose government of Francesco Crispi, sought to make Ethiopia a protectorate. The Negus resisted and war ensued. Ultimately, an Italian force some 15,000 strong under the command of Major General Oreste Baratieri moved forward in February 1896. On 1 March, near the northern town of Adwa (also known as Adua or Adowa), it met with an Ethiopian force under the personal command of Menelik. The resultant battle saw the invaders experience 'the bloodiest defeat ever suffered during the nineteenth century by a white colonial force at the hands of native enemies'.[77] This, from the Italian perspective, caused the humiliation of the entire country at the international level. One young writer who was later to gain much fame agreed and three years later phrased it thus:

> On the 1st of March, 1896, the battle of Adowa was fought, and Italy at the hands of Abyssinia sustained a crushing defeat. Two results followed which affected other nations. Firstly, a great blow had been struck at European prestige in North Africa ... Secondly, the value of Italy as a factor in European politics was depreciated.[78]

There were riots in the cities which the army had to put down. The Crispi government was swept away. There were, though, longer-term repercussions in the shame and frustration the defeat at Adwa created in Italian consciousness. Francesco Crispi died in 1901, but charged though he was 'with the cost of the most opprobrious failure of Italian expansionism' ever, his reputation was later resurrected. He had been, according to Fascist propaganda, 'the "bearer" of the great-power conscience of modern Italy' and was credited with the invention of a truly 'Italian' style of imperialism.[79] Indeed, at a ceremony held in Rome in 1924 to commemorate him, one of his successors, a certain Benito Mussolini, recalled that even though he had but a 'vague impression of those events, because I was still a young man', he had nevertheless 'suffered a lot for the battle of Adua'.[80] It had become a 'shame that had to be wiped away one day or another'.[81]

Chapter Two

The Sawdust Caesar

> The contribution of Benito Mussolini
> To political theory was teeny.
> Only his desire to make a splash is some
> Explanation of *The Doctrine of Fascism*.[1]

* * *

Benito Amilcare Andrea Mussolini, *il duce del fascismo* (Leader of Fascism), was, and still is, often considered a buffoon. According to the historian Carlo D'Este, he is 'universally regarded as an almost comical stereotype of a blundering dictator, a petit-bourgeois hick from the provinces ... whose inept leadership and lust for power led Italy to disaster'.[2] Needless to say, perhaps, there was more to him than that stereotype would have us believe.[3] However, and as was noted by contemporary commentators, he had neither a settled political philosophy nor any heroic background prior to assuming power in 1922:

> Unlike Vladimir Ilyitch Ulianov (Lenin) in Russia, he had no theory and no program. Unlike Mustapha Kemal Pasha in Turkey he was not a military hero and idolized savior. What these dictators had and were before they rose to power, Mussolini gradually made and became after his great ascent.[4]

Later scholarship has largely concurred in this analysis, concluding that the movement he founded and led, Fascism, had no consistent ideological basis other than radical nationalism and a toadying cult of personality based upon its leader. Sir Noel Malcolm encapsulated this incoherence, and did so rather brilliantly, as is noted above in the current chapter's opening epigraph.

Whilst spinning 'from point to point like a broken compass', Fascism did, though, evolve, or mutate, displaying several discernible phases. The last of these, what Alexander De Grand has identified as its imperial and racist phase,[5] is the one which will concern this narrative.

Writing in 1935, the American investigative journalist George Seldes, the Rome correspondent of the *Chicago Tribune* who had been expelled from Italy ten years previously for filing copy derogatory to the regime concerning the murder of the socialist deputy Giacomo Matteotti,[6] laid the transition to this phase at the door of the Great Depression. Indeed, Italy's slow recovery from this was arguably exacerbated by Fascist policies.[7] According to Seldes: 'Since the depression Fascism has come to a dead stop. All that it has had in the past four or five years is a record of broken promises, an unbearable debt burden, and the dynamic oratory of the Duce. But one cannot live on oratory alone.'[8]

Indeed not, but Mussolini had studied Machiavelli. Indeed he claimed in 1924 that he considered *The Prince*, which he had carefully read and reread, to be a work of reference for a ruler.[9] He therefore well knew that 'nothing makes a prince so highly esteemed as great deeds and setting rare examples'.[10] Given that one of his aims was the rebirth of Italy, and he constantly harked back to a mythical past[11] – 'everything calls Italy to the resumption of her imperial mission: the tradition of Rome, of Venice, and of Genoa'[12] – then 'great deeds' almost automatically formed a large part of *Il Duce*'s agenda.[13] That he might find such in the field of foreign affairs was evident from the early days of his rule.

Following the ambush and murder by persons unknown of an Italian general and his party on the Greek side of a disputed section of the border with Albania on 23 August 1923, Mussolini issued an ultimatum to Greece. Both in tone and content this was somewhat reminiscent of the Austro-Hungarian note to Serbia following the assassination of Franz Ferdinand. Like that earlier version, it was only partially accepted by the recipients and, similarly, that was an intended outcome. According to the Italian diplomat Raffaele Guariglia, Mussolini's reaction to the news of the murders was 'immediate, violent, and uncompromising. We were not allowed to seek a solution in the normal way. Mussolini wanted the occupation of Corfu.'[14] The opportunity afforded by the murders was unexpected but welcome; *Il Duce* wanted to act with force against Greece.[15] In the words of James Barros: 'Europe was being subjected to a new type of diplomacy, of cynical negotiation begun in bad faith.'[16] Thus the hurried exchange of diplomatic notes that followed were 'meaningless gestures and meant merely to impress or mesmerize the unknowing and the gullible with his [Mussolini's] feigned sincerity'.[17]

Diplomacy was necessarily hurried because, unlike Austria-Hungary in 1914, the Italians moved with extreme rapidity; on 31 August 1923 the *Regia Marina* bombarded Corfu city and landed an occupation force. Shortly afterwards, on 5 September, *Il Duce* attempted to justify this action by claiming that the island had belonged to the Republic of Venice for some four centuries before ownership passed, via a somewhat convoluted route, to Greece in 1864.[18] Though Italy eventually withdrew its forces from Corfu after a settlement was brokered, probably the biggest casualty relating to the whole affair was the credibility of the League of Nations, upon whose Executive Council Italy sat as a permanent member.[19] The League failed to restrain Italy after Greece asked for its help, and the Corfu Incident was seen as a serious failure, demonstrating as it did that a militarily dominant nation could overshadow one less powerful, and do so with a great degree of impunity:

> The settlement made a nasty smell. The Greeks were bitter, the Assembly [of the League] felt it had been betrayed and that the League had been degraded. Mussolini appeared to have triumphed in his assertion that where a nation was powerful enough it was justified in using force to further its interests and the League had no right to interfere.[20]

All in all, and although 'improvised and incoherent', whilst 'Mussolini's gunboat diplomacy failed to add Corfu to Italy's possessions ... it did successfully fulfil demagogic and propagandistic aims within the country.'[21] In fact Italy, before the advent of Fascism and in its so-called 'Liberal' incarnation, had form in the latter regard. The Italo-Ottoman War of 1911–1912, when Italy decided to add to her African empire by invading Ottoman-ruled Tripolitania, Cyrenaica and Fezzan (later Libya), was only entered into to satisfy the nationalist and jingoistic right wing that had become a powerful force in Italian domestic politics.

Italy had long coveted the territory and had taken pains diplomatically to try to ensure that it would eventually get it. It was, though, not enough for the politicians behind the adventure, prime minister Giovanni Giolitti and minister of foreign affairs Antonino Paternò Castello (Marchese di San Giuliano), to satisfy this long-standing territorial ambition by diplomacy. It had to be done by force of arms with famous victories reflecting the glory of Italy. It did not quite work out like that. Indeed, this conflict of choice on Italy's part may be reasonably viewed as a strategic blunder of massive proportions. In fact, and even though Italy eventually 'won' by getting the Ottoman Empire to come to terms, the failure to conquer the vast majority of the territory thus acquired triggered the Great Arab Revolt (*La Grande Rivolta Araba*).[22] This intensified when, on 23 May 1915, Italy entered the First World War – not on the side of its German and Austro-Hungarian allies of three decades, but rather on the side of Britain, France and Russia *against* Austria-Hungary (but not quite yet Germany. That came on 28 August 1916).

'Perfidy, like history does not know' was how Kaiser Franz Joseph of Austria-Hungary described it. Whether perfidy or not, this political and strategic realignment, and subsequent concentration of the Italian Army in the north-east of the country, exacerbated the revolt to the degree that Italy's hold on the newly acquired territory, such as it was, became tenuous in the extreme and confined to a few coastal enclaves.[23]

It is perhaps ironic that one of the fiercest opponents of the original Italian campaign to wrest Libya from Ottoman control was the then little-known socialist Benito Mussolini. When the war began, he was editing a small-circulation newspaper, *La Lotta di Classe* (*Class Struggle*) at Forli in north-east Italy. Being forthright in his opposition, and campaigning for a general strike, led to him being arraigned for obstructing the public authorities in the performance of their duties, advocating violence against persons and property, and inciting people to cause specific damage. He was sentenced on 23 November 1911 to one year in prison, subsequently reduced to five months. His fame spread because of the conviction and on his release in April 1912 he was appointed as editor of *Avanti* in Milan. He increased its circulation and, because he wrote a great deal of the content personally, greatly expanded his influence.[24]

Having fought in the First World War and abandoned socialism, he became involved in the post-war movement that was, to put it mildly, disenchanted with the outcome of the conflict as it pertained to Italy. The matter was complex but, stated very simply, many Italians considered that the several peace treaties imposed on the defeated Central Powers in 1919, and particularly the Treaty of Saint-Germain-en-Laye which dealt with Austria as one of the successor states to Austria-Hungary, were unfair. This was so because reassurances and guarantees embodied in the 1915 Treaty of London, under the terms of which Italy agreed to join the war, were later repudiated, particularly by President Woodrow Wilson. This applied principally with respect to the transfer of former Austro-Hungarian territory which Italy had designs on for one reason or another. Grievances against this 'mutilated victory' (*vittoria mutilata*), a term coined by the ultranationalist poet, writer and war hero Gabriele D'Annunzio, were successfully exploited and used to de-legitimise the entire political system as it then existed: democracy, socialism and liberalism were portrayed as failed systems. The alternative, Fascism, represented itself as best suited for government and, under Mussolini's leadership, conducted what was effectively an attempted coup d'etat on 28 October 1922.[25]

The March on Rome (*La marcia su Roma*) saw tens of thousands of fascists make their way to the Italian capital, threatening the seizure of power with violence. One senior army officer, general Pietro Badoglio, is reputed to have offered to disperse them with the proverbial 'whiff of grapeshot', stating that 'Fascism will totally collapse at the first fire'.[26] King Victor Emmanuel demurred, and instead appointed Mussolini prime minister of Italy on 31 October 1922. As such, he inherited the campaign to pacify or reconquer Libya.[27]

The difficulties of projecting force into the interior of the vast Sahara Desert, which had largely precluded the Italian Army from getting to grips with their enemies in 1911–1912, had now been eased following the technological quantum leap consequent upon the First World War. Perhaps the most important element of this related to aircraft. The Italians were the first to use aircraft in a military context in 1911–1912, although of course the models available were extremely basic. Nevertheless, the experience of, and developments in, aerial warfare proved of much value to them. Aircraft were used initially in the context of reconnaissance: as deserts are mostly devoid of vegetation they offer virtually no natural concealment from aerial observation. Thus it was found that they were fairly effective in that role. With rather less success they were also used for bombardment. There were 712 sorties by aeroplanes during the course of the Italo-Ottoman War in north Africa, during which 'several hundred' bombs were dropped, whilst airships sortied on 136 occasions and released 360 bombs.[28] The conclusion in respect of aviation reached after the conflict was that aeroplanes, although representative of a younger and less proven technology, were nevertheless faster, more manoeuvrable and much more versatile than airships, and thus had more to offer in the field of war in the future.[29] This was prophetic, and when combined with armed, and armoured, vehicles able to traverse the terrain they were indeed to provide the key to successful penetration of the desert. Indeed, drawing on their experiences, the Italians were the first to use integrated mobile air and ground units, dubbed *compagnie auto-avio sahariane*, for desert warfare in the 1930s.[30]

The Italian reconquest (*reconquista della Libia*), which was adjudged complete in 1932, was a brutal business. Some indication of its harshness may be gauged by noting that, according to figures compiled by Italy, the population of Cyrenaica dropped from 225,000 in 1928 to 142,000 in 1931.[31] Giorgio Rochat calculates that between 1923 and 1936 the number of dead in Cyrenaica was between a lower limit of 30,000 and an upper of 70,000.[32] Angelo Del Boca estimates that the total deaths in both Tripolitania and Cyrenaica were in the order of 100,000.[33] Whichever figures are the more accurate, it is indisputable that the slaughter was on a large scale. A further technique that had appeared during the First World War, and that was in evidence during the Italian campaign, was chemical warfare.

> Phosgene and mustard gas were used in Libya by the Italian air force on a number of occasions between 1923 and 1931, although not systematically or in large quantities, to give greater effect to the bombing of the people and their livestock in the inland desert regions.[34]

Indeed the internationally famous aviator Italo Balbo, a member of the *quadrumviri*[35] and the man who effectively headed Italy's aviation ministry from 1926 to 1933, opined during the course of a speech to the Chamber of Deputies on 29 March 1927 that aircraft and chemical weapons formed a 'natural union' for bringing death and destruction to non-combatant populations.[36] Balbo was far from being the first to identify this 'natural union'. For example, the British military theorist Captain Basil Liddell Hart stated it thus in 1925: 'If, then, gas seems destined to replace the bullet and the shell, so equally does the aeroplane appear likely to supersede the gun as the means of projection . . .'[37]

Practical exponents, as distinct from theorisers, had advocated similar methods for dealing with rebellious colonials. Colonel T.E. Lawrence, *aka* 'Lawrence of Arabia', wrote of the matter in early August 1920 in relation to insurrections against British rule, under a League of Nations mandate, in Mesopotamia (later Iraq):

> It is odd that we do not use poison gas on these occasions. Bombing the houses is a patchy way of getting the women and children, and our infantry always incur losses in shooting down the Arab men. By gas attacks the whole population of offending districts could be wiped out neatly; and as a method of government it would be no more immoral than the present system.[38]

Winston Churchill, at the time heading two military departments as secretary of state for war and for air, was in accord with this thinking. On 29 August 1920 he wrote to the chief of the air staff, Sir Hugh Trenchard, asking for experiments to proceed in relation to chemical-filled bombs: 'especially mustard gas which would inflict punishment upon recalcitrant natives without inflicting grave injury on them'.[39] Despite Churchillian urging, and notwithstanding the popular notion that the British actually employed chemical warfare in Mesopotamia at that time, such methods were never in point of fact put into practice.[40]

That they were, however morally reprehensible, nevertheless effective to a degree was demonstrated in the northern portion of Spanish Morocco (*Protectorado español de Marruecos*). Acquired by Spain in 1912, the territory encompassed the Rif, also anglicised as Riff or Rif Mountains. This was, from the colonial power's point of view, a topographically challenging area populated by extremely 'recalcitrant natives' in the shape of the local Berber population led by Abd el-Krim. Resistance to foreign rule was constant, and under Krim's leadership the Confederal Republic of the Tribes of the Rif (*República Confederada de les Tribus del Rif*), also known more simply as the Republic of the Rif (*República del Rif*), was declared in 1921.[41] Efforts to impose colonial rule, the 1921–1926 Rif War, saw Spain's Army of Africa (*Ejército de África*) resort to extensive use of chemical warfare using both air-dropped bombs containing mustard gas and phosgene and artillery shells with similar ingredients. One of the few historians to study the subject, Sebastian Balfour, concluded that 'the chemical war against Abdel Krim's supporters severely weakened their resistance. On top of the casualties of conventional battle ... the chemicals caused extreme suffering and want amongst Moroccan soldiers and civilians.' However, he also points out that 'it did not have the effect that its apologists naively expected – the immediate surrender of the enemy'.[42]

Like many states, Spain at that period had an army air force, the *Aeronáutica Militar*, and a naval equivalent, the *Aeronáutica Naval*, rather than a dedicated, autonomous, organisation such as Britain's Royal Air Force which, founded on 1 April 1918, pioneered the concept. The major European powers eventually followed suit, Germany and France, the former constrained by the Treaty of Versailles, forming the *Luftwaffe* and *Armée de l'Air* in 1933 and 1934 respectively, whilst the United States and Japan maintained separate army/navy air arms until after the end of the Second World War. The Bolsheviks created the Main Directorate of the Workers' and Peasants' Red Air Force in May 1918, but Russia was mired in civil war until 1923.[43] Italy was, however, relatively quick to follow the British example with the establishment of the *Regia Aeronautica*, by royal decree, on 28 March 1923.[44]

The creation of an independent air force boosted Italian aviation in every context with aircraft becoming, in the words of Fernando Esposito, 'a technototem of the fascist order'.[45] This was reflected in several famous feats, probably the most notable being the *Crociera aerea del Decennale 1933-XI*[46] (Decennial Air Cruise of 1933-XI). The cruise involved Italo Balbo, in celebration of ten years of the *Regia Aeronautica*, personally leading a trans-Atlantic flight of twenty-five Savoia-Marchetti S.55X flying boats from Italy to Chicago and back.[47] Despite losing one aircraft to an incident during an attempted take-off in the Azores on the return leg, it was a remarkable achievement by any standard. Indeed, it was rather too remarkable for *Il Duce*. Jealous of Balbo's fame, and fearful that he was plotting to supplant him, Mussolini promoted him to the unique rank of

Maresciallo dell'aria (air marshal) and then promptly shunted him out of the country to be governor-general of Libya.[48]

Balbo is generally considered to have been the 'father' of Italy's independent air force. There was no paternal equivalent in respect of the weapon he considered to form a 'natural union' with it, although the *Servizio chimico militare* (Military Chemical Service) came into being on 31 May 1923 under the aegis of the *Regio Esercito* (Army). Some two years later, and in order to centralise efforts and improve collaboration, it became a unified organisation responsible for aspects of chemical warfare in all three armed forces. Colonel Demetrio Helbig of the air force, a distinguished chemist in his own right, was appointed as deputy director.[49]

Fascist Italy invested heavily in chemical warfare, with one of the most important installations constructed being the *Città della Chimica* (Chemical City) situated some 50km from Rome in the forests of Monti Cimini around Lake Vico. Occupying an area of over 20 hectares, the site included bunkers, underground warehouses, barracks, offices and accommodation for several hundred civilian scientists and technicians producing mainly phosgene and mustard gas.[50]

As well as these supposedly complementary weapons systems, Italy possessed an indigenous intellectual, theoretical, basis for their futuristic deployment. The influence of the publication, in 1921, of General Giulio Douhet's *Il dominio dell'aria* (The Command of the Air) has been, and still is, subject to much scholarly disputation, but it was undoubtedly one of the first published works to advocate strategic bombing.[51] It may well have been the source of Balbo's belief, mentioned earlier, that aircraft and chemical weapons complemented each other perfectly. Douhet certainly thought so:

> In general, aerial offensives will be directed against such targets as peacetime industrial and commercial establishments; important buildings, private and public; transportation arteries and centers; and certain designated areas of civilian population as well. To destroy these targets three kinds of bombs are needed – explosive, incendiary, and poison gas – apportioned as the situation may require. The explosives will demolish the target, the incendiaries set fire to it, and the poison-gas bombs prevent firefighters from extinguishing the fires.
>
> Gas attacks must be so planned as to leave the target permeated with gas which will last over a period of time, whole days, indeed ... It is easy to see how the use of this method, even with limited supplies of explosive and incendiary bombs, could completely wreck large areas of population and their transit lines during crucial periods of time when such action might prove strategically invaluable.[52]

Douhet was translated into, amongst other languages, French, German, Russian and English, and widely disseminated.[53] However, and as stated, whether or not it influenced other thinkers, and to what extent, is disputed.[54] Further, and although not based on observable effects nor on a balanced analysis of evidence of any sort,[55] strategic bombing, and the combination of aircraft and chemical warfare, seemed to offer an alternative to the blood, gore and suffering which had pertained during the seemingly endless attrition of the First World War. One of the leading British military theorists and historians of the 1920s and 1930s, Major General J.F.C. Fuller, considered such methodology irresistible:

> I believe that, in future warfare, great cities, such as London, will be attacked from the air, and that a fleet of 500 aeroplanes each carrying 500 ten-pound bombs of, let us suppose, mustard gas, might cause 200,000 minor casualties and throw the whole city into panic within half an hour of their arrival. Picture, if you can, what the result will be: London for several days will be one vast raving Bedlam, the hospitals will be stormed, traffic will cease, the homeless will shriek for help, the city will be in pandemonium. What of the government at Westminster? It will be swept away by an avalanche of terror. Then will the enemy dictate his terms, which will be grasped at like a straw by a drowning man. Thus may a war be won in forty-eight hours and the losses of the winning side may be actually nil![56]

Startling and alarmist as such prognostications might now appear, that they were taken with a high degree of seriousness was evident. For example, in the late 1930s the UK government issued gas masks to the entire civilian population, at a cost of 'approximately £5,000,000',[57] and evacuated children from urban areas in 1939. Forecasts of this nature also neglected to take into consideration the likelihood of reciprocity when facing a peer-adversary; as the Duke of Wellington had informed a nineteenth-century proponent of chemical warfare, 'two could play at that game'.[58] The then future British prime minister Stanley Baldwin's 1932 phrase that 'the bomber will always get through' is often quoted. Less often mentioned is his somewhat bleak assessment that: 'The only defence is in offence, which means that you have to kill more women and children more quickly than the enemy if you want to save yourselves.'[59] Such doom-laden forecasts also discounted, during a time of rapid technological advances, the possibility of defensive measures being developed.

On the other hand, against a non-peer enemy, where there was no prospect of retaliation in kind nor any possibility of effective defensive measures, then attacks of the type outlined would inevitably prove effective. That this was so had already been clearly demonstrated; targeting urbanised civilian populations differed only in scale, rather than principle, from aerial attacks on the villages and livestock of 'recalcitrant natives'.

Some three years after completing the reconquest of Libya, Mussolini decided to play the 'place in the sun' card.[60] He did so in an effort to distract the populace from both the problems of ongoing economic depression, and the unfulfilled expectations that his regime had itself engendered in them. His pretext for this course was the so-called Wal Wal Incident of late 1934, when a clash occurred between Italian and Ethiopian forces at the Wal Wal oasis (*l'oasi di Ual Ual*) in eastern Ethiopia near the border with Italian Somaliland (*Somalia italiana*).[61] Although essentially trivial in itself, and despite Italy and Ethiopia having a recently (1928) signed 'Treaty of Friendship, Conciliation and Arbitration',[62] Mussolini used it as the basis for an outpouring of populist bombast justifying his decision to invade Ethiopia. The most succinct description of this comes from Ian L. Campbell:

> The rationale for the invasion that Mussolini delivered depended on his audience. The land-hungry peasants were told that they would be settled in their millions in great fertile tracts of empty land that would be theirs for the asking. The liberals were told that it would be a civilising mission. The military were told that it was to be revenge for the battle of Adua ... Businessmen were regaled with stories of the riches to be earned from the untapped Eldorado of the Horn of Africa.[63]

Mussolini was also able to garner the support of the Catholic Church. Pope Pius XI, with whom *Il Duce* had agreed the Lateran Treaties in 1929,[64] supported the war against Ethiopia. His cardinals and bishops, whose views were reflected in sermons across the country, justified the aggression as a 'Holy War', indeed a 'crusade', against the 'heretics and schismatics' of the Ethiopian Orthodox Church.[65] Given the huge investment in the venture, in every sense, *Il Duce*'s regime was unlikely to survive its failure. Indeed, determined to avoid Crispi's fate of some forty years previously, Mussolini decreed in December 1934 that all and every means should be used in pursuit of its goal: 'the destruction of the Abyssinian armed forces and the total conquest of Ethiopia'. To this end the use of armour and aircraft was central, and he specified that the invaders must have an 'absolute superiority of artillery and gas'. These orders also stipulated that the attack must begin at the start of October 1935.[66]

When the practicality of putting these matters into effect was studied by the commanders of the air force, and maps of the territory to be attacked were reviewed, the means at hand were found to be somewhat lacking. This was particularly so with respect to chemical ordnance. A meeting of the General Staff convened on 14 January 1935 decided that the small 21 kg bombs which had been used during the 'policing' operations in Libya would be useless in Ethiopia: they were 'too small to be effective in the [east] African environment'.[67]

An alternative, and theoretically more efficient, means of releasing the chemical was therefore decided upon: mustard gas would be delivered by aircraft fitted with spraying equipment. However, the Autonomous Armament Office of the Ministry of Aeronautics (*Ufficio autonomo armamento del Ministero dell'aeronautica*) based at Furbara near Rome, which was responsible for the study and testing of aeronautical materiel, disapproved this notion. According to Ferdinando Pedriali, such methodology would have been 'almost more dangerous for the crews than for the targets'.[68]

Instead, on 10 February the Autonomous Armament Office informed all concerned that a new weapon had been put into development. Following successful testing, this became operational as the *bomba C.500.T*, with 5,000 being ordered in May. Of the same dimensions as a 500 kg high explosive bomb, the final version

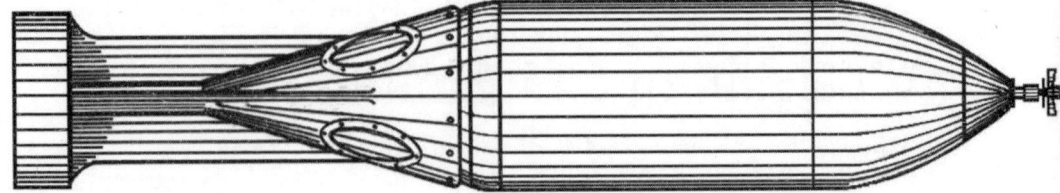

The *Bomba C-500.T*: '*C*' = chemical filling; '*500*' = external dimensions equal to 500kg HE bombs (460mm × 2,455mm); '*T*' = timed fuse (propeller-driven). Developed specifically for the Ethiopian invasion, it weighed 280kg and contained 212kg of *iprite* (mustard gas) plus a bursting charge.

Source: Ferdinando Pedriali, 'Le armi chimiche in Africa Orientale: storia, tecnica, obiettivi, efficacia', in Angelo Del Boca (ed.), *I Gas di Mussolini: Il fascismo e la guerra d'Etopia* (Roma: Editorio Riuniti, 2017), p. 124. (Illustration © Charles Blackwood)

weighed 280kg and contained 212kg of *iprite* plus a bursting charge. Two could be carried externally under a bomber aircraft such as the Caproni Ca.101. Each weapon was fitted with an adjustable, propeller-operated fuse that could be set to detonate at a set altitude. Experimentation showed that a C.500.T[69] which burst 500m above ground level created a contaminated zone roughly equivalent in diameter to that altitude.[70] Their use was somewhat complicated by the necessity of checking wind direction at ground-level first. This could only be done from the air by dropping a smoke-bomb and observing the effect. Later testing demonstrated that given precise calculation of aircraft speed, wind speed and wind direction, exploding the bomb at an altitude of 250m created a high-concentration 'dispersion ellipse' of some 650m × 150m on the ground.[71]

It seems almost superfluous to point out that in regards to its approach to chemical weapons generally with regards to Ethiopia, and particularly in evolving this new device specifically for use there, the Fascist government was demonstrating clear intent to violate the 1925 Geneva Protocol. This document, to which both Italy and Ethiopia (though the latter had no chemical warfare capability) were signatories, specifically prohibited recourse to such methods.[72]

This was merely a 'scrap of paper' to Mussolini who, in his Top Secret directive of 30 December 1934, had declared that the 'problem of Italian-Abyssinian relations' has:

> become a problem of strength; a historical problem: which must be solved by the only means by which these problems were always solved: by the use of weapons ... Having decided on war, the objective can only be the destruction of the Abyssinian forces and armies and the total conquest of Ethiopia. An empire cannot be made otherwise.[73]

Thus only by brute force could the Gordian knot of Italian-Abyssinian relations, which he had himself tied, be cut. As he was to later put it, the purpose of the Ethiopian campaign was 'to settle once and for all the great account which had been left open since 1896'.[74]

Chapter Three

'A Terrain of Crag and Precipice'

Amateurs talk tactics, professionals talk logistics.[1]

* * *

In setting out to recreate a version of the *Imperium Romanum* in Africa, Fascist Italy had perforce to first resurrect one of that empire's most notable achievements. As an American commentator put it: 'like Caesar's legions, these modern Romans had to build their roads in order to fight'.[2] In fact the roads and other communications in those colonial territories which would provide the jumping-off points for an Ethiopian campaign, Eritrea and Somalia, were deemed either non-existent or totally inadequate:

> When Emilio De Bono disembarked at Massawa [on 16 January 1935] the preparations which had been made before his arrival were absolutely inadequate for their purpose ... The equipment of Eritrea, in respect of harbours, roads, economic organization, and military strength, had to be multiplied a hundredfold, and not by an indefinite date, but within a very brief space of time, specified and established almost as a dogma: October, 1935.[3]

De Bono was, as appointed by Mussolini, the commander-in-chief designate of the attack on Ethiopia.[4] Although he had a distinguished career in the Italian Army, serving in the Italo-Ottoman (1911–1912) and First World (1915–1918) Wars, reaching the rank of major general by the close of the latter conflict, he was not chosen for his military expertise. It was rather his Fascist credentials which appealed to *Il Duce*, who wanted a Fascist war, under his personal direction, in which a large proportion of Italy's combatants, if not a majority, should be drawn from the ranks of the Fascist militia: the *Milizia Volontaria per la Sicurezza Nazionale* or MVSN (Voluntary Militia for National Security) better known as Blackshirts.[5] Mussolini's stated reasoning was that the involvement of the Blackshirts would demonstrate popular approval of the venture.[6]

De Bono was a member of the *quadrumviri* and had held a number of important offices in the Fascist regime. These included (1 February 1923–31 October 1924) being joint chief of staff (with Italo Balbo) of the MVSN. He was also governor of Tripolitania (Libya) from 1925 to 1928, and colonial minister from 1929 until 16 January 1935, the latter date being when he stepped ashore at Massawa, whereupon he became high commissioner for East Africa and, as already noted, C-in-C designate.[7]

Earlier, in mid-1932, De Bono had formulated a plan for undertaking offensive operations against Ethiopia, which he disseminated on 29 November 1932 to Mussolini and the Army General Staff. This 'Memorandum regarding offensive action against Ethiopia' (*Memoria per un'azione offensiva contro l'Etiopia*) proposed limited operations on a relatively small scale by a force some 85,000 strong, largely composed of *ascari* and Blackshirts, supported by around 100 aircraft.[8] It posited, as Rochat pointed out, operations involving minimal risk, cost and complexity.[9] The inevitable corollary, given that it advanced a colonial-style campaign with narrow and limited objectives, was that it would have minimum impact and effectiveness in terms of smashing the armed forces of Ethiopia and occupying its territory on anything like a large scale.[10] That the latter object was what Mussolini desired became clear, at least to De Bono if he is to be believed, in the autumn of 1933. According to his account: 'The Duce had spoken to no one of the coming operations in East Africa; only he and I knew what was going to happen.'[11]

The General Staff of the Army opposed the plan as being far too limited in terms of the expected end result. They were, indeed, unenthusiastic about the entire operation, being concerned about the despatch overseas of a large military force at a time when Nazi designs on Austria, a part of Hitler's quest for uniting Germans under his rule,[12] and which Mussolini was instrumental in assisting Austria to resist, were ongoing.[13] However, one of the predominant reasons for Army hostility was that the higher command saw De Bono and his ministry as infringing upon their prerogatives. Marshall Pietro Badoglio, a former chief of the general staff and now governor of Tripolitania and Cyrenaica (Libya) took particular umbrage at the proposed reallocation of resources from his command without consultation. Indeed, the Army's senior officers perceived that the intention was to supplant them entirely, with the replacement being a totally 'Fascist' institution. This belief was not unfounded: an unnamed senior official of the Colonial Ministry is recorded as telling Brigadier General Quirino Armellini that in the coming war against Ethiopia 'we will demonstrate that we can do without the General Staff'.[14]

This was, of course, the stuff of fantasy. It arguably paralleled the notion that Ernst Röhm, the leader of the Nazi Brownshirts, held for his *Sturmabteilung* (SA) to absorb and replace the German military. Or at least he did until Hitler had him shot on 1 July 1934.[15] Mussolini took less drastic action, merely realising that if the war were to succeed then the full cooperation of the General Staff, and the Army more generally, would be essential. Since he also wanted the matter, as De Bono phrased it, 'settled no later than 1936', then it followed that the invasion plan would have to be dramatically recast and scaled up.[16]

It was indeed, and whilst it is not proposed to deal with it in detail this involved a massive investment of resources in improving communications and infrastructure in Eritrea and, to a much lesser extent, Somalia. The former possessed only one half-decent port, at Massawa (*Massaua*), through which all men and materiel would need to pass. This was, according to De Bono, inadequate for the purpose.

Indeed, in his published account of his time in command he argued that Massawa 'had almost ceased to be a port with the building of the Khartoum and Port Sudan railways'.[17]

Given that the railway in question, from Khartoum via Atbara to Port Sudan, had been completed in 1906, then De Bono's account suggested Massawa had been moribund for decades.[18] This is, however, contradicted by a 1931 report

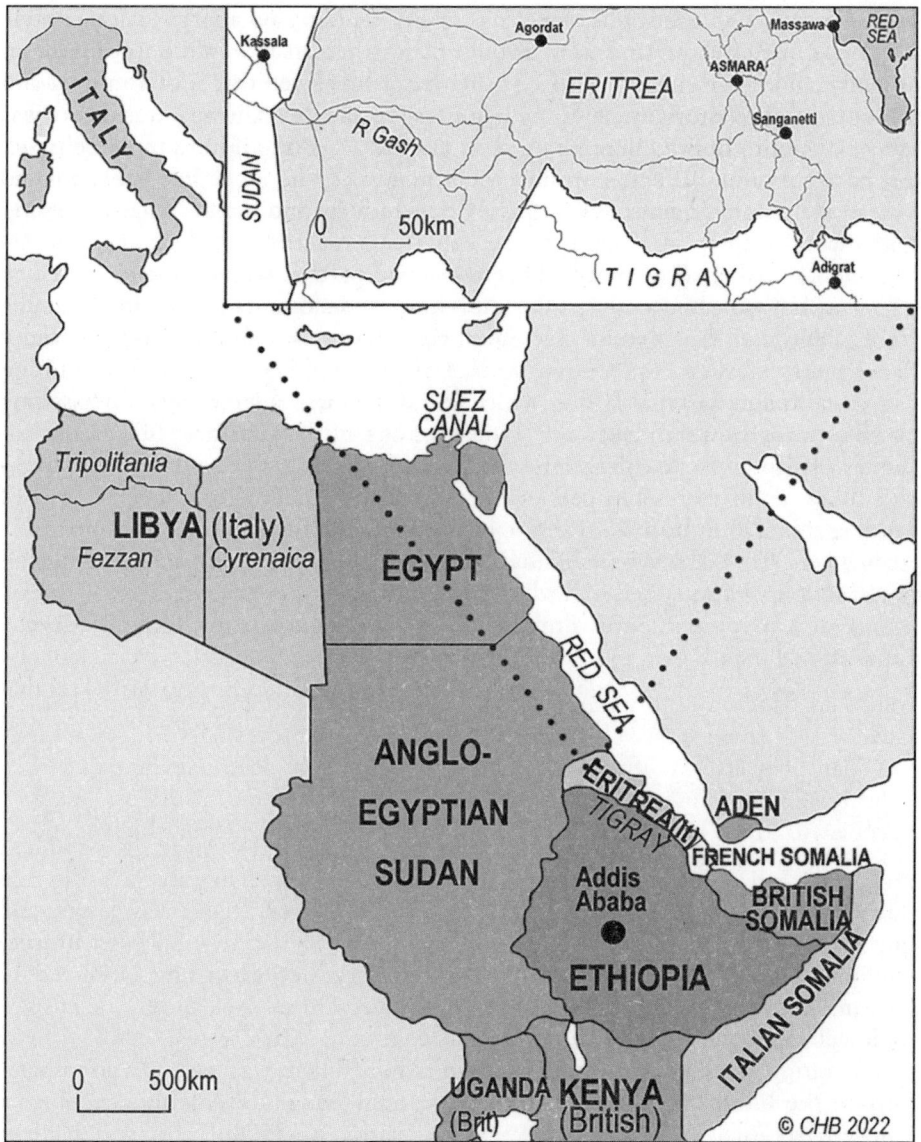

East Africa showing Ethiopia and (inset) Eritrea: the northern front. (© *Charles Blackwood*)

by the US Consul at Aden, Carlton Hurst. Using official Italian sources he calculated that: 'During 1929 entrances at the port of Massaua registered 597,600 tons net, and 71,500 metric tons of merchandise was unloaded. Shipments from that port during the same year amounted to 86,100 metric tons. A total of 224 vessels were engaged in this trade, out of which 183 were of Italian nationality.'[19]

If Massawa was perhaps not quite the complete backwater De Bono claimed, it would still be mightily stretched in terms of building up a large army with all its impedimenta in Eritrea. His account states that 'matters were improved by widening one of the quays and lengthening a breakwater'.[20] Communications from the port to the interior of the colony were also poor. There was a narrow-gauge (600mm) railway which ran from the port via Asmara, the capital city, to Agordat, a total of 310km. This line, according to Hurst, conveyed 98,171 tonnes of goods and 99,952 passengers in 1929 and 11,564 tonnes and 111,463 passengers the following year.[21] De Bono reckoned it 'a magnificent piece of engineering, but of very small capacity'. This he blamed partly on its rolling stock being obsolete, but mainly because of the steep gradients along its mountainous route: 'It is enough to say that in 120 kilometres there is a difference of level of 2,471 metres.'[22]

The situation as regards roads was also difficult, although, again according to Hurst's report, there had been some attempts at improvement: 'The Government has also constructed a network of wagon roads comprising approximately 275 miles of highways and 650 miles of narrower military roads.'[23] Notwithstanding this, De Bono was of the opinion that none of the roads, including the main artery from Massawa to Asmara, could be classed as practicable for mechanical traffic. He explained that whilst it was true they were used by a few score of motor-cars, which represented normal traffic, not one was asphalted. There were other impediments:

> all had dangerous turns and steep gradients, while only certain stretches were wide enough for vehicles to pass. There were a few small bridges, with a span of twelve or fifteen feet, but none that really deserved the name of bridge; so that during the rains there were often lasting interruptions, and to cope with these it was necessary to resort to various expedients which would have been impossible in the case of intensive traffic.[24]

The position in Somalia, where General Rodolfo Graziani was appointed governor general and commander-in-chief in February 1935, was worse. In fact, so poor were the communications in that territory that, according to his recollection, the role assigned to him by the General Staff was purely defensive: 'quiescence on the shores of the Indian Ocean'.[25]

The rationale behind this was comprehensible. There was basically no railway beyond the line begun in 1918 from the capital, Mogadishu, which eventually reached Afgooye in September 1924, a distance of 29km. This was further extended, however, so that by September 1927 it had a total length of 113km,

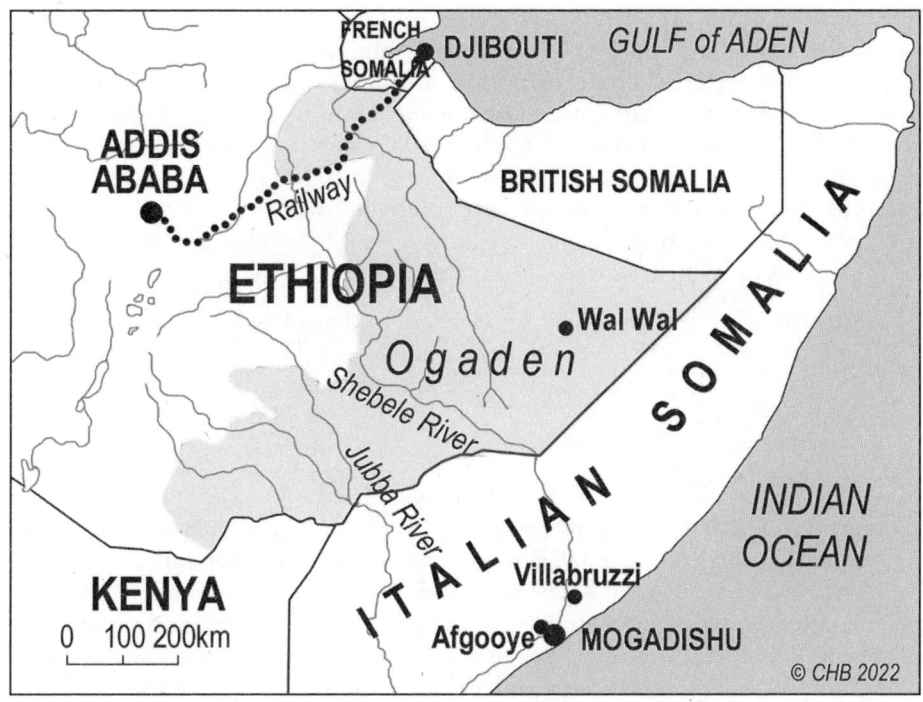

Somalia and Ethiopia: the southern front. (© *Charles Blackwood*)

connecting with the agricultural settlement of Villabruzzi (*Villaggio Duca degli Abruzzi*).[26] The absence of even a rudimentary railway network meant that roads of a sort were constructed, although these were of poor quality with concomitant limitations. Indeed, there was only one road in the entire colony which was ballasted, and that paralleled the railway from Mogadishu to Afgooye.[27] As Graziani later put it: 'An offensive action from the South, in the main direction of Harar about 1,300 kilometres from the coast of the Indian Ocean and having to cross an area absolutely devoid of resources through the arid Somali bush, was not to be envisaged without adequate and powerful equipment for the transport of men and vehicles.'[28]

He had, though, a reputation to maintain.[29] Determined to play more than just a supporting role to De Bono's operations in the north, he conceived a methodology whereby his forces could indeed operate across and through the 'arid Somali bush' into the Ogaden. Despite being 'arid', the area, essentially a vast plateau about 900m above sea level, also suffered from heavy seasonal rainfall which could turn the ground to mud. The British Army had pioneered the use of road-locomotives (traction engines) for towing trailers during the South African, or Second Boer, War of 1899–1902.[30] Now Graziani followed suit, utilising a later generation of equipment that promised much greater flexibility. The requirement was for vehicles that would prove capable of surmounting the difficulties of the muddy and uneven surface of natural slopes, the recessed and steep slopes of wadis, and to move whatever the terrain.[31] Bypassing the regular chain of command, but with the consent of Mussolini and using Colonial Ministry funds, Graziani ordered 185 Caterpillar tractors (crawlers) and 200 tracked trailers directly from the United States.[32] Each unit, of one tractor and two (sometimes three) trailers, could transport a 20 tonne load at a maximum speed of around 14km per hour (8mph).[33] As he retrospectively phrased it:

> The vehicles, loaded in America on specially equipped and hired steamers, arrived with regularity and were put ashore and set in motion.[34] With the same spirit of initiative, provision was made for the collection of fuels and all other materials from India, South Africa, and Japan. Thus the small southern army was placed in a position to take the offensive ... with enough logistical support to operate over extended distances of several hundred kilometres from their bases. The troops were in fact able, with the Caterpillar logistic trains, to manoeuvre both strategically and tactically.[35]

Graziani's 'small southern army', when up to strength, was to be based around two infantry formations: the 1st Libyan Division (*Divisione indigena Libia I*) and the 29th *Peloritana* Infantry Division.[36] These were supported by further units, including the six-battalion Somali Native Corps (*Corpo indigeni somali*)[37] and later (and of minimal military value) by the Blackshirt 'Tevere' Division.[38] When the troops marched they would be followed by the *treni caterpillar* (caterpillar trains), mobile storehouses from which they could draw as necessary.[39] In order to provide air cover for these movements, and for supporting the offensive generally, fifty-four airfields were constructed in Somalia. This was almost twice as many as the twenty-nine built in Eritrea, despite the latter being the jumping-off point for the main effort.[40]

In fact, De Bono assembled a force many times greater than Graziani's; in terms of sheer numbers, it constituted the largest ever assembled for an African war.[41] Between February 1935 and January 1936 seven regular army infantry divisions, plus five Blackshirt divisions, were despatched to Eritrea from Italy and encadred in four Army Corps plus supporting formations.[42] That wasn't the end of it, however, as around 100,000 civilian labourers were also sent; the problems of terrain on the northern front required a different solution from those applied to the southern front (see below). All in all, some 460,000 fighting men were transported to East Africa, where, of course, plus their support and administrative 'tail', they had to be maintained.[43] This necessitated a colossal effort, all of which ultimately depended upon a sea line of communication with a single, and highly vulnerable, choke-point at the Suez Canal.

Although under effective British control, the canal had always been an international waterway: 'from the outset [the Suez Canal was] the object of international agreements which culminated in 1888 in the Constantinople Convention guaranteeing freedom of transit and navigation under perfect equality to all vessels of the world in time of peace and war'.[44] All well and good, but this guarantee had been comprehensively breached during the First World War when the canal was closed to ships belonging to the Central Powers.[45] Indeed, it might be argued that the British authorities had previous form in this regard; during the Spanish-American War of 1898 they successfully delayed Spain's attempts to reinforce the Philippines.[46]

The danger from the Italian perspective wasn't that initiating a war with Ethiopia would automatically bring on a conflict with Britain as such, but rather that it might attract economic sanctions from the League of Nations which the British and French would attempt to enforce using their military and naval power. That Italy was intent on a conflict was clear as early as February 1935, even though attempts at peaceful settlement were still, at least ostensibly, ongoing under the auspices of the League. Italy was of course 'negotiating' in bad faith, and when the final impasse came on 5 July 1935 with the indefinite adjournment of the Italo-Ethiopian arbitration commission, the prospect that Britain might become involved began to definitely exercise the minds of the British politicians. Indeed, on that day the British government cabinet secretary, at the instigation of prime minister Stanley Baldwin, contacted the service chiefs. He 'wished them to bear in mind the military implications of Britain's carrying out the requirements of Article 16, the sanctions article, of the League of Nations Covenant'.[47] The chiefs of staff responded on 30 July, stating that the application of sanctions would almost inevitably lead to war with Italy, as would any efforts to interrupt her communications. Furthermore, the possibility of war required the active cooperation of other members of the League, France in particular, and this must be arranged in advance.[48]

That Britain was perceived as being unfriendly towards Italy's ongoing concentration of forces in Eritrea and Somalia was commented upon by De Bono, particularly with regard to the movement of aircraft:

> In the beginning a few squadrons of aeroplanes were sent out by air. This system was said to be the best, and it was the quickest; but even towards the end of February [1935] we could no longer absolutely count on it. Our machines were obliged to land at Cairo, then at Khartoum, where the authorities, both English and Egyptian, subjected them to strict inspection.
>
> Truth compels me to say that the British Governor of Khartoum and the Resident at Kassala [eastern Sudan close to the border with Eritrea] were always extremely uncivil where I was concerned. The vague but persistent menace of measures to be taken to our detriment was already in the air; so that for every reason it was advisable to keep to the safer method, which was to send the machines out by steamer.[49]

The situation paralleled in many ways that of 1911, when so-called 'Liberal' Italy had declared war on the Ottoman Empire and invaded what became Libya. Although both states disapproved of the Italian campaign, British and French policy had been, in essence, fairly simple: strict neutrality. This followed from their wish to do nothing that might reinforce Italian adhesion to her Triple

Alliance partners Germany and Austria-Hungary. The rationale behind this policy was, in Winston Churchill's analysis, because Britain and France had need to 'gain Italy against the darkening German menace'.[50] Once again then, a 'German menace' was 'darkening' the European scene and so, as before, Britain and France were trying to 'gain' Italy. Thus Mussolini was fairly certain, and definitely prepared to gamble, that neither Britain nor France would take action. He is recorded as claiming that if forced to make a choice between Italy and the League of Nations, Britain would choose Italy.[51] He was well aware that both states wanted to maintain good relations and that the vital interests of neither were directly threatened by an Italian invasion of Ethiopia. This was so despite the British having substantial colonial territories in East Africa, which shared significantly longer borders with Ethiopia than French or Italian possessions did. What he didn't know was that Britain's armed forces, and the Royal Navy particularly, were ill prepared for conflict in any event.[52] Nevertheless, and to quote the words of Arthur J. Barker, 'with a quarter of a million men on the far side of the [Suez] Canal in an area where they could hardly get enough drinking water and certainly not enough food, Mussolini had provided a hostage for any maritime power that chose to attack her'.[53]

If Mussolini was prepared to, as the phrase has it, 'bet the farm' on the conquest of Ethiopia, the possibility that this could fail and, perhaps more importantly, provoke a war with Britain exercised the minds of several important figures.[54] Chief amongst these was the King of Italy, Victor Emmanuel III, whose opposition was such that he went so far as threatening to abdicate, according to Alberto Sbacchi.[55] If so, then this particular top-down threat to the regime was never made good, whilst all the forces that the state could command were enlisted to nullify domestic threats from the other direction. On 9 February 1935 the minister of the interior, Guido Buffarani, despatched instructions concerning the treatment of those who opposed Mussolini's policy regarding Ethiopia: 'defeatists had to be found, repressed and punished with rigour'. The expression of negative opinions incurred the danger of being 'physically attacked, sent to prison, or confined'. Sbacchi records 1,424 political confinements, 2,577 imprisonments and 936 special police investigations being carried out in 1935 by OVRA, the Fascist secret police.[56]

Negative opinion wasn't confined to the political sphere, but was also a reflection of the pertaining economic situation. Unemployment remained high during the period of military mobilisation and those in work found their earnings falling behind as prices increased.[57] This was of little or no consequence to *Il Duce*, who prioritised preparations for the invasion above all else. De Bono recounted one example of this, quoting a telegram from Mussolini in respect of purchasing lorries and quadrupeds for the theatre: 'As for transport, I give you more than carte blanche.'[58]

Mussolini was, at least according to his son-in-law and at that time foreign minister Galeazzo Ciano, to disparage De Bono in 1942 by referring to him as 'an old idiot'. Expanding on this, he opined that 'he has always been an idiot and now he is also aged'.[59] If cliché be forgiven, a considerable amount of water had flowed under the Fascist bridge by then and none of it in the right direction from the perspective of *Il Duce*. Indeed, the 'spirit of the Nation', which had been 'sure of its radiant future under the guidance of Il Duce'[60] had by then been deflated somewhat and this may well have soured his outlook. In any event, he certainly had no cause to complain of De Bono's efforts some seven years earlier. Indeed, in the relatively short period from his assuming command in Eritrea in January 1935 to the deadline for action in October, and given the vagaries of the climate,[61] a considerable amount was achieved under his auspices. This included expanding the port of Massawa, the improvement and construction of over 1,000km of roads – principally upgrading that between Massawa and Asmara, and constructing four parallel secondary routes – and enhancing, so far as was possible, the railway with passing places for two-way operation. The requisite organisation and infrastructure for feeding, watering and accommodating a force that would approach half a million soldiers, plus 100,000 civilian labourers and 80,000 animals, was also created. Depots and warehouses for military materiel had to be built and stocked, and a communication system comprising hundreds of kilometres of telegraph and telephone lines established. The 'caterpillar' solution adopted by Graziani in Somalia was unsuitable for the mountainous terrain of Eritrea where it bordered the Ethiopian region of Tigray (*Tigrai* to the Italians). Indeed heavy, tracked vehicles would destroy the roads so several thousand wheeled vehicles had to be sent from Italy, plus tens of thousands of tonnes of fuel to allow them to move. Such large-scale mechanisation, with 3,250 vehicles arriving in July–August alone, required both fixed and mobile workshops for maintenance purposes.[62]

All in all, the scale of the Italian effort in Eritrea and Somalia was astonishing, and the rapidity with which it was accomplished may, as Brigadier General Longo says in the official history, have wrong-footed foreign critics.[63] De Bono, no doubt with an eye on his chief, put such successes down to Fascism having radically transformed Italy to the extent that its people were no longer those who had been defeated at Adowa. Rather, they were now stimulated by 'the unsurpassed spirit of devotion to the Duce and to Fascism'.[64] The results on the ground of this 'devotion to Fascism' portended Italy's ultimate intention with respect to Ethiopia. In Britain a report by a committee under the chairmanship of Sir John Maffey, a former governor general of Anglo-Egyptian Sudan, delivered on 18 June 1935 argued that: 'The chief result of Italian sabre-rattling has been to intensify and confirm Ethiopian suspicions of Italy (always latent since Adowa), and also to make world opinion watchful and suspicious. In Ethiopian eyes Italy stands fully revealed as the enemy . . .'[65]

No amount of devotion could, though, at least before the event, overcome the communication problems that De Bono's Eritrea-based forces would encounter once they entered Ethiopia. These were of a high order: the landscape has been picturesquely described as being 'a terrain of crag and precipice, where Nature seems to have lost her temper with the landscape or to have become demented'.[66]

Another author pronounced the country as 'The Switzerland of Africa' and went on to list Ethiopia's 'allies against which tanks, airplanes, and poison-gas will be useless':

> sun-stroke; burning waterless deserts; towering peaks; gorges and ravines a mile deep; no roads; wide rivers to be bridged; sand storms; lack of sanitary drinking water; poisoned wells; tropical downpours that make the ground slippery as soap; insects, whose bites cause irritation, disease, and death; malaria and other tropical maladies; and the pressure of high altitudes.[67]

There were, of course, roads through this fearsome topography, at least of a kind. One foreign correspondent's description of the trans-border Asmara to Adigrat road, which ran for some 200km, is revealing:

> It is well engineered and its first lap is comparatively easy going. Part of its surface is tarred, but from Sanganetti [Mes-hal Wedekele, Eritrea] to Adigrat it resembles the teeth of a saw set into the side of the mountain ridges. How many hair-pin bends it contains I do not know, but in 31 miles [around 50km] of it there have been counted 1,700.[68]

Ethiopia also possessed a single, and vitally important, railway which connected Addis Ababa with Djibouti, the principal port-city and capital of French Somaliland (*Cote francaise des Somalis*). Constructed over the years 1897–1917, this metre-gauge, single-track line ran for some 785km and constituted landlocked Ethiopia's only outlet to the sea. Its construction reduced the length of time it took to travel from Djibouti to Addis Ababa, and vice versa, from six weeks to three days.[69] Given its line of travel, however, it was of no use at all to an invader moving in from Eritrea.

Such were the physical difficulties faced by De Bono's command, difficulties which would, of course, be compounded by the fact that they would also be facing an alerted enemy.

Chapter Four

'Fascism believes neither in the possibility nor the utility of perpetual peace'

The League could ... be no more successful than the Great Powers were willing to make it.[1]

* * *

Aside from the difficulties occasioned by Ethiopia's geography, which according to Fuller's analysis meant that 'strategically [it] is like a porcupine bristling with quite exceptional difficulties',[2] there were two other factors that served to deter Italy from invading: the military and the political.

In terms of the former, Haile Selassie, who as Negus (King of Kings or Emperor) since 1930, was head of state, head of government and the ultimate holder of executive, judicial and legislative power, could theoretically mobilise considerable military force.[3] Italian intelligence reckoned they would face around 280,000–350,000 Ethiopians, but there was practically no army as such. Or at least not one on the European model. This was so because, according to Evelyn Waugh, and as Haile Selassie had explained to him, Ethiopia was 'a mediaeval state, a cohesive whole held together by the intricate bonds of feudalism'.[4] Whether he actually said this or not is open to question, but there's no doubt that as a statement it was largely accurate. Therefore, and reflecting the society from which they sprang, these troops would be raised by regional rulers, the Rases, to whom they owed allegiance. Not all Rases, however, were necessarily loyal to Haile Selassie and they pursued their own financial and dynastic interests. The British diplomat Sir Rennell Rodd, who had experience in Ethiopia and was Ambassador to Italy from 1908 to 1919, described the country and its government in the following terms:

> [It] consists of a number of kingdoms or principalities, the ruler of one of which from time to time has established his authority as overlord or king of kings. When he has been a strong man ... he has undoubtedly ruled over the whole country, and treated the other princes or rasses [sic] as mere vassals. The central Government ... hardly exercises the control over certain sections of the country.[5]

Those Rases who were loyal would send contingents but, despite having great personal fighting skills, these possessed little in the way of modern equipment or adequate training. Stuart Emeny, War Correspondent for the *News Chronicle*, described encountering a body of these men:

> Fierce warriors, many of whom had never seen a motor car or a white man before, swarmed into the capital [Addis Ababa], singing their war songs and brandishing swords and spears. I tried to pass a contingent of them in my car in the town one day but I received such menacing looks that I waited until they were well out of the way before going on … Barefooted, wild and bearded, many of them had dyed their normally white robes a pinkish brown in muddy streams on the march up as a camouflage against Italian marksmen. At one time there were over 40,000 of them in the city. They besieged the Gebbi (palace) shouting for the Emperor, clamouring for guns and ammunition, and boasting their bravery.[6]

That there were indeed 'guns and ammunition' available to distribute was down to the Negus. Shortly after his accession, a purchasing commission was despatched to Europe in an attempt to import modern equipment. The pace of this effort was increased in 1934 and, although sources vary, by the following year Ethiopia's forces possessed around 200,000 rifles, 250 machine guns of various types, plus small quantities of light and anti-aircraft artillery. Much of this had been imported from Belgium, Czechoslovakia and Germany, but some was also sourced further afield in Japan.[7] There was, though, no medium or heavy artillery, and the miniscule air force in late 1935 totalled 'ten flyable planes and eighteen pilots, the new ones with less than 150 hours total time'.[8] This unit was commanded by the African-American aviator John Robinson, although none of the aircraft was equipped for combat or bombing.[9]

Foreign assistance, via a Belgian Military Mission, had also been enlisted in respect of training an elite unit responsible directly to the Negus: the Imperial Guard.[10] The Belgian government was, however, to withdraw these personnel when war broke out, although a replacement of twelve officers comprising an 'unofficial' mission was to arrive in their stead. Even so, the Imperial Guard, which by 1935 totalled about 5,000 officers and men in four infantry battalions, a machine-gun company and a squadron of cavalry, was largely insignificant in the grand scheme of things.[11] Much the same could be said of other foreigners who travelled to Ethiopia, although one recent study describes the Italian government as being 'paranoid' about the prospect.[12] Perhaps it was because, as De Bono remarked, 'in their relations with the Abyssinian chiefs these European mercenaries continued to depict us as the people who were defeated at Adowa'.[13]

Other than supposedly making disparaging remarks about Italian military prowess, these foreigners could have, with one exception, little impact. Their number is estimated at about 200, of whom around 115 were medical, Red Cross personnel and the like, with the rest being military advisers and adventurers of one kind or another. This latter category embraced three Americans (including Robinson, as mentioned above) and the twelve Belgians. Twenty Swiss, thirteen

British, eight Germans, six French, five Austrians, four Swedes, two Russians, one Cuban and one Italian (later captured and shot for treason) also fought on the Ethiopian side.[14]

Six Turks also fought in Ethiopia, the most important of whom was Mehmed Vehib: the exception referred to above. Now aged 60, and also known as Vehip Pasha or Wehib Pasha (in English), and Weib (or Wehib) pascià to the Italians, he was a former general in the Ottoman Army who had fought in Tripoli (Libya) in 1911–1912, in the 1912–1913 Balkan Wars and the 1914–1918 First World War. Exiled from Turkey, and with his citizenship revoked, he was in Egypt in the spring of 1935, but travelled to Ethiopia in early June. At the end of that month Haile Selassie seemingly offered to appoint Vehip Pasha as commander-in-chief of the Abyssinian armies. If so, then this didn't come about. Rather, he was despatched in September to the southern (Somali) front as chief of staff to the Ras commanding there.[15]

If De Bono was correct in stating that 'European mercenaries' were intent on painting Italians in a poor light militarily, then their efforts were attended with some success, at least according to the previously quoted Emeny: 'The faith of Abyssinia in the League of Nations and in the belief that Great Britain, in particular, would come to her assistance was pathetic. Equally touching was the belief of everybody from government officials to the Ethiopian man in the street that if necessary they could thrash the Italians single-handed.'[16] He went on to add that 'They seemed incapable of appreciating the overwhelming strength of a modern Great Power equipped with mechanised transport, tanks, aeroplanes, poison gas and unlimited ammunition.' He was, of course, writing retrospectively, and whilst the pre-war confidence amongst the Ethiopians he noted may have been 'pathetic', it was not necessarily ill-founded.

The brainchild of US President Woodrow Wilson, the League of Nations was 'intermeshed' with the peace treaty signed in 1919 following the defeat of Germany in the First World War. In setting it up, Wilson got the agreement of the four principal Allied Powers that had emerged victorious: the British Empire, France, Italy and Japan. Thus the Treaty of Versailles, as with the several other treaties imposed on the defeated Central Powers,[17] contained a 'Covenant' containing the League's constitution and the agreement of the victorious nations, including, of course, the US, to join it. Many of the provisions of the peace treaty would be administered by the League. As Wilson conceived it, the League of Nations would be an organisation before which nations would bring their complaints and grievances, whereupon it would investigate such matters and render a peaceful judgment.[18] Headquartered at Geneva, the League would have a Council with five permanent members – the 'Representatives of the Principal Allied and Associated Powers' – plus four more 'selected from time to time and at its discretion' by an Assembly consisting of all the members.[19] To Wilson's chagrin, however, the American Senate refused to ratify the Treaty of Versailles and consequently the United States never became a member.[20]

There were forty-two founding members in 1920, with elements of the British Empire accounting for six of them.[21] Ethiopia was not an original member, but sought formally to join on 1 August 1923. The prime mover behind this was Ras Tafari, who was then responsible for foreign policy and was heir apparent, and regent plenipotentiary, to Empress (*Negiste Negest* or Queen of Kings) Zawditu. Despite some difficulties, and a great deal of Franco-British-Italian self-interested political manoeuvring, the application succeeded and thus on 28 September 1923 Ethiopia became only the second African state to join.[22] There were those who opined that this should not have happened, one such being Winston Churchill, who later stated that: 'No one can keep up the pretence that Abyssinia is a fit, worthy and equal member of a league of civilised nations', and insisted that admitting the country to the League was a mistake.[23] Churchill was at that time also a firm admirer of Mussolini and his regime, and remained so 'to the brink of World War II'.[24] He was, though, very much in his 'wilderness years' during the period in question, so his opinions counted for little. They certainly had no influence upon the British government, which was publicly committed to the idea of collective security as embodied in the League, and which would fight a general election with that notion as a central plank of its appeal in November 1935.[25] Whilst that was for the future, Ras Tafari, who had become Haile Selassie in 1930, and his government placed their faith in Article 16, the sanctions article, of the League of Nations Covenant.[26] That they had every right to do so, as a full member of the League, is undeniable. But whether or not their faith in 1935 was naïve is questionable. Certainly, the League had acquired a somewhat chequered record by that date.

Indeed, it was the case that, as with the previously discussed 1923 Corfu Incident, the League had proved largely impotent when confronted with an aggressor who refused to play by the rules. Probably the most glaring example of this had manifested itself in respect of Japan's military operations in Manchuria in 1931. Attacked and unable to defend itself, China appealed to the League of Nations and the United States for assistance. These appeals proved useless and a Japanese puppet state was carved out of Chinese territory; named Manchukuo (the Manchu State), it promulgated its Declaration of Independence on 18 February 1932. Although the League condemned Japan's actions, it did little else other than send an inquiry commission to China under the leadership of a British diplomat, the Earl of Lytton. The Lytton Commission issued its report in September 1932 and recommended that the League refuse recognition of Manchukuo and proposed measures to re-establish the status quo. China accepted these recommendations. Japan did not, and withdrew from the League in March 1933.[27]

Manchuria was a very long way from Europe (and Africa) and Japan was a dominant Asian power. Indeed, the only state that might have been able to apply economic or other pressure on Japan was the United States of America. This would, of course, have been difficult and likely to have led to war. If the judgement that 'The League could ... be no more successful than the Great Powers were willing to make it'[28] is accepted, then it is perhaps unsurprising that it failed in respect of the Manchurian affair.

Much the same, certainly in terms of distance from European centres of power, could be said to apply to another war where the League was unable, or failed, to meaningfully intervene: the three-year conflict between Bolivia and Paraguay known as the Chaco War of 1932–1935.[29] Virtually unknown today, the conflict was a territorial dispute between two League members. According to one historian of the conflict, the lack of League involvement was likely due to none of the Great Powers having any interest in the matter, and the opposition of Argentina, Brazil and the United States to their intervention. The League apparently would have liked to become involved in seeking to end the conflict 'but not enough to risk alienating anyone'.[30]

On the other hand, that mere distance from Europe was not necessarily an insuperable obstacle was demonstrated when the League was involved in arbitrating and settling a dispute between Colombia and Peru. Dubbed the Leticia War, this was a short-lived conflict over territory in the Amazon rainforest that lasted from 1 September 1932 to 24 May 1933. By way of contrast with the Bolivia-Paraguay war, both the Brazilian and United States governments were supportive of League intervention, and the combatants were also agreeable.[31]

An earlier success, and one rather closer to home as it were, had occurred in the case of the 'War of the Stray Dog', also known as the 'Incident at Petrich', the 'Demir-Kapu Incident' or, more formally, the Greek-Bulgarian Incident of 1925. This involved a skirmish on 19 October 1925 in the Demir-Kapu pass near the Bulgarian border town of Petrich, which may or may not have involved a stray dog, between Bulgarian and Greek troops. It escalated to the extent that Greek forces advanced some distance into Bulgaria, which, having been on the losing side during the First World War and thus disarmed, found itself unable to resist. It complained to the League. More importantly, three Great Powers – Italy, France and Britain – coordinated their response and put diplomatic pressure on Greece. This led to it effectively backing down and accepting arbitration and a settlement under the League's auspices. Beck makes the point, though, that the main role of the League in this instance was to act as an 'instrument offering the great powers a channel through which they could act *as and when they wished* [original emphasis]. The coincidence of great powers interests was a vital factor...'[32] As the British politician and historian Herbert Fisher wrote in 1935: 'The League of Nations can be no better than the member states of which it is composed. If they wish for peace, the League provides machinery by which peace may be better secured and maintained, but League or no League, a state which is resolved on war can always have it.'[33]

This is somewhat akin to an international version of the 'good chap' theory of British government. As the authors of that notion put it: 'We have long assumed that those who rise to high office will be "good chaps".'[34] Italy under Mussolini was not, however, a 'good chap'. Whilst this was perhaps not as blindingly obvious before late 1935 as it was later to become, Mussolini made no bones about his, and thus Fascism's, attitude to matters of peace and war. Consider, for example, an extract from an article he put his name to, and which first appeared in the 1932 edition of *Enciclopedia Italiana di Scienze, Lettere e Arti* ('Italian Encyclopaedia of Science, Letters and the Arts'). This piece was more widely published in booklet form thereafter as *La dottrina del fascismo* ('The Doctrine of Fascism'), and was translated into several languages.[35] It stated that 'above all',

> Fascism believes neither in the possibility nor the utility of perpetual peace. It thus repudiates the doctrine of Pacifism – born of a renunciation of the struggle and an act of cowardice in the face of sacrifice. War alone brings up to its highest tension all human energy and puts the stamp of nobility upon the peoples who have the courage to meet it. All other trials are substitutes, which never really put men into the position where they have to make the great decision – the alternative of life or death.[36]

This cod-philosophy, whilst indicative of intent, was, of course, mere words. Deeds are, proverbially, what count and the build-up of forces in East Africa in 1935 was definitely a deed that counted mightily. Given this, and the League's mixed history, then it is arguable that those Ethiopians who placed their faith in it were indeed being somewhat gullible.[37] This is accentuated when considering that they were being openly threatened by one of the four Great Powers holding a permanent seat on the League's Council.[38] Further, it was becoming plainly evident that Italy was ruled by a dictator with the 'mentality of a gangster',[39] who negotiated in bad faith and to whom supposedly binding commitments were mere 'scraps of paper' which counted for nothing. On the other hand, and according to the account of George Steer: 'Haile Selassie ... believed that the words of Treaties, that the pledges of one nation to another meant something.'[40]

Indeed, and aside from those obligations incumbent upon Italy as a member of the League of Nations, there was also the 'Treaty of Amity, Conciliation and Arbitration' with Ethiopia which had been signed at Addis Ababa on 2 August 1928. As per its terms, the parties agreed under Article 2: 'not to engage, under any pretext, in action calculated to injure or prejudice the independence of the other'.[41] Both countries were also signatories of the 'Geneva Gas Protocol' which dated from 17 June 1925,[42] although they became so at different times. It came into force so far as Italy was concerned on 3 April 1928, whereas Ethiopia didn't accede until 20 September 1935: the period when an Italian invasion appeared, and indeed was, imminent.[43] This, though, was irrelevant given that the Protocol prohibited the use of chemical weapons, as Ethiopia had none.[44]

That Italy intended to break or ignore these various treaties and obligations had become obvious, the Geneva Protocol excepted, from early in 1935. As previously mentioned, this would effectively force France and Britain into an excruciatingly difficult and mutually exclusive choice. If they supported Ethiopia via the League, then this would push Italy closer to Germany. On the other hand, a blind eye turned to Italian aggression would severely damage the system of collective security that the League embodied at a time when it was needed *vis-à-vis* Germany. There was actually a third theoretical alternative, inasmuch as it might be possible to avoid making that choice via attempts at compromise. This, though, had the potential to lead to the worst of all outcomes: the League destroyed and Italy on Germany's side. It is probably fair to say that few French and British diplomats or politicians realised this, or at least acknowledged it, at the time.[45]

Chapter Five

War in the 'Old-Style'

This is a European campaign on small war communications ... This is an enormous peace manoeuvre against a skeleton enemy supplied with a few live rounds to make it interesting.[1]

* * *

The invasion force assembled by De Bono was, in the considered opinion of Britain's 'Alchemist of War', the highly influential Captain B.H. Liddell Hart,[2] essentially traditional: 'It was ... in form and in outlook, an old-style army which was shipped out from Italy to Eritrea in 1935. Mechanized vehicles and aircraft were no more than a trimming to the masses of infantry ... They began the invasion of Abyssinia after the style of the invading hosts in 1914.'[3] Indeed so, and one might go even further back and say that the infantry advanced into Ethiopia in much the same style as had their grandfathers in 1896. Apart from the 'trimming' mentioned, one of the major differences was that they did so in much greater strength both qualitatively, for they were well equipped, and, more obviously, quantitatively. For when, in obedience to Mussolini's direct order of 29 September 1935, De Bono's forces crossed the frontier at 05:00 hours on 3 October 1935 they numbered around 100,000 men organised into three Army Corps.[4] There was no declaration of war. Nor was there any initial resistance as these forces, deployed in three columns, moved into Ethiopia. Each column had an initial, separate, objective. The right or westernmost column, comprising the Second Army Corps under Major General Pietro Maravigna, headed for Adowa of evil memory, whilst in the centre the Eritrean Corps, largely made up as the name suggests of locally recruited troops commanded by Lieutenant General Alessandro Pirzio Biroli, had the town of Enticcio as its initial target. On the left of the Italian advance was Lieutenant General Ruggero Santini's First Army Corps, with Adigrat as its goal. Each of these objectives was approximately 40km from the Eritrean border as the crow flies, although the distance marched was probably half as much again given the winding nature of the roads they used. Although each column moved separately, the total combined width of their front was around 70km. As might be expected, with the example of Adowa and what might happen to small columns in his mind, De Bono ensured each had sufficient strength to ensure that whatever else might happen, it would not suffer a similar fate.[5]

Inevitably, manoeuvring such a mass of men and materiel through difficult terrain rendered the effort ponderous; whilst large formations provided safety,

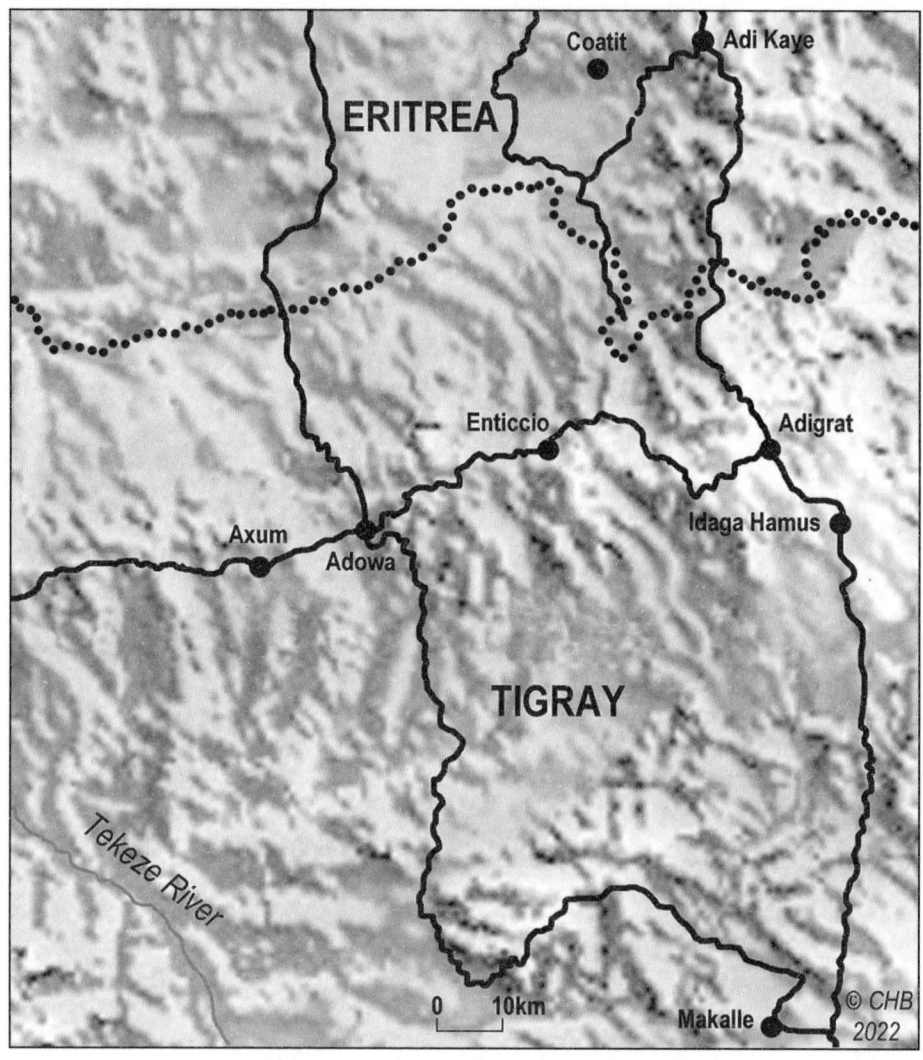

Key points on the northern front. (© *Charles Blackwood*)

they created logistical problems. Much work had been done in improving, or even creating, roads on the Eritrean side of the border, but nothing could be done in Ethiopia in advance of the assault. Consequently, these masses of troops, plus their impedimenta and supporting arms such as artillery, found themselves attempting to progress along basic tracks. Some sections were only passable to mule trains and the like, and thus much effort had to be put into improving them so that vehicles could pass. There was little in the way of opposition, and Italian air supremacy meant that forward reconnaissance could locate enemy positions and attack them. The town of Adigrat was targeted on the first day of the advance and bombed. Enemy formations that were located in the open were strafed, but the rugged terrain made it difficult to observe and attack any units that concealed themselves. De Bono's operational plan, much like the force to action it, was conventional: 'My plan of operations was based on the necessity of occupying simultaneously, and as quickly as possible, the Adigrat-Adowa position, and of organizing and fortifying it in readiness to sustain any possible attack.'[6]

The great prize psychologically, and thus in propaganda terms, was, of course, Adowa and whilst Eritrean troops were at the forefront of the advance, it would not do to have them get there first: 'Adowa, it goes without saying, had to be reconquered by Italian troops.'[7] It took three days to reach the town, but at 10:30 hours on 6 October a battalion of Italians attached to the Second Army Corps entered Adowa without a fight.

They did not, however, remain there in force, but passed through to take up positions to the south.[8] De Bono telegraphed Mussolini immediately this information was confirmed. *Il Duce* was naturally enough delighted: 'The announcement of the reconquest of Adowa fills Italian souls with pride. My high praise and the gratitude of the nation to you and all the troops.'[9]

The Italians had encountered very little in the way of resistance during their unwieldy advance. This was due to Haile Selassie ordering his forces to back away from the frontier in order to demonstrate to the world in general, and to the League of Nations more particularly, who the aggressor was. A second propaganda victory, to add to that of gaining Adowa, came Mussolini's way with the defection to the Italian cause of the Negus' son-in-law.

Haile Selassie Gugsa, who held the rank of *degiac* (*dejazmach*),[10] or army commander, in Tigray, commanded around 10,000 fighters based on the town of Makalle (Macalle Mek'ele), the provincial capital. He had been 'groomed' by the Eritrean colonial regime for some time, a matter which took the form of bribery and promises of preferment under future Italian rule. This appealed to him as he held a grievance against the Negus. The latter had declined to elevate him to the position of Ras and the overall governorship of Tigray; instead he held just the eastern portion and in a subordinate position at that. Such elevation he considered his right, and believed it had been unjustly denied him, which led to great resentment on his part.

In any event, on 11 October he arrived at the town of Idaga Hamus (Edaga Hamus), some 15km to the south-east of Adigrat, where he encountered the advanced units of the First Army Corps. He brought with him around 1,200 men, despite his previous promise that his entire command would follow. This did not deter Italian propaganda. A widely syndicated report, from the 'Field Headquarters, Italian Armies on Northern Ethiopian Front', and dated the day of the defection, stated: 'Haile Selassie Gugsa, first cousin of former Emperor John of Ethiopia and a relative of the present Emperor, said today he would fight with his 15,000 riflemen in the Italian Colonial Army.'[11]

Del Boca, who covers the defection in detail, argues that whilst this episode caused some demoralisation amongst Ethiopian troops, Gugsa's defection had no

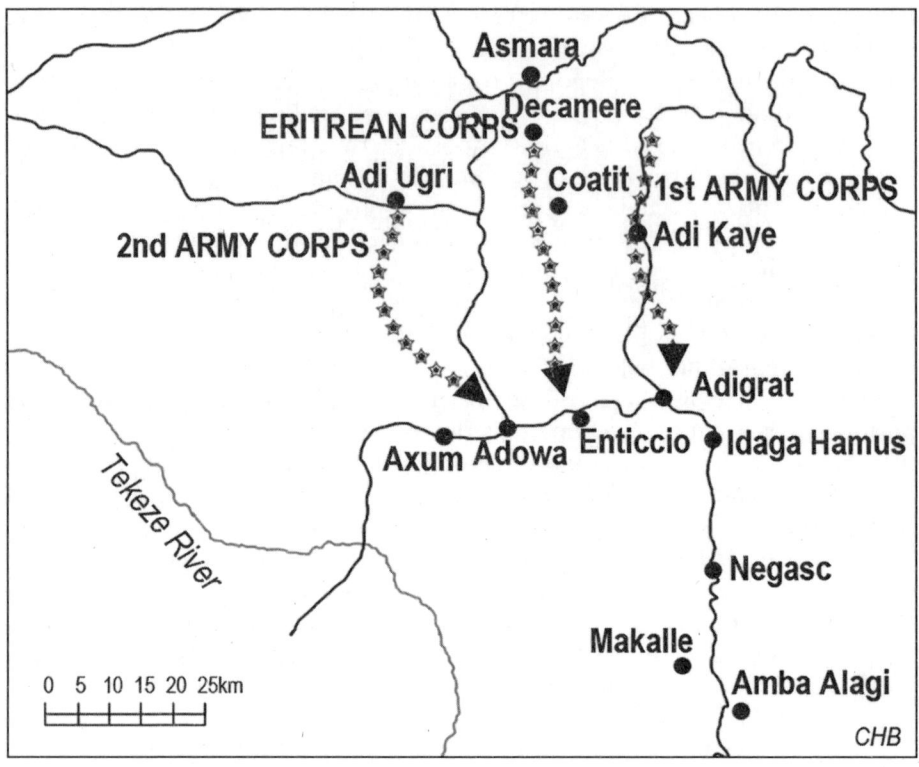

The initial Italian advance from Eritrea. (© *Charles Blackwood*)

major effect on the course of the war.[12] The manner of it did, though, cause some friction between De Bono and the government in Rome, particularly since Gugsa had jumped the gun somewhat. He was only supposed to defect when fighting around Makalle was taking place, thus effectively gifting the town to the invaders, and there was 'discontent' in the Italian capital because the capital of Tigray was not quickly occupied.[13] This was mitigated somewhat on 13 October by the capture of the Holy City of Axum (Aksum) on the right flank of the advance, which De Bono visited two days later.[14] This was a place of incalculable cultural and historical significance, being home to the fabled Ark of the Covenant. Further, and according to Ethiopia's founding mythology, it was where Menelik I, son of the Queen of Sheba and King Solomon, founded the Solomonic Dynasty which still ruled in the person of the Negus, Haile Selassie.[15] Thus the 'symbolic-religious value' of Axum had 'political resonance and weight' and possession of it also helped secure the Italian right wing.[16] Axum itself, however, was not occupied as De Bono, aware of the sensitivities involved, prohibited military personnel from entering the place.[17]

Mussolini, however, wanted De Bono to capture Makalle, which was about 40km south of Adigrat and some 20km from the Italian advanced position at

Idaga Hamus. This was a step too far for De Bono. As he explained it in his memoirs:

> I should not have had much difficulty in sending a detachment of natives to occupy Makalle. In all probability this little operation would have been successful; but it would have been difficult to keep the troops replenished, and impossible to hold the position. The actual situation of the enemy was by no means clear. The two or three battalions that I could have sent (I could not have sent more) would have attained the objective; but afterwards? ... I was never able to forget (and no calm and qualified judge should forget) the restrictions imposed upon me by logistic necessities.[18]

Major General Fuller, who was not to arrive in the theatre until 17 October, described the matter rather more succinctly: 'the inevitable happened. The weight of the army in front set such a strain on the communications that, although supply did not actually break down, the advance had to be halted.'[19] During this hiatus, fighting was restricted to minor operations aimed at eliminating small pockets of Ethiopian troops in the occupied zone, whilst forward movement was restricted to short-range reconnaissance probes, generally carried out by *ascari*. The rest of the army concentrated on road-building, creating defensive positions, bringing up artillery and constructing the necessary logistics base to support a further advance.[20] Mussolini was forced to accept the situation, informing his commander on the spot:

> Agree that [you] must not march on Makalle before organizing your rear and before receiving my orders ... Intensify defensive system in the lines Adigrat-Aksum-Adowa, extending to the right ... My orders will reach you when the European situation has cleared up in respect of sanctions, and above all, Anglo-Italian relations ...[21]

Il Duce's final sentence pertained to the fact that on 5 October 1935 the Ethiopian government had officially asked the League of Nations to intervene. As a United Press (UP) report of that date explained:

> Ethiopia today demanded that the League of Nations punish Italy for invading her borders; that the punishment take the form of military force to halt Italy's conquest of the country.
>
> It was the first time in the history of the League that the dangerous Article XVI (providing military punishment for an aggressor) had been invoked.
>
> It is understood that the basis of the categorical demand for sanctions is the 'brutal facts' of Italian aggression.[22]

The multitudinous complexities behind the deliberations of the League, and within and between the governments of its members, need not concern us overmuch here. Suffice to say that despite British and French reluctance to alienate

Mussolini, the League's Council branded Italy as an aggressor.[23] What this might mean in reality was far from clear at that time, but there was nothing like unanimity on the matter and this was particularly so with respect to the two foremost powers. Indeed, as one of the leading authorities on the international crises of the 1930s put it: 'The Ethiopian crisis was as much a crisis in Anglo-French relations as in Anglo-Italian relations.'[24]

What counted the most, though, was the effect that any decision to impose sanctions would have on Mussolini. The impact of the campaign on the Italian economy was already large. According to Cardoza's analysis, the deficit increased eightfold whilst increases in taxation meant prices soared. Further, Italy's military budget allocation up until 1938 was spent in 1935.[25] The hard-pressed population was further encouraged to donate towards the cost of the war, with such appeals being couched in terms of it being a 'patriotic duty' to give for the nation.[26] A contemporary German analysis of the country's economic situation noted that: 'Italy suffers more severely from a shortage of raw materials than any other big power in Europe.'[27] Clearly then, effective economic sanctions might hurt, though how much remained to be seen.

The British military theorist and writer J.F.C. Fuller, who had described himself as 'a trained soldier' and 'a full-blooded Fascist', was despatched to the theatre of impending war in September 1935 as a special correspondent for the *Daily Mail*,[28] a newspaper that has been described as being 'virtually Mussolini's house journal in London'.[29] Whilst en route to Eritrea, he was invited to an interview with Mussolini in Rome on 7 October. This had been set up by the leader of the British Union of Fascists (BUF), Sir Oswald Moseley, who had visited the Italian leader in August. According to an MI5 report, the visit had been arranged in order to decide 'the attitude to be adopted by the BUF during the crisis'.[30]

Il Duce arranged for Fuller's onward travel via troopship before they discussed the current situation in respect of the League of Nations. According to his diary account, Fuller told him that at worst the League might impose sanctions 'which were not sanctions at all', before explaining that the hostility of the British press towards the Italian invasion was due to 'Jewish influence'.[31] In his later, book-length, treatment of the war, he wrote: 'At that time I do not think he thought sanctions would be imposed; anyhow I feel that he was doubtful.'[32]

Mussolini was famously never wrong, at least according to the ubiquitous slogan – *Benito Mussolini ha sempre ragione* [Benito Mussolini is always right] – that had festooned Italy since it was first coined in 1926.[33] If so, then this precept had now been tested to the limit and beyond. Sanctions would inevitably take time to be effective, and this was not a factor that was on Italy's side. For although the initial operations had been successful, with an advance of some 40–50km (as the crow flies) on a 70km front achieved with negligible loss, the pace had been positively laborious. It also followed that further advances would lengthen the invaders' supply lines and make matters worse. Nevertheless, forward movement had now become essential. Mussolini wrote to De Bono on 20 October informing him of the latest political developments and his analysis of them. This included information that the British and French had no intentions of attempting to blockade Italy or close the Suez Canal but, he added, 'I have little faith in either of them.' He went on: 'In any event, a certain period of time will pass before there is any move from economic to military sanctions.' After outlining a series of proposals – 'some minimal requests' – he had put to the French foreign minister, Pierre Laval, in the certain knowledge that they would be rejected by Ethiopia, he set out what was now required in the theatre of war. The main thrust of this was that time was of the essence in several contexts, including the fact that an international arms embargo on Ethiopia had been lifted on 11 October:

> it is necessary to adapt our military action in both manner and time. There will be no complications in Europe before the British elections, set for mid-November. By that date all of Tigray up to Makalle or beyond must be ours ... a month of time is at your disposal. While waiting for my order, which may reach you between 1 and 5 November, continue the occupation of the territory ... I also have a duty to remind you that with the end of the arms embargo, large quantities of modern weapons and ammunition are arriving in Ethiopia, so time works against us ... delaying the occupation of Makalle for too long will embolden our enemies ...[34]

That *Il Duce* had quickly begun to lose faith in De Bono as a military leader is evidenced by his despatch to the theatre of Alessandro Lessona and Marshall Pietro Badoglio, minister of the colonies and the chief of the General Staff respectively. They had arrived on 19 October and held discussions with De Bono as well as going on tours of inspection.

Fuller, having travelled to Eritrea alongside Badoglio, met with the Italian theatre commander on the evening of 20 October at his HQ at Coatit (Qua'atit, Quatit) just inside Eritrea. He described the final portion of his journey there from Adi Kaye (Adi Keyh, Addi Qeyh), a distance of around 26km, as having taken place over a 'secondary road ... which beggars description'.[35] He found De Bono to be 'a pleasant, active little man of about seventy years old, and by reputation I knew him to be an astute politician'.[36] However, and as he later wrote, 'It was then that I began to see that this was not a military campaign.' In support of this he offered several 'brief extracts' from diary entries written contemporaneously:

> The forces in front represent a pumpkin on a slender stem ... This is a European campaign on small war communications ... This is an enormous peace manoeuvre against a skeleton enemy supplied with a few live rounds to make it interesting. ... On this front 30,000 men in three columns would be ample ... Whoever planned this campaign must be a strategical lunatic ... No proportion between supply and tactical power ... It would appear that all this is a tactical demonstration to terrify the Negus.[37]

He also added of De Bono: 'I doubt whether he will last long.' Eight days later Fuller's diary offered further elucidation on the situation as he saw it:

> the Italians are operating with a large army of the World War model instead of mobile columns, because the shadow of Adowa still glooms in the offing, and because they wish to impress the Abyssinians with their overwhelming strength. If General De Bono's army is not a political instrument, then, in my opinion, it is nothing at all; for it certainly is not a mountain warfare instrument as we understand it ...[38]

In his judgement, rendered retrospectively, he re-emphasised that what he was seeing was not a military operation but rather, and in fact, 'a political one – persuasion on the spot by a show of force, instead of at a distance by the threat of its use'.[39]

Fuller's assessment, and despite his fervent Fascist beliefs he remained an acute military analyst, was undoubtedly accurate in terms of description, but wrong with respect to operational philosophy. Mussolini wanted a military rather than a political solution, and even though he acted the part of 'a human dynamo, charging the battery with an electric current',[40] the means to this end were, as Fuller accurately observed, distinctly lacking. Indeed, if he thought that Lessona and Badoglio would criticise De Bono over what was perceived in Rome as his slow, uninspired performance, then he was to be initially disappointed; the two military leaders and the politician basically agreed. As De Bono explained to *Il Duce*, 'their Excellencies Badoglio and Lessona' had approved his plan which was to 'march in strength on Makalle by the 10 November'.[41]

This was not at all to the liking of *Il Duce*, who wanted the attack to be brought forward by seven days. In this he had the backing of the chief of staff of the Italian Army, General Federico Baistrocchi, who argued that the plan of conquest could not ignore the 'political-economic-military triad' and the consequent need to give maximum speed to its implementation. He pointed out to his leader that this was being disregarded in De Bono's operational planning.[42]

Several messages were exchanged in respect of the matter, with the political situation obviously exercising those in Rome and the logistical difficulties troubling those on the spot. On 25 October De Bono was informed that: 'The European situation has not improved and the lessening of tension is purely formal,'[43] and on 29 October Mussolini sent an official instruction: 'To synchronise the political exigencies with the military I order you to resume action objective Makalle-Takazze [Tekeze River] the morning of 3 November. The 3 October all went well, now it will go better. Reply.'

De Bono's reply was all that could be expected from a dutiful Fascist: 'Action will be resumed 3 November with objective Makalle.'[44] He was as good as his word, and the advance began at dawn and proceeded along the main routes through the terrain, such as they were. The only difficulties encountered on the ground related to the poor state of the roads and, on the following day, intense rain which caused extensive flooding.[45] The air force also had its problems owing to the rugged nature of the ground and the tracts of wooded country, which might conceal enemy forces. Another issue related to 'the absence of emergency landing-grounds, which compelled the machines to take off and land in aerodromes well to the rear, thus greatly restricting their freedom of movement'.[46]

There was, though, some concurrent manoeuvring, of the distinctly political kind, occurring in Rome. The apparent concordance established between De Bono, Badoglio and Lessona in Africa evaporated when the latter duo got home. For it was on 3 November that both submitted highly critical reports. Lessona reckoned De Bono to be uncertain, timid, irresolute and unfit to exercise command. Badoglio concluded that under its present commander the expeditionary force was 'substantially static in spirit and function' and that De Bono gave the impression of 'a tired man' who was disheartened, with concomitant repercussions on his ability to analyse military situations.[47]

Fuller, who had moved to Adigrat on 3 November, managed to attach himself to the headquarters of Santini's First Army Corps on the left of the Italian line. This was the spearhead formation, with the other two corps advancing in echelon to protect its right flank. On 4 November he caught up with them at the village of Negasc (Negash), which was about 40km south of Idaga Hamus and around 60km from the objective, Makalle. He noted that from Negasc onwards there was no road at all, merely a track 'plunging down a precipitous gulley'.[48] The main operation was halted at Negasc for two days in order to attend to improving communications, although there was no sign of any opposition, and two days after that, on 8 November, Makalle was entered without resistance.[49] Once again Fuller pondered upon the meaning of what was happening generally, and the significance of capturing Makalle in particular:

> And what is the significance of this event? From the military point of view there was no strategy, no tactics – not a shot was fired. Yet, from the political, the results may be startling, because Makalle gives practically the whole of Tigre to Italy, and with Tigre to gamble with, who can say what will happen at Geneva?[50]

Mussolini was less interested in what the taking of Makalle might mean in Geneva and, whilst thrilled with pride over it, wanted further action and quickly. To De Bono, the occupation of Makalle 'represented a good step forward, and nothing more'. Indeed, he judged that capturing the place had actually worsened his situation which, 'regarded from the logistic and strategic standpoint, was not so favourable as it had been'. For the near future he wanted to consolidate what had been gained thus far and improve the road, and only then advance 'in the principal direction: Amba Alagi-Ascianghi'.[51] However, on 11 November he received a directive from his leader: 'On the right bring Maravigna's [Second] Army Corps to the front on the Takazze [river] and with the native [ascari] divisions march without hesitation on Amba Alagi while the national [Italian] divisions remain at Makalle. Reply.'[52]

Before considering the response, it is interesting to note Mussolini's choice for spearheading the advance he ordered. Fuller divided the invading force into five categories: *ascari* or regular native units; native levies; regular conscript units composed of Italian soldiers; Blackshirts; and armed labourers. He regarded the *ascari* as 'the spear point of the Army' who, 'because he was the only trained fighter in this war ... bore the brunt of every action'. The drafted native levies on the other hand were dismissed as 'no more than armed riff-raff'. The conscripted, regular Italian soldier came in for only slightly higher praise. These men were, he observed, at a disadvantage compared to the *ascari* owing to poor training and lack of that 'horse sense for war which comes only with long service'. The contempt that many of them had for smartness or appearance was remarked upon, especially where it applied to weapons and equipment: 'From the state the rifles and machine guns of many units were in, I should say that a high percentage must have been inoperative ... I never once saw rifles piled. Instead they were thrown down in the dust even if it was inches deep.' The Blackshirts looked like 'the "Pirates of Penzance" after having sacked Petticoat Lane'. They had no discipline but were rather animated by 'not so much *esprit de corps* as *esprit de* stunt'. He concluded that:

> In spite of their glitter and glamour, their terrifying badges and knives, they are not soldiers. They may be good sub-machine-gunmen, street fighters and town sackers, but they are not soldiers. I doubt whether they could ever carry out a skilful attack or stubborn defence ... What they are here for is obvious. They are the war chorus of the Duce, and the troubadours of his cult.

By way of contrast the armed labourers, being 'the base of all military operations', received lavish praise:

> Without hesitation, I can say that these sturdy peasant folk and townsmen stand in a category by themselves. Split up into little groups along the mountain sides, sweltering on the plains, burnt black by the sun, swept unceasingly by clouds of dust, sleeping in small shelters and living on the simplest of fare, they worked with a will and a cheerfulness which were beyond all praise. Such was the base, surely the most unconsciously heroic any army has ever had.[53]

That De Bono's immediate intent was to concentrate on utilising the last mentioned, and indeed augmenting them with troops, rather than the first, was made clear in his reply to Mussolini's telegram of 11 November. He contended that it would be a mistake to advance on Amba Alagi, even if using *ascari* alone, and he enjoined *Il Duce* to remember:

> that we have at present a line of operation over 500 kilometres in length of which more than a third is bad track. Further 100 kilometres are still liable to ambush, which calls for special security measures. The positions occupied

three days ago are not yet organized for defence and no heavy field guns have yet arrived there. My reserve is divided into gangs for work on roads.

De Bono's lengthy message went on to argue that Amba Alagi had no strategic importance and was vulnerable tactically because it could be completely surrounded. Occupying it in isolation would create a detached point without possibility of replenishment, against which enemy forces 'now assembling' could act in one body. If they did so and obtained a success, even partially so, this might have very injurious results. He pointed out that as the commander on the spot, and after having consulted his subordinates and those dealing with logistics, it would be 'playing the enemy's game' to advance precipitously. He finished by stating his belief that 'at this moment the military situation must have precedence over any other consideration whatsoever'.[54]

Mussolini had little alternative than to acquiesce. His reply recognised the 'validity' of the reasons pertaining to a 'reasonable halt' and urged his theatre commander to 'rapidly systematize [his] lines of communication'.[55] There matters rested, as it were, and on 16 November De Bono left his HQ at Adigrat to tour the front. His considered opinion, which he communicated to Rome in the early hours of 17 November, was that because of the precariousness of the logistic situation, the difficulties of which were defined as immense, an adequate period of time to overcome them was required.[56]

Upon his return to Adigrat later that day, however, he found a personal message from *Il Duce* awaiting. Mussolini, fortified no doubt by the critical reports of Lessona and Badoglio, had concluded that De Bono was too prudent, too much of a time-waster, and generally lacked the necessary thrust to successfully manage the campaign. He would therefore replace him.[57] The message communicating this decision was sugar-coated, at least to a degree:

> With the reconquest of Makalle I consider your mission in East Africa completed, a mission that you carried out in extremely difficult circumstances and with results that point you in the present and in the future to the gratitude of the Nation. Your indisputable and everywhere recognized merits will be explicitly consecrated with deeds. I believe that this message of mine will not surprise you too much because you know from experience that every cycle of activity must be concluded at a certain point, that a little rest is needed and that luck should not be too much demanded when this has been propitious for some time. I inform you that I have chosen Marshal Badoglio as your successor. While waiting to see you again, I embrace you with unchanged cordiality.[58]

As has been mentioned, it had been De Bono's Fascist credentials which originally appealed to *Il Duce*, who wanted a Fascist war with a large proportion of the combatants on the Italian side drawn from the ranks of the Blackshirts. That he had acknowledged Italy's most effective troops were, as also discerned by Fuller, the regular *ascari* has been noted. Now he had dismissed his Fascist general and replaced him with an Army commander in the expectation that he would somehow overcome the difficulties which had so encumbered De Bono. Moreover, this had to be accomplished quickly; aside from the threat of sanctions and the yet-to-be-encountered enemy armies, there was the Ethiopian monsoon to contend with. This starts in June and runs through to September, meaning of course that Badoglio had roughly eight months of campaigning left. Given that it had taken a little over a month to advance around 150km to Makalle, and that Haile Selassie's capital, Addis Ababa, was around 750km further south, over brutally difficult terrain, this was asking a lot. Unless, of course, Badoglio introduced a different tactical model.

Chapter Six

Graziani

In the Ogaden it rains intermittently in September and October, after the rains have stopped on the high plateau. The dry sandbeds become torrents for a day or two, and the pink earth along the Ogaden tracks a spongy pulp. A mechanised column sinks into the mud and sometimes remains engraven in the earth after it has dried, so quickly does the mud turn into rock again in the Ogaden.[1]

* * *

The change of command could not take effect immediately as Badoglio was in Italy. Accordingly, De Bono remained in post until his replacement arrived at Adigrat on 30 November.[2] The incoming C-in-C had made an important decision the day before, however: strict censorship would apply from then on in relation to the various foreign war correspondents operating with the Italians, and they were to be kept well away from the front. This applied to Fuller too, so despite his acknowledged Fascist beliefs and his connections with high-ranking members of the regime, he was prevented from returning to Adigrat.[3] De Bono's operational plan had baffled the British officer, who had calculated, or rather guessed, as he confessed, that the massive advance into Tigray was a feint. It was, he concluded, designed to threaten the Ethiopians from the north and thus draw the majority of their forces away from the southern part of the country where the main effort would be made.[4]

In fact, and as has been discussed, Graziani in Somaliland had been assigned an essentially passive role, although he had refused to accept it as such and intended to attack. This was despite Mussolini telling De Bono explicitly that he was to 'order Graziani to remain absolutely on the defensive'.[5] His command, though, lacked necessary materiel, in terms of men, hardware and munitions, and with only twenty aeroplanes at his disposal, his options were limited. De Bono had already accepted, prior to the commencement of hostilities, a point Graziani had made about the distance between the two fronts making synchronous action both impossible and unnecessary.[6] Thus operations from Italian Somaliland were conducted entirely independently from those in the north.

To that end, and despite his materiel handicaps, Graziani had formulated a plan in early September. Operation No. 1 (also known as *piano Milano*) postulated an attack in three operational sectors. In the left, or western, area Dolo, the 'half-Ethiopian, half-Italian town on the Juba river', was to be fully occupied, an operation described as only requiring the invaders to climb over a clay wall.[7]

Some 200km to the north-east of Dolo there was to be a double drive, of around 100km initially, into Ethiopia. The right hand, or eastern, thrust had Shilabo as its target, whilst to its left was planned a push along the course of the Shebeli river to capture Kelafo. This would give the invaders control of an important communication route. Shilabo, being deemed an important target, would be subjected to a surprise attack by a motorised detachment, with the infantry element conveyed in about forty lorries.

Finally, the goal of the right-hand advance was Geregube, located some 85km north-north-east of Shilabo. This objective was about 140km inside Ethiopia and about 20km from the Wal Wal oasis. The capture of Geregube would clear the way to the fortified position of Gorrahei (Korahe), some 18km south of Kebri Dahar on the Fafen river, where a large Ethiopian force was garrisoned. It was proposed to bring this to action with a surprise attack whilst the air force would carry out reconnaissance and bombing as required.[8]

On 3 October orders went out to put the plan into action, although the move on Shilabo had to be postponed as the vehicles to carry it into effect had not yet been assembled. There were other difficulties too, in particular with the weather. As the journalist George Steer, who visited and was familiar with the area, described it:

> In the Ogaden it rains intermittently in September and October, after the rains have stopped on the high plateau. The dry sandbeds become torrents for a day or two, and the pink earth along the Ogaden tracks a spongy pulp. A mechanised column sinks into the mud and sometimes remains engraven in the earth after it has dried, so quickly does the mud turn into rock again in the Ogaden.[9]

A certain degree of journalistic hyperbole perhaps, but nevertheless a decent sketch of the consequences arising from volatile meteorological conditions. Just how unpredictable these could be was noted by Norman E. Fiske, the official American Military Observer with the Italian Army, who recorded how one officer was searching for possible water sources without success when 'suddenly, under a clear sky, water began pouring down the dry river bed, evidently from heavy rains miles away'.[10]

Even with the weather permitting, the Italian probes, whether planned or actual, were necessarily small in scale given the available resources. They were also relatively unambitious, although the attack on Geregube had the potential to develop into something more important given that it was a nodal point, a crossroads. The town fell on 5 October after a minor battle and preparations were undertaken to move on to Gorrahei, a key position in relation to possession of the Ogaden owing to its abundance of wells in an otherwise largely arid region. It was also an important junction on the road towards Degeh Bur and Harrar, these being some 180km and 360km away to the north-north-west, as the crow flies, respectively.

The significance of the place being as obvious to the Ethiopians as to the Italians, the former had ensured that it was as well defended as possible. The 2005 Italian General Staff history describes the location's defensive 'pivot' as 'a fort located in the centre of a vast open plain'. This 'entrenched camp' was elliptical

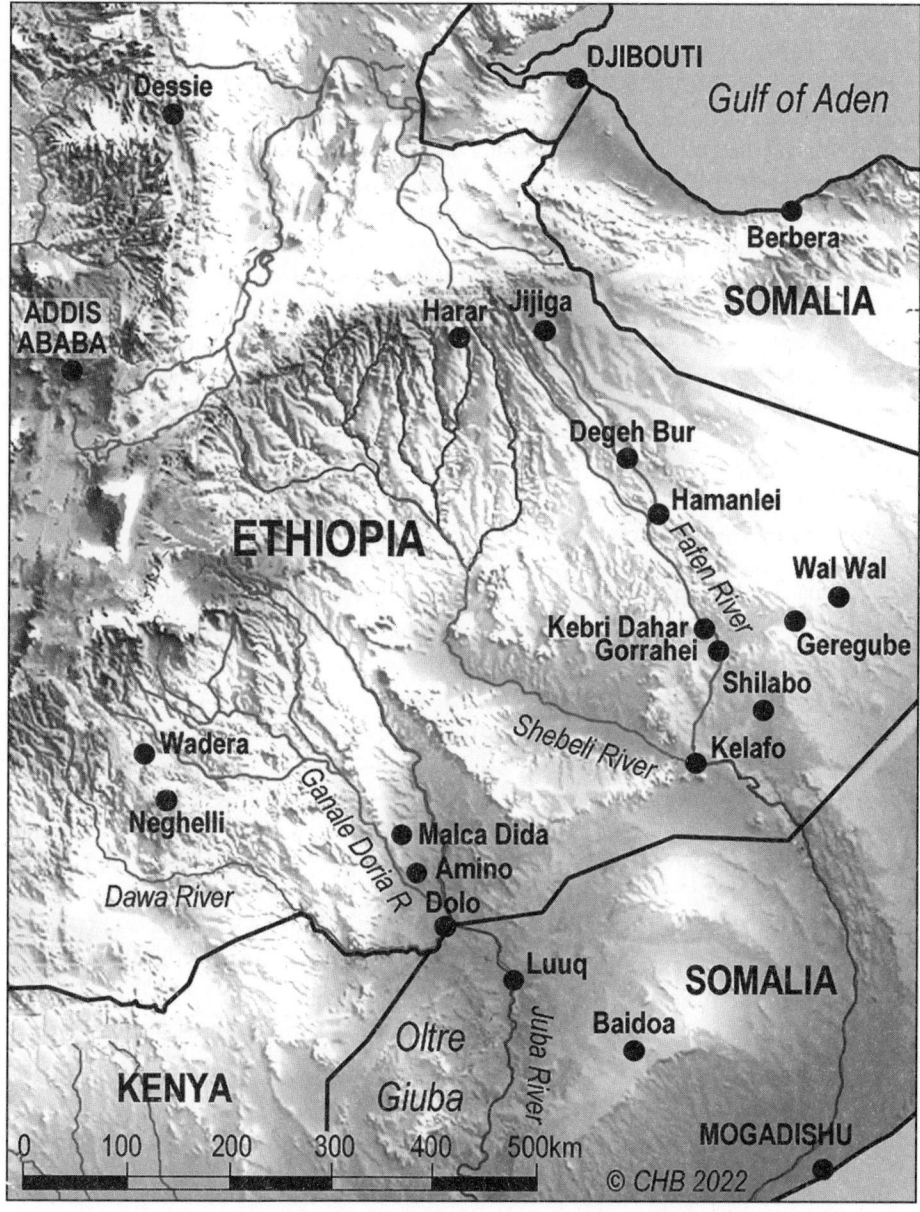

Key points on the southern front. (© *Charles Blackwood*)

in shape, with the long side oriented north–south, and surrounded by two lines of entrenchments for riflemen and machine-gunners. Subterranean excavations were also constructed to provide shelter from air attack. Detached works were connected via deep walkways, and the whole was surrounded by a thick *zeriba* improvised from thornbushes. The garrison numbered some 3,000 men, and the Italians estimated that in addition to their rifles, there were forty-eight machine guns and three Oerlikon 20mm automatic cannon available to the defenders, plus an unspecified number of small calibre anti-tank guns.[11] Steer, who visited the place shortly before it fell, reckoned, however, that there were no anti-tank guns apart from the Oerlikons. He also claimed there were only four machine guns and about forty 'machine-gun rifles'.[12]

The rain thwarted an early move on this objective. In fact, it was only in early November that serious moves to attack were initiated. These began with an aerial bombardment over three days, 2–4 November, before two mechanised columns, consisting of tanks and armoured cars, accompanied by lorry-mounted infantry, advanced the next morning. The objective was to attack from the east and the north, but early reconnaissance flights on 5 November reported that the area had been evacuated. A patrol, pushed ahead to approach the camp, arrived just before noon and confirmed that the enemy had indeed abandoned the position.

Information subsequently obtained from a prisoner revealed that the three days of bombing, against which the Ethiopians had no defence, had severely shaken the morale of the garrison and they had cracked completely when their commander, Afawarq Walda Samayat, had been seriously wounded on 2 November. His condition worsened and, without his authority, discipline broke down completely. Thus, the erstwhile defenders retreated northwards towards Degeh Bur, taking Samayat with them. He was to perish on 5 November whilst travelling.[13]

Even though the vast majority of the Ethiopian forces had escaped, along with most of their equipment, this was a significant gain for the Italians. Pursuit of the fleeing enemy began early on 6 November by one of the columns under Colonel Pietro Maletti. This was spearheaded by two platoons of L3 tanks, eleven in total, and five Fiat 611 armoured cars, plus 300 *dubats* (locally recruited Somali regular soldiers) in lorries, driving north along the eastern bank of the Fafen river in rapidly deteriorating weather.[14] Kebri Dahar was reached the next day, with only minimal resistance from Ethiopian rearguards being encountered. The advance halted on 7 November, not through enemy action but rather because violent storms rendered the tracks, such as they were, impassable to vehicles and knocked out radio communication. These conditions also affected their retreating enemy and after Maletti resumed the advance on 10 November, his motorised force found itself closing on a large enemy body the next day at the wells of Hamanlei (Anale), some 70km south of Degeh Bur. George Steer recorded what happened next, or at least that version of events as was related to him by the pursuees:

> Maletti had caught the Ethiopians ... the tanks roared after them over tufted sandhills, zigzagging round the treacherous crumbling dongas, and crushing

thornbush. The tanks, slit narrowly in front for eyes, were half blind in the dust which their tracks knocked up ... the drivers, sweating, shoved up their lids and shot forward, spitting a chain of fire [...] the Ethiopians understood cover perfectly. Not a man could be seen in the dirty dust-clouded bush.

A tank moved up to a little hill to inspect. It fidgeted this way and that. Twenty Ethiopians were lying in the roots of thorn trees forty yards [36m] away. At the top the driver stopped. Nothing visible. A head in a suffocating crash helmet bobbed up from the tank. 'We thought it was a cruel animal,' the soldiers told me, 'we dared not shoot.'

The driver got out. It was a two man tank ... The machine-gunner got out, as the Ethiopians held their breath and pressed closer into the thorns.

'Kill them,' whispered their officer. Twenty shots from the Fusil Gras.[15] 'They fell very slowly to the ground, like sand off riverbanks,' the soldiers told me. They did not dare to approach the tank ... another tank came up, stopped its engine, could not see in the track dust. It shouted to the other tank – no reply. 'We think they wanted to know what was wrong, and could not see,' said the soldiers.

Again the men got out. Another volley, and they slipped to the ground. But the Ethiopians dared not approach. There might be more men in the tank, they thought.

A third tank came up and in a businesslike manner the driver got out to fix chains on one of the others. His machine-gunner was meant to cover him, but the guns were fixed in a traverse of 15° pointing in the wrong direction. The driver fell dead: they think they wounded the machine-gunner, I don't know how.

Many of the Somalis in the lorries were shot down as they tumbled off them into cover. A wicked fire out of the bush mowed them through before they could use their guns.[16]

The Italian account, as contained in the 2005 General Staff history, is concise to the point of terseness: 'The situation became critical with the three tanks being put out of action, and in the late afternoon the column was forced to fall back on Gabredarre [Kebri Dahar] after suffering significant losses of almost 60 per cent.'[17] By way of contrast, Colonel Maurizio Parri's account, in his history of Italy's armoured forces, devotes several pages to the incident. It is described as developing into a gruelling struggle, lasting over nine hours, which proceeded from attempts to recover a single, bogged-down tank. This was eventually abandoned as losses mounted, and the air force was tasked with destroying the three vehicles to prevent them being used by the enemy – an attempt that failed.[18]

Though small in scale, the operations to take Gorrahei and the subsequent pursuit to, and minor battle at, Hamanlei are of some interest in terms of larger lessons. Certainly, the initial stage points up the underdeveloped, or indeed non-existent, tactical coordination between Italian air and ground forces. A 1937 assessment by the US Army General Staff Military Intelligence Division described the attack on Gorrahei thus:

> the air force carried out its bombing operations prematurely and prior to the arrival of the ground columns... The severe air bombardment killed a dozen or so Ethiopians, wounded the commander, and caused an evacuation of the town and withdrawal, before the Italian ground forces could make their presence felt. This was hailed in some quarters as a decisive triumph for the air – the first battle won by an air force alone. Actually it destroyed the opportunity for a decisive victory and probable elimination of the Ethiopian forces involved. The Italian ground commander charged with the operation had no control over the air attack. It was to have been coordinated by GHQ and is a rather outstanding instance of failure in cooperation.[19]

Italian difficulties were not, though, exclusively doctrinal. The loss of the three tanks on 11 November might indicate poor tactical deployment but, as Colonel Parri argues in his historical account, the vehicles also suffered from 'intrinsic technical limitations'.[20] These are described by Steer above and were undoubtedly exacerbated by the operational environment. Major Fiske, the official American Military Observer, commented:

> The light fast tanks, so widely heralded in the first months of the Abyssinian campaign, proved to be valueless in the Somaliland fighting. The high brush was an obstacle that could not be overcome. The tanks could not operate independently in advance of the foot troops. The Abyssinians soon found out about their limitations and would set fire to the brush and thus overcome the personnel by smoke. The lack of visibility from the tanks made it impossible to maintain direction, formation or contact. They could be employed only as accompanying tanks in support of the infantry and since the hostile position was seldom accurately located the infantry usually had to protect the tanks and derived very little support from them.[21]

Even given these limitations it has been argued that with a little more 'dash and daring' the Italian columns could have pushed on for 70km to Degeh Bur. Indeed, this momentum might have taken them another 170km north to Jijiga and then on to the vitally important city of Harar, some 100km to the west. Possession of the latter would have facilitated interdiction of the 'vital arteries for the flow of supplies to Ethiopia': the road from Berbera in British Somaliland to Jijiga and, perhaps even more critical, the railway from Djibouti to Addis Ababa.[22] This optimistic, perhaps overoptimistic, analysis comes from Anthony Mockler, who posits that it was achievable because, prior to the clash at Hamanlei: 'The Ethiopians were demoralized and disorganized, and the Somali clans were ready to take part in what was from their point of view another round, Italian-officered, of the centuries-old struggle against the Christians of Ethiopia.'[23]

There is some contemporary corroborative evidence that this latter assertion was accurate. According to one of the four foreign correspondents with

Graziani's forces, the Austro-Hungarian-born journalist Demeter Ödön, better known as Edmund Demaitre, the Somali fighters, dubbed the 'Lions of Juba', were particularly warlike:

> So they come ... young and old ... all moving like an interminable flood towards the camps where the Doubats, the native attacking forces of the Italian, are recruited. It is not just a question of avenging insults, pillages and raids. It is not a question of earning five lira a day ... What is far and away more important is that war in any form represents for the Somalis the most noble, worthy and significant manifestation of life; the most honourable endeavour, the most poignant and virile of physical and moral emotions.[24]

He added to his description by noting that: 'The sight of blood makes them literally drunk, and they massacre their enemies mercilessly. They are not, however, cruel. They kill quickly and never make their victims suffer.'[25] Whilst there is undoubtedly a degree of journalistic licence in such broad-brush characterisations, fighting between Islamic Somalis and their traditional Christian Ethiopian enemies was always likely to be a no-quarter affair.

Having said that, not all the non-European troops who fought for the Italians in the southern campaign were Somali. Rochat reckons that around 25,000–30,000 were locally recruited *dubats*, a term reserved for them. *Ascari* is a word of Arabic origin and refers to Eritreans, Libyans and Yemenis, several battalions of whom were imported, as it were, to reinforce the *dubats*.[26]

There is, though, one other point to ponder regarding Demaitre's claim about the *dubats* killing quickly and without cruelty. Whether accurate or not, this was meant to highlight the difference between them and their opponents, for it was believed that the Ethiopians indulged in, certainly with regard to European sensibilities, barbaric practices. For example, Steer, who was pro-Ethiopian, related how the corpses of the Italians who died during the affair of the three tanks were 'mutilated and distributed among the local Ogaden'. He also notes that the machine-gunner from the third tank, who was captured, 'died of starvation and thirst after three days of the sour camel's water of the Ogaden'.[27] Given the ubiquity of the 'atrocity stories' that filled the Italian, and international, press at that time, then the 'machine-gunner' might have been considered fortunate.[28] Such stories had been common currency, in Italy at least, since the Battle of Adowa and there is no doubt that at least some of the stories pertaining to that conflict were well founded.[29] The Fascist propaganda machine maintained that such atrocities were still being practised, and indeed provided what they considered compelling evidence that this was so.[30]

Be that as it may, and even given that the Somali troops who would have spearheaded the putative advance on Harar were well motivated and skilled, it seems improbable that the relatively weak columns Graziani could have mobilised would have been sufficient to successfully penetrate so far. Nor, if they succeeded in doing so, could they have easily been sustained. The weaknesses in Italian tactical air-support and armoured forces have already been mentioned, and added

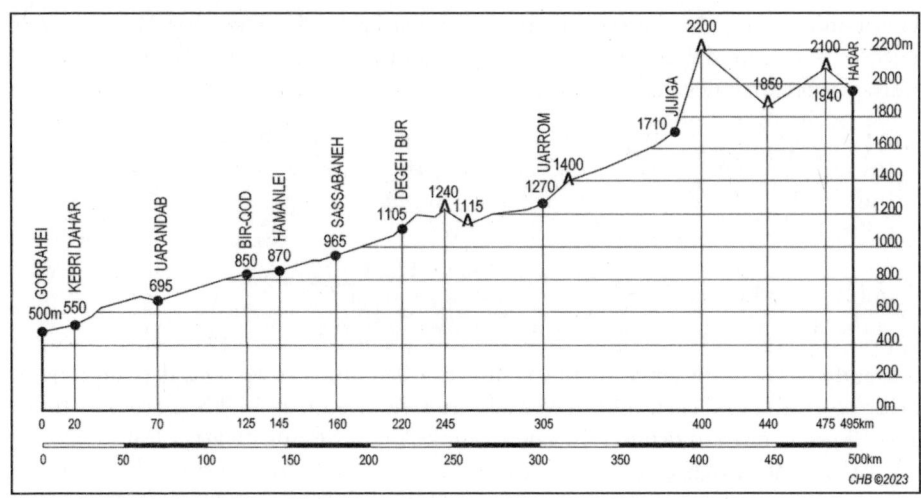

A graphic rendering of the route from Gorrahei to Harar, clearly indicating the ever-increasing elevation. (© *Charles Blackwood*)

to these was the forbidding terrain that would have to be traversed. There was, of course, a further factor too: the enemy. Shortly after their repulse at Hamanlei, intelligence sources began indicating that a strong Ethiopian force was concentrating around the town of Neghelli [Negele Borana or Neghelle] about 300km to the north-west of Dolo.[31]

Italian intelligence in respect of their enemy was massively facilitated by the fact that Ethiopian radio communications were compromised. Under the auspices of the 15th Battalion of Engineers, some 140 listening and direction-finding posts were deployed to intercept enemy traffic.[32] Ethiopian ciphers had already been cracked by the Special Interception Section of the Italian East Africa Command, set up in Asmara in 1935 and headed by a disloyal Ethiopian and three Amharic-speaking Italian officers. These men were able to break the military cipher, which utilised 100 Amharic syllabic groups, as well as its diplomatic counterparts. Thus, messages from the Ethiopian Foreign Ministry to its representatives abroad were also being read.[33]

Thanks to the insights gained by such methodology, Italian intelligence was able to estimate that the Ethiopian army around Neghelli numbered between 35,000 and 50,000 men, and that it was poorly equipped with heavy weaponry.[34] Commanded by Ras Desta Damtew, it was expected to advance on Dolo along the courses of the Ganale Doria river and, some 40km to its west, the roughly parallel Dawa river. Utilising these water courses was tactically astute inasmuch as they offered cover in respect of bombing and aerial observation along the entire route and, of course, were sources of water for both men and animals. In addition, the Italians considered that by following the line of the Dawa their enemy would thus close in on the border with British-ruled Kenya. This, it was estimated, mattered because they believed that the authorities there would likely provide aid and military advice. Suspicion was also harboured in relation to perceived British designs on that portion of Italian Somaliland which abutted the Kenyan frontier, known as Oltre Giuba [Jubaland, Trans-Juba]. This roughly 93,000 sq. km territory had formerly been British-ruled, but was handed to Italy in 1925, the transfer being a part of the 1915 Treaty of London which survived.[35]

Whilst there is no evidence that the British had designs on Italian territory, or that they would offer assistance to Ras Desta's army, the threat that force posed was real enough, although the direction in which it would act was uncertain. Its most likely move was, however, conjectured to involve outflanking Dolo from the west, which would allow it to operate along the Juba river, the source of which was the confluence of the Dawa and Ganale Doria, towards Luuq, some 65km to the south-east. There was a large Italian logistic base and airfield there, and it was an important waypoint in respect of communications between Mogadishu and Dolo.

Graziani was therefore forced to conceive a plan to counter the prospective enemy advance, and to protect the area around Baidoa in particular, where he sited his HQ. As well as being an important communication node, Baidoa was the location of a significant source of fresh water, and the centre of a growing distribution network that was vital to sustaining his army in an otherwise generally arid landscape.[36] By mid-November Graziani had more men than did Ras Desta: some 27,000 Italian and 30,500 indigenous troops with 320 lorries to provide them with mobility. His equipment situation was also fairly strong, with 129 artillery pieces, 38 armoured cars and 21 tanks, plus 75 aircraft of various types.[37] The situation was also improving as reinforcements of all types arrived.

But Graziani did not intend to wait: rather, he intended to strike the enemy forces pre-emptively. However, locating concentrations of the enemy army was difficult since the Ethiopians took elaborate precautions to avoid being detected by aerial reconnaissance by, for example, marching only after dusk and staying under cover in the dense bush during the day. The herds of cattle that accompanied the Ethiopian force, rations on the hoof as it were, were also concealed in much the same manner. What did threaten to 'embarrass' Desta in this regard, though, was the presence of two Red Cross units, one Canadian and the other Swedish, which were attached to his force and, given their status, made no attempt to conceal themselves. The Ethiopian commander attempted to ensure these units stayed well away from his army.[38] Although the Italians were unaware of the precise intentions of Ras Desta, estimates of time and distance indicated that his force would not be likely to cross into Italian territory before sometime around the first week in December. Events in an entirely different sphere intervened in the meantime, however, as on 18 November 1935 the League of Nations imposed sanctions on Italy.[39]

Chapter Seven

'a small masterpiece'

The Italians dropped countless bombs, but from [17 December] they also dropped gas bombs, which rain like hail. The smell of gas does not allow you to stay in the trenches. Dr Hylander warned us to be careful as this is poisonous gas. The injuries, even slight ones, produced by this gas, always swell greatly to the point of becoming, by infection, great wounds.[1]

* * *

Italian suspicions, and indeed worries, with respect to British intentions had an effect on their deployment of forces during November 1935. The 2005 General Staff history notes that, until clarification of the 'political situation with England' (*la situazione politica con l'Inghilterra*) was obtained, Mussolini ordered a Libyan division that had been scheduled for transference to Somalia instead to remain in place and indeed, along with two others, move up to the western border of British-ruled Egypt.[2] This sabre-rattling worried the General Staff, whose members considered that a war with Britain would be catastrophic for Italy.[3] In any event, and in lieu of the 1st Libyan Division which was retained to threaten the British and Egyptians, a significantly inferior military force, the 6th Blackshirt 'Tevere' Division, was despatched to reinforce Graziani.[4]

The likely British posture as regards Italy was hardly clarified by the General Election held on Thursday, 14 November 1935 in which the incumbent coalition National Government, under prime minister and Conservative Party leader Stanley Baldwin, was returned with a huge majority. The government's manifesto, as published in *The Times* of 28 October 1935, had stated: 'In the present unhappy dispute between Italy and Abyssinia there will be no wavering in the policy we have hitherto pursued. We shall take no action in isolation, but we shall be prepared faithfully to take our part in any collective action decided upon by the League and shared in by its Members.'[5]

As one scholar later asked: 'But which policy?' The second sentence was also vague and indeed the statement as a whole left, as it would be termed today, considerable wriggle room for the British government.[6] It was also the case, though, that the election had been held in the shadow of the so-called Peace Ballot or, more properly, 'A National Declaration on the League of Nations and Armaments'. This 'First British Referendum' was carried out between November 1934 and June 1935, and 11,640,066 adults, an estimated 38.2 per cent of the population over 18, participated.[7] Questions such as 'Should Great Britain remain a member of the League of Nations?' and 'Do you consider that, if a nation insists on attacking another, the other nations should combine to compel it to stop –

(a) by economic and non-military measures (b) if necessary, military measures' elicited substantial majorities in favour.[8] It was unsurprising then that the Baldwin government claimed that 'The League of Nations will remain, as heretofore, the keystone of British foreign policy.'[9] Although Baldwin could claim an unarguable mandate for backing the League of Nations, he had cautioned Parliament the previous year in respect to the implications of such policies:

> The moment you are up against sanctions, you are up against war. I have probably put in as much work on these subjects as any Member of this House for the last 12 years, and one of the many conclusions to which I have been driven is that there is no such thing as a sanction that will work that does not mean war, or, in other words, if you are going to adopt a sanction you must be prepared for war. If you adopt a sanction without being ready for war, you are not an honest trustee of the nation.[10]

Mussolini had publicly affirmed that he was, effectively, in full agreement with Baldwin: in September 1935 *Il Solco Fascista*, the newspaper of the provincial fascist federation of Reggio Emilia, had thundered that 'Sanctions mean war – millions of deaths – the recasting of the European map.'[11] Whether in reality sanctions inevitably meant war or not remained to be seen at that time, but what it all essentially boiled down to was that Britain now faced a choice: 'between the League busting Mussolini or Mussolini busting the League'.[12]

Il Duce was, of course, intent on the latter, but from his perspective the more protracted the operations in Ethiopia, then the greater the chance of the situation escalating out of control. Fuller reckoned the decision to impose economic sanctions brought about a fundamental change in the way the invasion was conducted:

> No longer was it now possible to rely on a slow penetration of the country; instead action was demanded even if of a ruthless kind; for were sanctions to be extended to oil, or were the Suez Canal to be closed, as was daily demanded in the British press, the war must collapse and with it in all likelihood the entire Fascist regime. In short, the economic blockade not only compelled Mussolini to fight for the conquest of Abyssinia but for his political existence in Italy.[13]

Later analysis has largely confirmed this view. As one authority on Fascist Italy's foreign policy and military strategy worded it:

> What had originally been a Fascist enterprise planned on the sly had been transformed by League opposition into a national cause. Singled out for punishment by a satiated and selfish West, 'proletarian' Italy was now ready for sacrifice ... men flocked to the colors, and women rushed to common collection points with wedding rings and other gold artifacts to help defray the huge expenses of the war.[14]

It was, of course, one thing for those in Rome to demand that the invasion be expedited, even with 'ruthless' action, and quite another to translate such pronouncements into action on the ground.

The first to adopt 'ruthlessness' was Graziani, engaged as he was in attempting to blunt the forthcoming attack by Ras Desta. In support of this, twenty-four aircraft were transferred to Luuq by the first week of December 1935, their task being to first locate the approaching Ethiopians and then to machine gun and bomb them. Their targets were not just the men, however; the herds of animals were also to be attacked as a priority, for without them the enemy troops would go hungry.

Finding these targets was difficult as long as the Ethiopians maintained discipline. According to Steer's account, it was a lack of this that gave away their locations. He relates how Air Brigadier General (*Generale di brigata aerea*) Mario Bernasconi, who headed the Italian Somaliland Mixed Air Brigade (*Brigata aerea mista dell'Aviazione della Somalia italiana*), personally flew at low level, 90m, above areas where an enemy presence was suspected. Many of the Ethiopian troops, being confident of hitting such an easy target, 'blazed away from the bush'. In fact, it is extraordinarily difficult to shoot down an aircraft with small arms fire. Their defiant attempts to do so meant 'Desta's secret was out ... the bulk of his forces was mapped and fixed.'[15]

On 14 December Negele, which was considered to be of importance as an Ethiopian base, was attacked by fifteen Caproni Ca.101 bis bombers based at Luuq. This strike, according to the 2005 General Staff history, utilised bombs filled with mustard gas.[16] The second volume of the 2005 work (*Allegati* – Attachments), which contains copies of relevant documents, reproduces a telegram dated 15 December 1935 in which Graziani, obviously retrospectively, asked Badoglio and Lessona for 'maximum freedom' to use 'asphyxiating gases' (*gas asfissianti*) against the 'barbarous hordes' he was facing.[17] Two days later he was informed that he could now use gas-filled bombs wherever he deemed them useful.[18] He immediately did so. Ras Desta communicated it to the Negus:

> The Italians dropped countless bombs, but from [17 December] they also dropped gas bombs, which rain like hail. The smell of gas does not allow you to stay in the trenches. Dr Hylander warned us to be careful as this is poisonous gas. The injuries, even slight ones, produced by this gas, always swell greatly to the point of becoming, by infection, great wounds.[19]

Further gas-bombing was carried out on enemy detachments located along the Ganale Doria river over the period 23–25 December, and on 30 December aircraft dropped twenty-one gas bombs on the area around Malca Dida.[20] Situated on the west bank of the Ganale about 20km north-west of Amino, this was now, and had been since 22 December, the location of the Swedish Red Cross field hospital where Dr Fride Hylander, mentioned above, worked.[21] The attack was led in person by Bernasconi, who reported the results to Graziani in the following terms:

> Today 4 IMAM Ro.1 aircraft bombed Abyssinian camps and a field hospital in Malca Dida. Leaflets were also launched. Subsequently, six Caproni

aircraft in two passes bombed the enemy, dropping a single 250kg bomb, six 100kg bombs, ten 50kg bombs, four 31kg bombs, thirty-two incendiary bombs and twelve 21kg mustard gas bombs.[22]

This particular raid was carried out in direct retaliation for the alleged treatment of Lieutenant Tito Minniti and Sergeant Livio Zannoni.[23] The circumstances around this notorious case are as follows: after their withdrawal following the clash at Hamanlei on 11 November, the Italians constructed an airfield at Gorrahei from which they carried out reconnaissance and bombing missions. On 26 December 1935 one of these flights, involving an IMAM Ro.1 biplane, was over Degeh Bur when it was hit by enemy fire and forced down. The two-man crew, pilot Minniti and photographer Zannoni, survived the forced landing but were then attacked, although whether by soldiers or locals incensed at Italian bombing is disputed. In any event, the outcome was the death of Zannoni during the firefight and the capture of Minniti. The unfortunate pilot was subsequently tortured, emasculated and finally beheaded, with his and Zannoni's severed heads carried on spears to Harar.[24] That, at least, was how the matter was portrayed by the Italians; the facts surrounding the fate of Minniti in particular are still disputed to this day.[25]

The chronology pertaining to the above events is mainly of interest because it serves to demonstrate the falsity of the assertions that chemical weapons had been used in Ethiopia only minimally, and in retaliation for the gruesome fate of the two aviators.[26] This is so because mustard gas had been used prior to their being downed, both before and after Graziani had asked for, and received, clearance to use it. Indeed, the subsequent delegation of this usage to his air force commander occurred some ten days *before* the incident that is supposed to have provoked the question in the first place. Rather than the use of gas, it was the deliberate bombing of the Red Cross site that was a direct consequence of that event. This was explained in the leaflets, with Amharic text, that were dropped during the bombardment, as mentioned by Bernasconi. Translated into English these read: 'You have transgressed the laws of kingdoms and nations by killing a captive airman by beheading him. According to the law prisoners must be treated with respect. Do not touch them! You will consequently receive the punishment which you deserve. Graziani.'[27]

Forty-two people, patients and Red Cross personnel alike, perished.[28] Exactly why a conspicuously marked hospital was targeted is unknown. Steer believed that it was meant to 'clear foreign witnesses out of the way while illegal methods of war were being used by the Italians'.[29] Graziani's subsequent explanations are obviously mendacious, but it forms only one example of a definite pattern of similar behaviour.[30] By way of defending such attacks, the Italians were to claim that the Ethiopians exploited the Red Cross insignia for military purposes, which included the use of marked ambulances to transport weapons and ammunition.[31]

Graziani's wilful destruction of the field hospital was a bit *too* ruthless for Mussolini. Not that he objected to it as such, and certainly not on humanitarian grounds, but rather because at a time of political sensitivity in respect of sanctions it aroused widespread international condemnation. He wrote to Badoglio two days after the event explaining this:

> The news of the bombing of a Swedish Red Cross hospital on the Somali front has raised a great feeling in that country ... which our enemies will make full use of ... this is extremely harmful. No one more is more in favour of a hard war than I ... and in this case I have given to you recent instructions, but the game must be worth the candle and the necessary retaliation must be intelligent. If in order to disperse ten more Abyssinians we throw the opinion of the world against ourselves and force reservations upon our few friends, we are only making our task more difficult. Issue strict orders so that Red Cross facilities are diligently respected everywhere.[32]

It was the case, however, as already noted, that this command was to be honoured more in the breach than the observance. In any event, those who survived the attack on the facility at Malca Dida withdrew to Negele, taking their surviving patients and equipment with them. This, of course, left Ras Desta's force with greatly reduced access to medical facilities at a time when they were suffering mightily from air attacks, and had probably been reduced to around 10,000 effectives.[33] As well as initiating attack from the air, Graziani devoted significant resources to defensive works. Dolo was entrenched and surrounded with 64km of barbed wire, positions were dug for 150 artillery pieces (although there were only enough guns to fill a third of them), and searchlights were installed to aid any nocturnal battle. He also ordered the construction of fortified camps around Mogadishu and other localities on and near the coast, and deployed large numbers of men to guard them.[34]

Graziani did not, though, intend to remain on the defensive, and was planning to take the fight to the enemy on the ground. On 6 January 1936 he informed his superiors that he considered Ras Desta's 'great strategic offensive' to be paralysed. He considered that the Ethiopian force was stranded some 360km from its base and suffering 'critical logistical conditions' whilst being 'daily tormented by our aerial actions and land attacks'. It was 'unable to attack our fortified positions'. Aware that he was supposed to be acting defensively, he couched his proposed offensive in terms of attracting the enemy to his front. Always ambitious, although prey to 'persecution mania' and eternally suspicious that his superiors were intent on ruining his career,[35] he also indulged in a modicum of self-praise for his efforts thus far:

> one day the statistical data will highlight the efforts made to amass on this front, about 700 kilometres from the sea with biblical roads and suffocating heat, an operational body of about 28,000 men, half of them white. Only then will it be possible to evaluate the effort, without which Oltre Giuba and northern Somalia would surely have been lost.[36]

In truth his logistical accomplishments had been substantial, and he was able to assemble a force behind Dolo of about 25,000 men, plus armoured vehicles and lorries to provide rapid mobility, whilst in the meantime continuing to probe with smaller, air-supported, units. The deficiencies in tactical coordination between aircraft and ground units, as noted earlier during the attack on Gorrahei, had been rectified by attaching air force officers to the army. Equipped with radios, these officers could call on air support as required, both for ground attack and supply purposes.[37]

On 10 January 1936 Graziani issued orders for the advance and thus began what was dubbed the Battle of Ganale Doria. The attackers advanced in three motorised main columns with the entire strength of the Somaliland Mixed Air Brigade in support. Chemical weapons were freely used, including both phosgene and mustard gas, as required. From 12 to 20 January the air force carried out 141 bombing and 49 reconnaissance and strafing sorties. There was some resistance but in the main Ras Desta's army melted away. Neghelli was attacked with gas and incendiaries on the morning of 20 January, just a few hours before the arrival of the truck-mounted troops who had travelled some 300km in ten days.[38]

One of the pilots involved was Vittorio Mussolini, a son of *Il Duce* who was remembered by one of the latter's mistresses, Margherita Sarfatti, as 'the family dunce'. She also recalled that during the Ethiopian war 'Vittorio enjoyed bombing the enemy, then flying low so that his crew could machine-gun the survivors'.[39] That this was indeed the case is evidenced by Vittorio himself, who published an account of his exploits. Of the attack on Neghelli he wrote:

> Neghelli is soon a sea of flames. The population flees to the surrounding bush. Black microbes can be seen from above running swiftly through the open areas, escaping in all directions; even the clouds of dust raised by the fugitives can be distinguished ... Oh, the hellish joy of the aviator, who sees the target jump when hit! Anyone who has never experienced this terrible destructive voluptuousness does not know exactly what man is made of. In these moments there is no place for human pity ... the enemy country is bombed, devastated metre by metre, eviscerated. Everywhere ruins and smoke from the fire. Incendiary bombs give more satisfaction, at least you can see fire and smoke. We burned the whole area well, but there were already no more people ... The survivors got a good volley and the Abyssinians were on the ground. It was a lonely manhunt, as usual, and the aircraft searched every hole sniffing out the Abyssinians. It was a very funny job, with a tragic effect, but beautiful.[40]

Italian propaganda made the most of this rapid and victorious advance. Graziani became a hero, fêted as the 'Lion of Neghelli' in the newspapers, and was indeed later awarded the aristocratic title Marquis of Neghelli by the king of Italy.[41]

According to Fuller, who along with all foreign journalists had been 'literally interned in Asmara, not being even permitted to leave the precincts of that town' since 10 December 1935,[42] this 'great Italian victory' had been proclaimed on 12 January. His account, based on official information, went on:

> on the 12th and the succeeding days, Ras Desta was heavily defeated in a battle called after an affluent of the Juba-Ganale Doria, and driven in rout beyond Negelli. As it had now become normal procedure in the Italian official communiques 5,000 Abyssinians were stated to have been killed, another 5,000 being added to this figure on the 27th.[43]

Fuller's analysis of the battle, although it was 'an exceedingly important one' in his estimation, and its operational context was, however, highly critical:

> For over three months General Graziani had been toiling with his Harar operation, now he and presumably a considerable part of his main army had been pulled several hundred miles in the opposite direction; consequently, though he had gained a tactical victory he had simultaneously suffered a severe strategical defeat.[44]

This was so because Graziani could profitably advance no further. Indeed, although an airfield was quickly established at Neghelli from where air strikes continued to be launched, the nearby town of Wadera being bombed with mustard gas on 25 January for example, he terminated his advance once the place had been reached.[45] Thus, later analysis has mostly tended to confirm Fuller's opinion, with Del Boca reckoning that whilst the Battle of Ganale Doria could be 'considered a small masterpiece (*piccolo capolavoro*) from a logistical and tactical point of view', it was essentially a sterile exercise.[46] Rochat agrees:

> Basically, the threat from Ras Desta was not so serious as to force Graziani to stop the offensive against Harar ... In reality, Neghelli was a group of huts (according to the Touring guide) and, more importantly, it was an end in itself; the lack of roads made it impossible to continue the offensive towards the plateau and more important objectives ... When he returned to take charge of the offensive on Harar, the only decisive target for the outcome of the conflict, it was already late and the means were scarce.[47]

The 2005 General Staff history disagrees, however. The author argues that the outcome represented the first authentic Italian success in East Africa, and was thus notable in the moral and propaganda contexts. This was, though, not the least of it and according to his viewpoint, it was an operationally important battle to have fought:

> Examined from the strategic point of view, there is no doubt that the positive outcome of the manoeuvre had freed the left flank of our deployment from a threat that could potentially have assumed considerable proportions ... In fact, it had neutralized the most important and dangerous enemy mass, while at the same time ensuring our possession of almost all of the vast territory of [southern Ethiopia].[48]

Longo also argues that an advance on Harar in January 1936 was not achievable with the means at Graziani's disposal. Identified as lacking in particular were 'the efficient Libyan Division' and 'suitable vehicles', particularly the Caterpillar tractors and trailers purchased in the United States.[49]

Whatever its operational/strategic implications, the battle was won, even if during its course about 1,000 Eritrean *ascari* defected to the enemy.[50] It did, however, serve to demonstrate, as argued by theorists and prophets such as Fuller, that what the latter termed 'totalitarian' tactics, indeed totalitarian warfare, had arrived. This was a new form of making war utilising, above all and as Fuller saw it, scientific methods. As he wrote in one of his articles, published whilst the conflict was still under way: 'The Italian High Command has had the vision and the courage to develop a new technique of war from the weapons and appliances which science and industry have placed at their disposal.'[51]

One might add that it had also demonstrated a total disregard for international law, particularly in terms of the 1925 Geneva Protocol regarding the prohibition of 'Asphyxiating, Poisonous or other Gases' and respecting the Red Cross. Graziani had then established the efficacy of this methodology tactically, although in January 1936 his feat had yet to be emulated by his commander-in-chief. For Badoglio, despite having immensely greater resources than pertained on the Somali front, was not having anything like the same success.

Chapter Eight

'The Awful Warning'

THE AWFUL WARNING

France and England (*together?*): 'We don't want you to fight, but by jingo if you do, we shall probably issue a joint memorandum suggesting a mild disapproval of you.'   [*Punch*, 14 August 1935]

* * *

If Mussolini had expected his appointment of Badoglio to rapidly make things happen on the northern front, then he was to be disappointed. His worries and discontent only increased in early January 1936, given that no apparent progress had been made in the two months or so following the occupation of Makalle on 8 November the previous year.[1] It was the case that the invasion force in Tigray was highly unlikely to be militarily defeated, but the stasis there was not replicated in the political sphere; the threat of an extension of sanctions to coal and oil and – the perennial worry – the potential closure of the Suez Canal continued to chafe.

Badoglio also knew, although not in detail, that enemy forces were manoeuvring on his front in order to attack. As Rochat points out, given the dearth of records and written accounts on the Ethiopian side, then information on their forces and operations mostly derives from Italian sources.[2] Italian intelligence, particularly via its ability to intercept and decipher Ethiopian radio signals, was, however, generally well informed. Analysis of enemy intentions pointed to them seeking to isolate Makalle and advance in three areas, the object of the exercise being to split up the Italian front and defeat its parts in detail.

To carry out this plan three armies were assembling. The largest, the Army of the Right under the command of Ras Mulugeta Yeggazu, numbered over 60,000 men and was concentrating in the area of Amba Aradam. A second force, the Army of the Centre, with about 40,000 men commanded by Ras Kassa Hailu and Ras Seyoum Mengesha had advanced upon the Giba river, whilst a third, the Army of the Left, under Ras Imru Haile Selassie (a cousin of the Emperor) containing 40,000–50,000 men was progressing across the Tacazze river.[3] Whilst the manpower of the Ethiopians was undoubtedly exaggerated, and probably greatly so, the invaders nevertheless faced a formidable force, although one that laboured under the weight of several disadvantages, the most important of which was that the Ethiopians had no answer to Italian air supremacy other than concealment, which was of no avail in relation to large fixed targets such as towns.

One well known incident in this regard relates to Dessie, situated around 270km south of Makalle as the crow flies. It was here that the Negus had arrived on 30 November 1935, and from where he intended to lead the defence of his country. It was also the site of several medical facilities, including the Tafari Makonnen Hospital, also known as the American Hospital because it was operated by American Seventh-Day Adventist missionaries, which Haile Selassie visited on 1 December.[4] Five days later it was severely damaged during an Italian air raid, an attack witnessed by the American war correspondent Linton Wells. Wells was in Dessie with his wife, aviator and fellow journalist Fay Gillis Wells, where they were, rather incredibly, combining a commission from the *New York Herald Tribune* to cover the Ethiopian war with their honeymoon.[5] He wrote a detailed account of what he saw:

> Fay ... raised her hand, pointed, and said casually: 'Well, look who's here – Italian airplanes.' Looking toward the north I made out five Italian three-motored Capronis limned in the sky. As the roar of their engines reached our ears pandemonium broke loose around us. Natives began to scatter in all directions, firing their guns indiscriminately. I never have seen such panic. To me it was obvious that our move was to reach the American hospital compound, which was marked with twenty big Red Crosses. Some were painted on the tops of buildings and tents; others made of red and

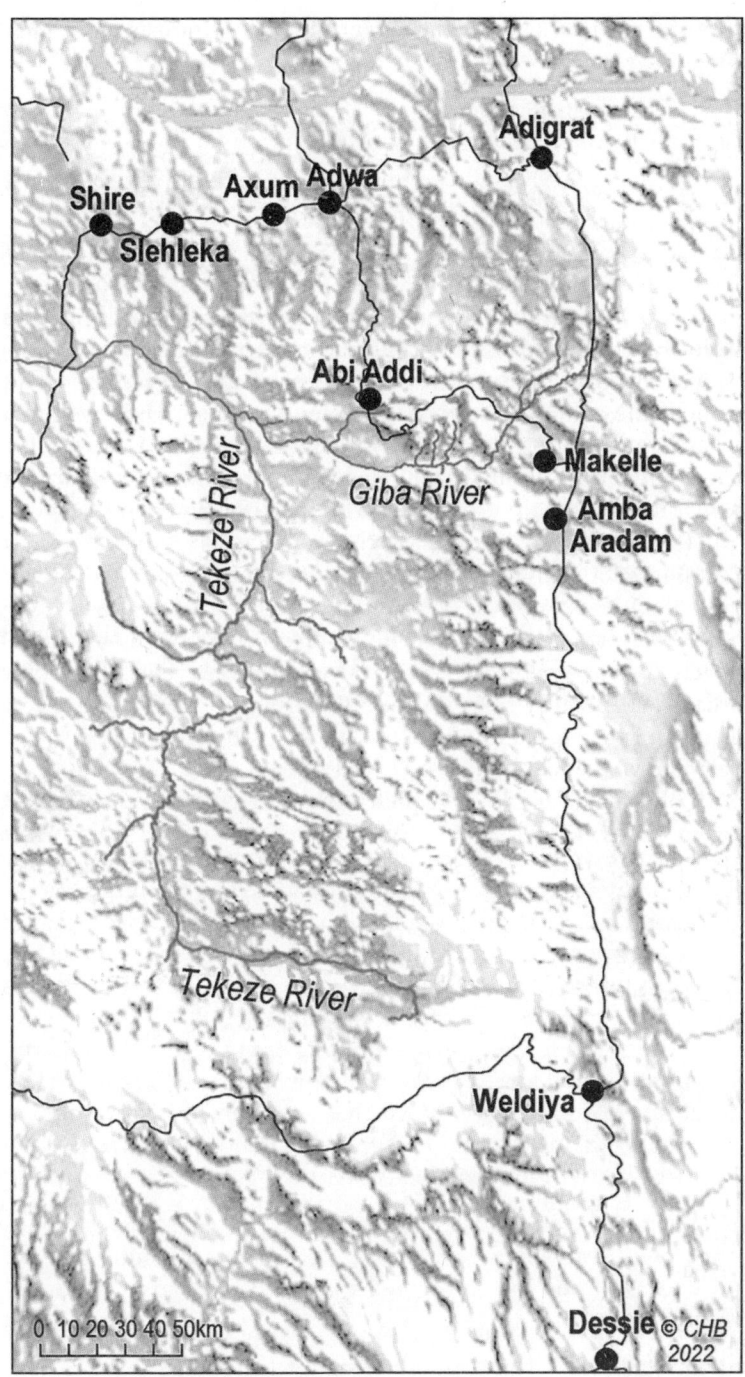

Key points on the northern front. (© *Charles Blackwood*)

white bunting stretched across the ground; all were unmistakable and easily visible from the air.[6]

Sending his wife towards the hospital, Wells decided to run to their car and retrieve his guns before joining her. Whilst doing so he was hit in the shoulder, although not seriously, by a stray round from the indiscriminate firing going on and so rapidly changed direction. Having reached what he considered comparative safety, and being reunited with his partner in the doorway of the main hospital building, he continued to observe the attackers:

> By now the five Capronis were circling overhead at an altitude of about 6,000 feet [1,800m] and dropping clusters of incendiary and 100-kilogram high explosive bombs on the town, hoping, of course, to blast the Emperor beyond any further hope of annoyance. Simultaneously, the few antiaircraft batteries were pounding away ineffectually and the natives continuing to fire rifles and pistols with careless abandon. It sounded like a spectacular Fourth of July celebration, but after the first few minutes we hardly heard it... After a sixteen-minute bombardment, moderate quiet was restored as the five planes disappeared behind a mountain to the east and within a few minutes Fay and I were back at our tent comparing notes with our colleagues. No bombs had dropped in the compound, but it was apparent that the village outside had taken an awful licking. We could see that the Emperor's headquarters were still intact and assumed that he was safe.[7]

But the attack was far from over.

> Before we could ascertain the casualties, someone shouted, 'Here they come again,' and we looked up to see and then hear the roar of ten planes, five other buzzards having joined the first five ... Now hell did pop, for instead of directing their attentions on the town, they seemed to concentrate on the hospital compound. Fortunately, the high explosive bombs landed on the edges of its twenty acres, but the 2-pound incendiaries, about the size of a water tumbler, burst all around us and ignited, giving forth a heat which scientists say is in excess of 6,000° Fahrenheit [3,300° Celsius]. Certainly those which burned a few feet away from us were uncomfortably warm. The trouble with an air raid is that you never know what in hell to do or where to go in the absence of a deep dugout which is not likely to cave in and bury you alive ... it seemed to me that the safest place in the world was in that hospital building with the red cross painted on its roof.[8]

Wells related how the next fifteen minutes were a repetition of the previous sixteen, until 'comparative quiet descended upon the community as the warbirds flew away'. He remarked that it seemed the attack was 'over for today' before relating that 'it wasn't':

> Those scum had simply slithered out of sight to give us a chance to come out in the open and within seven minutes they were back overhead raining death

and destruction upon us again. This time bombs hit Red Cross tents and the hospital where Fay and I had been standing but a short time before. When they burst into flames, we all rushed forth to save them, but practically all medical supplies and the operating room of the hospital were destroyed. Throughout this shindig, our chief concern had been for the safety of a thousand or more gallons of gasoline loaded in trucks around which inflammable shells were falling with disconcerting closeness. Fortunately, they didn't explode and later in the day we buried the petrol tins in the ground at a safe distance from the camp. By the time the fires were under control, the Italians had called it a day and disappeared into the north.[9]

The whole episode was characterised by the American, who had seen much of war and strife in his career as a correspondent, as 'the most contemptible, disgusting and inhumane act of warfare it has ever been my misfortune to watch in twenty odd years'.[10] Aviation historian Roberto Gentilli has calculated that the raid was conducted from an altitude of 1,000m and that 48 100kg bombs, 1,518 1kg incendiary bombs, and 330 2kg fragmentation bombs were dropped over its course: a total of 7,698kg of ordnance.[11]

This was, in 1935, a massive air attack[12] and it certainly attracted its fair share of press reports, most of which were highly critical. In fact, the attack on an American-run hospital, as reported by an American journalist, was, unsurprisingly, headline news in the US. This was of concern to the Italian government because *not* antagonising the US administration, nor public opinion there, was considered crucial. The US, as a non-member of the League of Nations, did not apply sanctions of any kind, and during 1935 supplied a little over 10 per cent of Italy's oil imports, although in the last quarter of the year this had risen to 17.8 per cent.[13] The rest came from a number of other countries, and by 12 December ten of them had informed the League that they were willing to embargo oil for Italy. These included the Hashemite Kingdom of Iraq, the Netherlands (a big oil producer via their colonial holdings in what is now Indonesia), Romania and the USSR, who collectively provided 74.3 per cent of Italian imports.[14]

Clearly then, American oil was an increasingly vital commodity for Italy, and had the US government, whether in conjunction with the League or unilaterally, made the decision to cease exporting oil to Italy, then the latter would have quickly been crippled. Even a restriction of the supply, which as noted had increased massively in October and November 1935, would have been highly damaging.[15] Indeed, Cristiano Ristuccia calculates that had the Roosevelt administration taken a 'hard line' by only supplying Italy with average monthly, peacetime, levels of oil, then 'Italian industrial production would have come to a complete stop in March 1936 ...'[16]

There were, however, several reasons why an American oil embargo was unlikely, although not all were necessarily obvious to Mussolini at the time. As De Felice points out, Roosevelt was up for re-election in 1936 and there were a significant number of largely pro-Fascist Italian-American voters in the US. He also observes that even if the major oil companies abided by a ban, this was unlikely to have been observed by the independents, who could have easily made up the difference, their daily output being some 80,000 tons whilst Italian daily consumption was 8,000 tons.[17] Further, Breckinridge Long, the US Ambassador to Italy from 1933 to 1936, was also against oil sanctions.[18] A friend and confidant of the president, and an admirer of Mussolini, his position as laid out in November 1935 was dead-set against the notion:

> I am motivated entirely by the desire to see the United States out of this war. I believe that an emplacement of an oil embargo on oil will get us involved in it. Mussolini is wrong and has been wrong from the start ... Let me implore you to continue the policy of allowing Italy – and Ethiopia – to buy the same quantities they have bought in normal times.[19]

Whilst it is unlikely that a single air raid would have induced the US to change its policy, it is clear that the Department of State did not wish to make much of the affair. As a memorandum to secretary of state Cordell Hull phrased it: 'In view of all the circumstances ... it would appear to be wise to refrain from making any protest to the Italian government at this time.'[20] In any event, the decision on whether to impose oil sanctions on Italy was scheduled to be taken at a meeting of a committee of the League in Geneva on 12 December 1935.[21]

We shall come to that shortly, but it is worth noting that Longo categorises the bombing of Dessie as one of the most important, and certainly one of the largest, such operations of the entire conflict. With the objective located 2,000m above sea level, and surrounded by mountains around 1,000m taller, attacking the town involved navigating a return flight of almost 1,000km over testing terrain. These difficulties were, however, offset by the importance of the objective: it was the seat of the Ethiopian command, with the Negus himself in residence along with his political-military leaders. This resulted in the 'the installation of numerous anti-aircraft weapons' whilst the area 'was also occupied by thousands of armed men heading north'. Thus, it is argued, Dessie was a legitimate target, with the attacks directed at government buildings, the airfield, the telephone exchange and the like. Destruction of civilian infrastructure, along with civilian casualties, was collateral damage.[22]

Claims that the American Hospital, in particular, had been targeted were laid at the door of 'a large group of foreign journalists' who had followed on the heels of the Negus and his entourage. Additionally, Longo argues that aerial reconnaissance reports had repeatedly pointed out that much of the tented camps, the infrastructure of the airfield and even areas of cleared land were marked with the red cross.[23] Nevertheless, in this interpretation the foreign reporters 'did not miss the opportunity' to describe the bombing as:

> an indiscriminate attack on a 'defenceless' city, emphasizing in particular that the hospital under the aegis of the American Red Cross, with some

European volunteers, had been hit. Their articles were accompanied by a series of photographic images that showed impressive scenes of destroyed barracks, around which, however, the people who appeared there were clearly soldiers and not civilians. In the following days, as a result of the emotionally exasperated reaction from vast sectors of world public opinion, expertly fed by the press, the aerial activity suffered a stagnation in the context of bombing ...[24]

In other words, public opinion in the western democracies, or rather Italian fear of what it might lead to in terms of influencing their governments, resulted in a curtailment of the bombing of targets such as Dessie. As has been discussed earlier, the French government was determined to avoid estranging Mussolini at almost any cost, no matter what public opinion might demand, whilst the British government, largely through the force of public opinion, appeared much firmer. This had been exemplified in a speech by the experienced politician Sir Samuel Hoare, who had been appointed Britain's foreign secretary in June 1935 albeit he had little foreign policy knowledge.[25] On 12 September 1935 he addressed the League General Assembly at Geneva:

> I will begin by reaffirming the support of the League by the Government I represent and the interest of the British people in collective security ... the League stands, and my country stands with it, for the collective maintenance of the Covenant in its entirety, and particularly for steady and collective resistance to all acts of unprovoked aggression.[26]

That this was more form than substance was not appreciated at the time. Prior to speechifying, Hoare had held 'long talks' on 10 and 11 September 1935 with his French opposite number Pierre Laval, who had assumed the office of prime minister as well in June 1935. In terms of the Ethiopian situation, both men 'excluded the idea of war with Italy as too dangerous and double-edged for the future of Europe'.[27] Neville Chamberlain, the chancellor of the exchequer, made similar observations. He was accustomed to writing to his unmarried sisters on a weekly basis and on the day Italy invaded he told one of them that 'the French are determined not to fight and we are not going to act without them'.[28]

The quandary Britain faced was, retrospectively, well expressed by Winston Churchill: 'The Prime Minister had declared that Sanctions meant war; secondly, he was resolved that there must be no war; and, thirdly, he decided upon Sanctions.'[29] A devilish puzzle indeed, but one that Britain's foreign secretary, who as head of the MI5-run British Military Mission to Italy in 1918 had bribed a young journalist named Benito Mussolini to the tune of £100 per week for pro-Allied articles, might have solved.[30]

Hoare and Laval met on 7 and 8 December in Paris and further discussed what had now become the Italian invasion and, more pertinently, how the war might be brought to a close diplomatically. Arnold J. Toynbee characterises the meeting as an affair where Laval, who was in touch with Mussolini, employed 'consummate diplomatic skill' in order to draw Hoare 'into an ever-closer partnership in a game which the British Secretary of State seems never fully to have understood ...'[31] Possibly this was so, although later scholarship has tended towards an explanation around Hoare being badly briefed.[32] What might have counted for more was that he was accompanied by Sir Robert Vansittart, his permanent under-secretary. Vansittart's perspective on, and consistent attitude to, British policy towards Italy was straightforward. As he set it out the following year:

> Mussolini has made his first advances to his fellow dictator across the Alps; but unless we drive him into an active and offensive co-operation with Hitler, we are entitled to hope that he will not be anxious to take the high road to Berlin. We shall have to compromise with Mussolini, for we can never compromise securely or even live safely with Dictator Major [Hitler], if we are at loggerheads with Dictator Minor [Mussolini].[33]

The foreign secretary's room for manoeuvre was also restricted by prime ministerial fiat: 'the burden of Baldwin's instructions was to prevent war by whatever means'.[34] The outcome, as Hoare was to recall it, was that: 'By the evening of [8 December] agreement had been reached between us on a threefold basis.'[35] This agreement, known as the 'Hoare-Laval Plan' or 'Hoare–Laval Pact', basically offered Mussolini 'about two-thirds of Abyssinia in return for the evacuation of Italian troops'.[36] It was, as Crowcroft has observed, and on balance, a 'plausible solution to Italian demands'. This was so because, as he points out, Rome would achieve its imperial objectives whilst at least part of Abyssinia remained independent. Mussolini was prepared to accept it, and the Abyssinians had little choice on the matter. It was even consistent with the Covenant of the League of Nations, which mandated the settling of disputes through conciliation.[37]

According to the celebrated writer and journalist Genevieve Tabouis, Laval decreed on 6 December that nothing whatsoever must appear in the French press in respect of his negotiations with Hoare, nor of their outcome. Being distinctly hostile to Laval and to Fascism, she saw this as an opportunity, writing some years later that: 'I wondered if this was not exactly the chance I had been waiting for. If I should manage to publish an account of the plan twenty-four or forty-eight hours before the final draft was completed, I might be able to ruin its chances ...'[38]

Whilst her explanation of how she pieced together the contents of the plan is unconvincing, and rightly so given she was undoubtedly protecting a source inside the Ministry of Foreign Affairs, she and fellow journalist André Géraud (who wrote under the name *Pertinax*), working independently, produced accurate accounts combined with withering criticism. These appeared in *L'Oeuvre* and *Echo de Paris* respectively on 9 December and, perhaps aided by the fact that Géraud was also the Paris correspondent of the *Daily Telegraph*,[39] the news was not long in crossing the Channel. It created a political storm. As the then little-known Conservative MP for Stockton on Tees, Harold Macmillan, was to remember:

> at the time, those who were not behind the scenes could not know what were the reasons for Hoare's sudden change of front, involving a surrender to Laval and a betrayal of the policies to which we were all so recently and so decisively pledged. At the same time, we were almost overwhelmed by the public reaction: first stupefaction, then shame and anger.[40]

The very well connected Soviet ambassador to Britain, Ivan Maisky, who was also excluded from being 'behind the scenes', was similarly baffled. As his diary entry for 14 December put it:

> The situation becomes more and more mysterious. On 11 September Hoare made his famous speech in Geneva, in which he resolutely stated that from now on British foreign policy would be the policy of the League of Nations ... I had assumed that loyalty to the League of Nations remained very much in the interests of the British government. And all of a sudden, the Hoare-Laval 'peace plan' appears in Paris! A plan that marks the most brazen, most impudent betrayal of the League! And when? Three weeks after the election. And at what precise moment? The moment of the manifest failure of the Italian army in Abyssinia and of ever-increasing problems for Mussolini at home! It is beyond understanding! What's it all about? Who is to blame?[41]

Who indeed? One man who was very much 'behind the scenes', Neville Chamberlain, had little doubt who was to blame:

> nothing could be worse than our position. Our whole prestige in foreign affairs at home and abroad has tumbled to pieces like a house of cards. If we had to fight the election over again, we should probably be beaten & certainly would not have more than a bare majority. Sam's reputation is damaged – perhaps irretrievably. I am told that our supporters in the house ... say he can never recover his position among foreign nations and therefore he had better go and so help the [government] back to its feet ... All that is to be taken as a measure of the disaster that has befallen us.[42]

One of the 'supporters' mentioned, the Conservative backbench MP Robert Boothby, later described the issue and the outcome: 'The public reaction to the Hoare-Laval proposals for the dismemberment of Abyssinia was spontaneous, widespread, and wholly creditable. It was one of disgust. Mr Baldwin was quick to discern that this was no ripple on the waters. He dropped Sir Samuel like a hot potato ...'[43]

The resignation of Hoare on 18 December 1935, albeit with the promise of rapid restoration to a Cabinet position if he went quietly,[44] and the speedy repudiation of the Hoare-Laval Plan by the British government, probably saved Baldwin's premiership. Laval was not so fortunate. His part in it all was a major factor in persuading the Radical elements of his government to withdraw support; he was forced to resign on 22 January 1936.[45]

The greatest disaster, though, was reserved for the League. The choice that Britain was faced with, as outlined by Vansittart in July, between 'the League busting Mussolini or Mussolini busting the League'[46] had effectively been made, albeit it was Hoare and Laval who had mostly done the 'busting'. In any event, the League of Nations was now, to quote A.J.P. Taylor, shown to be 'an empty sham'.[47] Perhaps Martelli put it best:

> The Hoare-Laval Plan was the death-blow to collective action. It revealed the real face of the League and showed the flimsiness of its facade. The sheep-like battalions of small States, in whom the attitude of Britain had instilled a certain courage, on seeing their leader turn tail, broke and scattered for cover. Disillusionment, defeatism and demoralisation set in, and though efforts were made to rally the Geneva forces, their fighting spirit had ebbed and they had no heart for further battle ... The proceedings at Geneva were no longer taken seriously ...[48]

In truth the cartoon entitled 'The Awful Warning', published in the London satirical magazine *Punch* on 14 August 1935, had proved all too prescient and all the League could do, as Churchill was to phrase it, was continue imposing 'such half-hearted sanctions as the aggressor would tolerate'.[49] The meeting in Geneva on oil sanctions was held on 12 December, but it took no action pending a decision on the 'merits of the new proposals put forward by France and the United Kingdom'.[50] As we have seen, the British quickly disavowed the 'proposals' and in any event the Ethiopians totally rejected them as having no merit whatsoever. They further declared that, having been 'taught by cruel experience', they were 'firmly opposed to all secret negotiations'.[51]

The abrupt repudiation of the Hoare-Laval plan rather caught Mussolini on the hop, too. *Il Duce* had approved the outcome it advocated, and had even planned a meeting of the Fascist Grand Council where he would have announced a great victory.[52] Deprived of a political solution to the conflict, but reassured that the threat of meaningful collective action by the League of Nations, and particularly by the British, had receded, the Italian government and high command knew now that Italy would gain only what it could conquer.

Although the unexpected collapse and disappearance of the Hoare-Laval proposals had come as a surprise, Mussolini's decisions in the diplomatic sphere were usually based on solid information about his opponents. This was obtained from compromised British and French diplomatic ciphers, which had yielded to the attacks of the cryptanalysts in the army's Military Information Service (*Servizio Informazioni Militari* – SIM) led by General Vittorio Gamba. Working largely with pencil and paper, as there were no machines to assist with processing and analysis, Gamba's codebreakers read much British and French diplomatic traffic, which gave some insight into the political processes ongoing in London and Paris.

With respect to these signals, there was a second string to SIM's bow in Section P (*Sezione P*): the Extraction Section (*Sezione Prevelamento*). This was basically a team of burglars headed by an officer of the *carabinieri*, Major Manfredi Talamo, who specialised, with inside assistance, in infiltrating the embassies of foreign powers and removing documents and the like. These were then photographed and returned in quick time, leaving no trace of the operation.

Both the French and British embassies naturally received increased attention during the Ethiopian campaign which, David Alvarez tells us, allowed *Sezione P* to often place 'secret documents on Mussolini's desk within twenty-four hours of their arrival from London or Paris'. He goes on to state that 'The haul from the British embassy included several diplomatic and consular codes, a naval attaché cipher, the India Office Cipher, and the Interdepartmental Cipher.'[53] Documents from the British embassy, which included 'the heavy set of twenty-four books containing the diplomatic cipher' had been removed, photographed and replaced in July 1934 by the brothers Francesco and Secondo Constantini, the latter being a live-in servant at the place. Exemplifying the 'wilderness of mirrors' world of espionage, the Constantinis, who operated only for money, were also working for the Soviet Union.[54]

Italian intelligence also operated abroad with a good deal of success, one prime example being the acquisition of the 'Maffey Report'. On 18 June 1935 the British Foreign Office had received the report of a committee put together under the chairmanship of Sir John Maffey, the permanent under-secretary of state for the colonies and former governor general of Sudan. This committee had been assembled in order to evaluate British interests in Ethiopia à propos an Italian invasion, and it concluded that these were not of a magnitude to trigger military action in preservation of the status quo. It did not, however, take into account the broader matter regarding the weight to be given, *vis-à-vis* British interests, in preserving and upholding the authority of the League of Nations. The report also determined that the Ethiopians were not overawed by Italian military strength, and would not therefore concede much in negotiations, even if pressed:

> The Ethiopians have shown no sign of yielding to the Italian demands because of any fear of Italian military strength. The chief result of Italian sabre-rattling has been to intensify and confirm Ethiopian suspicions of Italy (always latent since Adowa), and also to make world opinion watchful and suspicious. In Ethiopian eyes Italy stands fully revealed as the enemy; and the Emperor could not hope to command acceptance for any peaceful settlement with Italy which would be humiliating to Ethiopian pride and independence, even if he were pressed to do so by disinterested foreign Powers anxious to see peace preserved.[55]

The Italian embassy had acquired a copy of the report soon after its release via the depredations of Captain John Herbert King, a Foreign Office cipher officer, who was passing documentation to foreign powers.[56] Mussolini thus had inside knowledge regarding what Britain was likely to do. He calculated that he could therefore afford to bluster and bluff, and did so. Nevertheless, and despite all the advantages enumerated, his decision to launch a full-scale invasion of Ethiopia, and then persist in the matter, involved a massive gamble. Neville Chamberlain put the matter succinctly in December 1935:

> By putting his great army on the other side [of] the Suez Canal Mussolini has tied a noose round his own neck and left the end hanging out for anyone with a navy to pull. It would seem incredible that in such a position he should venture to attack us, and in the end I don't believe he would. Yet one can't absolutely exclude the possibility with such a man and he loses no opportunity of letting it be known that such is his intention though always by agents who could easily be disavowed.[57]

Although military action was Italy's only choice of gaining anything following the collapse of the Hoare-Laval Plan, the situation in that regard was, as already mentioned, not entirely propitious. The invaders were suffering from, as Longo called it, 'operational stagnation'.[58] Thus December 1935 proved to be a somewhat eventful month, in both the diplomatic and military spheres. In fact, and with the advance of large Ethiopian forces northwards to engage the invaders, it presaged much more in the latter context.

What this meant was that before attempting any further conquest, Badoglio would have to repel the counter-attacks. In this regard he would use all available means. Accordingly, on 20 December the acting air force commander, Air Brigadier General Mario Ajmone Cat, was directed to attack the enemy with mustard gas as well as conventional bombs.[59] Two days later, on the morning of 22 December 1935, the first two *bomba* C.500.T to be used in East Africa were dropped in a remote valley away from the front in order to field-test their adjustable fuses.[60]

Chapter Nine

Keeping Mussolini awake at night

we had by now become accustomed to bombing. But that morning they didn't drop bombs, but strange drums (*fusti*) that broke as soon as they touched the ground or the water of the river, and threw a colourless liquid around them. Before I could realize what was happening, a few hundred of my men had been struck by the mysterious liquid and were screaming in pain as their bare feet, their hands, their faces blistered.[1]

* * *

Badoglio did not intend to conduct a war of attrition to wear down the opposition. Rather, his operational objective was to bring on a great pitched battle, or a series of them, to ensure the rapid and total annihilation of the enemy armies.[2] First, though, he had to ensure the security of his own forces, and to that end ordered the construction of fortified positions south of Makalle that would serve both as a platform for further operations to the south, and to stop his adversary. He was well aware that his enemy were fine troops, skilled at infiltration and courageous in assaults. On the other hand, they were grossly deficient in terms of supplies, heavy weapons and ammunition, and thus, being essentially unsupported light infantry, were unable to successfully overcome fortified positions. Nevertheless, Makalle was a worry. In occupying it, 'political needs had not taken into account military ones', and the left wing of the Italian front was now in a potentially dangerously isolated situation.[3] It was then heavily fortified, with the consolidation of the entire Italian front being conducted over the first two weeks or so of December 1935. Mussolini was informed of the necessity of 'seriously organizing in order not to be in the air as we are now, and then following up on military operations'.[4] As Del Boca remarks, Mussolini did not seemingly pick up on the allusion to things being 'up in the air' and replied a few days later pointing out the desirability of advancing to Amba Alagi. He was obviously unaware that this position was now occupied by Ras Mulugeta Yeggazu's command.[5]

It was, though, on the right, westernmost, portion of the Italian front that the first Ethiopian attack manifested itself in the Tembien region, an area that borders Tigre to the north of the Tekeze river. Given the forbidding topography of the Tembien Massif, control of the mountain passes along the route Adi Gebru–Inda Aba Guna–Shire–Slehleka was vital. The first-named was some 8km north of the Tekeze as the crow flies, whilst the last, similarly calculated, was about 30km to the west of Axum. There was a motorised Italian unit stationed along the road, such as it was, close to the northern bank of the river. Under

Major Luigi Criniti, and about 1,700-strong in terms of personnel, it was composed mainly of *bande*: the Eritrean levies that Fuller had dismissed as 'no more than armed riff-raff'. In a supporting role, and encamped around 5km south of Inda Aba Guna, were eight L3/35 light tanks of the *10° Squadrone carri veloci «Esploratori del Nilo»* (the 'Explorer of the Nile' Fast Tank Squadron), plus a contingent of *bande* under Captain Ettore Crippa.[6]

The Ethiopian plan was for two columns, each of around 2,000–3,000 men, to advance across the river around 15km apart. One column would move directly on the enemy along the road whilst the second progressed secretly through the mountains in order to interdict that road as it traversed a pass at Inda Aba Guna (Dembeguina to the invaders). The first indications that the latter manoeuvre had been successful came at around 07:30 on 15 December, when Crippa heard the sound of intense small-arms fire to the north. He calculated that the skirmish involved a pair of trucks, escorted by about 100 *bande*, which had departed at 06:00 after delivering fuel to his command. He sent a single tank commanded by Sergeant Major Giuseppe Bruno along the road to investigate; arriving at the pass, it was obvious to Bruno that a powerful and well armed Ethiopian formation had succeeded in ambushing the trucks and escort.[7]

Bruno knew that his single poorly armed tank stood no chance in any sort of action, and instead retired to report on the situation. Crippa decided to deploy his whole force, sending a single tank on ahead with the rest following under his direct command. This proved to be a mistake: after driving 'a few kilometres', the leading tank of the main force, commanded by Bruno, discovered the tank that had gone ahead 'immobilized in the bush due to the breaking of a track, with the left hatch torn off and the crew massacred'. When Crippa arrived, he ordered the bodies removed from the vehicle before having it destroyed with explosives to prevent its use by the enemy. The force then pressed on until it reached the position of the original ambush, where the two trucks were still burning on the road. Here contact with the enemy was made.

The situation, from the Italian point of view, swiftly deteriorated. Crippa was hit and mortally wounded almost immediately and his second-in-command, Lieutenant Franco Martelli,[8] was machine-gunned shortly afterwards, leaving Sergeant Major Bruno as the senior survivor. He was to rediscover, via painful experience, what had already been established on the southern front in early November: the Italian L3/35 light tanks were exceedingly vulnerable vehicles. Indeed, the Ethiopian troops, although they had never seen a tank before, quickly identified their weak points.[9] Perhaps chief amongst these was the turretless configuration, which meant that the twin 8mm machine guns had an extremely limited firing arc of around 15 degrees. They were also cramped, although only crewed by two men, and fragile inasmuch as the tracks were unsuitable for rough terrain – and in Ethiopia even the so-called roads through the mountains were rough. To deal with the tanks, the Ethiopians divided themselves into small groups and, staying clear of the machine guns, surrounded them. Climbing onto the chassis, they bent the barrels of the weapons by striking them with heavy

Il Duce announcing victory over Ethiopia on 5 May 1936 from 'Mussolini's Balcony' on the Piazza Venezia, Rome. (*Author's Collection*)

Mussolini and Marshal Pietro Badoglio. (*Author's Collection*)

General Emilio De Bono in North Africa in 1935. Mussolini's initial choice as C-in-C for the Ethiopian campaign, he was replaced in December 1935. (*Author's Collection*)

Marshal Pietro Badoglio, De Bono's replacement, brought the war to a conclusion with his entry into Addis Ababa on 5 May 1936. (*Author's Collection*)

Badoglio observing the Battle of Amba Aradam (Enderta), which was fought between 10 and 19 February 1936. (*Author's Collection*)

Badoglio in 1943 with Allied war correspondents after he replaced Mussolini as Italy's prime minister. The American writer Richard Tregaskis, wearing the glasses, is to his immediate left. (*Author's Collection*)

Graziani addressing his officers in Somalia-Ogaden. (*Author's Collection*)

Graziani as defence minister of the RSI. He was awarded the Iron Cross I and II class by decree of the Fuehrer on 7 October 1944. (*Author's Collection*)

Graziani at his trial in 1950. Sentenced to nineteen years' imprisonment on 2 May 1950, he was freed on 29 August the same year. (*Author's Collection*)

Galeazzo Ciano in 1939. A pilot during the war with Ethiopia, the 'second most important man in Italy' was married to Mussolini's daughter and became Italian foreign minister. He was shot in 1944 for 'betraying' his father-in-law. (*Author's Collection*)

Mussolini, Hitler and King Victor Emmanuel III in May 1938. (*Author's Collection*)

Vittorio Mussolini, son of *Il Duce* and 'the family dunce', was a pilot during the Ethiopian war. He 'enjoyed bombing the enemy, then flying low so that his crew could machine gun the survivors'. (*Author's Collection*)

Colonel Vittorio Ruggero (*left*) and Sergeant Major Francesco de Martini (*right*) at Beilul, Eritrea, in 1935. Behind them are some of the 'dogs of war' recruited in Yemen for the lorry-borne 'flying column' across the fearsome Danakil Desert to take the town of Serdo. (*Author's Collection*)

Haile Selassie, Emperor of Ethiopia. (*Author's Collection*)

Haile Selassie at Dessie, 6 December 1935, manning an Oerlikon anti-aircraft gun. (*Author's Collection*)

(*Above left*) Ras Desta Damtew, commander of an army which attempted to thwart Graziani's designs in Somalia. His force was defeated at the Battle of Ganale Doria. (*Author's Collection*)

(*Above right*) Ras Getachew Abate commanded the Imperial Guard at the Battle of Maychew. (*Author's Collection*)

(*Right*) Ras Imru Haile Selassie. Probably the most successful, and certainly the most cunning, Ethiopian commander, Ras Imru is said to have 'kept Mussolini awake at night'. (*Author's Collection*)

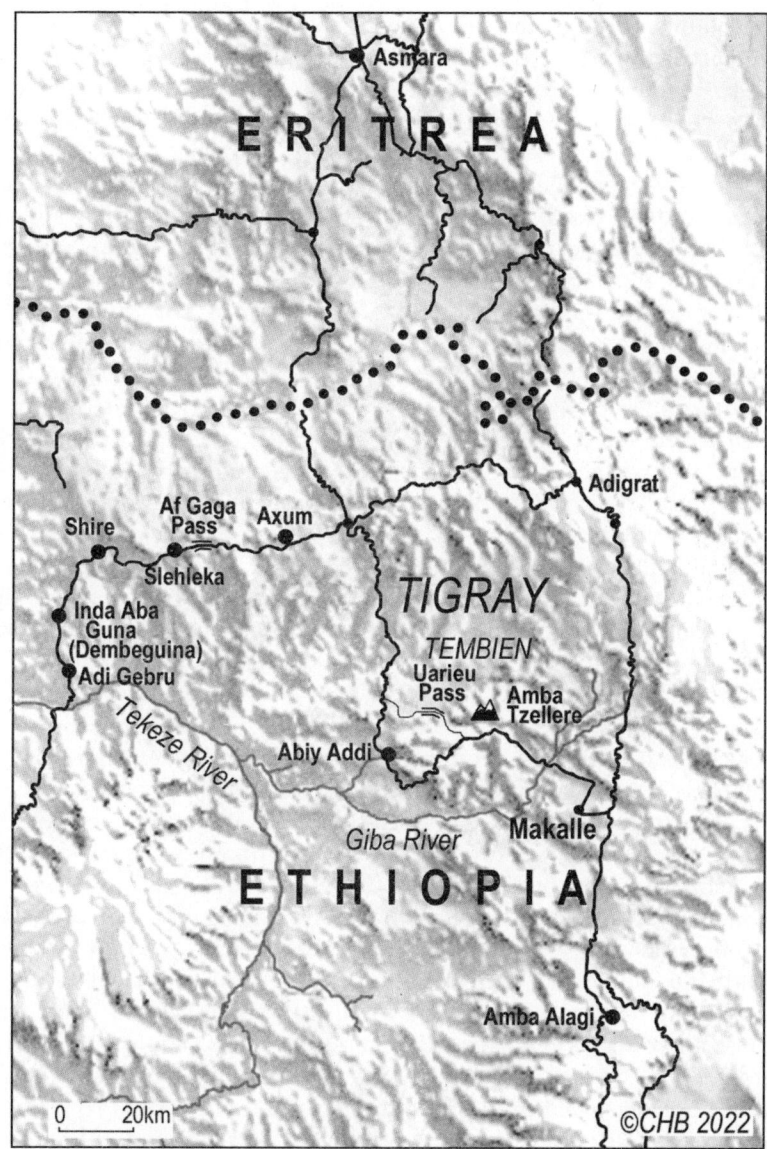

Key points pertaining to the Ethiopian counter-offensive. (© *Charles Blackwood*)

stones (or attempted to), and fired through the vision slits to kill the crew. These tactics were successful and put all the vehicles out of action with most of the personnel killed. This action was still in progress when it was interrupted by the arrival of Major Criniti and his retreating force, which included infantry. These were deployed and managed to clear the road sufficiently to allow the retreating column to get past the ambush-point and through the pass.

Pursued and harassed by the Ethiopians, Criniti successfully brought his command to Shire, arriving there around midnight on 15/16 December. The cost of the day's fighting had been severe. Sources differ somewhat, but Longo, quoting official reports, states that Italian fatalities amounted to nine officers and thirty-three NCOs and other ranks.[10] In addition, 270 Eritreans perished.[11] In total, 1,420 survivors, of whom 125 were seriously wounded, reached Shire, where there was a friendly, albeit small, garrison. Badoglio was determined to avoid battle in the open field. Therefore, rather than pushing forward a force to Shire, he ordered the contingents there to withdraw some 30km to Slehleka, where there was entrenched an entire Italian division, the *24ª Divisione fanteria 'Gran Sasso'*.

Fuller, 'interned' at Asmara along with all the other correspondents, related how a rumour reached the press office concerning 'a considerable engagement' which had taken place on the Tekeze river. Further uncorroborated information trickled in to the effect that two columns of Ethiopians had forced an Italian detachment about 1,000-strong back from the river and had 'cut it to pieces' in the 'pass of Dembeguina'. On 19 December the press corps were informed that the casualties resulting from the engagement had amounted to 'more than 500 Abyssinians killed', whilst Italian losses had been '272 killed and 29 wounded'. These figures, their ratio 'irreconcilable with normal statistics', were, he opined, ominous because they 'suggested massacre'.[12] When he worked up his notes and despatches into book form he reckoned that whilst tactically the battle was 'but a small affair', in strategic terms it was 'of marked importance, for it broke the Italian front'.[13]

Later analysis has tended to confirm this view. Longo details how in the days following the engagement more than 20,000 men advanced across the Tekeze and spread north-east. On 18 December they reached the border with Eritrea, threatening to extend the war into the colony, and posing a danger to the Italian forces at Axum and Adua by interdicting their already tenuous lines of communication. Badoglio, fearful for the 'Gran Sasso' Division in the face of these large numbers, ordered it to evacuate Slehleka and retreat to Axum, destroying any materiel they couldn't take with them. This operation, a 60km journey via an abysmal, winding road was conducted 'in difficult and extremely uncomfortable conditions' in two stages and with 'exasperating slowness': a rate calculated at just 2km per hour. Fortunately, perhaps, the retreating column remained unmolested, arriving in the entrenched camp of Axum exhausted but intact.[14]

Aside from the large-scale repercussions of the clash at Inda Aba Guna (the *Battaglia al Passo Dembeguina* to the Italians), this episode revealed serious problems with respect to the tanks. This went beyond their inherent flaws, as already detailed, and extended into doctrinal matters: how they were used. As Rochat points out, the manner of their unsupported deployment remains 'incomprehensible', and their destruction 'amplified the Ethiopian success'.[15] One result was that on 1 January 1936 the Ministry of War issued 'Rules for the Employment of Tank Units', the third point of which stated: 'It is a serious mistake to launch tanks without them being preceded by light and fast elements (motorcyclists, cyclists or horse-riders) charged with the triple task of exploration, security, and reconnaissance of the terrain.'[16]

Nor was the air force held to have distinguished itself. Despite carrying out multitudinous reconnaissance flights, it failed to detect the whereabouts of Ethiopian troops numbered in the several tens of thousands. This failure undoubtedly owed a great deal to the skill with which the Ethiopians concealed themselves – moving mainly at night and only in small dispersed groups during daylight[17] – much was also due to a lack of specific training in the matter.[18] Badoglio expressed himself dissatisfied that the reconnaissance missions had been carried out conscientiously.[19] Further, there were problems with the command structure. General Giuseppe Valle, chief of staff of the air force based in Rome, had intended to take personal command in Eritrea and appointed Brigadier Mario Ajmone Cat as his chief of staff. Until Valle arrived, Ajmone Cat, despite being the senior air force officer in the theatre, was then chief of staff to an absent commander, and so lacked the authority to impose his will on his subordinates. According to Rochat, this gives a significant glimpse into the confusion in the military chain of command,[20] which wasn't settled until January 1936 when Ajmone Cat obtained overall command. There was, though, a caveat to this.

The air force was, doctrinally, heavily influenced by the work of the air-power theorist General Giulio Douhet, whose seminal work *The Command of the Air* (*Il dominio dell'aria*) first appeared in 1921.[21] The book maintained that victory in modern war could be achieved by having command of the air, and that using air power strategically would be decisive: 'Bombing the population ... will cause the citizens to petition their leader to end the war, bringing about peace.'[22] Douhet's influence, and how far it extended, is still a matter of debate, but it can safely be said that Ajmone Cat was an adherent of 'Douhetism'.[23] As he wrote in 1951: 'Our Douhet's mind saw ahead; what he predicted; reality confirmed. If he had been listened to, we could have done then what others did later, and at our expense.'[24]

But Badoglio wasn't a man who listened, or if he did, he wasn't convinced by 'Douhetism' in the context of the Ethiopian campaign. His requirements involved utilising methods not covered in 'Douhet's ruminations'.[25] Therefore what he demanded, and got, was a new doctrine based around effective inter-force cooperation or, in other words, tactical support.[26] This was perceived as a step backwards by air-power purists, who criticised the loss of autonomy that resulted from subordinating the service to the needs of the army. One of these critics was General Giuseppe Valle in Rome. Valle had, as noted above, originally wanted the theatre air force command, but didn't take it up as it would have meant him being subordinated to the army commander.[27]

In fact, Valle had proposed in early 1935 that the air force install itself well away from the army in five large bases constructed on the Red Sea coast. This was not a realistic project: the heat in that area was intolerable to most Europeans and the difference in altitude between any such bases and the operational area was around 2,000m, which would have to be overcome on every sortie.[28] Moreover, whilst the air force would have liked to escape army control, and devote itself to attacking strategic targets, these were practically non-existent in the Ethiopian context.[29]

So it was that Ajmone Cat was prepared to adapt to Badoglio's needs, and went on to organise a streamlined system of communications whereby air support for ground formations could be quickly called upon. This was further complemented by internal air force communication, which enabled reconnaissance flights to call in attacks by bomber formations if they spotted enemy concentrations.[30]

In December 1935, however, and since Badoglio initially refused to send his land forces out from behind their fortifications, blunting the Ethiopian advance became the exclusive preserve of the air force. To that end, and as has been related, Ajmone Cat was ordered to utilise mustard gas, which led to the testing of two C.500.T bombs on the morning of 22 December 1935. These being deemed successful, six more were dropped on the area of the pass at Inda Aba Guna that afternoon. It is perhaps worth noting at this point that authorisation to use mustard gas was not granted by Mussolini until 28 December.[31] This gives some indication of the seriousness with which Badoglio viewed the situation. In fact, the above attack was merely the precursor to a heavy bombardment of the Tekeze river fords that took place the next day, when twenty-eight C.500.T bombs were dropped. This latter attack served to demonstrate, however, that there were problems with the ordnance and its delivery system. Ten bombs failed to release, and of those that did, only nineteen detonated at altitude, the remainder hitting the ground where some at least failed to explode.[32]

Ethiopian eyewitness testimony to this event exists. Collected, along with similar evidence, by Angelo Del Boca and first published in 1979, it comes from Ras Imru Haile Selassie, the commander of the attacking force:

> It was a terrifying sight ... I myself escaped death by chance. It was the morning of 23 December, and I had just crossed the Tekeze, when some aeroplanes appeared in the sky. The fact, however, did not alarm us too much, because we had by now become accustomed to bombing. But that morning they didn't drop bombs, but strange drums (*fusti*) that broke as soon as they touched the ground or the water of the river, and threw a colourless liquid around them. Before I could realize what was happening, a few hundred of my men had been struck by the mysterious liquid and were screaming in pain as their bare feet, their hands, their faces blistered. Others, who had quenched their thirst at the river, writhed on the ground in agony that lasted hours. Among those affected were also farmers, who had brought the herds to the river, and people from nearby villages. Meanwhile, my under-leaders had surrounded me and asked me for advice, but I was stunned, I didn't know what to answer, I didn't know how to fight this rain that burned and killed.[33]

Ras Imru was by then in his early seventies and was recounting an incident which had taken place some thirty years earlier. Such reports are fraught with difficulty:

as the distinguished English newspaperman and writer Antony Howard once remarked: 'It has ... been, consistently, my experience that there is no more flawed source for recalling the events of yesterday than human recollection.'[34] Quite so, and few would argue with him. But inconsistencies in Ras Imru's account, as highlighted by, for example, Ferdinando Pedriali, do not invalidate it even though the latter has argued that they 'give the impression that he was not a direct witness of this attack'.[35]

Those points which impressed themselves most upon Pedriali in this regard include the fact that the effects of exposure to mustard gas are delayed, rather than immediately apparent, as described by Ras Imru, and that he failed to mention those bombs which burst at altitude and aerosolised their contents.[36] Ultimately, though, whether Ras Imru had to some extent misremembered or not is irrelevant: the attack took place and, along with substantial high-explosive bombing and strafing, formed a part of the Italian attempt to interdict the road along which he was moving men and supplies. That this force might succeed in reaching, and attacking, Italian supply bases and routes in Eritrea was something that kept Mussolini awake at night.[37] But if *Il Duce* was worried, then so was Badoglio, who, according to his later account, feared it was all part of a 'vast offensive plan' to circumvent the entrenched camp of Adua-Axum and invade 'our colony of Eritrea'.[38] He knew also that any such incursion, even if only partially successful, 'could have shaken his military prestige to its foundations'.[39]

On 23 December there was also a more conventional attempt at dislocating Ras Imru's advance to the north, when an ad hoc mixed Italian column some 12,000-strong was ordered to advance back along the road from Axum towards Slehleka. This was an attempt to seize the initiative by attracting, and then engaging with, enemy forces who would otherwise be making mischief elsewhere. It took two days for the column to reach the Af Gaga pass, just a few kilometres from Slehleka, where an encounter battle with an enemy force estimated to be 8,000-strong took place.[40] Heavy air support was provided, which prevented the Ethiopians from concentrating and broke up their attacks.

One of the pilots engaged in strafing operations was an Italian-American named Vincent Patriarca, whose exploits later featured in the debut edition of a short-lived US magazine. Readers were told that the Italian airmen had been warned that if captured by the enemy they would be 'skinned alive' and have their 'hearts cut out'.[41] Also involved was the writer and 'super-Fascist' Alessandro Pavolini, a volunteer member of a bomber squadron (*squadriglia aerea 'Disperata'*) commanded by Mussolini's son-in-law, Galeazzo Ciano.[42] This unit also hosted Vito Mussolini, a nephew of *Il Duce*. In his history of the squadron, Pavolini describes how one of the fighter pilots involved, Attilio Allavena, was forced to land after his aircraft was hit by rifle fire. His comrade Luigi Vaschi, in an effort to save him from capture, landed his own biplane fighter nearby but came to grief in doing so. Both pilots were unhurt, and set off on foot towards the Italian position. This, though, was some 20km away, so aircraft circled above them in an attempt to prevent the Ethiopians from following them. As Pavolini recorded, the crew of his trimotor bomber did 'their utmost to protect them in their escape', engaging in an 'air-ground mêlée' (*mischia aeroterrestre*) with their machine guns.[43]

Patriarca, in a fighter, recorded in his recently discovered and published diaries his own attempts to save the downed fliers:

> I see some soldiers falling hit by my shots, they had come very close to the two and I have to be very careful to aim well. I keep circling and hitting others who try to reach the pilots ... others fall back looking for a place to protect themselves. I am about to start yet another attack but am starting to run out of fuel, I check the indicator and I have just 15 minutes of flight, it is not even enough to return to Asmara ... with deep sadness I take a painful decision, I swing my wings to salute the two unfortunates, hoping that our troops arrive in time to save them and I head towards Asmara.[44]

Unfortunately, as he went on to relate: 'Their bodies were found after three weeks, crucified on a tree, with their testicles removed and stuck in their mouths, which were sewn with wire, their hearts torn out and probably eaten. According to local beliefs this rite transmits the strength of the enemy.'[45] Cultural anthropology fallacies and barbarism aside, the fighting on Christmas Day did see the Italians victorious in the tactical sense inasmuch as the Ethiopians ceased to attack them. On the other hand, the Italians ceased to advance, so the outcome might best be described as inconclusive, although Pedriali does credit it with 'inducing Ras Imru to renounce the project of crossing the Eritrean border in force'.[46]

Ras Imru's incursion, although it might have caused insomnia in certain quarters, was, of course, only one of several such attempts at repelling the invaders. At the same time as the fight at Inda Aba Guna was taking place, the Ethiopian Army of the Centre, commanded by Ras Seyoum Mengesha and Ras Kassa Hailu (on the left and right respectively), was also advancing. It had crossed the Giba river south of Abiy Addi, the latter being an important caravan-route nodal point around 60km south of Adwa, and was attempting a pincer movement to encircle the place.[47] Badoglio could not retreat far here, as he had done at Slehleka, as it would have exposed the route from Adigrat south to Makalle. Rather he reinforced the area with an *ascari* division (*2ª Divisione Eritrea*) and a Blackshirt division (*2ª Divisione CC.NN. '28 Ottobre'*), directed the air force to smash the advance, and asked that two further divisions be sent to the theatre from Italy (Mussolini in fact sent three).[48]

On 20 December an Ethiopian formation advancing directly on Abiy Addi from the south was repulsed, but it was less easy to deal with those that infiltrated through the mountainous, bush-covered terrain to occupy positions to east and west of the town. An attempt on 22 December to dislodge those occupying the nearby mountain of Amba Tzellere, using six battalions of *ascari*, failed, despite being supported with three batteries of artillery and aircraft. These supporting arms were largely ineffective because of the terrain. In fact, the fighting mainly devolved to hand-to-hand combat with cold steel. Italian losses – dead, wounded and missing – came to around 200.[49]

Curiously, there arose within the Italian command a difference of opinion as to which side emerged victorious from this clash. Those on the spot at the time determined that 'despite the valour and the heroic sacrifice of the officers and the most loyal Eritrean *ascari*, the enemy managed to maintain the occupation of the amba ...'[50] Therefore, with an Ethiopian force in possession of this commanding position, it was necessary to abandon Abiy Addi and move to prepared positions further north. Badoglio, in his memoirs, disagreed:

> Despite the happy result of the action, the commander considered it necessary to withdraw the victorious troops ... This decision, resulting from a completely personal appreciation of the local situation, did not allow us to draw from this combat the results that the heroic behaviour of the troops would have allowed us to achieve. In particular, by renouncing the occupation of Amba Tzellere, we allowed the enemy, as soon as reinforced ... to firmly establish itself on the amba, which later forced us to abandon the dominated positions at [Abiy Addi] and to withdraw on those of the Uarieu [Worsege] Pass, which were much less favourable than those of [Amba] Tzellere.[51]

Later scholarship has generally concluded that Badoglio was wrong.[52] There is, though, little doubt that he was a worried man at that period. As Arrigo Petacco aptly put it: 'He had arrived in Eritrea to give greater impetus to the advance and instead he had been forced to retreat and abandon to the enemy much of the territory that De Bono had conquered.'[53]

The Italian retreat to the Uarieu Pass, about 10km almost directly north of Abiy Addi, was completed by 27 December and resulted in a lull in the ground fighting, the Ethiopians limiting themselves to harassing operations. Thus, the Italian front had not been breached and their losses, the vast majority of them *ascari*, were relatively light at just over 1,000.[54] If, at least from the Italian perspective, all was relatively quiet in terms of action on the ground, the opposite was the case with respect to the air force. Forty-eight Caproni bombers and seventy-two fighters of various types were kept occupied in bombarding and strafing from low altitude Ethiopian positions, or suspected positions. The ordnance dropped by the heavier aircraft included 112 C.500.T bombs, which were also used to contaminate wooded areas where the enemy were thought to be lurking.[55] Gentilli calculates that on the northern front as a whole, including the areas where the Ethiopian Army of the Left was operating, 261 C.500.T bombs (each containing 212kg of *iprite*) were dropped between 22 December 1935 and 18 January 1936.[56] Although the effects of this aerial campaign cannot be accurately measured, it appears to have gone some way to deterring the Ethiopians from attempting to assault the Italians at the Uarieu Pass. Badoglio may have later complained that, as a defensive position, it was inferior to that at Amba Tzellere, but possession of it brought on a fight that was one of the most crucial battles of the whole war. For on 19 January 1936 Badoglio turned to the attack. As Fuller worded the matter: 'the campaign had now reached a stage where it was no longer possible to advance in Great Wall of China formation'.[57]

Chapter Ten

An 'African Thermopylae'

the enemy was betting everything on his only great card: if he managed to force Passo Uarieu before evening, he would have cut Makalle out. 'Hold on, my Sommo ...' Bombings, strafing, reconnaissance, single-seater, two-seater, all series of trimotors. Reconnaissance equipment removed for fragmentation bombs ... and on the besieged Blackshirts, tonnes and tonnes of cartridges, water and bread; delivered with parachutes, and in their absence padded bags.[1]

* * *

Despite the heavy bombing, both conventional and chemical, of the Ethiopian armies south of the Uarieu Pass, and indeed elsewhere, their build-up remained threatening. It is clear that on this occasion there had been a widespread failure of Italian intelligence. Indeed, the scale of the enemy operations across the whole northern front had taken Badoglio completely by surprise, as he informed Rome on 30 December 1935.[2] He was, at that time, attempting to fully grasp the scope of their intentions, and to discover the direction of their main thrust and where it might be made, and which of the several offensive movements might have been feints. As he summarised it in his account of the war:

> Was it a question of isolated actions and initiatives of the various Rases or was it a vast offensive plan directed by the Negus? To operate, that is, against our right and centre to circumvent the entrenched camp of Adua-Axum, to break our front by aiming in the direction of Hawzen[3] and invade, with the mass of forces, the Eritrean Colony? It was still hard to say: One could have been incredulous about the enemy's ability to implement such a vast strategic plan; but, given the situation as it had emerged, one had to act with great caution until its clarification.[4]

Great caution was, though, not what Mussolini wanted. Rather he desired action whilst, contradictorily, ordering suspension of the use of mustard gas on 5 January unless 'necessitated by supreme need for offence or defence'.[5] Badoglio protested and, no doubt feeling the 'supreme need', ignored the directive: 113 C.500.T bombs were dropped between 6 and 18 January 1936.[6] He did, however, follow instructions not to bomb the Djibouti-Addis Ababa railway in order to avoid international – for which read French – repercussions.[7] There was also the matter of the 20 per cent share that Italy had held in the line since January 1935.[8] Otherwise he remained on the defensive, communicating a situation report to his senior commanders on 7 January, informing them that 'for the eventual offensive from the Makalle sector, an action is envisaged aimed at seizing the Amba Aradam'. This, he explained, would constitute robust flank support and form 'a serious threat to the enemy's flank and rear' and 'allow us to develop a profitable offensive action'. Indicating that he was still unsure of what the enemy was planning, or when they might attack, he added: 'I reserve orders on the basis of the development of the situation.'[9] A missive expressing similar sentiments was despatched to *Il Duce* on 11 January, evoking a response three days later that was far from sympathetic. Badoglio was reminded that he now had at his disposal no fewer than fifteen divisions (including those on the southern front) and he was urged not to wait passively for the enemy to attack but to seize the initiative and dominate them.[10] Badoglio had already decided on that line, issuing orders on 15 January for offensive action. The object of the exercise was to engage with and fix the Army of the Centre, then exploit this by launching a full offensive against Ras Mulugeta Yeggazu's Army of the Right south of Makalle.[11]

Proverbially it is said that the victors get to write the history, and whilst this adage is undoubtedly fallacious generally, it has to be admitted that it applied in the current context. For, when Badoglio did order an advance, on 19–20 January, he dubbed the ensuing combat the First Battle of Tembien (*La Prima battaglia del Tembien*).[12] According to Rochat, this was so as to avoid recognising the Ethiopian offensive of December 1935, which had pushed his forces out of Abiy Addi, as a battle proper.[13]

Badoglio's initial move was a bid to isolate from each other the two Ethiopian armies to his front, the Army of the Centre and Ras Mulugeta Yeggazu's Army of the Right. To that end a strong force advanced some 10km south from Makalle with the limited objective to interdict the valley in which ran the Gabat river. Once this was achieved, then east–west communication between the two Ethiopian armies was effectively blocked and they could not easily or quickly reinforce each other.[14]

At dawn on 20 January the offensive against the Army of the Centre began with a pincer movement by the 2nd Eritrean Division. This was divided into two widely separated columns, with the main mass on the left, the intention being to encircle Melfa to the south-west of the Italian line. In support, the contingents that had been garrisoning Addi Zubbaha and the Abaro Pass also moved forward. In addition to these powerful assaults, backed up with abundant air power and artillery, albeit encountering fierce resistance from the off, a demonstration or feint was to be made on the far right of the Italian front by the garrison defending the Uarieu Pass. Commanded by 57-year-old Major General Umberto Somma, an army officer who had been wounded during the First World War, this contingent mainly comprised Blackshirts of the '28 October' Division (*2ª Divisione CC.NN. '28 Ottobre'*). In accordance with Badoglio's plan, *Console Generale*[15] Filippo Diamanti led a column from the pass early on the morning of 20 January. This was composed of two battalions of Blackshirt infantry, reinforced by a company of machine-gunners, making a total of 48 officers and 1,484 troops.[16]

Key points relating to the First Battle of Tembien. (© *Charles Blackwood*)

With orders not to engage in combat, Diamanti led his column south towards Abiy Addi for around 3km before turning about and, completely unmolested by the enemy, returning to his starting point. All personnel were reported to be back within the defences by 22:00 hours.

The first day of fighting was accounted a success by the Italians. Both arms of the 'pincers' had succeeded in advancing towards their objective, the left-hand column being about 8km from Melfa, whilst repelling counter-attacks and causing 'huge losses'. The Ethiopians had been compelled under heavy bombardment to fall back generally, and their attempts to outflank the left-hand column to the west had been thwarted.

The morning of 21 January saw the fighting renewed, and once again *Console Generale* Diamanti sallied forth with his Blackshirts along the road to Abiy Addi. What happened next was the subject of much contention concerning who was responsible, but basically, the column went around twice the distance it had the

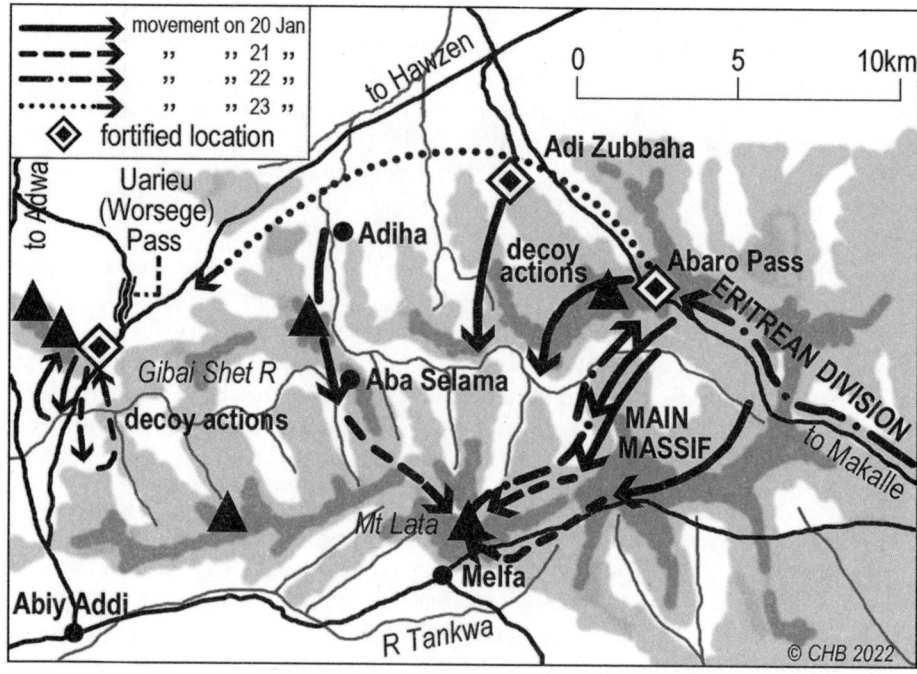

Military movements during the First Battle of Tembien. (© *Charles Blackwood*)

previous day and found itself in contact with a large body of Ethiopians and in deep trouble. Rochat sums up what happened succinctly: 'Diamanti's column, with 1,500 Blackshirts, pushed too far, was encircled by the Abyssinian forces and overwhelmed; in the desperate retreat 23 officers, 87 ascari and 245 Blackshirts fell, as many were wounded, the greatest losses of Italian soldiers of the whole war.'[17]

This was grim, but the implications were even more so. The hot-pursuit of Diamanti's column brought the Ethiopians to the Uarieu Pass, which constituted a relatively weak point in the Italian line. It was defended by about 3,000–4,000 personnel, three-quarters of them Blackshirts; they were equipped with artillery and machine guns, but they were not well off for ammunition. Moreover, it was, as Badoglio was to state, not a particularly good naturally defensive position since it was overlooked by high ground. Rudimentary, dry-stone fortifications had been constructed, including two 'forts', but the biggest problem with the site was its lack of water. According to Longo, the nearest source was 4km distant, and there were only 1,200 litres on hand to be shared by the entire garrison. This latter problem in particular had been missed during an inspection of the site by the commander of III Army Corps on 1 January.[18] Seemingly almost by accident then, a large Ethiopian force had found, and was moving on, a place that was poorly sited for defence and was manned by second-rate troops, who only had limited amounts of water and ammunition. This all might have been relatively unimportant had not the pass also been a critical point in the Italian line: something else that seems not to have been appreciated before the event. Indeed, the taking of it would have allowed Ras Kassa's troops to outflank his enemy completely and – Badoglio's worst nightmare – move on towards Hawzen, thus severing Italian communications with Makalle.

Between 21 and 24 January the defenders bravely withstood relentless Ethiopian assaults on their positions, although they did not do so unaided. Realising the danger, and forced to contemplate the ruin of his campaign and, along with it, his military career if he were forced into a general retreat, Badoglio reacted fast. He despatched a message to the commander on the spot: 'Hold on, my Somma; today the Blackshirts will cover themselves with glory'[19] – and more importantly ordered all available resources to be deployed in support. The 2nd Eritrean Division was redirected and sent to the rescue, although given the terrain and the distance, it could not conceivably intervene rapidly. But the air force could, and Alessandro Pavolini recorded their efforts:

> the enemy was betting everything on his only great card: if he managed to force Passo Uarieu before evening, he would have cut Makalle out. 'Hold on, my Sommo ...' Bombings, strafing, reconnaissance, single-seater, two-seater, all series of trimotors. Reconnaissance equipment removed for fragmentation bombs ... and on the besieged Blackshirts, tonnes and tonnes of cartridges, water and bread; delivered with parachutes, and in their absence padded bags.[20]

There are some doubts as to how effective in reality the air-dropping of provisions was, water supplies in particular,[21] but there is little disagreement concerning the efficacy of the air-ground attacks. Pavolini doesn't, of course, mention the use of mustard gas, but Gentilli calculates that between 19 and 24 January nearly 19 tonnes were discharged over the northern front via C.500.T bombs.[22] Some of these weapons at least were used directly on the battlefield, rather than at a safe distance from the Italian positions,[23] and the last ten days of January saw their usage increase until they amounted to 22 per cent of all aircraft-launched ordnance.[24] The climactic day for the air force was 23 January, when approximately 20 tonnes of conventional bombs, 10 tonnes of mustard gas and 4.5 tonnes of supplies were delivered.[25]

This massive aerial intervention, plus the fact that the outnumbered defenders possessed machine guns – 'machine-gun fire is concentrated infantry fire'[26] – crushed the assaults with few losses to those manning the extemporised fortifications. The pressure eased on 23 January when the impetus of the attackers waned, which was unsurprising given what they were subjected to. Indeed, their experience evokes Belloc's famous lines brutally summarising the imbalance in military power between European and African forces that existed in 1898: 'Whatever happens we have got/The Maxim Gun, and they have not.'[27] In any event, the next day the 2nd Eritrean Division finally arrived, meaning the affair was effectively over.[28]

This battle, or perhaps siege may be a better term, came to represent for Italy what the 1836 Battle of the Alamo did for Texans or the 1879 Battle of Rorke's Drift for the British. Fascist propaganda made sure of that. It was, as Rochat points out, 'the most dramatic (and publicised) moment of the campaign'.[29] One of the participants on the Italian side was the writer and poet Filippo Tommaso Marinetti, who had a twofold role: 'actual combat on the front line and endless propaganda speeches'.[30] He also had a succession of poems glorifying the conflict printed in the *Gazzetta del Popolo*, which were then collected and published as *The African Poem of the '28 October' Division*.[31] An unnamed journalist, writing in praise of Marinetti's eloquence, dubbed the combat they celebrated as an 'African Thermopylae',[32] with the Blackshirts playing the role of Spartans.[33] Unlike the latter, however, or indeed the defenders of the Alamo, their modern equivalents mostly survived: the losses suffered by the garrison over the period 22–24 January were twenty-seven dead and seventy-five wounded.[34]

One of those who didn't survive, being killed on 21 January, went on to become widely celebrated as a national hero and Fascist martyr. To quote Del Boca: 'the one who received the greatest tributes and honours, and who entered by right into the pantheon of the fallen of the Fascist revolution, was the Torinese cleric Father Reginaldo Giuliani'.[35] The priest-soldier *Padre* Giuliani, who exemplified, albeit in exaggerated form, the coincidence between some developments in the Church and those 'secular experiences that were to lead from patriotism to Fascism',[36] was a Dominican friar. He had served in the First World War and then, aged 48, enlisted in the Blackshirts to fight in Ethiopia.[37] Indeed, whilst all the fallen Blackshirts became, in the words of a 1936 song penned by the futurist poet Umberto Bottone (*aka* Auro D'Alba), 'the pillars of the Roman empire', Giuliani received special mention.[38]

In addition to providing a great propaganda coup, with the Blackshirts indeed being 'covered in glory', the denial of the Uarieu Pass to the Ethiopians, who had withdrawn by the morning of 24 January, marked the effective end of the First Battle of Tembien. But who had won? Longo opines that the most realistic summary of the outcome was that penned by Major Giuseppe Bottai, then serving in the army but a well known writer who went on to serve as a minister in Mussolini's government.[39] He wrote on 2 February 1936:

> We are stuck. The action, which had its driving force in the Tembien, is over. Or rather: a failure. The heroic behaviour of the '28 October', of the 'Gruppo Diamanti', our decisive advance ... the greater losses suffered by the enemy (over 5000 dead), they are not enough to convert a failed action into a victory. The enemy is not conquered; we didn't win. We exhaust ourselves in the status quo. We languish in the provisional ... an attack on the left had been decided ... typical positional warfare project. We should have left these positions and participated in the operation. The plan has now been abandoned.[40]

Similar judgements were being levied from above as well. The under-secretary for war and chief of staff of the army, General Federico Baistrocchi, sent a memorandum penned by his deputy, Alberto Pariani, to Mussolini on 28 January. This was scathing about the leadership exercised on the northern front, implicitly by Badoglio:

> Any conception cannot have adequate development if those who have to implement it are not fully convinced of it.
>
> Now, while it seems that everything is fine in Somalia from the point of view of the leaders, the same cannot be said for Eritrea.
>
> One gets the impression that, on this front, a static mentality has taken root for which the solution of the problem is based more on time than on action.
>
> The difficulties of the terrain, the mobility and aggression of the enemy, have made them lose the initiative; operations must be resumed at any cost.
>
> All leaders must have the inner conviction that they are entrusted with solving the problem exclusively based on the need to defeat the enemy.
>
> One desire for all: of battle thoroughly pursued – relentlessly – with the clear vision that only in this way will we be able to defeat this enemy who is valiant but not powerful, who has daring but not tenacity of purpose, quick to be enthusiastic but also to become demoralised, which is strong on the Eritrean front.
>
> In any case: decide early because there is no time to waste.[41]

Mussolini did decide, and Badoglio was kept in position, although the fact that he remained in danger of being replaced by Graziani was common knowledge.[42] There can be no doubt that the Ethiopian offensive had badly shaken him, particularly since it had come perilously close to success. In an unusually candid admission, he wrote in his account of the war that he had indeed foreseen having to retreat from Makalle. He had gone so far as to order plans drawn up to evacuate about 70,000 men and 14,000 pack animals, plus 300 artillery pieces and a huge volume of stores 'along a single road, which was still under construction'.[43] It would have been a disaster, and that it had been avoided was, in itself, a victory of sorts. One advantage that had been gained, though, was knowledge on the Italian side of how their enemy fought, and consequently how they might be successfully combated. This was a matter that the C-in-C also addressed in his memoirs. The Ethiopian army, he pointed out:

> like the [Ethiopian] people, possessed an innate warrior spirit which, at the right moment, could always be a powerful spring ... I thought, the Abyssinians had made some progress and therefore some surprises were to be expected in the conduct of the war and on the battlefield. I did not have a clear and precise idea of what the Abyssinian army really was, and only by observing what had happened up until then could I draw an exact assessment of the situation.[44]

Whilst Badoglio pondered his options, the battering of the Ethiopian forces continued, via large-scale gas and high-explosive attacks delivered by the recently reorganised air force. This had, of course, proved its worth during the recent operations, and ground-air liaison had been good. Indeed, and in a reversal of the tactic evolved on the Somali front, whereby army units were accompanied by air force liaison personnel, now army observer officers with specific knowledge of the tactical situation, and able to distinguish between friendly *ascari* and hostile Ethiopians, flew in the bombers.[45]

Nevertheless, and despite their army having suffered heavy casualties,[46] Ras Kassa and Ras Seyoum were convinced they had won a victory:

> To Kassa's headquarters they brought all the machine guns and rifles that they had lifted from the battlefield. At the cave mouth everything was counted and counted again, so wonderful was this victory. Over a hundred machine guns; two thousand, eight hundred and fifty-four rifles. And on the positions which they had taken there were fifteen mountain guns and about ten mortars. Kassa, the Old Testament scholar, felt truly that he had smitten them hip and thigh.[47]

Fuller quotes a communique issued by the Negus which claimed that the Italians had been driven back and 'pursued to destruction'. The booty claimed amounted to 29 guns, 175 machine guns and 2,654 rifles, as well as convoys of ammunition, mules and many prisoners.[48] Steer added that, confident though the Ethiopians were, they 'did not bother to inspect their cartridge-belts'.[49] This was a highly pertinent point because ammunition and supplies in general, or rather the lack thereof, constituted a serious problem. Nor was it one easily solved, for France controlled the port of Djibouti and restricted Ethiopian imports; in return the Djibouti–Addis Ababa railway was spared Italian attack.[50] An example of *perfidious français*? Arguably so, dependent on perspective, of course, but even if the French authorities had actively encouraged the ingress of supplies, the 785km, single track, metre-gauge line to Addis Ababa was an easy target, albeit a sensitive one. Either way then, Haile Selassie would struggle to supply his armies in the field. Even so, those confronting the Italian invasion force in the north still held their positions at the end of January 1936, and were not likely to easily yield them.

Badoglio was then under severe pressure to come up with a solution. There was, of course, the political drive from Rome for offensive action, which was not altogether disconnected from the phenomenal financial strain Italy was suffering; a second year of war would have been disastrous for the national economy.[51] Operational requirements also dictated rapid action before the start of the main Ethiopian rainy season (*Kiremt*), which occurs roughly from June to September. During this period campaigning would become difficult if not impossible, likely extending the war into a second year.

However, with the outcome of the First Battle of Tembien having largely stabilised the front, in early February Badoglio was finally in a position to move onto the offensive. His initial objective was Amba Aradam – 'a mountain that formed a terrible natural fortress on the 'imperial' road to the south[52] – around and upon which was based the strongest enemy army under Ras Mulugeta. So confident was the Italian commander that he would prevail that on 9 February the journalists previously confined to Asmara were called to his command post at Enda-Eyasus near Makalle.[53] One of those formerly resident at Asmara was sure that Badoglio was correct in his assumption. He was to write that:

> Whilst Marshal Badoglio was preparing for a set-piece battle, Ras Mulugeta, the Negus' leading general ... instead of breaking away and extending the guerrilla war, perpetrated the egregious blunder of massing against Makale and so offering his opponent a target to strike at. This was to play directly into the Marshal's hands; for had he not done so the vast preparations made would have been completely wasted.[54]

Chapter Eleven

Amba Aradam

The famous battle for the conquest of Amba Aradam ... was never fought ... The 30,000 defenders had in fact escaped the encirclement at night. More surprisingly, there weren't even any fortifications on the hill because the Ethiopians hadn't bothered to dig any. But, without fortifications, there are no legends to tell. Thus, in view of an imminent visit of high hierarchs, princes and dukes, the Alpine troops were forced to build forts and trenches with their hands to show to guests (and to be immortalized in photographs).[1]

* * *

Badoglio's preparations were vast in scope. For the Battle of Amba Aradam, also known as the Battle of Enderta, he would employ the I[2] and III[3] Army Corps, comprising three infantry and two Blackshirt divisions plus support contingents. The 1st Eritrean Division formed the reserve and the offensive would be supported with 280 artillery pieces.[4] As Steer remarked on the level of organisation:

> In English [sic] military theory, which is reputed to be over-careful, each division is believed to need a road of its own for supply. Badoglio, for the battle of Amba Aradam, used one road between Adigrat and Makalle to feed two Army Corps. Evidently he had time to prepare and to store food. His road was not subjected to bombardment. He could use it in day-time, for there was no need to be afraid of the air.[5]

This mass of artillery was required for both the bombardment of enemy positions and direct support at the tactical level. The last was considered crucial in stopping, or at least mitigating, the 'offensive impulse of the Ethiopian masses' before they reached Italian positions.[6] Included in the gunners' ordnance were shells loaded with arsine,[7] but it was the air force that deployed by far the greater volume of chemical munitions. Gentilli calculates that between 30 January and 14 February 1936 aircraft dropped 204 C.500.T bombs, containing nearly 44 tonnes of mustard gas, on the northern front.[8]

One of those on the receiving end of this fearsome bombardment – for every tonne of gas there were 3 tonnes of high explosive and fragmentation bombs[9] – was Alejandro del Valle (Alejandro Ramón Narciso del Valle y Suero). A foreign mercenary in the service of Ras Mulugeta, described by Steer as a 'Cuban machine-gunner',[10] his account of the matter was only published some sixty years after the event:

> From arriving at Amba Aradam we were bombed every day, but without great damage because we had excellent shelters; we remained virtually

immune until the release of gas. When the planes took off from their airport we could see them clearly, so there was no need for an air raid alarm. Taking off, the planes circled the airport and then headed for our mountain. Since the Amba Aradam was high, when they got close to the mountain the planes were so close to the ground that many times the faces of the pilots could be seen. The gas was sent down in large bombs, similar to 200-litre drums. When these drums were dropped from planes, they made a dull blast as they hit the ground, then the gas dispersed in the air for about 500 metres and the entire contents spread at the impact site.

I had no experience or knowledge of asphyxiating gas and it was only later that I discovered what it was: the gas had a pungent smell of garlic and about two hours after inhaling it there was a terrible itch in the upper respiratory tract, so intense that we felt the desire to scratch our lungs, then a violent cough was unleashed that lasted for days, and this occurred every time we inhaled it. Those that were close to the impact point of the barrels were much worse off; many died a few hours after inhaling the gas, others a few days later, depending on the amount of gas they came into contact with. On the feet, hands, face and other exposed parts of the body, the burns were terrible, after a couple of days people were losing pieces of meat. You couldn't see the gas, you could only smell it, which was much more intense in low places, such as gorges and ravines. At night the smell disappeared, but reappeared the next day as soon as the sun rose. Of course, we had no gas masks or any defence against this type of bomb, and I believe that the only thing that saved us from complete destruction was the altitude we were at.[11]

This description of '200-litre drums' hitting the ground tallies closely with that of Ras Imru at the Tacazze river, indicating that at least some of the bombs were still failing to explode at altitude and thus properly disperse their contents. However, and whether or not its fuse or burster charge malfunctioned, the C.500.T wasn't dropped indiscriminately. Pedriali concludes that, during the course of the war overall, 80 per cent were used for creating what were termed 'C Barrages' (*Sbarramenti C*): barriers to interrupt enemy communications and movements, particularly at bottlenecks such as fords and passes. Some 10 per cent were dropped directly on encampments and troop concentrations, whilst only 6 per cent were used tactically, although that percentage was greater during the assault on Amba Aradam.[12] They could not, however, be used on positions or ground which it was intended to occupy or cross.[13] That was so because mustard gas, which has been dubbed 'the king of battle gases', is extremely persistent, persistency being 'an expression for the length of time during which a chemical agent remains and exerts its effect on the place where it has been released'.[14] Although mustard gas can exert its effects for decades,[15] this is very much dependant on climate and most accounts relate how, in Ethiopia, it only remained effective for a matter of days.[16] It would certainly have retained its potency for the duration of the battle, which began on the morning of 10 February with a two-pronged thrust intended to encircle the mountain, III Corps to the west and I Corps to the east.[17]

This flat-topped 'rocky bastion', as Longo calls it, measured around 8km east–west and 3km north–south, and reached a maximum height of 2,756m.[18] Situated some 16km south of Makalle, its northern and eastern sides are steep and difficult to ascend, whilst those to the south and west slope more gently and are easily passable. Ras Mulugeta had ordered his men to dig in on and around the mountain, making it the centre of his defensive dispositions; Steer writes of him sending a message to Ras Kassa stating that 'I am turning my mountain into a castle.'[19] It was certainly well defended with, it is estimated, around a quarter of the Army of the Right deployed there. Judgements on how large that army actually was at that time vary widely. Rochat reckons that there were nowhere near 80,000 men – 'as hagiography dictates' – but more like half of that, with 'a fair number of machine guns, a few small calibre artillery pieces, and big supply problems'.[20] Given the areas of dense vegetation, plus the numerous ravines and caves, found in, on and around Amba Aradam, the Ethiopians had little difficulty in concealing themselves from aerial reconnaissance.

The first day of the advance met with no opposition, and difficulties on the second day, 11 February, were largely caused by torrential rain. Then, III Army Corps remained static, both to secure its position and to deceive the opposition with respect to the direction of the main attack. This deception was enhanced by the apparent course of the 'Sabauda' Division, on the left of I Army Corps, which appeared to have Anseba, some 20km to the east of Amba Aradam, as its goal. Similarly, the Blackshirt '3 January' Division, which was paralleling that advance some 12km closer to Amba Aradam, looked to be marching directly southwards towards Afgol. In any event, for the second day of the operation, both divisions restricted themselves to moving forward to occupy high ground south of the Gabat river. To their rear, the 'Pusteria' Alpine Division advanced to fill the position vacated by the Blackshirts, and this manoeuvre was followed in turn by the 1st Eritrean Division, which tracked the *alpini*.

Still Ras Mulugeta held back from deploying forces to offer resistance, continuing to concentrate on reinforcing the positions on Amba Aradam. Badoglio's operational plan involved getting both corps into a position from where they could quickly complete the encirclement of the mountain, so at first light on 12 February the advance was resumed across the board. The 'Sabauda' Division on the left wing of I Army Corps again met no resistance and, hindered only by the persistent bad weather, advanced further to the south towards Anseba. The Blackshirts to its west were not so lucky, though. At first light, and just as it was about to resume the advance in two columns, the '3 January' Division was attacked simultaneously in front and on the right flank by an enemy force estimated to number several thousand. The attackers were supported by small-calibre artillery and machine guns, and they are credited with extreme rapidity of movement. They were, however, contained and repulsed by the concentrated fire of the corps artillery, which swiftly came into action. Consequently, at

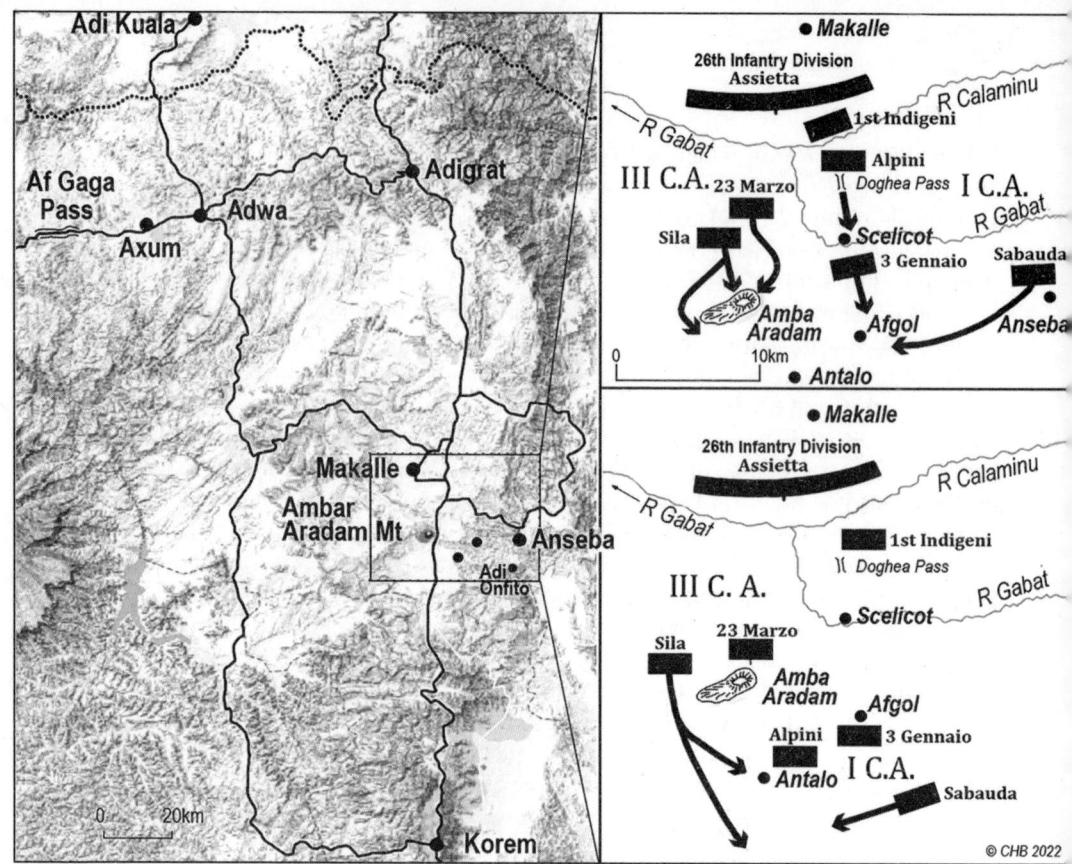

Compound map showing the Battle of Amba Aradam. (© *Charles Blackwood*)

09:00 hours the Blackshirts were ordered to resume the advance. This command was, however, as Longo discreetly puts it, 'not promptly implemented'. The division was, he continued, 'not susceptible to new momentum'.[21] The American military observer at Badoglio's HQ, Major Fiske, was rather less subtle, if not entirely accurate as regards chronology: 'The Black Shirt Militia organization were not very effective. The "3 January" Division failed to get forward the first day and had to be relieved. Thereafter it was employed at road construction until February 15th when it took over the position of the "Sabauda" Division after the latter advanced to resume the attack.'[22]

Indeed, at 11:00 hours the corps commander ordered the Alpine Division to relocate and replace the Blackshirts, whereupon forward movement was restored against strong enemy resistance. Nevertheless, and even with reduced air force support given the continuing bad weather, by the evening of 12 February the day's objectives had been attained. III Army Corps had also advanced, with the 'Sila' Division in the lead and the Blackshirts of the '23 March' Division backing them, and despite also encountering some stiff resistance had prevailed in attaining its goals for the day.

Badoglio now ordered an operational pause so that gains made thus far could be consolidated. Communications required improvement, as the '3rd January'

Blackshirts discovered when they were put to the hard labour of road-building, and the heavy artillery needed to be brought forward to support further advances. Badoglio's general order issued on 13 February restated his aim: 'It is my intention to proceed with the envelopment from east to west of Amba Aradam, to make it fall, and then proceed according to the circumstances.' The heavy artillery was ordered forward to support I Army Corps in particular.[23] The intention was to resume the offensive two days later, on 15 February, when the encirclement would be completed. The enemy, however, had other ideas, and launched a series of attacks on both Army Corps on the morning of 13 February. The Italian tactics, designed to counter the 'offensive impulse of the Ethiopian masses', proved successful, and the attackers could not prevail against the divisional artillery and machine guns deployed defensively.

The crucial day of the battle would, though, be 15 February, when the encircling manoeuvre began at 07:00 hours with a simultaneous advance by the 'Sabauda' and 'Pusteria' Divisions on the left, and the 'Sila' on the right. Daylight, however, brought thick fog, which hindered the use of aircraft and artillery, but had the advantage so far as the attackers were concerned of concealing their movements. Thus there was no Ethiopian reaction until, at about 10:00 hours, visibility improved and counter-attacks were mounted on both advances. These were, once again, defeated by concentrated artillery and machine-gun fire and the use of tactical air support. A total of 189 aircraft in twenty-four squadrons were available and deployed, delivering nearly 14 tonnes of high explosive and fragmentation bombs onto enemy positions and formations.

Yet this did not discourage or prevent further repeated attempts to counter-attack. In fact Badoglio reinforced the 'Sila' with a battalion of Eritrean troops from the reserve after it was subjected to several strong attacks between 11:00 and 14:00 hours, and by 17:00 hours the division had reached the objectives assigned to it to the south of Amba Aradam. The pincers, however, had not closed. The 'Pusteria' Alpine Division, forming the right wing of I Army Corps' advance, had moved westward to close in on the south-eastern slopes of the mountain, leaving it to the 'Sabauda' Division to complete the encirclement. However, and according to Longo due to the 'irresolute command' of that corps, the fierce resistance and the difficulties of the terrain, there remained a gap of some 3km between the 'Sila' and 'Sabauda' Divisions that evening.[24]

It mattered not. Ras Mulugeta had already decided to abandon the 'castle', and his army had begun retreating southwards, 'hastily and messily', in the early afternoon. This retreat swiftly turned into a rout when the air force pounced. During their advance, the Ethiopians had avoided air attack by moving at night and concealing themselves during the day. Now their discipline crumpled and the men simply massed along the road south, making an unmissable target to all available aircraft, which bombed and strafed at will: 'for three consecutive days they were chased by the air force and mustard gas'.[25] As one who participated in this 'hunt' put it: 'the planes waited for them, like hunters ... To spot the prey, it was no longer necessary to search ... The enemy fled in disorder along the route ... but along a single road which narrowed at the fords, and ran along the bottom of valleys, which inevitably thickened them.'[26]

On the first day of this aerial pursuit, 16 February, 72 tonnes of bombs were dropped, the highest amount in one day of the entire campaign.[27] Over the period 16–18 February, eighty-four C.500.T bombs, delivering around 18 tonnes of mustard gas, are recorded as being deployed.[28] Dr John H. Spencer, the American legal adviser to Haile Selassie, reckoned that 'the demoralization which set in with the systematic campaign of spraying poison gas over the countryside spread like the Black Death through the troops on the northern front'.[29]

To add to the already severe woes of the fleeing horde, the local tribespeople along their route also turned on them. This was not necessarily because they were in sympathy with the Italians, but more likely because the predatory, locust-like nature of Ethiopian troops was notorious. As Steer remarked: 'Whenever they saw a field of beans, corn or maize, they were down on it like a troop of monkeys: it was stripped and eaten raw.'[30] Now those who had seen the devastation of their crops, upon which they were dependant, were in a position to take revenge.

How many perished during this joint effort at massacre is impossible to compute, but amongst them was Ras Mulugeta. For what it's worth, and taking the battle and the pursuit together, the Italian estimate of total Ethiopian casualties was 20,000.[31] In any event, Steer recorded how 'Starving and waterless and rotting with wounds, a few thousand men struggled into Korem on Lake Ashangi at the end of February.'[32] Italian losses were insignificant by comparison: 134 officers and men killed and 523 wounded, whilst the 'indigenous' troops, as they were termed, suffered sixty-two killed and eighty-three wounded. These figures included those killed in a 'friendly fire' incident on 12 February when aircraft inadvertently bombed troops of the 'Sila' Division, killing twenty-seven and wounding seventy-six.[33]

That Badoglio had won a famous and important victory was, and is, undeniable, and Fascist propaganda went into overdrive. As one modern author has accurately noted, 'everything about the Fascists was bombastic and mock-heroic',[34] and the portrayal of the Battle of Amba Aradam proved no exception. Indeed, the facts were brutally twisted to suit the Fascist narrative. In this version of events, it was the Blackshirt '23 March' Division that had captured Amba Aradam whilst being led in person by a member of the Italian royal family, General Filiberto of Savoy-Genoa, the Duke of Pistoia. Elements of the division had climbed up the steep north face of the mountain, reaching the summit at 17:30 hours, before courageously defeating the enemy entrenched there and raising the now bullet-shredded tricolour of Italy to signify their victory. That at least was the version which appeared in contemporary official accounts, although Fiske debunked it in his report: 'The "23 March" Division took little if any part in the fighting but on February 15th, when the artillery had blasted the top of AMBA ARADAM and the PUSTERIA and SILA Divisions had attacked both flanks and rear it was given the honor of "capturing" the mountain without resistance.'[35]

It is probably true to say that few Italians got to see Fiske's reports, and once again it fell to Del Boca to publish the real story long after the event. He got this from journalist and writer Italo Pietra, who had been a junior officer in the Alpine Division in 1936.[36] On the 50th anniversary of the invasion of Ethiopia, the left-wing newspaper *l'Unita* dubbed the official version 'farcical' and recounted Pietra's testimony:

> The famous battle for the conquest of Amba Aradam ... was never fought. The future journalist, then a young officer of the Alpine troops, went to the assault of a mountain in which there was not even an Abyssinian. The 30,000 defenders had in fact escaped the encirclement at night. More surprisingly, there weren't even any fortifications on the hill because the Ethiopians hadn't bothered to dig any. But, without fortifications, there are no legends to tell. Thus, in view of an imminent visit of high hierarchs, princes and dukes, the Alpine troops were forced to build forts and trenches with their hands to show to guests (and to be immortalized in photographs).[37]

In his telegram informing Mussolini that the battle had been won, Badoglio acknowledged that the Blackshirts had indeed been the ones to raise the flag: 'The national flag flutters on Amba Aradam hoisted by a unit of the first division of Blackshirts "23 March" commanded by HRH Duke of Pistoia.'[38] However, that he failed to endorse, or even include, the propaganda version in his account of the war is judged by Longo to be evidence of his desire not to feed the long-standing resentment the army felt for the Blackshirts.[39] Such resentment is understandable, given that it was actually troops of the Alpine Division who had first reached the top of the Amba.

Whichever units took the credit for the success, it was clear that the overwhelming firepower the Italians could bring to bear had been the decisive factor. This would, though, have been of little utility had not the Ethiopians provided a target. Fuller's retrospective analysis around how the Ethiopians would have been better served by 'extending the guerrilla war' rather than 'massing' to fight conventionally was then, on the face of it, eminently sound, but it was obviously not an evaluation arrived at by Ras Mulugeta before the event.

On the other hand, his fellow commander, Ras Imru, had adopted just such a methodology following the fighting at the Af Gaga pass on Christmas Day 1935. Realising, and certainly fearing, that the objective of the Ethiopian Army of the Left was to cross into Eritrea in force, Badoglio had deployed IV Army Corps – comprising two divisions, the 5th Infantry 'Cosseria' (*5ª Divisione fanteria 'Cosseria'*) and the Blackshirt '1 February' (*5ª Divisione CC.NN. '1 Febbraio'*) – to garrison the passes along the border. As already noted, the combat at Af Gaga had impressed upon Ras Imru the futility of attempting to fight conventionally against an opponent able to deploy much superior firepower and who possessed total command of the air.[40] Instead, as he explained it to Angelo Del Boca in April 1965, he broke up his force into highly mobile detachments of 400–500 men, which waged irregular warfare on the two Italian divisions and raided the main supply routes between Eritrea and northern Ethiopia. The most widely publicised of these small-scale encounters, certainly on the Italian side, was that which occurred in the early hours of 13 February 1936, whilst Badoglio was proceeding to envelop Amba Aradam, and became known as the 'Gondrand Worksite Massacre' (*Eccidio del cantiere Gondrand*).[41]

This took place at the 'No. 1 Road-builders' Labour Camp of Gondrand and Co.', which was situated some 10km south of the Mareb river near a village named Mai Lahla (Rama). Populated by civilians employed by the *Società anonima nazionale Gondrand*, a private company under contract to the Italians, the camp consisted of two large marquee-tent dormitories for the workers plus several wooden huts to accommodate the managerial staff, offices, stores and the like. The whole was surrounded by a flimsy barbed-wire barrier mounted on 'fragile' poles but was otherwise undefended, apart from fifteen rifles distributed amongst some of the Italians. Several hundred metres away outside the fence was a brick-built, semi-subterranean magazine containing 3 tonnes of gelignite for road-building operations. The camp was in the charge of two engineers, Cesare Rocca and Roberto di Colloredo Mels, the former accompanied by his wife Lidia (or Lydia) Rocca-Maffioli, and there were reckoned to be around eighty-five persons asleep there on the night of 12/13 February. Being far away from the fighting front they slept easy.

At around 05:00 hours, and on the direct orders of Ras Imru, according to his later statement, the camp was attacked by an Ethiopian detachment estimated to be around 100-strong. The intruders, having got inside the wire unnoticed, then entered the tents where, it was later adjudged, they despatched the majority of inhabitants with spears and swords. Those in the huts were awakened and, as some of them at least were armed with revolvers, they tried to put up a fight. The noise, particularly when the attackers somehow detonated the gelignite store, killing about forty of their own number in the process, alerted units nearby who moved to investigate. The earliest arrivals, at about 07:00 hours, discovered a gruesome scene. Alberto Pollera,[42] a colonial officer of long experience, who was based in Eritrea and headed the Political Bureau of II Army Corps, reported seventy-four Italian dead initially, many with horrendous wounds and mutilations. Amongst the dead were both Cesare Rocca and Roberto di Colloredo Mels, who had apparently committed suicide by revolver shot to the brain rather than be captured, and Lidia Rocca-Maffioli. She, it was adjudged, had been despatched by her husband to prevent her capture, as had her Ethiopian maid. Two Italian workmen, Alfredo Lusetti and Ernesto Zannoni, were taken as prisoners; both survived to be freed at the end of the war.[43]

The strict censorship instituted by Badoglio, which would ordinarily have kept the episode secret, was deemed inapplicable in this case. Del Boca calculates that this was because too many Italian civilians had died for it to be suppressed and, because they were civilians rather than soldiers, it provided a shocking example of the behaviour of the 'barbaric and bloody' regime Italy was fighting to remove. A formal complaint was raised with the League of Nations in this regard, containing several gruesome photographs detailing the mutilations suffered by the victims. It included a list of the names of sixty-eight Italians who perished, but made no mention of Eritreans or Ethiopians.[44] Italian internal propaganda naturally went into overdrive, and the following year the Futurist poet Ignazio Scurto published 'The Song of Lydia' (*Il cantico di Lydia*).[45] This was written in memory of Lidia Rocca-Maffioli, and it earned him recognition at the 'Poets of Mussolini's Time Award' (*Premio Poeti del tempo di Mussolini*) ceremony.[46]

Italian reprisals were equally barbaric and just as bloody as the massacre itself, and indeed more so. One of the most notorious, but merely one of many, was documented by the writer Ennio Flaiano, who was in Ethiopia as a lieutenant of the engineers. During his tour he compiled a notebook – 'in fact a sort of diary'[47] – in which he recorded:

> On 7 March [1936] a detachment of Spahis [Libyan troops also known as zaptié] of the II Army Corps arrived in Adi Onfito to search some tucul [circular houses]. They found objects belonging to the engineer Rocca (killed with his wife in the Gondrand massacre). The inhabitants who had already obtained permission for free movement from other troops are killed en masse. The women and men barricaded in the church are slaughtered. A woman, the most attractive, is possessed in a circle and an ember is introduced into her sex: an ember from the fire used to burn the Coptic headman. Then the church is cleared of the corpses. It is decided to burn them.[48] Some militiamen ... are about to undertake the disgusting enterprise when a poor sick woman is found in a box, her eyes wide with terror. She is placed with the others near the stake. A centurion sees her and shouts: 'But she is alive!' The soldier answers: 'No, captain, she is almost dead.' In any case, the woman, saved from the fire in the evening went there the next day. She died that night.[49]

As Flaiano wrote in the same book, the *zaptié* remembered how the Italians had utilised *ascari* in Libya, and, unable to distinguish between Eritreans and Ethiopians, indulged in revenge. This playing-off of colonised peoples against each other was, he noted, 'the elementary secret of good Imperialism'.[50]

Chapter Twelve

The Second Battle of Tembien and the Battle of Shire

Alpine units and Blackshirts of the Eritrean Army Corps with surprise action climbed the massive Uorc Amba this night, which constituted a solid position on the right flank of the advance on Abbi Addi. The opposing garrison was caught in the dark, and overwhelmed after poor resistance.[1]

* * *

Badoglio's victory at Amba Aradam had changed the operational situation to one of potentially great advantage to the Italians. The destruction of Ras Mulugeta's army had obviously removed a powerful Ethiopian force from the equation and the possession of Amba Aradam meant an attack on the Army of the Centre, under Ras Kassa (now promoted above Ras Seyoum), could be mounted from a flanking position. Indeed, there was the possibility of completely encircling it to the south.

There was another major Ethiopian force under the direct command of the Negus in the north, but this was based around Dessie, around 270km south of Makalle. However, on 20 February Italian intelligence discovered that Haile Selassie had departed the town and, along with the Imperial Guard, was moving northwards. Although this force, which would likely be augmented as it moved north, to an estimated total of about 30,000 men, presented no immediate threat, it was thought that it might advance to the strategically important area of Amba Alagi. Situated some 40km south of Amba Aradam as the crow flies, and part of a massif over 3,000m in elevation, possession of it would interdict the road south through the Alagi Passes, of which there were three. Knowledge of what the Negus might be attempting came from interception of the messages he had exchanged with Ras Kassa and, indirectly, Ras Imru; the latter was out of direct radio contact, with messages taking anything from five to eleven days to get through in either direction.[2] On 19 February, after learning something of the outcome of the Battle of Amba Aradam, but not the full extent of the rout, Haile Selassie ordered them both to withdraw their forces to Amba Alagi. Ras Kassa disagreed with this order and did not obey. Further, the several days of argument and discussion between the Ras and the Negus which ensued, all by radio and all intercepted by Italian intelligence, convinced Badoglio to move before Ras Kassa did.[3] Ras Imru, although his guerrilla activities were of concern, was more or less contained, whilst preparations for neutralising him continued.

Having got the measure of his opponents, as he thought, on 21 February Badoglio issued a set of tactical instructions to be used in the forthcoming operations, with special reference to II and IV Army Corps, which had not been engaged in the recent battles.[4] He intended an offensive with three main objectives. Firstly, he wanted to take possession of Amba Alagi, which would preclude any advance past that point by the Negus' army, and also prevent the escape of Ethiopian forces to its north. His second purpose was to encircle and smash Ras Kassa's army and then, finally, do much the same to Ras Imru's army. To achieve these aims he would use massive force and overwhelming firepower. Indeed, virtually his entire command, now consisting of five Army Corps, would be deployed. He was to state in his memoirs that this was the largest military manoeuvre ever attempted in colonial warfare, and this was undoubtedly the case. All five infantry corps would be advancing simultaneously in multiple directions, whilst backed by massive artillery and aerial support and reinforced with tanks.[5]

Badoglio also shuffled his forces, moving the 'Sila' Division from III to I Army Corps and replacing it with the 1st Eritrean Division on 16 February. The plan was for III Army Corps to advance westwards from the region of Amba Aradam in an attempt to block Ras Kassa's retreat, and Badoglio calculated that the Eritreans were better suited for movement through the difficult terrain than were Italian troops or Blackshirts. During this manoeuvre the corps would be supplied from the air, as there were no roads.

If III Army Corps was to be the 'anvil', then the Eritrean Corps would provide the 'hammer' by advancing from the north on Ras Kassa's army and pushing it back. Whilst these forces engaged and attempted to annihilate their enemy, I Army Corps was directed to advance south along the route to Amba Alagi, improving the road as it went.

Several hundred kilometres to the north-west, and in what would effectively be a separate campaign dubbed the Battle of Shire (*La battaglia dello Scire*), the plan involved IV Army Corps advancing south from its positions guarding the Eritrean border with the intention of getting behind Ras Imru's army, based around Slehleka. At the same time II Army Corps would move westwards from its lines around Axum and move through the Af Gaga Pass, the intention being to catch the enemy in a pincer movement and obliterate him.[6]

The logistical effort required to maintain the Italian forces in northern Ethiopia and Eritrea, let alone allow them to conduct offensive operations, was mind-boggling. On 23 February Badoglio summarised his command for Mussolini as containing 11,230 officers and 13,825 non-commissioned officers, who together directed 233,546 Italian and 53,510 Eritrean and Libyan troops. In support of this multitude were 75,816 pack and draught animals, 5,719 lorries and waggons, and 1,854 'special vehicles' (water tankers, field kitchens and the like), which had to keep the soldiery fed and watered, as well as supply ammunition for their weapons: 293,318 rifles, 21,492 handguns, 7,407 machine guns, 1,904 flamethrowers and 30 mortars. Heavier ordnance was also required for the 877 artillery pieces of various calibre, and the whole transport apparatus had to be kept supplied with fuel, as did the 1,088 motorcycles, 156 tanks and 43 other armoured vehicles.[7] Given the scale of effort required to supply and sustain such forces in the field, the road convoys could assume gigantic proportions. One who had a bird's-eye view, Alessandro Pavolini of the *Disperata* bomber squadron, described the hundreds of nose-to-tail trucks he saw on the road south to Axum as resembling the beads on a rosary (*Rosari di autocarri*). He included a photograph of them, captioned 'the truck rosary' (*Il rosario degli autocarri*), in his book.[8]

Supported by 196 aircraft of the *Regia Aeronautica*, the Second Battle of Tembien, as it was called, did not actually start at H-Hour on D-Day, 27 February 1936. In fact, I Army Corps, comprising three infantry and one Blackshirt divisions,[9] plus supporting units, had already marched south in three columns following the conclusion of the fighting at Amba Aradam. It was thus already closing in on its objective, the Amba Alagi Passes, on that date. Similarly, the two-division-strong III Army Corps, consisting of the 1st Eritrean Division and the Duke of Pistoia's Blackshirts,[10] had moved west and taken up positions to the south of Abiy Addi, where Ras Kassa's army was concentrated. This corps was then situated as to block that army from retreating southwards. The formation that would attempt to force just such a retreat, the Eritrean Army Corps, encompassed an Eritrean division and a Blackshirt division as its core formations.[11]

II Army Corps, based around three divisions, two infantry and one Blackshirt,[12] included a contingent of Libyan *spahis*. As mentioned, this formation was tasked with advancing westward along the road from Axum towards Slehleka, whilst the two-division[13] IV Army Corps moved south from the border with Eritrea. The object of the exercise as it pertained to these two corps was the destruction of Ras Imru's army.

Thus, on the morning of 27 February the columns of I Army Corps merely moved forward to complete the last stage of their journey. They went entirely unopposed, with the only impediments to their movement being the rugged terrain. Accordingly, at around 11:00 hours on 28 February the tricolour was raised on the summit of Amba Alagi: an event of some moment given a previous battle there had been the precursor to Adua.[14] Aside from its propaganda value, possession of the mountain, and with it control of the adjacent passes, meant that Badoglio's first objective for the Second Battle of Tembien had been met.

The second was not so easy. The outcome of the battle for the Uarieu (Worsege) Pass in late January had left the Ethiopians in possession of high ground, specifically the 2,400m Amba Uork (Werk Amba, Work Amba) situated some 2km west of the pass. This twin-peaked prominence effectively interdicted the route that the Eritrean Army Corps needed to advance along, and was believed to be held by some 500 Ethiopians equipped with modern machine guns. Rather than bombard and gas this garrison out of existence, the corps commander General Allesandro Pirzio Biroli decided on a more subtle approach. An ad hoc group was assembled, consisting of forty-five *alpini*, sixty Blackshirts and twenty-five *ascari*, all of whom were skilled in climbing. The plan was for the

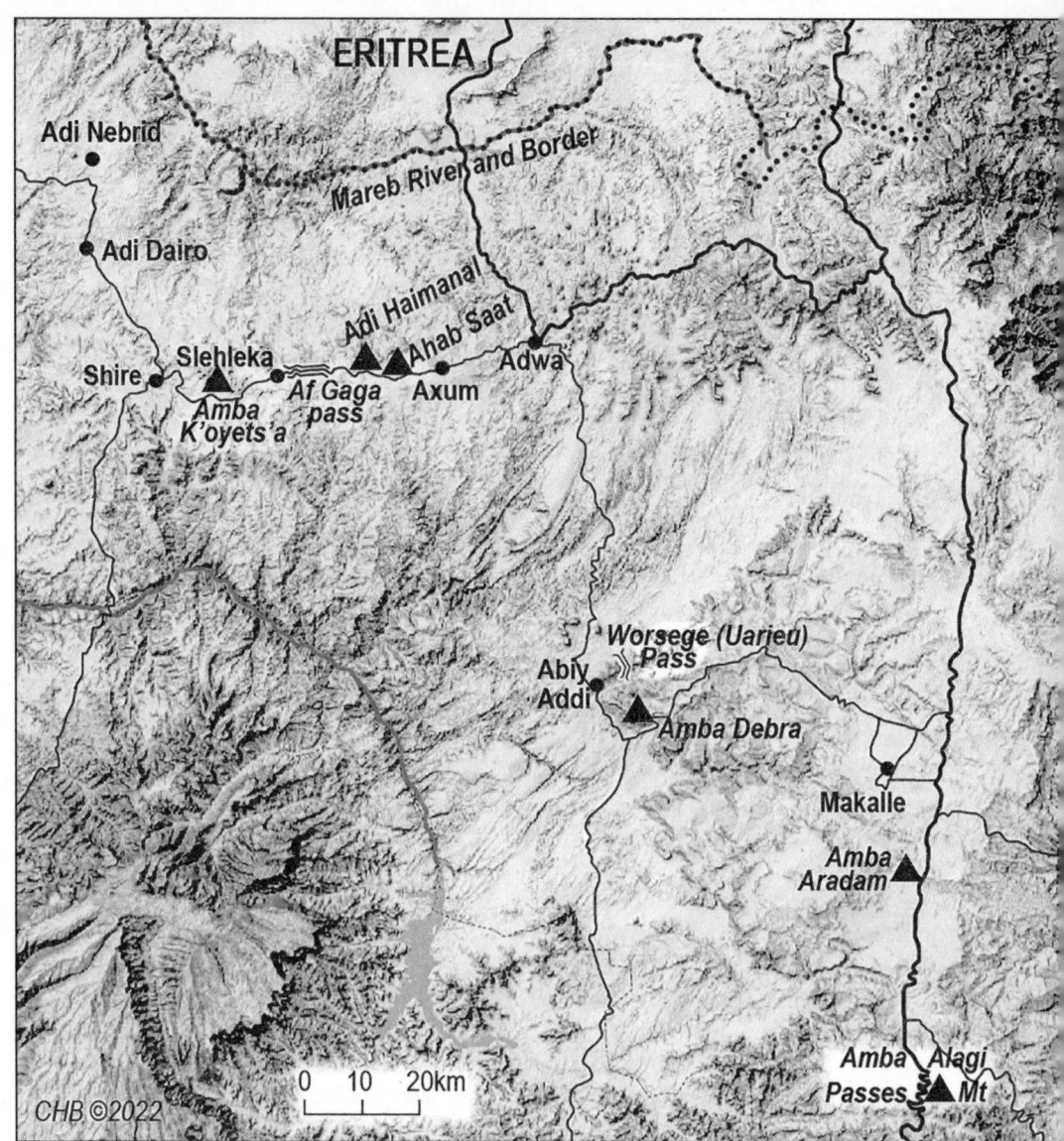

Key locations pertaining to the Second Battle of Tembien and the Battle of Shire. (© *Charles Blackwood*)

Alpine troops and fifteen Eritreans to scale and attack the southern peak, whilst the Blackshirts and ten *ascari*, under the command of *capomanipolo* (Lieutenant) Tito Polo, attempted its northern counterpart.[15] Polo, reputedly a former smuggler from the north of Italy, remarked to one of his colleagues that the Ethiopians atop the mountain 'won't be smarter than the Swiss customs officers. These are people who sleep at night and we work at night.'[16]

Like the Swiss, the Ethiopians were indeed asleep. Badoglio recalled in his memoirs that two teams set out at 03:00 hours and successfully overcame 'very great difficulties in a dangerous climb in darkness up the steep and rugged sides of the mountain'.[17] Steer, who was not present and so must have got the story

Ras Kassa Hailu fought at both the First and Second Battles of Tembien. (*Author's Collection*)

Ras Mulugeta Yeggazu perished at the hands of Ethiopian tribespeople during the retreat of his defeated army from Amba Aradam. (*Author's Collection*)

Ras Nasibu Zeamanuel. Ras Nasibu fought on the 'southern front' against Graziani, the latter defeating his forces during the Battle of the Ogaden. (*Author's Collection*)

Ras Seyoum Mengesha. Forces under his command played significant roles in the First and Second Battles of Tembien. (*Author's Collection*)

Italian troops in front of Amba Aradam in 1936. Ras Mulugeta had ordered his men to dig in on and around the mountain, making it the centre of his defensive dispositions. Between 10 and 19 February 1936 the Italians encircled the defenders, forcing them to withdraw. (*Author's Collection*)

Amba Aradam lies some 16km south of Makalle. This flat-topped 'rocky bastion' measured around 8km east–west and 3km north–south, and reached a maximum height of 2,756m. Its northern and eastern sides are steep and difficult to ascend, whilst those to the south and west slope more gently and are easily passable. (*Author's Collection*)

Amba Alagi. A strategically important point some 40km south of Amba Aradam as the crow flies, and part of a massif over 3,000m in elevation. (*Author's Collection*)

Amba Alagi. An Italian column passing the mountain, showing how, if it fell into enemy hands, the road south would be interdicted. (*Author's Collection*)

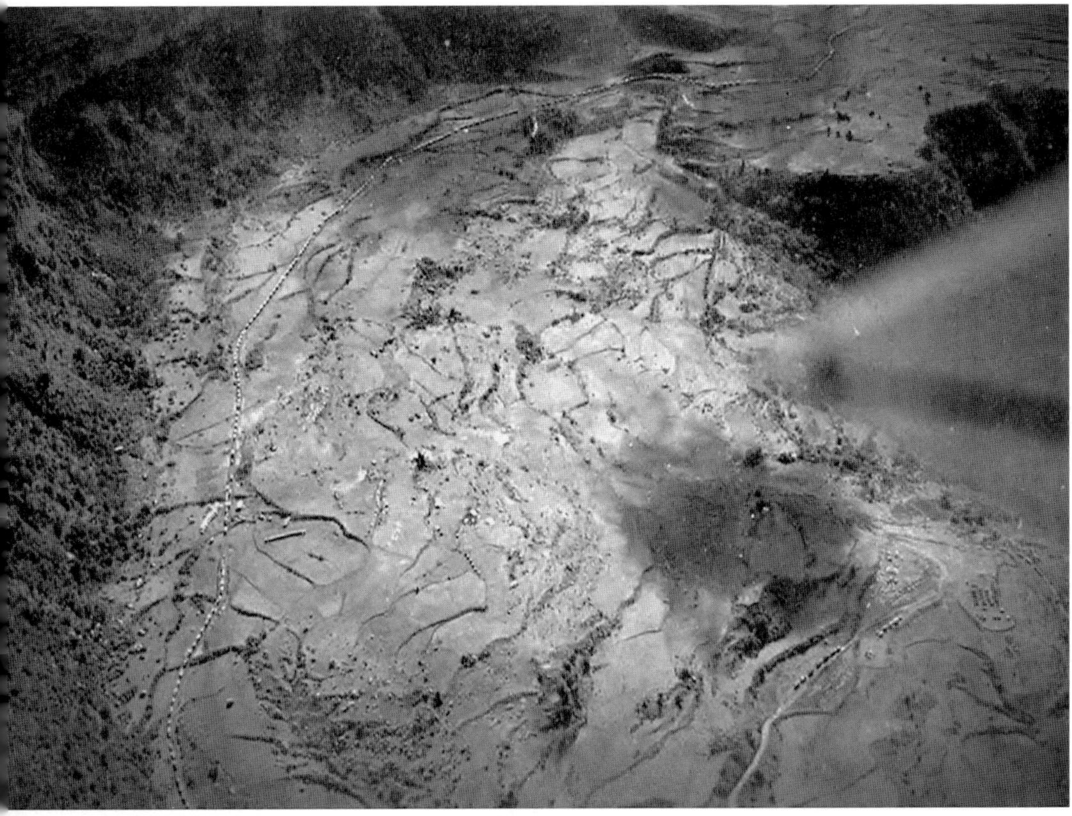

(*Opposite, above*) Amba Uork. In the early hours of 27 February 1936, 'when all the Ethiopians throughout the Empire were sleeping', a group of Alpine troops and Blackshirts climbed the steepest side of Amba Uork. As Badoglio's report put it: 'The opposing garrison was caught in the dark, and overwhelmed after poor resistance.' (*Author's Collection*)

(*Opposite, below*) Road building. In setting out to recreate a version of the *Imperium Romanum* in Africa, Fascist Italy had perforce to first resurrect one of that empire's most notable achievements. As an American commentator put it: 'like Caesar's legions, these modern Romans had to build their roads in order to fight'. (*Author's Collection*)

(*Above*) Rosary of trucks. Alessandro Pavolini of the *Disperata* bomber squadron described the hundreds of nose-to-tail trucks he saw on the road below as resembling the beads on a rosary (*Rosari di autocarri*). (*Alessandro Pavolini*)

(*Left*) Fascist propaganda: A postcard advertising the *82° Battaglione CC.NN. 'Benito Mussolini'*. The symbolism is obvious. (*Author's Collection*)

Types of aircraft used in East Africa. Top: Caproni Ca.101. Middle: (*left*) Caproni Ca.111; (*right*) Caproni Ca.133. Bottom: (*left*) Savoia Marchetti SM.81; (*right*) IMAM Ro.37.
(*Alessandro Pavolini*)

The *bomba C.500.T* was developed in early 1935 especially for use in the conquest of Ethiopia. Each round contained 212kg of mustard gas and was set to air-burst via an adjustable, propeller-operated fuse that could be set to detonate at a given altitude.
(*Author's Collection*)

A pair of C.500.T bombs slung under a Caproni Ca.101. Testing demonstrated that exploding a single bomb at an altitude of 250m created a high-concentration 'dispersion ellipse' of mustard gas measuring some 650m by 150m on the ground.
(*Author's Collection*)

An aeroplane, possibly an IMAM Ro.30, over Amba Alagi. (*Author's Collection*)

The airfield constructed near Makalle. (*Author's Collection*)

second-hand, probably from Ras Kassa's Russian adviser Colonel Feodor Konovalov (of whom more shortly), portrayed the subsequent events thus:

> Pirzio Biroli had prepared ... a surprise of extraordinary daring and skill. In the early hours of February 27, when all the Ethiopians throughout the Empire were sleeping, a company of Alpini and mountain-climbing Blackshirts were sent out from the Uarieu Pass to climb the steepest side of Uork Amba. They were loaded lightly, with rifle, dagger and hand-grenades. They reached the top just before dawn, walked through the first circles of the garrison of Uork Amba, who snored in their shammas around the white ashes of their camp fires – for the Ethiopians roll themselves up at night and lie heavy. Then they scattered their whole cargo of grenades. The garrison ... about 500 men, woke in sudden panic believing that the mountain was taken, so violent was the noise of battle near its centre. They fled down the Amba sides.[18]

A grossly simplified and truncated account undoubtedly, but it conveys the essence of the matter. At 06:00 hours six battalions of Italian infantry advanced through the Uarieu Pass with the object of encircling Amba Uork in order to secure it against counter-attacks. This proved a wise move; Ras Kassa reacted violently to the loss of the mountain, throwing forward masses of troops in an effort to dislodge the invaders. However, and despite some fierce hand-to-hand fighting on occasion, the Italian machine-gunners were able to repulse all assaults. Having suffered numerous casualties to no effect, the Ethiopians eventually withdrew.[19] As Badoglio informed Mussolini late in the afternoon of 27 February: 'Alpine units and Blackshirts of the Eritrean Army Corps with surprise action climbed the massive Uork Amba this night, which constituted a solid position on the right flank of the advance on Abbi Addi. The opposing garrison was caught in the dark, and overwhelmed after poor resistance.'[20]

The Ethiopian army was now in grave danger of being surrounded, although it seems Ras Kassa was largely unaware of this and concentrated on attempting to fight-off the enemy advancing from the north. Only on the morning of 28 February, when III Army Corps overran part of his rear area, was it that 'his servants came running to tell him of the mass of men to his south'.[21] That was the day when, to quote Longo, 'the pincer manoeuvre conceived by Badoglio would see its maximum development'.[22] Pirzio Biroli had been handed operational command of both corps to complete this encirclement, and at 12:30 hours on 28 February he therefore ordered a column of the Eritrean Corps to move on Amba Debra on the eastern end of the Ethiopian positions. His main force, however, advanced past Amba Uork and to the west of Abiy Addi, whilst III Army Corps moved northwards in the opposite direction.

The air force, operating Savoia-Marchetti SM.81 *Pipistrello* trimotors in tactical support, gave the enemy no rest: 100 tonnes of high explosive and thousands of fragmentation bombs were dropped on 28 February. Heavy strafing was also much in evidence.[23] Given that Italian forces were expected to occupy much of the ground in contention, then mustard gas was not used.[24] Nevertheless, Steer posits that the *Regia Aeronautica* was the decisive arm in this particular battle and, indeed, more generally:

> The most cruel effect of aviation on the Ethiopian was that it destroyed his traditional response to his leaders. Instead of assembling for mass security around their leader ... they scattered now in a frantic dash for individual security ... Italian air supremacy made of the Ethiopians a rabble which could not think for itself. It demolished, in fearful explosions and vibrations of the solid earth, the aristocracy which was the cadre of their military organisation.[25]

Steer also states that it was on 29 February that Ras Kassa consulted with Colonel Konovalov, who advised an orderly retreat 'before it was too late'.[26] This cannot be right date-wise, inasmuch as the western elements of the two corps joined hands in the early hours of that day at a point some 3km west of Abiy Addi.[27] By that time those Ethiopians who were going to escape to the west had already done so; their resistance on 28 February was described as being 'reduced to fragmentary actions, which confirmed the lack of a clear and precise operational concept'.[28] At 12:00 hours on 1 March Badoglio sent a telegram to Mussolini, which he said should be released to the press:

> The battle of Tembien is won. Ras Kassa's army, pressed from the north by the Eritrean Army Corps and from the south by the III Army Corps, desperately tried to escape the grip that closed around it, attacking both towards the Uarieu Pass and on the flanks of the III Corps. In fierce combat the enemy was put on the run with very serious losses of men, quadrupeds, weapons and materials. Enemy groups managed to escape to the west, chased by our air force. Other groups wander, without direction, and under continuous attack. Thus, after Ras Mulugeta, the Abyssinian army of Ras Kassa has disappeared.[29]

Indeed, the Second Battle of Tembien, as Badoglio later dubbed it, ended with the destruction of Ras Kassa's army as a coherent force. The air force set out to annihilate the remnants fleeing west, but they largely avoided the fate of Ras Mulugeta's army by moving at night and in small groups towards the Takeze river, which they hoped to cross in order to head south. In anticipation of their arrival, eight T.500.C bombs were dropped on the fords on 28 February.[30] In terms of casualties, the battle cost the Italians a total of 581 dead, enumerated as 34 officers, 359 Italian troops and 188 Eritreans. Ethiopian dead were estimated to be about 8,000.[31] Badoglio's second objective had been achieved and he had already, on 27 February, moved his GHQ to the Axum area, the better to conduct the Battle of Shire (*la battaglia dello Scire*) against Ras Imru's army.[32]

According to Badoglio's post-battle report,[33] his opponent was estimated to have just over 30,000 men in the region, with the vast majority based in the area around the Amba K'oyets'a (*Monte Coietzà*) massif. Situated some 12km west of the Af Gaga Pass, and about 9 from Slehleka (as the crow flies), this feature dominated an important communications nodal point. The commander-in-chief planned a two-stage battle following a preparatory phase aimed at implementing complex logistical measures. Foremost among these was the carrying out of roadworks, thus enabling the concentration of IV Army Corps on the Ethiopian-Eritrean border. Even more intricate measures would be required once that corps began to advance south over particularly forbidding ground, since this involved traversing a vast, largely unknown region of broken terrain. The entire area was poor in resources, particularly water, and covered by thick thorny vegetation that would make the march slow and painful. To at least partially overcome these difficulties, the corps would be supplied by air. Major Fiske, the American military observer, particularly noted this facet of the Italian campaign:

> In the last three months of the campaign the Italian supply service frequently resorted to air transport to take care of the supply needs of troops operating beyond the possibility of supply by motor and animal transportation. At one period during 21 days of fighting the aviation dropped to the combat troops 385 tons of supplies; over 500 tons were dropped in all. A number of airplanes were especially fitted for transporting supplies. The supplies were packed in padded canvas containers carrying about 200 pounds each and were dropped from the airplanes attached to inexpensive parachutes of treated cotton material. It was not possible to salvage these parachutes for subsequent use as there was no transportation to bring them back. The troops usually kept them as souvenirs.[34]

The first part of Badoglio's plan, to begin on 29 February, involved II Army Corps advancing westwards towards its objective of Amba K'oyets'a. Simultaneously, IV Army Corps would move on Adi Dairo via Adi Nebrid, these places being some 45 and 35km to the north-west of Amba K'oyets'a respectively. The second part of the plan was dependent on subsequent events, mainly, of course, the reaction of the enemy, and the C-in-C would deal with the situation as it arose within his overall concept of concentrating the two corps against the enemy forces. He reserved to himself these further decisions, which would be made according to the circumstances surrounding the situation as it developed. In order to increase the firepower of II Army Corps, he redeployed 149 artillery pieces from the Makalle sector and these, after a 'rapid and exemplary march of 500 kilometres', reached the area on the afternoon of 29 February.

That was also the date when the offensive began; at dawn on 29 February 1936 the two corps moved off from their start lines. Ras Imru knew they were coming. He was the only Ethiopian leader to have organized an efficient intelligence service, among which members of the clergy at Axum featured heavily. He was therefore aware of the composition, location and armament of II Army Corps, although he was oblivious in respect of the artillery reinforcement mentioned. He had also been warned by sources in Eritrea that IV Army Corps had, from 20 February, started towards the Mareb river.[35]

According to Steer, Ras Imru had considered any threat from the north to be minimal, given the nature of the country there. However, when he learned that there were thousands of troops, with tanks, assembling on the border, he felt that he must act quickly against II Army Corps. Due to the delays in respect of his communications, this decision was made in ignorance of the fate of the armies of Ras Mulugeta and Ras Kassa. Steer reckons that if he had realised their fate, and how it had been brought about tactically, he would not have risked battle.[36]

II Army Corps advanced from the starting point, about 5km east of Axum, with two divisions, the 'Gavinana'[37] and Blackshirt '21 April',[38] forward in column formation, the latter in the lead. The third, 'Gran Sasso',[39] was in reserve, along with the III Eritrean Brigade, and so following to their rear. Intelligence reports indicated that there were no enemy in the vicinity, so flank guards were not utilised.

The corps marched along the only road towards Slehleka until at noon the Blackshirts moved to the right to occupy the heights of Ahab Saat. The 'Gavinana' took their place at the front and continued to advance on Salaclacà. It was when they reached a position near the town at 13:00, a small valley under the heights of Adi Haimanal, that the Ethiopians struck.

The terse prose of the official report records that 'a hard fight ensued that lasted until night, but the enemy was everywhere stopped and counterattacked'. The Italian advance was also stopped and they were forced to form a defensive line, the Blackshirts moving to the left of the 'Gavinana' and the reserve, 'Gran Sasso', taking up position to their right. The Ethiopian attacks were pressed home with courage and determination. Longo talks of the Italians forming squares with a *risorgimentale*, that is a nineteenth-century, flavour (*quadrato di sapore risorgimentale*).[40] Both Steer and Del Boca mention that, according to non-official Italian sources, the mêlée became so close and involved that the field artillery was forced to fire at point-blank range, hitting both attackers and defenders on occasion.[41] Once again, though, the sheer firepower that II Army Corps was able to deploy meant that, however determined their attacks, the Ethiopians could not prevail. They nevertheless continued to press their assaults, particularly on the flanks of the Italian deployment, throughout 1 March, by which time the 149 guns which had been sent from Makalle came into operation. In addition, the air force carried out tactical missions in support of the ground troops, the upshot being that all the Ethiopian attacks failed. Badoglio recorded that intelligence confirmed the presence of numerous enemy forces in the Amba K'oyets'a area, but also suggested that Ras Imru might be about to order a retreat. He commanded an immediate advance on 2 March so as to take advantage of this, but General Pietro Maravigna, the corps commander, demurred. His command needed time to reorientate from a defensive to an offensive mode, and was not in a position to advance *en masse*, although some small gains were attained.

The delay occasioned was used to advantage by Ras Imru, for Italian intelligence had been correct. He had indeed decided to retire, particularly given that another army corps was bearing down on his left flank, although still some distance away. He therefore ordered that, whilst contingents of troops would remain to harass II Army Corps, the bulk of the army would retreat in good order, and at night, towards the fords of the Takeze river.[42] So it was that when the Italian advance resumed at first light on 3 March, it was unopposed. As Badoglio's report put it:

> at dawn on day 3, the army corps resumed their march and the enemy, shaken by the fighting sustained in the previous days ... and threatened from the north by the IV corps, now close, did not accept battle and the retreat towards the Takeze began: a retreat which, hammered without rest by the air force, soon turned into a chaotic and disordered flight. And so with the destruction of the army of Ras [Imru] the battle of the Scire ended like the others, victoriously.[43]

Even if the operational plan had not worked out as intended, and the majority of Ras Imru's men escaped, the last Ethiopian army on the northern front had now left the field. It was, as Badoglio notes above, to suffer unmerciful aerial bombardment whilst attempting to cross the Takeze, although, perhaps curiously, mustard gas does not appear to have been employed; Gentilli records no usage between 28 February and 16 March.[44] Longo attributes this to political, rather than military, necessities, which is a theme we shall return to in the next chapter. Nevertheless, it was estimated by the Italians that in crossing the river the Ethiopians suffered as many casualties as they had during the battle, making a grand total of 6,000–8,000 overall. Their opponent's figures for killed and wounded were much lower, and came mainly from the 'Gavinana' Division: 856 Italian officers and men, plus 12 *ascari*.[45] IV Army Corps suffered no battle casualties at all, having arrived only after the fighting was over.

The conclusion of the Battle of Shire represented a major achievement for Badoglio. The forces under his command had successively defeated, and driven from the field with severe losses, three Ethiopian armies. These constituted the main body of their enemy's military force, leaving only one important military formation to overcome: the Imperial Army under the Negus, which was south of Amba Alagi but believed to be advancing northwards.

Chapter Thirteen

Serdo and Gondar

In the Danakil, kids, even calves, were transported and parachuted through the air ... This was the first case of transporting live animals to supply units on the march. Given the tropical temperature of the region, no butcher's meat would have endured transport.[1]

* * *

The non-use of mustard gas to attack Ras Imru's retreating army has been, as noted in the last chapter, posited as being politically motivated.[2] The politics revolved around the fact that a meeting of a committee of the League of Nations was scheduled for 2 March 1936. This would discuss extending sanctions in respect of Italy, for, as Baer put it, 'oil sanctions were not yet dead'.[3] At least not quite, and in any event and perhaps unsurprisingly, nothing substantive came of it. It cannot be said, though, that this meeting was definitely related to the deployment of mustard gas, or rather the lack thereof. In any case, 'respect' for international law did not prevent Badoglio's command from rapidly violating it, albeit in another context.

On 4 March a Red Cross Field Hospital, organised under the auspices of the British Ambulance Service in Ethiopia (BASE), was heavily bombed.[4] Set up two days earlier at Alamata, some 20km to the south of Korem, the hospital consisted of several tents and vehicles, and was in the charge of Dr John Melly, with Dr John Macfie as second-in-command. According to the latter's later account, the site chosen was apparently perfect:

> an immense level stretch of ground extending far over the plain, dry and covered by coarse grass. On each side at a convenient distance ran small streams in shallow furrows from which to obtain water. It seemed an almost ideal site. There was not a hut, or a tent, or even a tree for miles. So here, we pitched our tents, trusting implicitly in the good faith of the Italians, which hitherto we had no cause to doubt. From above we must have looked blatantly conspicuous and isolated.[5]

During the hospital's first two days of existence, Italian aircraft overflew the site on several occasions. Reports from these flights, which included information that they had been subjected to fire from the ground, led the Italian air force commanders to erroneously conclude that Ethiopian forces were using the Red Cross symbols to camouflage military activity. In the early afternoon of 4 March, therefore, they attacked the hospital. The raid lasted for about 30 minutes and was described by Macfie:

> not less than forty high explosive bombs fell, and a great number of incendiary bombs; but we were spared 'gas' bombs. It was an entirely one-sided affair. From our camp not a shot was fired; indeed, not a shot could be fired because, I believe, the few rifles we had for our guard had not been issued. The fellow could come down as low as he liked and risk nothing. It made one angry to think that such things could be done with impunity.[6]

Melly wrote that there could be no doubt that the attackers knew exactly what they were attacking: 'The 46 ft. square Red Cross flag had a direct hit. There is no possible question of doubt as to the absolute deliberation of the attack. Practically all the tents and lorries are also clearly marked with Red Crosses.'[7] The potential repercussions of this raid must have been evident to Badoglio, which explains why he sent a telegram marked 'absolute maximum precedence' to Mussolini on the night of 4 March explaining the rationale behind it:

> Yesterday our aircraft sighted in the immediate vicinity of the South Abyssinian camp of Korem, a column of lorries unloading crates and baggage marked with the Red Cross. Upon descending to investigate, the aircraft was hit by violent anti-aircraft fire near the Red Cross camp. When it returned today, the aircraft was again hit by anti-aircraft fire and damaged in the fuselage. Consequently, the target was bombed, and it was noted that much dense smoke was produced confirming the hypothesis that it was an ammunition deposit.[8]

There was perhaps a second reason; according to Steer, one of the bomber pilots in question was none other than Vittorio Mussolini. In fact, Steer accuses him of being the pilot responsible for the 4 March attack: 'A criminal strain must run in the family', he opined.[9] Longo also mentions his involvement during the reconnaissance stage, and of his aircraft being hit by ground-fire, which led to the decision for immediate destruction of the site.[10]

Although the hospital was comprehensively destroyed, with thirty-five tents, including the operating theatre centrepiece, being lost, remarkably only five patients died and no British personnel were harmed. There were also journalists in the vicinity, so the attack made headlines in the UK and questions were asked in the House of Commons.[11] However, as Baudendistel remarks, the British government was well aware that an Italian victory was in the offing and this, combined with the fact that no British national had been hurt, led the Foreign Office to take a low-key approach.[12] In addition, much more serious political events had intervened rather closer to home. Indeed, the European diplomatic situation was completely upended on 7 March. As Winston Churchill remembered it:

> At ten o'clock on the morning ... the German Foreign Minister summoned the British, French, Belgian, and Italian Ambassadors to the Wilhelmstrasse

to announce to them a proposal for a twenty-five-year pact, a demilitarisation on both sides of the Rhine frontier, a pact limiting air forces, and non-aggression pacts to be negotiated with Eastern and Western neighbours ... At noon on this same March 7, 1936, two hours after his proposal for a twenty-five-year pact, Hitler announced to the Reichstag that he intended to reoccupy the Rhineland, and even while he spoke German columns streamed across the boundary and entered all the main German towns. They were everywhere received with rejoicing, tempered by the fear of Allied action.[13]

But there was, of course, to be no Allied action. This was the first of several 'capitulations' to Hitler.[14] The effect was felt most in France. According to Franklin D. Laurens:

> The impact of the remilitarization of the Rhineland upon French thinking was earth-shaking ... Thereafter, the Italo-Ethiopian dispute took even more of a back seat to the German menace as a factor in the policy decisions of the Quai d'Orsay. Or rather, the plans which French statesmen formulated regarding the African conflict were made with both eyes on the Rhine.[15]

The attitude of the British government was encapsulated in the words of a memorandum drawn up by the recently appointed (following the defenestration of Hoare) foreign secretary, Anthony Eden: 'by reoccupying the Rhineland he [Hitler] has deprived us of the possibility of making to him a concession which might otherwise have been a useful bargaining counter'.[16] In comparison to Hitler's move, the bombing of a hospital in far-away Ethiopia was an event of singular insignificance.

The question as to why the *Regia Aeronautica* carried out such operations is not, I think, difficult to answer. It was, after all, the branch of Italy's armed forces that was most imbued with the 'Fascist spirit'.[17] Further, their enemy did not play by the book, as it were, and the Italians were seemingly convinced, and consistently if self-servingly argued, that the Ethiopians used the Red Cross as a convenient shield: 'the only clause of the Geneva Conventions which the Abyssinians regard as valid, and clamorously invoke on every occasion, is that which lays down that any persons taking refuge under the sign of the Red Cross should be secure from aerial bombardment'.[18] In addition, the 'uncivilised' character of Ethiopian warfare, with its atrocities and war crimes, was held to legitimise such actions.

Whether the British Red Cross Field Hospital was a legitimate target or not, the attack on it was only a small part of an ongoing airborne campaign presaging a large-scale Italian advance. Given that the majority of Ethiopia's armed forces had now been destroyed or dispersed, the possibility of a virtually unopposed advance along the main north-south communication routes leading to the capital, Addis Ababa, beckoned. The exception to this, of course, was the route through Korem, where the Negus' army currently lay.

In preparation for any such advance, on 8 March Badoglio ordered his logistics chief, Brigadier General Fidenzio Dall'Ora, to assemble over a thousand lorries in the area of Makalle. The intent, though premature, was to provide for a column that would drive straight on to Addis Ababa.[19] Dall'Ora has been described as 'a general of uncommon professional ability' and 'a man of exceptional tenacity', which, given his achievements, few would dispute.[20] No doubt burdening his overworked department a little more, Badoglio's order arrived whilst a somewhat peripheral operation, requiring significant logistical organisation, was under way.

This operation involved the despatch of a 350-strong lorry-borne 'flying column' across the fearsome Danakil Desert from bases at Assab and Beilul in Eritrea, with the target being the town of Serdo in Ethiopia's Aussa region. This area, the most fertile part of the Danakil, comprising a large alluvial plain some 300–400m above sea level, was ruled by Sultan Mohamed Jaio from Serdo, his capital.[21] Although nominally subject to the Negus, the remoteness of Aussa meant that the Sultan ruled autonomously over some 40,000 inhabitants. He was thought to be sympathetic to Italy and had had many discussions with Italian emissaries, although in fact he had never committed himself one way or the other. He would likely have been left in peace, at least for the moment, had it not been decided that an airbase at Serdo would prove strategically useful. Aircraft based there would threaten the right flank of the northern Ethiopian forces, with Dessie only about 200km away to the south-west; the Djibouti–Addis Ababa railway was also within easy range, albeit Mussolini had agreed not to bomb it. Further, the planned airfield would provide a connecting point between the northern and southern invasion fronts.

One of the officers attached to the Serdo-bound column was Colonel Vittorio Ruggero, a former military attaché at Addis Ababa and now head of the political bureau of the Supreme Command. Del Boca considered him, alongside General Dall'Ora, as 'perhaps the most capable man ... of all those who prepared and directed the war'.[22] The commander was Lieutenant Gianfranco Litta Modignani, who was now directing about 350 mercenaries hired in the ports of the Red Sea and the Gulf of Aden. The reason for utilising such men was the fairly high risk of failure: the Danakil is an absolutely waterless desert, interspersed with lava ridges featuring precipitous drops and rocks with razor-sharp edges, where the temperature can reach and surpass 50° Celsius. It was then 'not considered appropriate to jeopardize the prestige of the regular army'.[23] The journalist and aviator Vittorio Beonio-Brocchieri, who was involved in the escapade, reckoned that to rely upon 350 adventurers straight out of an Emilio Salgari adventure novel was putting the matter in the hands of destiny.[24] The mercenaries he described were indeed a mixed bunch: 'Somalis, Bedouins, Copts and Muslims, Abyssinian refugees and former raiders from the Danakil, escapees, vagabonds, pilgrims from Mecca, beardless boys and old pirates with sabred faces.'[25] Their supply needs would be met by the air force: 'constituted almost entirely of indigenous elements, the logistic supplies ... etc. were entrusted exclusively to a special formation of our aviation which had as its main base the Assab airport and which progressively established makeshift bases'.[26]

The column had set off originally on 19 January 1936, after four weeks' training, but was halted on 2 February. This first phase had resulted in several local tribes – famous for their violent hostility to outsiders,[27] but no doubt recognising *force majeure* when they saw it – submitting to Italian rule. The pause was to evaluate the 'positive repercussions' of this subjugation.[28] On 8 March Litta Modignani was ordered to complete the final 130km to Serdo, which was reached on the late afternoon of 11 March without opposition. One unique feature of the aerial logistics operation put in place to sustain the column was particularly noted by Paul Gentizon, the Swiss-born correspondent for *Le Temps*. He was to write how: 'In the Danakil, kids, even calves, were transported and parachuted through the air ... This was the first case of transporting live animals to supply units on the march. Given the tropical temperature of the region, no butcher's meat would have endured transport.'[29]

Ajmone Cat, in an article he penned the following year, didn't mention the goats. He did, though, record that the Danakil support operations, carried out by a single section of bombers, managed to transport 63 tonnes of material, 300 people and 'seventy head of live cattle'.[30] There was no need for the bombers to assume their traditional role as there was no fighting; the population were friendly or overawed. As the official Italian bulletin worded it:

> Our troops departing from Assab-Beilul, after a daring march of 350km, made particularly difficult in some places by, in addition to the torrid temperature, the conformation of the rocky terrain and the absolute lack of resources, reached and occupied Sardò, heart of the Aussa ... [where] on 11 March, the tricolour was hoisted over the residence of the sultan of the Aussa, Mohamed Yahio, in front of the deployed troops and the entire group of aircraft squadrons, lined up in the new landing field below. The population of the whole territory has joyfully welcomed our occupation, which seals the relations between Italy and the Aussa ...[31]

The occupation of Serdo, 'the mythical Sardo' (*la mitica Sardò*) as Del Boca calls it, had been a secondary Italian aim since the previous year.[32] Now, thanks to the airborne supply system under the direct command of Pilot Lieutenant Colonel (*piloti tenente colonnello*) Simon Pietro Mattei, who had studied the problem for several months, it had been achieved.[33] Italian propaganda made much of it. As Beonio-Brocchieri was to write from Serdo on the day of occupation: 'The Italian troops, who occupied this vast province with vigorous aviation assistance, have achieved a strategic result of great importance ... The centre of what remains of the North Ethiopian army is now within a half hour flight from our bases.'[34]

It cannot be said that the occupation of Serdo directly affected the course of the campaign. What it did demonstrate, though, was that with their mastery of the air, and their ability to exploit it in a meaningful way with respect to ground operations, there was no part of Ethiopia, vast though it was, that was outside the Italians' grasp. Gentilli makes the point that the Ethiopian campaign was in many ways a precursor to later, more famous, war-making methods.[35] Badoglio now

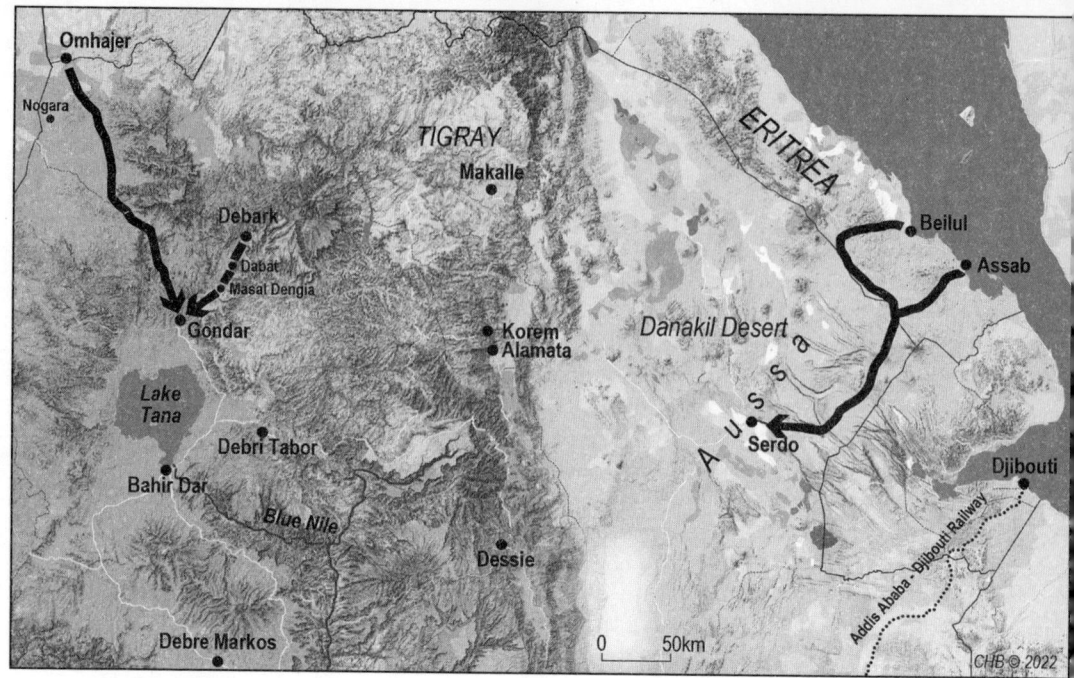

Peripheral manoeuvres. Lieutenant Gianfranco Litta Modignani's advance across the Danakil to Serdo, and Achille Starace's fast column to Gondar. (© *Charles Blackwood*)

intended to utilise these evolved techniques to defeat the Negus and his last army by moving directly south towards Korem. At this point in time there were no other organised Ethiopian forces in the north of the country. Despite this, or perhaps because of it, the curious business of the occupation of Gondar came about.

As earlier noted, Mussolini desired that the campaign in Ethiopia should be, above all else, a Fascist enterprise. He wanted a Fascist war, at least ostensibly under his personal direction, in which a large proportion of Italy's combatants, if not a majority, should be drawn from the ranks of the Blackshirts. In this he had been largely thwarted, although reality had been massaged somewhat on occasion as, for example, with respect to the 'famous battle for the conquest of Amba Aradam'. Now, and with the certainty of little or no opposition, the concept was to be boosted to ridiculous heights with the appointment of the secretary of the Fascist Party, Achille Starace, as leader of a 'fast column' (*colonna celere*) that would occupy the city of Gondar. This, according to Rochat, was the biggest such concession to the political needs of the Fascist regime that the army made during the entire war, as both Badoglio and General Federico Baistrocchi in Rome were largely successful in limiting the role of the 'Fascist hierarchs'.[36]

Gondar had no particular strategic importance with regards to the ongoing campaign, although it was linked to Asmara in Eritrea by a road of sorts that had been constructed by Italian engineers in 1904–1905.[37] This road had never been used by motor vehicles, but was nevertheless the chosen – indeed the only – route for the fast column that Starace was to lead. Many difficulties were foreseen, given the forbidding topography, which included mountain passes at altitudes of around 2,700m and the lack of knowledge as to whether vehicles could negotiate the track at all. The only positive factor was the near-zero probability of encountering any armed resistance.[38]

The column was formed on 12 March (some sources say 5 March) at Asmara and comprised three battalions of the 3rd Regiment of *Bersaglieri* (*3° Reggimento Bersaglieri*), formerly part of the 'Sabauda' Infantry Division, plus a battalion of Blackshirts (the *82° Battaglione CC.NN. 'Benito Mussolini'*).[39] One suspects the latter was chosen for its name rather than any military prowess its troops might have been thought to possess. Also attached were an armoured car company, a motorised artillery group, machine gun-armed motorcycles, and engineers, which all together totalled 3,348 officers and men mounted in around 500 vehicles.[40] Full air support was also provided and a quartet of writers were in attendance; Giovanni Artieri for *La Stampa*, Paolo Caccia Monelli for *La Gazzetta del Popolo*, Ferdinando Chiarelli for *Il Giornale d'Italia* and Alberto Mario Perbellini for *Il Resto del Carlino*.[41] The column departed Asmara on 15 March and, driving on good roads, reached Omhajer on the Ethiopian border four days later. The next day, 20 March, it started towards its goal, which lay some 220km to the south-east as the crow flies. The column was formed up into four groups, with about half the armoured cars, the motorcycles and a battalion of *Bersaglieri*, plus engineers, in the vanguard. Close behind followed a second battalion of *Bersaglieri*, then came the Blackshirts, the artillery, the command along with a radio section, plus further engineers and the logistic services. The rearmost formation consisted of the third *Bersaglieri* battalion and the rest of the armoured cars. Each echelon was connected with the others, and with the command, by radio.[42] It was then quite capable of taking care of itself against anything but a major attack.

Badoglio was aware that Starace's *opera buffa* performance might well have embarrassing repercussions, particularly since Mussolini followed the operation closely; both Mussolini and Starace were former *Bersaglieri*. He therefore decided that in order, potentially at least, to safeguard the precious life (*salvaguardare la preziosa vita*) of the party secretary he would deploy some back-up. The III Eritrean Brigade, under Brigadier General Luigi Cubeddu, which had been engaged in pursuing the remnants of Ras Imru's army, was at Debark, a town some 85km to the north-east of Gondar. Cubeddu was now ordered to change direction and head for the same target as Starace, which basically meant covering the left flank of the latter's column.[43]

The advance, with the fast column extending along the track for about 15km, involved nothing in the way of fighting but did include a good deal of arduous road repair and several air-drops of supplies. On 31 March, the column having reached to within about 40km of the goal, the road became impassable and irreparable owing to landslides. Starace therefore abandoned his vehicles and, leaving a battalion of *Bersaglieri* to guard them, marched the rest of the way.[44] They reached Gondar on the morning of 1 April 1936 having suffered, since leaving Omhajer, casualties to the total of six dead and seven injured.[45] Starace actually arrived about half a day later than the III Eritrean Brigade. The latter, however, in order not to dim the glory of his achievement, had been ordered not to enter the town. Accordingly, at 10:00 hours the Italian flag was raised atop the Fasil Ghebbi (or Gondar Castle, *Castello di Gondar*), allowing Starace to message *Il Duce*:

> The Bersaglieri and Blackshirts have hoisted the Tricolour on Gondar, having overcome no slight fatigue with glad hearts and inexhaustible enthusiasm. The Duce has always been present and His name echoed endlessly across the impassable plains and mountains that we have crossed, clearing our way metre by metre. The enemy was deeply shaken by our advance, but rather than confront us he preferred to beat a hasty retreat. The motto – Usque ad Finem[46] – is engraved on our victorious black pennant but more decisive is our will to continue to shoot straight.[47]

Such epic toadying was, of course, quite normal within the Fascist hierarchy. Starace then turned his pantomime campaign into a heroic adventure via the 'incredible hagiographic report' – *La marcia su Gondar: della colonna celere AO e le successive operazioni nella Etiopia Occidentale* – that he penned and published.[48] It was, of course, all grist to the mills of Fascist propaganda, with one account claiming that: 'The epic enterprise will remain in the history of Italy as an example of audacity, extreme decision and contempt of danger.'[49]

Both columns, now under Starace's overall command, went on to advance a further 30km south on 11 April, reaching the shore of Lake Tana the following day.[50] As Ethiopia's largest lake, and the source of the Blue Nile, this was of particular interest to Britain.[51] That wasn't the end of operations for the combined columns. They went on to move towards, and occupy, several other towns south of the lake. These included Bahir Dar (24 April), Debre Tabor (28 April) and Debre Markos (20 May).[52] All these operations were concluded peacefully, inasmuch as the population submitted to Italian rule.

These movements were of little strategic value, and this was particularly so with respect to Starace's march on Gondar.[53] Conducted entirely for propaganda purposes, it violated one of the fundamental principles, indeed the 'master principle', of war: maintenance of the aim.[54] This basically holds that all efforts should be focused on the main object, with minimum combat power devoted to secondary efforts. The occupation of Gondar unarguably falls into the latter category, and if Badoglio had deemed it necessary then it could easily have been, and indeed effectively was, accomplished by Cubeddu's command. The most apt comment on the matter was, ironically and unwittingly, provided by none other than Mussolini himself in his reply to Starace's fawning telegram quoted above: 'I receive your greetings after the magnificent march on Gondar, which was TRULY FASCIST IN STYLE. I pay tribute to the officers and the troops'.[55]

Quite so!

Chapter Fourteen

The Emperor's Army

'There is nothing for Your Majesty to do but retire,' I answered, when the Emperor asked me for my views. The retreat was approved by his entourage ...[1]

* * *

Badoglio could afford to indulge Starace's, and Mussolini's, whimsicalities; he was to report at the end of March that the assets available to him during that month included nearly 8,000 'efficient trucks', 266,088 Italian officers and men plus 55,614 indigenous troops, and almost 900 pieces of artillery.[2] His difficulties largely revolved around bringing this huge preponderance of force to bear on the enemy. The thousand lorries he had ordered General Dall'Ora to accumulate around Makalle for an advance south would be unable to negotiate the 50km or so (as the crow flies) of road, such as it was, between Amba Alagi and Korem. Only south of the latter was the so-called 'Imperial Road' passable by vehicles as far as Addis Ababa via Dessie. Advance elements of I Army Corps and the Eritrean Corps, formations from the *Pusteria* Alpine and 1st Eritrean Divisions, had begun to traverse the route early in March, and had reached Maychew, some 20km directly south of Amba Alagi, towards the end of the month. The objective was Korem, but the poor state of the road meant logistical support was based largely on pack animals.[3]

The commander-in-chief was also concerned that the Negus and his army might adopt different methods from those of the armies he had recently defeated, particularly that they might resort to guerrilla warfare and adopt a delaying strategy rather than standing and fighting as a whole. If this were to occur, then the campaign might well be prolonged into June and the start of the rainy season, making further advances nigh on impossible until at least September, with all that entailed.[4] However, his worries on the latter score were, initially at least, relieved by none other than Haile Selassie himself, who had started to move his forces north to Korem at the end of February. This manoeuvre was discovered by the Italians, via radio interception, as was the operational purpose of the move. On 18 March Badoglio communicated this vital information to Mussolini:

> The situation between Lake Hashenge and Korem has radically changed in recent days. Two new facts have emerged: (1) In the above area there is a considerable concentration of enemy forces, including the imperial guard, totalling 50,000 so far. (2) A decision has been taken in a council chaired by the Negus to no longer retreat to Dessie, which would mean disbandment of

the army, but instead fight to the bitter end between Lake Hashenge and Korem.

This situation gives me the lively hope (*la viva speranza*) of being able to engage these enemy forces and inflict another sensational defeat on them. However, since this will not be a fight against a rearguard but a large battle, I have now made arrangements to have no fewer than forty battalions take part, plus masses of artillery of all calibres.

This brings with it the need to postpone the start of operations, given that 50 kilometres of road has to be built and that, for now, we have to utilise pack-animals to amass sufficient quantities of supplies, food and munitions. Preparations will be complete on 31 March and operations will start on 1 April. I foresee that the action, proceeding over difficult terrain with successive, uninterrupted, mountainous ridges, could last about ten days. I represent the above to your Excellency so that nothing is concluded until the completion of this grandiose act which could be truly decisive.[5]

In the meantime, and whilst the advance guards at Maychew were reinforced, the air force began sustained operations around Korem and Lake Hashenge. This included, according to Steer, the 'most intensive gas campaign of the war'.[6] Later research confirms the claim: between 16 and 28 March, a total of 153 C.500.T bombs, containing around 33.6 tonnes of mustard gas, were dropped.[7] This action prompted Princess Tsahai, the Negus' daughter, to send an open, and widely disseminated, telegram of protest to the Women's Advisory Council of the League of Nations Union:

For seven days without break [the] enemy have been bombing [the] armies and people of my country including women and children with terrible gases. Our soldiers are brave men and we know that they must take [the] consequences of war. Against this cruel gas we have no protection, no gas masks – nothing. This suffering and torture is beyond description, hundreds of [my] countrymen moaning and screaming with pain. Many of them are unrecognisable since the skin has been burned off their faces. May I appeal to the Women's Council of the League of Nations Union to protest against this criminal breach of the 1925 Protocol?[8]

Through wide circulation this message became famous. Of course, Italy denied using gas and responded with a counter-campaign concerning Ethiopian atrocities. The British position has been ably summed up by Steven Morewood: 'Although the Chiefs of Staff considered that Italy's clear infringement of the 1925 Geneva Gas Protocol could not pass without some rebuke, there was an unwritten assumption that as this had happened in the remote Horn of Africa against a backward people, it was not terribly serious.'[9]

Those on the receiving end were of a different opinion with respect to how 'serious' it was. Steer recorded that Haile Selassie's men became 'exhausted by the continual spraying with yperite, which burnt their shoulders and feet, blinded them, and burnt the mouths of their pack animals when they chewed infected grass'. He did not observe this at first hand, but rather got the story verbally from someone who did: Colonel Feodor Evgenievich Konovalov (Konovaloff).[10]

Konovalov was an anti-Communist, or White, former Russian military officer who had arrived in Ethiopia after the Bolsheviks assumed power. He went on to become one of the most important foreigners involved in training Haile Selassie's troops. Despatched north by the Negus on 22 July 1935, he stayed on as a military adviser to the Army of the Centre, witnessed the Battles of Tembien, and was involved in the precipitous retreat.[11] He drafted a semi-autobiographical account of his experiences, which he gave to Steer before the latter was expelled from Ethiopia on 16 May 1936.[12] Parts of his story were drawn on and used extensively in Steer's book, comprising indeed the entirety of Chapter XVIII.[13] Of historical importance, Konovalov's work has had what Clarke describes as 'a troubled history'.[14] In fact a much revised, and very pro-Fascist, version was later published in Italy.[15] Given the bias of this reworked version, and that he became involved in the Spanish Civil War on the side of Franco, then justifiable suspicions about where his allegiances really lay sprang up, although he has been largely absolved of playing a double game.[16] In any event, his near-contemporary account as published by Steer is, as the latter says, the only account by 'a European who saw it on the Ethiopian side'.[17]

Konovalov arrived at Korem on 20 March along with 'what remained of the armies of Ras Seyoum and Kassa, after the fatiguing retreat of three weeks'. The following morning he was informed by Haile Selassie that: 'I have decided to attack the Italians at their camp near Mai Chow [Maychew] ... before they have gathered in force.' The means to carry out this assault consisted, in the Russian's judgement, of between 40,000 and 50,000 men in total, equipped with 'about 200 machine-guns of every possible type, eight guns of 37mm calibre, one French 75mm [gun], six Brandt mortars and eight new Oerlikon anti-aircraft guns'.[18]

The Emperor's plan had, in theory at least, a good deal of merit. Ethiopian success would have been unlikely to have changed the war's final outcome but, as with the resort to irregular warfare, it might well have caused delays sufficient to prevent that outcome being realised before the beginning of the rainy season and the operational stasis that would follow.[19] On the other hand, Badoglio was attempting to build up sufficient forces south of Maychew to launch a further advance but was struggling with logistical issues given the lack of a decent road. Whilst the troops marched, their artillery, munitions and other essentials were carried by mules which had to be fed, their fodder being transported by yet other mules. Military priorities being foremost, animal feed became of secondary importance. This resulted in equine rations being cut to a single feed of oats per day, and sometimes not even that, causing the animals to become fatigued and in many cases perish.[20] The commanding officer of a regiment of *alpini* that had advanced to forward positions on 17 March recorded that, owing to the lack of mules, his men had to carry forward on their shoulders the ammunition for their mountain-guns, a fourteen-hour journey.[21] Still Badoglio kept pushing men

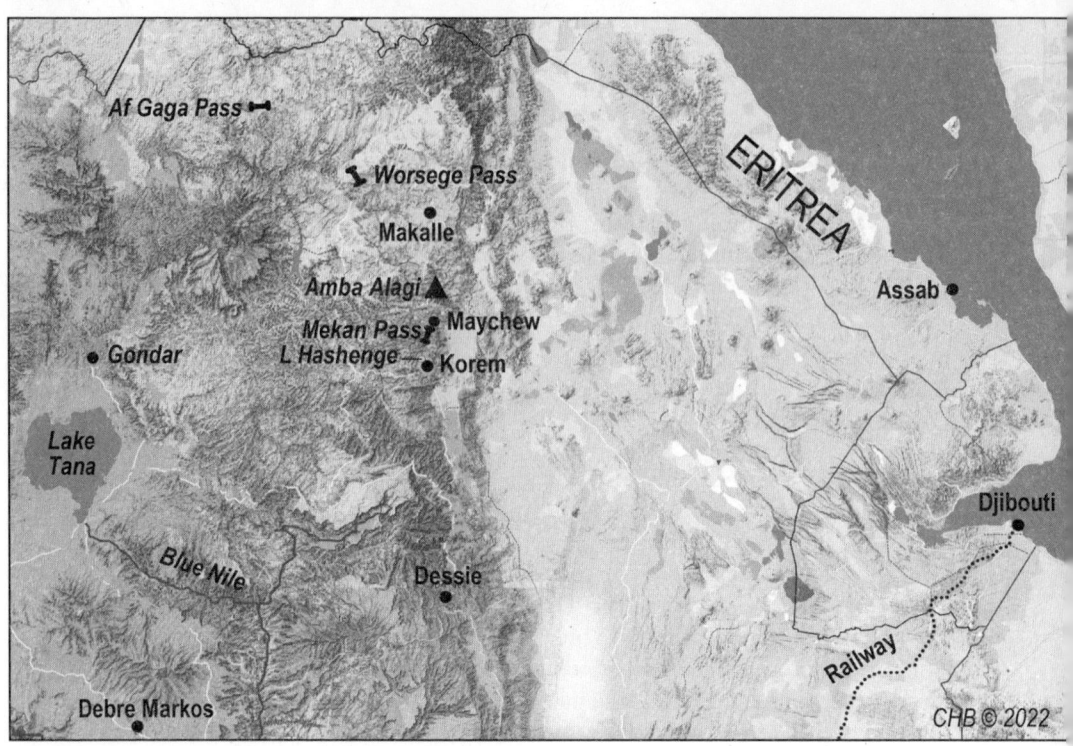

Key locations pertaining to the Battle of Maychew. (© *Charles Blackwood*)

forward; by the third week of March three divisions from two Army Corps, the *Pusteria* Alpine and the 1st and 2nd Eritrean Divisions, were deployed just to the south of Maychew along with artillery support.[22]

The total manpower of these three units and their support amounted to around 40,000 officers and men. Arrayed to their rear were the other divisions of I Army Corps, with a similar manpower total.[23] These would, though, find it difficult to move forward quickly if needed. The divisions at the front were, however, neither well dug in nor well supplied, and had the Ethiopian attack taken place on 21 March it could well have caused severe problems. Unfortunately, in respect of rapid decision-making and unlike Badoglio, Haile Selassie did not exercise authority over a cohesive force that would act promptly, or even at all, on his orders. Other than in the case of the Imperial Guard, he was obliged to work through the various Rases and leaders, each of whom commanded his own contingent of fighters. The Negus was no dictator, and so had great difficulty in getting all his supposed subordinates to cooperate with him or, indeed, with each other. Konovalov wrote that 'each day brought some new obstacle to delay the offensive' and remarked that during this period of inaction the Ethiopian forces were under constant air attack. He also noted that the three main Ethiopian commanders, who would each lead a column in the attack, were Ras Kassa, Ras Seyoum and Ras Getachew Abate. The first two had already suffered catastrophic defeats at the hands of the enemy. 'Why [led] by them and not by others of greater energy and capacity?' the Russian asked, rhetorically. His answer: 'Because the sovereign had to reckon with his feudal seigneurs of the

Empire although they had proved their ineptitude already and had lost the first part of the war. He had better men, but he could not use them.'²⁴

On 28 March Badoglio, unaware of his opponent's intentions, disseminated orders to his senior commanders in respect of the attack he was planning:

> The enemy troops reported to the north of Lake Hashenge seem to represent the last forces with which the Negus, who has direct command, intends to try to attack or, much more likely, to oppose our attack. We must also consider the possibility that the Negus wants to keep these forces in hand by withdrawing them before our attack, and then to use them at the right moment [...] In this situation it is my intention to perfect our deployment and logistical preparation in order to launch, in the most advantageous conditions, an attack on the enemy. In the meantime, to put ourselves in a position to repel any enemy offensive attempt on our front, or flanks, or along the line of operation; and keep ready to advance at any moment to turn into a rout any enemy attempt to retreat.²⁵

As noted, the Emperor had determined on the less likely option, as Badoglio saw it, although he struggled to have his decision implemented. Moreover, the defences that the Italian advanced detachments were able to construct were second-rate. Extending for around 10km, they lacked barbed wire and similar obstacles such as *cavalli di frisia* (logs studded with iron or wooden spikes), and, in the absence of sandbags, featured hastily constructed shallow trenches, low stone walls and sangars. Nor were the defenders able to rely on masses of artillery: only small calibre mountain guns and the like were readily available, and they had limited supplies of ammunition.²⁶

The interminable discussions and arguments in the Ethiopian camp only terminated on 30 March, allowing preparatory movements to begin on that date. For the attack Haile Selassie divided his force into four: three columns and the reserve. The left hand, westerly, column consisted of some 10,000 men under Ras Getachew, and had as its objective the positions held by the Alpine Division. The centre column of 15,000 men, commanded by Ras Kassa, aimed to penetrate the centre of the Italian line, defeat the 2nd Eritrean Division and advance through the Mekan Pass onto the village of Maychew. On the right a smaller force amounting to some 3,000–4,000 men under Ras Seyoum, would assault the positions held by the 1st Eritrean Division and attempt to outflank them, manoeuvring so as to threaten Maychew from the east. The reserve, which included about 5,000 of the Imperial Guard and amounted to around 10,000–15,000 men, was held back.²⁷

Thus the two opposing armies were roughly equal in terms of manpower. However, in terms of artillery they were very different; despite supply problems, the Italian front divisions were able to deploy about a hundred 65mm and 75mm guns against a mere handful possessed by their opponents.²⁸ Also, of immense importance defensively, they possessed about ninety heavy machine guns as well as having the inestimable benefit of the air force's 'flying artillery', which had seventy-five Caproni Ca.133 bombers and thirty-seven Romeo Ro.1 and IMAM Ro.37 reconnaissance/ground attack aircraft available for direct support.[29]

There is some dispute concerning whether or not the Ethiopian attack took the Italians by surprise. Del Boca, for example, has argued that because Badoglio was absent, and had to delegate operational command to General Ruggero Santini of I Army Corps, he failed to anticipate the assault.[30] It came at 05:45 hours on 31 March with attacks on all sectors of the Italian line, thus diverting attention from the main objective of the Mekan Pass, and involving tactics that were likened by one commentator to 'a human flood'.[31] Despite the ferocity and persistence of these attacks, only minor successes were achieved, with support from the Ethiopian artillery being described as 'meagre'.[32] It was not only meagre but ineffective, according to Colonel Konovalov:

> Our gunners had no idea of the objectives which they were supposed to bombard. They shot at random and sometimes hit their own men. The Ethiopians also attacked fortified positions without proper artillery preparation. Giving the order to his artillery to fire, the Emperor had said, 'Our men must hear their artillery shooting. It will give them courage and improve their morale.' The Italian works were generally stone walls, rather low – some were only two feet high. Only in rare places were these walls formed into turrets to hold machine-guns. If anybody in the Ethiopian army beside the Emperor had known how to fire artillery they could have been shot to pieces.[33]

On the other hand, Badoglio, writing in retrospect, reckoned that the assaults on positions defending the eastern portion of the Mekan Pass were 'prepared by the well-directed action of artillery and machine guns'.[34] Whether or not this was the case, the attack made some limited progress. Then, to add to the tribulations of the Ethiopians, between 07:30 and 08:00 hours the *Regia Aeronautica* made its appearance in strength, much to the relief of the *ascari* of the hard-pressed 2nd Eritrean Division.[35] These attacks, particularly with fragmentation bombs, were, according to the memoirs of the commander of the 1st Eritrean Division, very effective: 'from time to time we see thousands of white robes (*fute bianche*) swinging and stopping, uncertain whether to advance or retreat'.[36] Inclement weather and low cloud forced the aircraft to fly low, resulting in several being hit by anti-aircraft fire. A single Ro.1 was downed, while seventeen other aircraft were hit, of which four suffered serious damage. Three airmen were slightly wounded. One high-profile bomber pilot, Bruno Mussolini, the younger brother of Vittorio, was nearly killed when an Oerlikon shell exploded just behind him.[37]

During the fighting several of the 2nd Eritrean Division's batteries ran out of ammunition. However, notwithstanding Haile Selassie's early introduction of the Imperial Guard in an attempt to make progress in respect of penetrating the Mekan Pass, nowhere did the Ethiopian assaults make significant headway. Just as had proved to be the case at the earlier battles at the Af Gaga and Uarieu Passes, attacks by what were essentially unsupported light infantry against

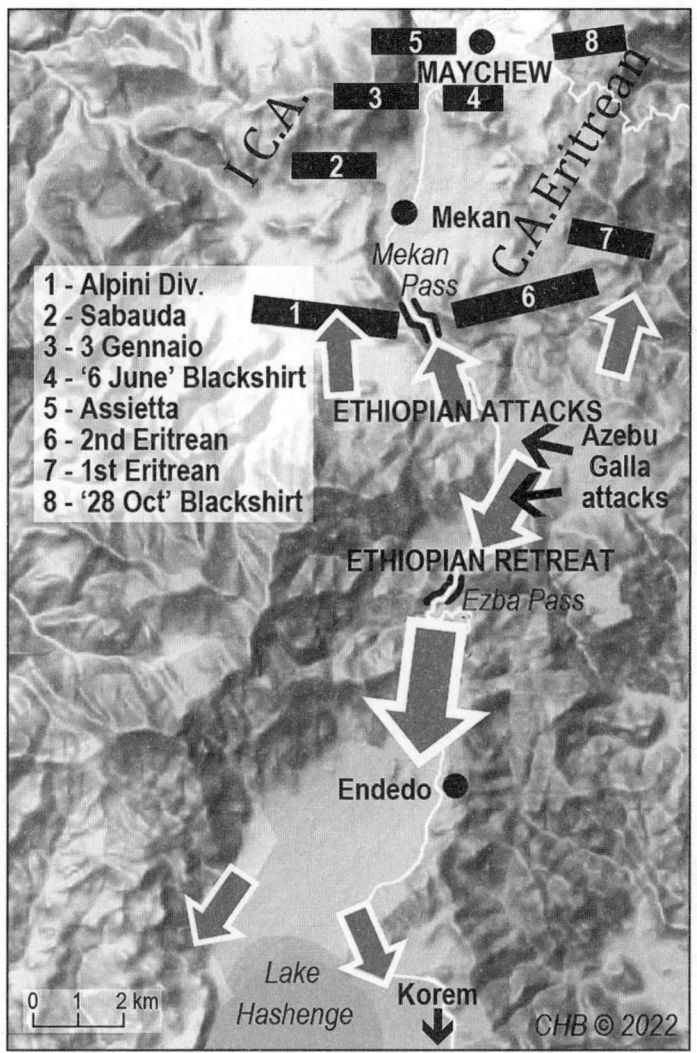

The Battle of Maychew. (© *Charles Blackwood*)

entrenched defenders supported by machine guns, artillery and aircraft proved difficult and costly.

In spite of suffering severe casualties, the Ethiopians continued again and again to assault the Italian line. Only at 18:00 hours, when daylight began to fade, did Haile Selassie order a cessation of operations and a withdrawal, although on some sectors the fighting continued for a further two to three hours.[38] The battle was effectively over after more than fourteen hours of fierce fighting and, to quote Konovalov: 'It was clear that the offensive had failed. What remained of the northern forces, the Emperor's own army, would not beat the enemy.'[39]

In terms of casualties, the Italians lost 21 officers and 68 men killed, whilst the figures for wounded were 47 and 244 respectively. These were overwhelmingly from the Alpine Division, whilst the two Eritrean divisions reported casualties amounting to 204 deaths and 669 wounded amongst the *ascari*.[40] Estimates of how many Ethiopians perished or were wounded vary widely. According to Konovalov, casualties were 'relatively small' but he gave no indication of what that meant.[41] General Gustavo Pesenti, commander of the 1st Eritrean Division, later wrote of 5,000 dead, whilst Badoglio offered 8,000.[42]

There is no way of arriving at an accurate figure of Ethiopian casualties, although the sheer amount of ordnance expended by the Italians would tend to suggest a fairly high number. Longo states that the 1st Eritrean Division fired 400,000 rounds during the fighting and had only fifteen cartridges for each rifle and two magazines for each machine gun at the end of the day, whilst their artillery had only fifty rounds per gun remaining. The 2nd Eritrean Division was worse off in that regard, having fired off their entire stock, whilst the Alpine Division had twenty rounds per gun.[43] In addition, it has been calculated that during the battle almost 32 tonnes of bombs of various kinds were dropped, and over 6,000 machine-gun rounds discharged, from the air.[44] Despite the fact that some accounts make the claim, no mustard gas was used.[45]

Konovalov says that the Emperor wanted to renew the offensive and in the afternoon of the following day, 1 April, asked the Russian for his advice. This was given entirely in the negative: 'There is nothing for Your Majesty to do but retire,' I answered, when the Emperor asked me for my views. The retreat was approved by his entourage ...'[46] The Italian bombers were mostly grounded that day because of heavy rain storms and a thick blanket of low cloud. Seven Ro.1 and Ro.37 biplanes did manage to make it into the air, however, discharging 200kg of high explosive and 1,500 machine-gun rounds at their opponents.[47]

Initially, and throughout 2 April, the Ethiopian withdrawal southwards was disciplined and orderly, being covered by sporadic attacks on the Italian positions in an attempt to discourage them from engaging in any pursuit. This succeeded to some extent, although Badoglio was fully engaged in reshuffling and resupplying his forces rather than pushing them forward immediately.[48] There was, though, no disguising the fact that the outcome of the Battle of Maychew (*battaglia di Mai Ceu*), also dubbed by some writers the Battle of Lake Hashenge (*battaglia del lago Ascianghi*) was catastrophic for the Ethiopians. Italian intelligence intercepted and decrypted a telegram from the Ethiopian Foreign Ministry in Addis Ababa, headed by Heruy Wolde Selassie, to the Ethiopian Legation at Paris which, from the content, was a copy of one sent to Dr Warqenah Eshete (*aka* Dr Charles Martin), ambassador to London.[49] It stated the matter plainly even if not entirely accurately in every respect:

> The military situation will become unsustainable: Only 5,000 Ethiopian armed men are at Lake Tana to oppose the advance via Gondor towards Gojjam [Debre Markos] and the capital. The advance of the enemy troops is

halfway between Assab and Dessie and there is no army to arrest it. Ras Imru's army is greatly reduced.

For the rest of the (disbanded) armies; they joined with the Emperor's army which is threatened with being surrounded and cannot find reinforcements. The Emperor will remain with it until his death. Then the empire will collapse. Get in touch with Eden immediately and confidentially disclose to him the gravity of the military situation and the imminent dangers. Let us know his opinion on immediate measures to be taken.[50]

The apparent faith that the Ethiopian government had in the British, and the hope that they would somehow come to their rescue, has been previously noted, and this telegram is surely an example of it.[51] Such appeals were, of course, in vain. Equally vain was the attempt of the Emperor's army to withdraw in good order. As had occurred following previous defeats, discipline soon disintegrated, resulting in a shambolic exodus from the field of battle. In Konovalov's words: 'When the Ethiopians march, the main object of each man is to pass all the others. This mob of people trying to thread its way through donkeys, mules and hundreds of other Ethiopians created an incredible disorder.'[52] The fate of this 'unbroken flood of humanity which surged towards Korem' along the bank of Lake Hashenge was also, as per previous experience, predictable. On 3 April 21.5 tonnes of bombs were dropped on the retreating mass, whilst three times that amount, as well as 30,000 machine-gun rounds, followed the next day when the *Regia Aeronautica* flew 155 missions. After that the rate progressively fell: for the four days between 6 and 9 April the figures for air-delivered ordnance were 24.7, 13.7, 8.0 and 1.2 tonnes respectively.[53] The final day of the aerial pursuit was 9 April, owing to the dramatic decline in useful targets. Thereafter the aircraft were mainly utilised in efforts to keep the advancing ground forces supplied.[54]

To add to the already grievous woes of the victims, they were also regularly attacked by bands of local people who had thrown their lot in with the Italians. Referred to as 'Azebo Galla', or just 'Galla' by the Italians, these *bande* had contributed to the destruction of Ras Mulgeta's defeated army and now reprised that performance.[55] To quote Konovalov once again: 'Our troops, scattered over a huge country, were completely demoralised by a chaotic retreat, by their defeat, by the attack of the Galla, and above all by the Italian aviation.'[56] Haile Selassie, despite the statement to the contrary in Heruy's telegram quoted above, did not remain with his army until death intervened. Rather, accompanied by his entourage, he journeyed south towards Dessie and then Addis Ababa.[57] He could not afford to tarry.

Badoglio wasted no time and on 4 April launched both the I Army Corps and the Eritrean Corps towards Dessie, with some 120 tonnes of supplies air-dropped to them as they went.[58] Thus, as his memoirs had it: 'Pressed by our troops, threatened along the way by the bands of Azebo Galla ... beaten by all the aviation ... the Abyssinian retreat turned into a disordered and ruinous escape.'[59] Badoglio was indeed triumphant, despatching a seven-page message to Mussolini on 4 April detailing his recent victories, although admitting there was 'no news of the Negus'.[60] He had every reason to be pleased with himself for there was now nothing, and nobody, to stop him. Perhaps Paul Gentizon, the correspondent for *Le Temps*, summed it up best of all: 'The Battle of Aschanghi decided the fate of Ethiopia.'[61]

In order to seal that fate, Badoglio issued further orders on 5 April. This was the date on which the two-division Eritrean Army Corps had taken Korem, following brief resistance from the local garrison. Now it was to advance on Dessie, some 150km distant as the crow flies and about 250km by road, with the view to taking possession on 15 April. Meanwhile I Army Corps, reinforced by units drafted from other sectors, would remain between Maychew and Korem whilst major efforts were put into improving the road between Korem and Amba Alagi. The Eritreans marched off on 9 April with their artillery, ammunition and heavy equipment carried by mules and the air force providing logistic support to the tune of about 18 tonnes of food daily.[62] They encountered no opposition, the only difficulties, apart from the high mortality rate amongst the pack animals, being caused by the bad weather, which created swollen watercourses and marshy ground. Overcoming these problems, the corps entered and occupied Dessie on 15 April without encountering the slightest opposition.[63]

The town had been prominent as an Ethiopian strategic centre, with the Negus basing his headquarters there until he moved north, and it was a nodal point in respect of several roads. Its importance now, so far as the Italians were concerned, lay in its context as a significant waypoint on the road to Badoglio's ultimate objective: the Ethiopian capital of Addis Ababa. The inhabitants of that city had learned of the defeat of Haile Selassie at Maychew on the morning of 13 April, when thirteen Ca. 133 and nine Ro.37 aeroplanes appeared in the sky above them. No bombs were dropped, only 100,000 leaflets announcing the Italian victory. In addition to proclaiming Italy's great triumph, these leaflets also informed the citizenry that slavery had been abolished throughout Ethiopia.[64] They had yet, however, to meet any of their new colonial overlords in person, although Badoglio was working on that.

Chapter Fifteen

Totalitarian Motorisation

On the Somali front, our imperial conquest was above all a war of means: victory in the strategic field had to go hand in hand with victory in the logistics field. In fact, the extension of the front required the totalitarian motorisation of the fighting units ...[1]

* * *

In early March, as previously mentioned, Badoglio had ordered a thousand lorries to be assembled at Makalle. His intention was for these to form the basis of a motorised column which, once the road between Amba Alagi and Korem was brought up to standard, would drive directly to Addis Ababa. Now, a month later, and given that the last organised Ethiopian army in the north had been destroyed, the operation became feasible and was unlikely to meet with any serious opposition. It was the case, though, that possession of the Ethiopian capital, of itself, might not be enough to end the war. In fact, and as Longo points out, the force delivered there would have found itself 'dangerously isolated in hostile territory', with all the implications that flowed from that situation.[2] This was so because whilst the north of the country had been cleared of enemy forces, or at least of the coordinated variety, the same did not apply to the south.

A significant army numbering some 30,000 men under the command of Ras Nasibu Zeamanuel was intact and deployed there, mainly around Degeh Bur and Jijiga, oriented towards preventing an advance by Graziani's command on Harar.[3] Neutralising the potential threat from any redeployment of this army, and it was considered 'not improbable' that Ras Nasibu would fall back to cover the capital,[4] would have required Badoglio to advance two or three army corps, or perhaps indeed the entire expeditionary force, far enough south to completely secure Addis Ababa. This in turn would have entailed organising a vast and complex logistic supply system over a considerable distance. All of this would have taken time, perhaps a great deal of it, and time was Badoglio's enemy: the rains, which would render the roads virtually impassable, were only a few weeks away.[5] There was, though, an alternative: engaging Ras Nasibu and defeating him in the south.

Following his success in the Battle of Ganale Doria, which had eliminated an Ethiopian army under Ras Desta, Graziani had been perforce mostly quiescent whilst he built up his forces and tended to his logistical requirements. This hiatus in operations had allowed the Ethiopians time to construct, under the supervision of Wehib Pasha, Nasibu's chief of staff, a system of supposedly strong fortifications and entrenched camps south of Degeh Bur, variously dubbed a 'second Verdun' or 'Hindenburg Line'.[6] Ras Nasibu was, however, not minded to act defensively, and so ignored the advice of Wehib and his aides,[7] who warned him against dangerously extending his supply lines. This advice followed his decision to redeploy around two-thirds of his available manpower towards the Italian lines which ran west–east from Danan, through Kebri Dehar and on to Geregube.[8]

Graziani, too, had been, as already described, offensively minded right from the start, despite his orders to 'remain absolutely on the defensive'.[9] As has also been illustrated, he ignored such instructions insofar as he could, although he was deeply irritated at playing second fiddle to Badoglio, whom, it may be recalled, he had been slated to replace in January 1936.[10] That he deeply resented his secondary status is demonstrated by his reply to a telegram received from the commander-in-chief on 3 March 1936, in which he was informed of Badoglio's great victories: 'Thus, in about twenty days, of the three Abyssinian armies of the north-front there are only a few remnants fleeing south.'[11] The reply was telling:

> I express to Your Excellency my subordinate and very warm congratulations for an ingenious manoeuvre which in twenty days completely destroyed three enemy armies. It is to be regretted that if I had been believed and fulfilled since a year ago in the requests made, and in the possibilities glimpsed, on this front, I would have now in turn been able to beat the armies of Bale and Ogaden, thus marking the end of the Italo-Abyssinian war. History will specify to whom to attribute this shortcoming. I have a clear conscience.[12]

No matter how keen Graziani was to steal Badoglio's thunder, he first had to overcome the logistical difficulties inherent in operating from Somalia – a matter about which he never ceased to grumble. In truth he had much to complain about, as the colony had simply lacked the infrastructure to support major military operations. The port of Mogadishu, through which most men and materiel had to pass, was some 630km from Gorahai, the logistical base for an advance on Harar, across a largely desert region. The situation was, of course, just as bad, if not worse, on the Ethiopian side of the border. For example, the road from the border-town of Ferfer to Kebri Dehar, the advanced base for the campaign, ran for some 280km and required the construction of nine bridges, three of them spanning over 65m, in order to make it usable for lorries. By the middle of March 7,000 military and civilian personnel and 700 lorries were involved in this project, which was scheduled to be complete by 10 April. To compound the difficulties the weather turned wet, slowing down the work. Graziani threw men at the problem and they worked day and night, in the darkness under the glare of vehicle headlights, until some 200km of ballasted road, with a crushed stone surface, was completed in just twenty days.[13]

Though communications, and therefore logistics, had been and remained problematical, Graziani's command had been steadily reinforced in terms of both manpower and materiel. For example, the infantry of the Libyan Division

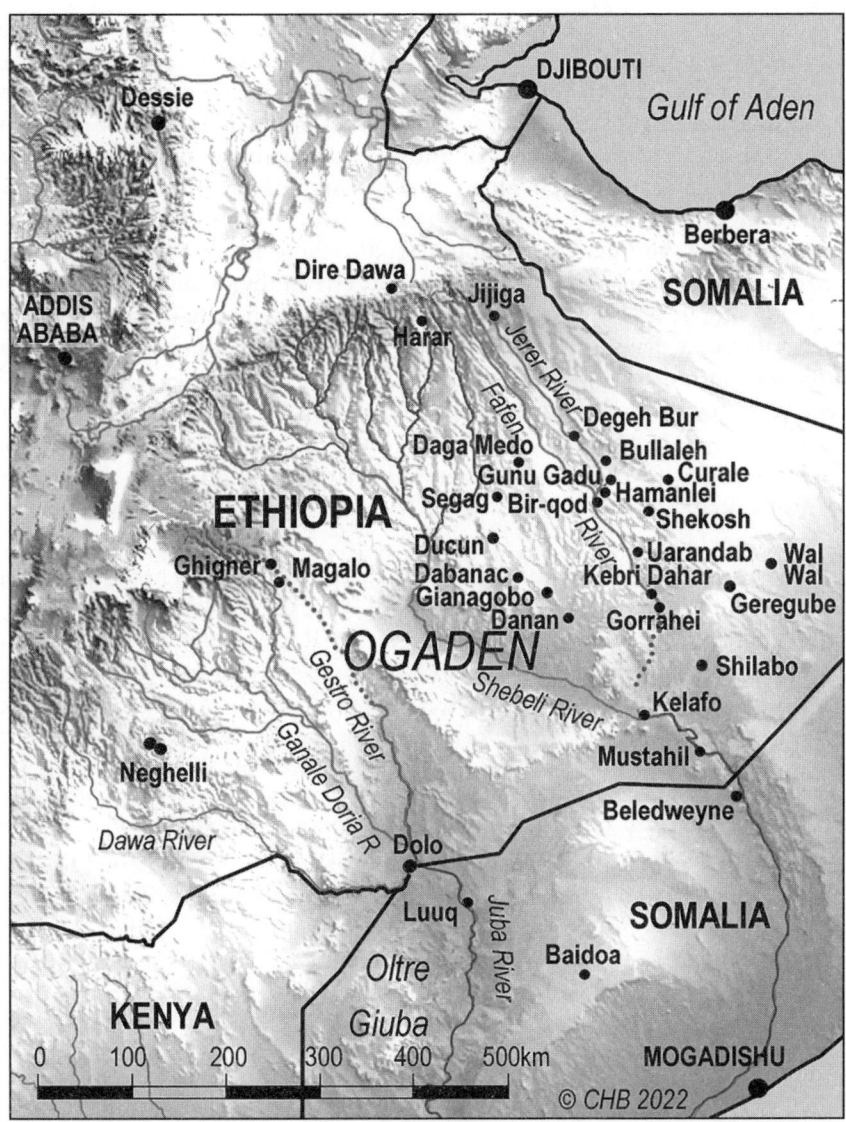

Key locations related to Graziani's advance from Somalia. (© *Charles Blackwood*)

(*Divisione indigena Libia I*), 8,870-strong,[14] finally arrived in Somalia in the first half of February and proceeded via Mustahil to Danan.[15] Arriving on 1 April at Mustahil, the division was reinforced with artillery and tanks, plus engineers and medical services, and a contingent of *dubats*.[16] The previous month a much smaller, and arguably rather more unusual, reinforcement had arrived in the shape of a detachment of 1,000 *Carabinieri*. Formed from volunteers, these were divided into four 'truck-mounted bands' (*bande autocarrate*) that had departed

Rome on 25 February 1936 and arrived in Somalia on 12 March.[17] The forward position for these 'bands' was Geregube on the right of the Italian line. Whilst it is the case that the *Carabinieri* had provided fighting units in previous conflicts,[18] their appearance in Somalia rather illustrates a point Fuller made about the Italian expeditionary force in general: 'the army was grouped together like a Lord Mayor's show. It contained a bit of everything, not because each bit was of tactical value, but because the whole was politically symbolic of a united Fascist Italy. In it was to be found every conceivable unit or bit of a unit.'[19]

Buttressing this theme somewhat, it is worth noting that a battalion-sized cohort of 'Forestry Militia' (*Coorte milizia forestale*) was also based at Geregube.[20] In terms of materiel, specifically vehicles, the southern front now possessed over 1,500 trucks plus 100 Caterpillar tractors with two trailers for each.[21] Further aircraft had also been sent to the theatre, including a Bombardment Group of fourteen Caproni Ca.133 that arrived in February. These brought to about ninety the total number of aircraft available to Brigadier General Ferruccio Ranza, the air force commander in Somalia, who had taken over from his predecessor, Bernasconi, in January.[22]

In contrast to the ground forces, the air force had remained heavily engaged following the successful outcome of the Battle of Ganale Doria in January, with continued efforts to prevent any possibility of Ras Desta's army regrouping. Between 10 February and 20 March several areas in the southern Ogaden, largely around Neghelli and along the Weyib [Gestro] river valley, were targeted, with 67.5 tonnes of bombs and 15,680 machine-gun rounds expended.[23]

Federigo 'Ghigo' Valli, the director of *L'Ala d'Italia*, an aviation magazine published monthly in Milan, was a volunteer pilot based at Luuq who took part in these missions. He wrote about one such mission that occurred in February, and published it in the April 1936 edition of his journal. Described as being 'From our pilot volunteer director in East Africa', the article was entitled 'Bombing of the Gestro: Magalo and Ghigner',[24] and in it Valli explained the rationale behind the attacks and the tactics used:

> Today's action has a reason for particular interest. Magalo and Ghigner stand on the upper Gestro as two junctions between Addis Ababa and the south. The road that borders the villages is the most important in the area. The proximity of the river, flowing even in this dry season and flanked by thick and tasty vegetation, makes it a transportation current. Water for livestock and for men ... The enemy has become smart. He is terrified of aviation. Pilots and reconnaissance observers must have the eyes of an eagle to discover the hidden objectives on the uneven ground. The Gestro area was targeted particularly ... Above all, it was wanted to divert a possible plan of concentrating livestock for transport and slaughter along the road that flanks the river. Aviation alone has had this task. The results were, as always, perfect ... the territory was searched with obstinate meticulousness. The vegetation along the Gestro covered the enemy and his large columns of

camels ... But the aviator has learned to see everywhere. We fly low, fragmentation bombs here and there in suspicious areas, then some machine gun fire and finally the enemy has been flushed out. This was just a salute by the reconnaissance, then the bombing began ... Thousands of camels laden with weapons and supplies were slaughtered and the armed men who led them were forced to flee again.[25]

There was, of course, no mention of chemical warfare in Valli's account, and it is in any case difficult to calculate the quantities of gas used on the southern front.[26] There is, though, evidence that over the period 16 February–30 March 11.8 tonnes of mustard gas and 6.4 tonnes of phosgene were discharged.[27] The vast majority of the mustard gas, deployed in a total of fifty-three C.500.T bombs, wasn't, however, used to discourage any reformation of Ras Desta's force. Rather, it was utilised against targets further north against which Graziani intended to advance. Indeed, he had ordered the air force to concentrate from 20 March on preparatory work for that offensive. In anticipation of this operation, General Ranza's HQ had moved to Gorahai on 14 March and started building up aviation strength there.[28] Mussolini, whilst displaying impatience for the attack to begin, had circumscribed the bombing campaign. This was conveyed in a message to Graziani of 11 March: 'No bombing of Addis Ababa, Dire Dawa and the railway; maximum freedom of action on Jijiga, Harar and south of this line; no freedom of employment, to date, of aggressive chemicals of any kind.'[29]

Whilst the prohibition in respect of the two cities and the railway was respected, the ban on 'aggressive chemicals' was less so. Indeed, Gentilli records sixteen C.500.T bombs being used in the northern sector on the date of *Il Duce*'s telegram[30] and on 25 March a further six were used on a section of the so-called 'Hindenburg Line' near Bir-qod.[31] On 30 March the air force turned from bombing towns such as Jijiga and Harar, which had suffered heavily, and began concerted attacks on the defences south of Degeh Bur. These included dropping a further twenty-three C.500.T bombs between 30 March and 10 April.[32]

Whether the aerial preparations for it were constrained or not, the question of when the ground offensive might begin was a matter that had begun to preoccupy both Mussolini and Badoglio, despite both of them knowing that Graziani's difficulties were immense. His earlier success in the Battle of Ganale Doria had involved advancing a relatively small force of around 8,000 men over a limited distance. Now he faced the much larger question of projecting an army of more than 35,000 men some 500km to Harar over very difficult terrain. These difficulties were, moreover, compounded by the unexpectedly heavy rain afflicting the theatre at that time. Nevertheless, and particularly after Badoglio's victory at Maychew, both men began pressing him further. In fact, the day after the latter battle the commander-in-chief sent a telegram urging Graziani to abandon caution: 'The Negus' army is retreating south. The I Army Corps and the Eritrean Army Corps, as well as all the aviation, are in pursuit. It is time to dare everything. I am sure that Your Excellency will be able to make the most of the situation.'[33]

The following day he received a similar message from Mussolini: 'Given the rapid course of events facing the North, I ask [you] if – with an effort of which [you are] always capable – it is not possible to anticipate [the attack by] even a few days.'[34] Angelo Del Boca reckons that Badoglio even went so far as to use a 'mocking tone' when he addressed Graziani as 'my old comrade in arms' in a further telegram along the same lines. The reply was icy: 'I thank your excellency for the cordial comradely appeal addressed to me, but ... allow me to state that it is not the Abyssinian military which prevent me from taking steps, but the logistics which are not yet at such a point to allow me to do so before the 15 [April].'[35] Mussolini adopted a similarly condescending attitude on the very eve of the offensive: 'Today 14 [April] our advance guard is about to reach Dessie. From an international perspective, the situation is also accelerating its pace. Dear Graziani [Caro Graziani], it is necessary not to delay any longer. I await the announcement of the start of the march on Harar.'[36]

Although it is easy to imagine him practically exploding with indignation, Graziani did not immediately reply. In the light of such a message, his determination to begin the offensive on 15 April, no matter what, becomes comprehensible. He therefore stood his ground when some of his subordinate officers, particularly Brigadier General Guglielmo Nasi heading the Libyan Division, argued that the atrocious weather combined with the logistical difficulties, pointed to a delay.[37] Accordingly, the columns into which the invasion force was divided began operations on the morning of 15 April, despite a violent storm grounding most of the air force.

The left column, which would advance from Danan under Brigadier General Guglielmo Nasi, was based around the Libyan Division reinforced with two tank companies, an artillery group, and engineer and other support units. The column also included a contingent of *dubats* commanded by a Blackshirt, Consul-General Franco Navarra-Viggiani. This sub-group was dubbed 'Navarra's fast column' (*Colonna Celere Navarra*). In addition, there were several irregular *bande* attached.

The central column at Kebri Dehar, commanded by Brigadier General Luigi Frusci, was composed of *dubats* supported by tanks and armoured cars, along with three artillery groups plus engineer and flamethrower detachments.

Striking from Geregube, the right column came under the command of a Blackshirt, Lieutenant General Augusto Agostini, commandant general of the Forestry Militia. Unsurprisingly then, the Forestry Militia Cohort formed a part of his command, as did the *Carabinieri*, along with contingents of *dubats* and support units.[38]

The aerial component, comprising about fifty aircraft flying from bases at Gorahai and Danan, was tasked primarily with supporting the advance tactically and attacking Ethiopian rear areas as required. In order to avoid friendly-fire incidents, the ground troops had been provided with large recognition sheets, which were to be laid out whenever necessary. Further sheets were provided for units to indicate enemy positions to aircraft. The air force was also assigned a role

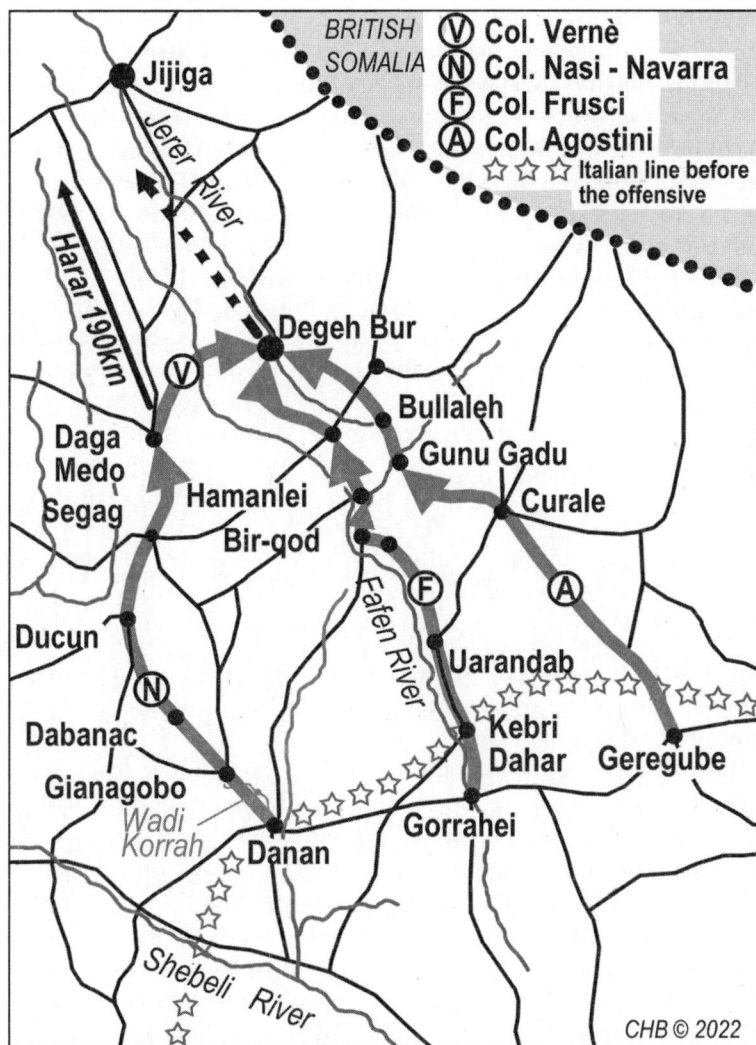

The Italian advance in three columns. (© *Charles Blackwood*)

in maintaining direct contact between Graziani's HQ at Beledweyne in Somalia and the advancing columns.[39]

Each of the columns had just over 500 lorries[40] for carrying troops and supplies, whilst 47 Caterpillar tractors towing 95 trailers moved behind them. A back-up system, using the remaining tracked prime-movers and trailers, was based at Gorahai ready to support the advance as necessary.[41] The operational plan involved the columns advancing from Danan, Kebri Dehar and Geregube, from left to right respectively, with the ultimate intention of converging at Degeh Bur, the vital focal point of the Ethiopian defence.

First contact with the enemy was made by the left column after it had advanced some 35–40km on the western bank of what one participant called 'the great furrow of the Wadi Korrah' and was approaching Gianagobo. Just south of there, where the wadi briefly bent more or less east–west before returning to its northwesterly course towards Dabanac, there was an Ethiopian force estimated at some 10,000–12,000 strong.[42] The eastern and, where it detoured, northern banks of the normally dry watercourse were pocked with natural caves surrounded by dense vegetation which had been cleverly utilised by the Ethiopian troops.[43] Thus, at 09:30 hours the invaders found themselves being subjected to large volumes of accurate fire whilst, because the wadi was in full spate from the incessant rain, being unable to get across and attack the enemy positions from flank or rear.[44]

There followed what Rochat reckoned to be 'the only real battle of the campaign', with, in a reversal of the situation that had obtained at Maychew and elsewhere, the Italians having to deal with strongly defended positions.[45] Even when the weather cleared enough for the air force to fly some missions, only five Caproni Ca.111 bombers, carrying about 600–800kg of ordnance apiece, managed to get airborne on 15 April. Three of them dropped 1.8 tonnes of high explosive and fragmentation bombs on the defences in the wadi, but the Ethiopians remained protected in their caves and continued to resist.[46]

The fighting continued much in the same vein throughout the following day, displaying similar characteristics to, and evoking memories of, the trench warfare of the First World War Battles of the Isonzo, according to Longo.[47] Hyperbole no doubt, but it was certainly the case that the Ethiopians could not be dislodged. In fact, Nasi was compelled to radio HQ and ask for reinforcements to be sent north along the far bank of the wadi, and thus to be in a position to attack the enemy from the rear. Graziani agreed, and a truck-mounted column of 2,000 *dubats*, with artillery and armoured cars in support, was withdrawn from Frusci's command and, under the command of Lieutenant General Vittorio Verne, the deputy commander of the 6th Blackshirt 'Tevere' Division, redeployed at Danan.[48]

The air force was able to operate in strength on 16 and 17 April. Over that period around 8 tonnes of high explosive and fragmentation bombs were dropped in the area occupied by the enemy, who were also treated to heavy aerial machine-gunning.[49] Forced to fly low in order to deliver their attacks, the aircraft came within range of defensive fire, which caused some casualties. One pilot hit and injured was the previously quoted Federigo Valli. The May 1936 edition of his journal recorded that: 'During the battle of Gianagobo our director, with an observer aboard a Ro.1, was hit by an explosive bullet. We fervently hope that he makes a complete recovery.'[50]

Although the Ethiopian force successfully resisted for three days all Italian efforts to dislodge and defeat them, given the Italians' massive superiority in terms of firepower, and the fact that the defenders could be neither easily reinforced nor supplied, there could only be one ending. It came on the afternoon of 17 April after the Libyan Division managed to finally cross the Wadi Korrah at

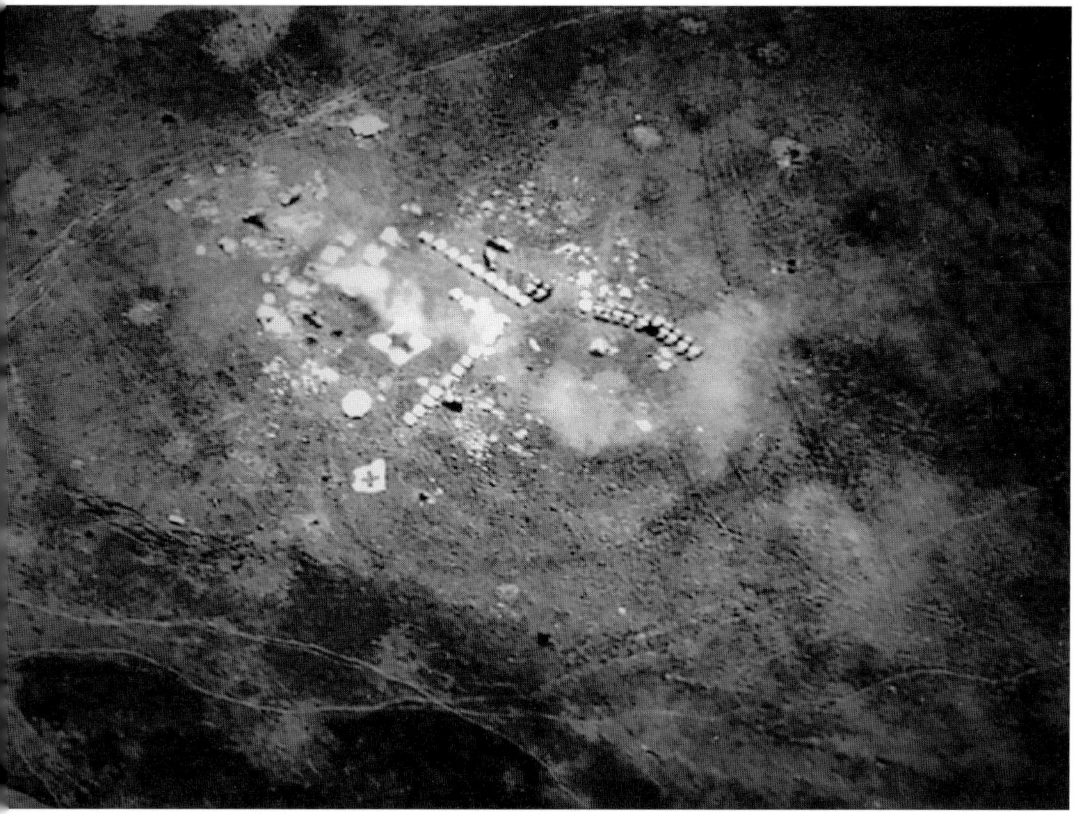

The British Red Cross Field Hospital near Korem, organised under the auspices of the *British Ambulance Service in Ethiopia* (BASE), under attack on 4 March 1936. (*Author's Collection*)

Gorrahei, on the southern front, under aerial bombardment in early October 1935. (*Author's Collection*)

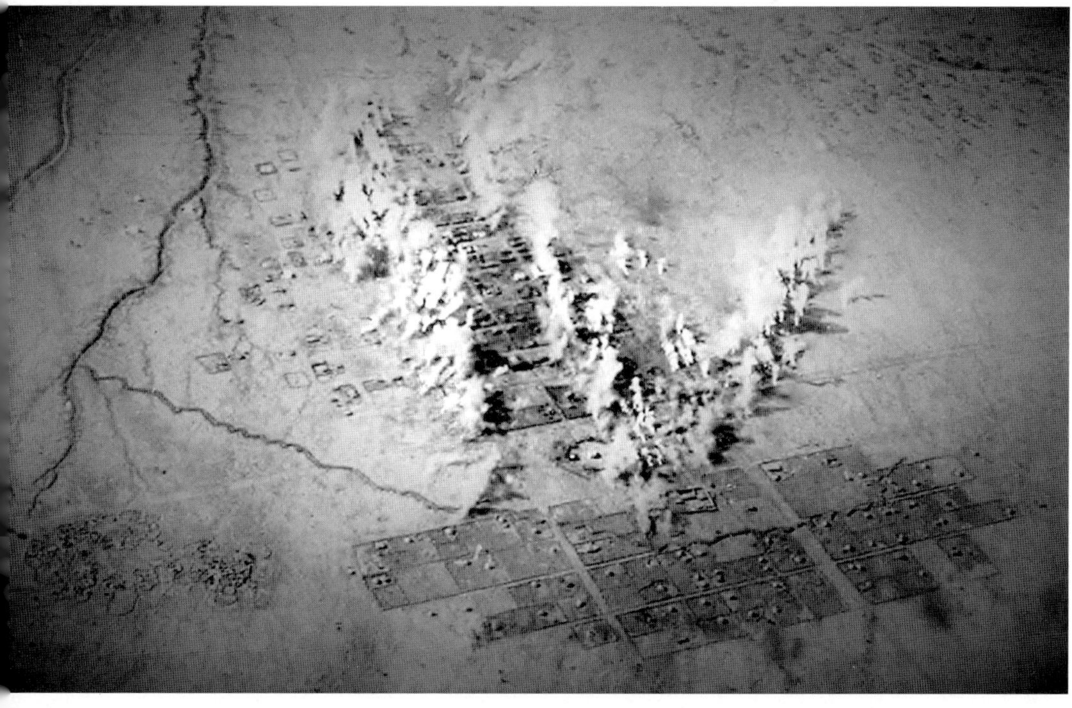

The L3/35 (or Carro Veloce CV-35) light tank (or tankette, as such vehicles were sometimes dubbed). Armed with twin machine guns and crewed by two men, they were used extensively by the Italians, although they proved vulnerable unless properly supported. (*Author's Collection*)

Infantry using a Fiat-Revelli Modello 1914 medium machine gun. (*Author's Collection*)

Strafing. Sergeant Bacio Gallini, aircraft machine-gunner. Gallini was killed during the Ethiopian campaign. (*Alessandro Pavolini*).

Lorry-mounted *dubats* in the Ogaden. (*Author's Collection*)

A postcard depicting mountain guns deployed by Alpine troops and transported by pack animals.
(*Author's Collection*)

... and an African version.
(*Author's Collection*)

A Pavesi P4 towing what appears to be a *Cannone da 105/28*. (*Author's Collection*)

The Pavesi artillery tractor was developed from an agricultural vehicle. With four-wheel drive and articulated steering, it proved highly successful. (*Author's Collection*)

A Caterpillar train. Bypassing the regular chain of command, but with the consent of Mussolini and using Colonial Ministry funds, Graziani purchased Caterpillar tractors (crawlers) and tracked trailers directly from the United States. (*Author's Collection*)

Each unit, consisting of one tractor and two (sometimes three) trailers, could transport a 20-tonne load at a maximum speed of around 14kph (8mph). (*Author's Collection*)

Described by one officer as *mastodontici autotreni* (mammoth road trains), the idea proved itself in practice in campaigning across the Ogaden, forming what were, in effect, mobile warehouses. (*Author's Collection*)

Fascist propaganda: 'The Fascist Revolution is not only Italy's privilege and effort, but the watchword and hope of the world.' Mussolini's message for the 11th Anniversary of the Revolution, 28 October 1933, on the dawn of the year XII. (*Author's Collection*)

Fascist propaganda: A highly stylised rendition by Achille Beltrame of Blackshirts of the '28 October' Division defending the Uarieu (Worsege) Pass between 21 and 24 January 1936. (*Author's Collection*)

Fascist propaganda: Ethiopian troops literally taking shelter under the Red Cross during the bombing of the British Field Hospital on 4 March 1936. (*Author's Collection*)

Fascist propaganda: Members of the '23 March' Blackshirt Division planting the flag atop Amba Aradam on 19 February 1936 after, under the leadership of Prince Filiberto of Savoy, courageously defeating the enemy entrenched there. (*Author's Collection*)

Prince Filiberto of Savoy, Duke of Genoa and Duke of Pistoia (*left*). Contrary to propaganda claims, the famous battle led by him for the conquest of Amba Aradam was never fought. However, in view of an imminent visit by Fascist hierarchs and royalty, forts and trenches were constructed to impress guests. (*Author's Collection*)

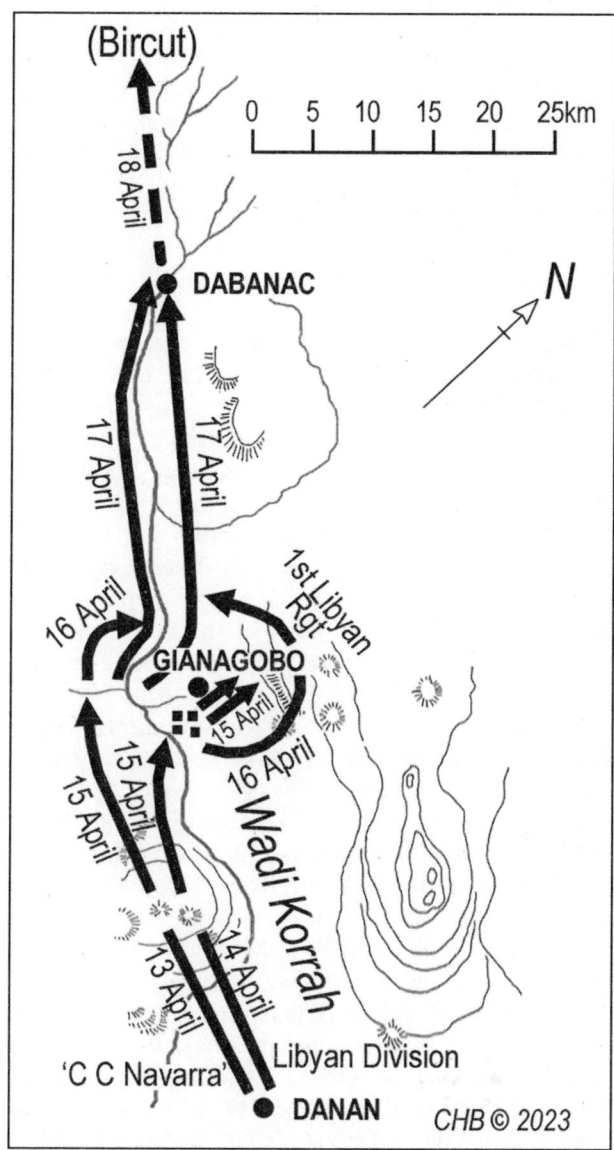

The Battle of Gianagobo. (© *Charles Blackwood*)

Dabanac and began directly attacking their opponents. Although they attempted counter-attacks, the only real option for the Ethiopians now was to leave their positions and escape into the dense bush. General Nasi arrived at Dabanac shortly after 17:00 hours and, acting on information from the air force that the enemy were retreating, ordered a pursuit. Verne's column had not been required and the Battle of Gianagobo was over.[51]

Graziani, who had moved his HQ to Kebri Dehar, reported on the clash to Mussolini and Badoglio on the same day. He noted the persistence of the enemy's resistance, and stated that they had to be 'flushed out' of their caves using 'tanks, flamethrowers and artillery'. He also reported that the enemy casualties were very high, but that there were 'few prisoners, according to the custom of the Libyan troops'.[52] Published Italian estimates claim that over 3,000 Ethiopians perished during the battle, whilst many others were lost during the retreat, and there were around 500 prisoners. Casualties on the attacking side, dead and wounded, were much fewer: 20 officers, a non-commissioned officer, 10 Italian soldiers and 707 Libyan and Somali troops.[53]

The action at Gianagobo and the Wadi Korrah wasn't, though, the end of the confrontation between the opposing forces. The bad weather had partially immobilised, and certainly slowed, the motorised element of Nasi's column so he sent the Libyan Division north to Bircot on foot. By way of a 32km forced march, it arrived at an oasis, encompassing several wells, some 12km from the village on 18 April. Unbeknown to the Italians, their march had been paralleled by contingents of Ethiopians retreating from Gianagobo, who were also headed for the wells. At first light on 19 April these contingents attacked, and a violent and disorganised mêlée ensued. Once again, however, superior Italian firepower was brought into play via the twenty guns of the 2nd Camel Artillery Group (*2° Gruppo Artiglieria Cammellata*) that had accompanied the division.[54] There was also aerial support in the shape of five R0.37 aircraft, which flew in rotation above the battlefield bombing and strafing enemy concentrations as they saw them or were directed by the ground troops.[55] Verne's column, having not been required at Gianagobo, had been redirected northwards towards Segag and was too far away to assist quickly. Nasi then called for assistance from Navarra's so-called fast column, which was about 20km south at Dabanac. This, though, was unable to move fast enough, leaving the Libyan Division to rely on its own resources. Fortunately for them, but not so for their opponents, these proved sufficient. The Ethiopians withdrew at about noon.[56] Italian casualties, dead and wounded, amounted to 189 in total, whilst those suffered by their attackers are unknown.[57]

Neither of the other two columns encountered initial resistance as they advanced. Frusci, however, moved only two battalions forward from Kebri Dahar to Uarandab, a distance of some 45km. This circumspect approach was prompted by the need to await the outcome of the struggle at Gianagobo, and was abandoned on 17 April when Graziani's HQ ordered the advance to resume in strength. Frusci's immediate target now was Hamanlei, some 70km to the north on the Fafen river, which he was expected to take on 22 April. Moving forward overnight in heavy rain, the column had covered over half the distance, some 45km over rough terrain, by the end of the next day without encountering opposition.

Agostini's column on the right was likewise restricted, sending only patrols forward on 16–17 April. These got as far north as Curale, over 100km distant from their start point as the crow flies, without discovering any enemy presence.

Again, and following Nasi's victory at the Battle of Gianagobo, the column moved forward on 17 April with the immediate goal being to reach Gunu Gadu on 22 April.[58]

The situation by 20 April was as follows. On the left, Nasi's column had advanced until it was just south of Ducun, whilst the Verne sub-column was further north at Segag. The central column under Frusci had reached Shekosh, about 85km north of its starting point in a straight line and over 100km by what passed for a road. By way of bringing Frusci's numbers back up following the detachment of the Verne group, Graziani sent him two battalions of Blackshirts from the 'Tevere' Division, one being composed of university students.[59] The right-hand column, following in the wake of its advance guard, was at Curale.[60]

The left and centre columns in particular had, and continued to have, great difficulties owing to the weather, which turned much of the ground to mud and caused multitudinous watercourses and wadis to become rushing torrents. This made rapid vehicular advances virtually impossible until the engineers could improve the roads and construct bridges over the worst of the watery obstacles. Such structures had, in some instances, to be heavy duty in order that the Caterpillar trains could cross; by 19 April four such bridges, each capable of bearing 27 tonnes, had been built for use by the central column alone. An officer with the Libyan Division, Major (later Lieutenant Colonel) Raffaello Micaletti, reported favourably on the Caterpillars crawlers and their trailers, which he dubbed *mastodontici autotreni*:

> as a reinforcement to its organic automotive section [the column] had mammoth road trains, suitable for covering all terrains, with an average speed no higher than that of man. These trains were providential because they relieved several distressing situations and even formed mobile warehouses, for the whole column, during the operations.[61]

It was sometimes found that the banks of watercourses were incapable of supporting bridges that would take the weight of a Caterpillar train. This necessitated detours to sites where that wasn't the case, which slowed the advance and consumed further resources.

Conversely, the heavy rain proved something of a bonus to Agostini's column on the right. The portion of the Ogaden it had to traverse contained fewer wadis and the like than was the case further west, so the going along a pre-existing, albeit overgrown, track was easier. A corollary to fewer watercourses was, of course, less water – or none at all. This could have meant supplying the column from bases further back in Somalia: a round trip for road-tankers of several hundred kilometres. That most of the personnel involved in the advance were Italian rather than, as was the case with the other columns, Arab or Somali could have exacerbated problems with any such shortage, as Europeans were far less accustomed to such privation. However, the matter was never put to the test, and with the aid of purifiers, filters and pumps the engineers were able to keep the column well supplied with water.

The air force meanwhile had been hammering known Ethiopian positions with high explosives and gas; on 20 April over 9 tonnes of *iprite* was delivered via C.500.T bombs on positions at Hamanlei.[62] The latter place, like Bir-qod some 10km to the south, was a bottleneck that lay directly in the path of the centre column.[63] Similarly, aerial attacks on locations at Gunu Gadu and Bullaleh, through which Agostini's column had to pass, were also mounted, whilst comparable positions pertaining to Nasi's advance, at Ducun and Dagamedo, received similar treatment. More generally, Ca.133 bombers were utilised for offensive reconnaissance sweeps which involved them in attacking enemy lorries, caravans and troop concentrations wherever they found them. Single-engine Ro.1 and Ro.37 biplanes were also utilised for the same role, dropping fragmentation bombs and machine-gunning targets of opportunity.[64]

All three columns resumed their advance on 23 April, with a significant success quickly gained on the left when General Vittorio Verne's lorry-borne contingent moved the 50km or so from Segag to Daga Medo to find it unoccupied by enemy forces. The position was considered important as Italian possession of it threatened the Ethiopian right flank, and this was recognised the next day when attempts to expel the occupiers began in the early morning. These were ultimately unsuccessful, but did cause a delay in the onward drive to Degeh Bur, where the Italian plan called for the three columns to converge.[65]

Matters were not proceeding according to plan with the centre column either, as it ran into difficulties attempting to break through enemy positions at the Bir-qod and Hamanlei bottleneck on 24 April. As had occurred at Gianagobo and the Wadi Korrah, the Italian advance was frustrated by a well armed and well concealed enemy force reckoned to be some 5,000-strong, although Steer states only half that number.[66] Artillery fire proved unable to dislodge them and despite significant aerial intervention, with twenty-four bombers and fifteen lighter aircraft dropping a total of 12 tonnes of ordnance, the Ethiopians continued to resist. They did so successfully, and the advance became uncoordinated, descending into numerous small-scale encounters.

Having thrown in his reserve without success, Frusci telegraphed Graziani at 16:38 hours to ask for help, requesting that he be reinforced with units taken from the right-hand column: 'Positions reached are held, despite a lively enemy reaction and activity that suggests a counterattack. Significant enemy forces. Our losses so far have been about fifteen officers and about 200 indigenous troops. I consider a contribution from Agostini to be indispensable.' The commander-in-chief was having none of it, brusquely dismissing Frusci's concerns and with them the request for assistance: 'I judge the situation ... normal, nor are the number of losses exceptional. The forces available ... supplemented by the air force, are sufficient to withstand any counterattack and above all to progress an advance at the right moment.'[67]

The 'right moment' was adjudged to be the next morning when a coordinated infantry assault, preceded by a brief but intense artillery barrage, was launched on the Ethiopian positions. Spearheading this attack were units of Arab-Somali soldiers, dubbed *coraggiatori* by the Italians. These 'encouragers' were armed only with sabres and hand grenades and, according to one correspondent, they 'went off like rockets'.[68]

What the attackers didn't know was that Ras Nasibu had finally taken the advice of his advisers to concentrate further back on prepared defensive positions, and had therefore ordered an overnight withdrawal. The assault therefore went in against 'tenacious and courageous' rear-guards only.[69] There was still some fierce close-quarter fighting, but against a hugely reduced enemy the attackers prevailed and began clearing the Ethiopian positions. This action included the use of flamethrowers of which, according to Frusci's later account, the Ethiopians had an 'insane terror' (*terrore folle*) believing them 'atrocious instruments of war'.[70]

The Battle of Birgot, as it was named by the victors, saw around a thousand Ethiopians killed, at least according to Italian estimates, and an unknown number wounded. Casualties on the other side included ten dead officers, with eleven wounded, whilst one Italian soldier had perished and fourteen suffered wounds. Most of the fighting had, of course, been undertaken by *dubats*, whose casualties amounted to 132 dead and 504 wounded, mostly from one battalion which suffered 40 per cent losses.[71] As well as capturing a fairly small quantity of Ethiopian weapons and ammunition, the Italians also repossessed the three tanks that had been knocked out on 11 November 1935, and recovered the machine gun removed from Minniti and Zannoni's aircraft, downed on 26 December 1935.[72]

Graziani's refusal to countenance reinforcing Frusci by transferring troops from Agostini's column, difficult in any event due to poor east–west communications, was likely influenced by the fact that the latter was engaged in a fight of his own on 24 April. Having advanced unopposed to a position some 8km south of Gunu Gadu the previous day, the column moved at dawn on 24 April with contingents of *dubats* leading the way. Intelligence indicated that they were facing around 1,000–1,500 Ethiopians dug in on the banks of the Jerer river, then in flood, around 2km east of the town. It proved impossible to confirm this by direct observation owing to the dense vegetation. Agostini's plan involved circumventing these defensive positions in an enveloping movement, with two of the *Carabinieri* 'bands' forming the northern arm, whilst the *dubats* attacked to the south. The remaining two *Carabinieri* units were tasked with preventing any attempt by the enemy to move reinforcements south from Bullaleh or east from Hamanlei, whilst the Forestry Militia cohort formed the reserve.[73]

The attack began at about 07:30 hours with artillery support until at 08:00 hours it halted temporarily whilst the air force bombed Ethiopian positions along the river. As an officer with the *dubats* described it:

> a real curtain of airplane bombs and artillery grenades stops us. From [08:00–08:30] we carry out our bombardment of destruction [...] We are all on the ground to prevent splinters from hitting us. The nine bombers, in a slow deadly carousel, circle around in the sky, depositing their load.

Finally, the half hour of anguished waiting is over and we can move forward again ...[74]

Unfortunately for the attackers, the holes and caves in the river bank, which had been camouflaged with vegetation, formed the real line of resistance and on these the bombardment had little or no effect. Graziani was later to write that the techniques of concealment utilised by the Ethiopians, and their skilful choice and use of these positions, were evidence of the influence of foreign military advisers.[75] Whether that was the case or not, the defenders were certainly tenacious. They continued to resist throughout 24 April, although began to withdraw under cover of darkness. The fighting resumed on the morning of 25 April with Agostini forced to throw in his reserves. He also, in attempts to neutralise an enemy 'holed up in formidable caves',[76] deployed artillery in a direct fire role 'stationed at minimum distances, often not exceeding 50 metres'.[77] Fire was also used: 'Petrol cans continually arrive and are poured on the caves. Then, with hand grenades, this is set alight and the caves become gigantic torches.'[78] Such tactics were brutal but effective, and by the late afternoon of 25 April the Battle of Gunu Gadu was over.

The outcome of these battles was significant. The scholar-soldier Brigadier General Carlo Fettarappa Sandri judged that 'the bitter battle of Gianagobo' shattered 'the right hand of Wehib Pasha's *petite Verdun*', whilst the other battles brought down both the centre and the 'left pillar of the powerful enemy defensive system'.[79]

Graziani reported that losses inflicted on the enemy were estimated at over 600 dead and wounded and that 'no Abyssinian has surrendered. The prisoners were all wounded.'[80] Accounts of the attackers' casualties vary according to source. Longo states these amounted to twelve dead (all officers) and nineteen wounded Italians, whilst the *dubats* sustained over 600 dead and wounded.[81] He urges caution, however, noting that Major Rocco Vadala of the *Carabinieri* claimed in his history of the battle that twenty-two of his colleagues had perished.[82]

Although the plan was slightly behind schedule, Graziani's campaign had achieved much in ten days, particularly, as he put it, against 'an enemy who resists fiercely everywhere, and is favoured by the terrain and by time ...'[83] Although he celebrated the contribution of the air force, and emphasised the fighting capabilities of the forces under his command, writing for example of how 'the *Carabinieri* ... at Gunu Gadu had their baptism of fire and wrote a new page of historical glory',[84] the campaign had, of course, been, as all successful campaigns have to be, founded on logistics. Within an operational area about 100km wide and 200km deep there were a total of 38,000 men, 22,400 *dubats* and *ascari* plus 15,600 Italians, as well as 4,800 pack animals. The men had to be kept supplied with ammunition and ordnance, and all had to be fed and watered, although, as noted, the latter problem was eased by the wet weather. The soldiers' rations alone had involved a daily forward movement of 50 tonnes of food of various kinds, transported in lorries. Fuel for these, as well as for the vehicles carrying most of the troops, also had to be provided. Following closely behind the advance were the Caterpillar trains, hauling, amongst other essentials, a further 180 tonnes of food corresponding to 172,000 individual rations. In addition to all that, the sick, injured and wounded had to be evacuated south.[85] One officer who participated dubbed these underpinnings, which as noted involved over 1,500 lorries, 'totalitarian motorisation': 'On the Somali front, our imperial conquest was above all a war of means: victory in the strategic field had to go hand in hand with victory in the logistics field. In fact, the extension of the front required the totalitarian motorisation of the fighting units ...'[86]

Despite these successes, Graziani felt that his efforts were under-appreciated and that the plaudits were all going to the northern front and Badoglio. His message of 25 April reflected this perception: 'Please give more prominence to the bitter and very hard battles that we have been fighting here for ten days ... Such greater prominence, as well as highlighting our titanic effort which will help us abroad, will also serve to keep up the morale of my subordinates because they make the comparison.'[87]

Graziani's resentment, which is surely not too strong a term, towards both Badoglio and the propaganda around his achievements would shortly be greatly exacerbated. For on the same day that the 'bitter and very hard battles' at Bir-qod and Gunu Gadu began, the commander-in-chief launched the manoeuvre that he calculated would completely terminate the war and, incidentally, totally eclipse anything that might happen elsewhere.

Chapter Sixteen

'The March of the Iron Will'

'Rome, May 7, 1936-XIV – His Majesty the King awarded the Duce the insignia of Knight of the Grand Cross of the Military Order of Savoy. The decree has the following wording: 'As Minister of the Armed Forces, he prepared, led and won the greatest colonial war in history, a war that he, head of the King's government, sensed and wanted for the prestige, the life, and the greatness of the fascist homeland.'[1]

* * *

Following the occupation of Dessie on 15 April, Badoglio had thrown all available resources, including medical personnel if his own account is to be believed, into creating or improving the road between Amba Alagi and Korem.[2] Only when this 'missing link' in communications was rectified could his plan for a massive motorised advance on Addis Ababa be put into action. As previously mentioned, on 8 March the commander-in-chief had tasked his logistics chief, General Dall'Ora, with assembling a thousand lorries at Makalle in preparation for this. Subsequently, on 6 April this order had been updated: Dall'Ora now had to collect 1,300 vehicles. Further, these had to be ready to move between 23 and 25 April as Badoglio intended to occupy the enemy capital by early May at the latest. Subsequent additions saw the number of vehicles rise to 1,725 of various types and capabilities; in other words, a heterogenous collection varying from heavy lorries to light vans and cars with just about everything in between. The drivers, too, were a mixed bunch, with a large civilian component.[3] Moving such a diverse motorised mass over nearly 400km, across rivers and over mountain roads in the bad weather the region was then suffering, would be no easy task even if it went totally unopposed militarily. Badoglio, though, discounted the potential for enemy resistance:

> On 23 April, I personally took command of our troops who were to occupy the Ethiopian capital. I thought it opportune to organize the expedition to Addis Ababa with considerable strength, although unanimous news indicated the complete collapse of the Empire, the exhaustion of its capacity for resistance and our peaceful march for the occupation of the city.[4]

Badoglio had reason for this confidence and, as noted in the last chapter, had pressed Graziani hard to move north across the Ogaden to impede any redeployment of Ethiopian forces from that area. He also, sensibly, hedged his bets in the north. This was achieved by organising the expedition into three columns, only one of which was actually motorised, that would approach the target along two separate routes. Their dates of departure were also staggered.

First off on 24 April was Lieutenant Colonel Mario De Meo's Special Group (*Gruppo Speciale Ten Col De Meo*) which consisted of four Eritrean battalions and a mountain artillery (*artiglieria someggiata*) contingent. This unit set off on foot along the 'Imperial Road' to Addis Ababa, a journey of some 350–400km by way of Debre Sina and Debre Birhan.

The next day Brigadier General Sebastiano Gallina left Dessie with his column (*Colonna a piedi Gen Gallina*) along an alternative and, at about 300km, slightly shorter route to the capital. Gallina's command consisted of the 1st Eritrean Brigade (*I Brigata Eritrea*) of four battalions, and two mountain artillery groups. It would march through rugged terrain via Uorra Illu–Leghedadl–Embertera along tracks completely impassable to vehicles.

The main event, as it were, began on 26 April when Major General Italo Gariboldi set the multitude of vehicles (*Colonna autocarratte Gen Gariboldi*) in motion. Forming the core of this command was Gariboldi's own 30th 'Sabauda' Infantry Division of two brigades, one Italian and one Eritrean. There were also three groups (eleven batteries) of motorised artillery, a tank squadron, a battalion from the Blackshirt '3 January' Division, and engineering units.[5] This column would follow in the wake of De Meo's Special Group but, given the poor quality of the road and the weather, was unlikely to catch up with, never mind overtake, it. Indeed, Badoglio reckoned that the Eritrean troops could march around 40km a day whilst the vehicles on the 'Imperial Road' encountered increasingly serious difficulties on what he termed a 'mediocre cart track':

> This track intended to connect the capital of the empire to one of its most important centres 400 kilometres away was without even a hint of embankment, with excessive slopes and very narrow curves, without any bridges or with bridges made with simple branches, through wide valleys, fording rivers sunken or swamped, overcoming mountains and climbing impervious passes, some of which are very difficult and at a very high altitude ...[6]

Despatching a massive convoy along a questionable road and through forbidding terrain eminently suited for defence was, despite Badoglio's confidence, risky. Mitigating this was the air force, which provided continuous support, weather permitting, via reconnaissance and patrol missions. Not only that, but it succoured the marching columns, whose operations were only made possible by air-dropped supplies. This was a technique that had taken time to perfect:

> the first large drops of food gave rise to rather serious inconveniences, such as for example the loss of a third, if not sometimes even half, of the food due to imperfect packaging by the Intendency, of inadequate manoeuvring by the airplanes, and the unfortunate location of the drop zone by the troops ... But no one, as far as we can tell today, would have imagined then that air transport in the logistic field, would have assumed the development and importance that they did in East Africa.[7]

The air force was not called upon to attack any significant enemy formations and, in fact, there was to be only one serious attempt at defending Addis Ababa by interdicting the advance. This effort was undertaken whilst the Emperor was still absent from his capital and, very basically put, without Haile Selassie's presence, and with the Italians getting ever closer, the Ethiopian government was rudderless and verging on, if not already, chaotic.[8] The denizens of Addis Ababa, particularly those of foreign extraction, were also panicking. Dr John H. Spencer, the Negus' American legal adviser, wrote that the foreign traders, mostly Armenians and Greeks, were the next to panic after the various, mainly Belgian, military advisers had fled on the Djibouti railway:

> By April 26 some 1,500 Armenians had fled to the French legation. Although there was a Greek legation in Addis Ababa, so many Greeks had demanded refuge at the British legation that Sir Sidney Barton, the minister, ordered the erection of a barbed wire enclosure for them as an additional gesture to allay their anxieties ... By this time the city was full of retreating soldiers, most looking wretched and begging for back pay. The government's response was: Ishshi naga.[9]

Despite this, an effort to 'organise the extreme defence of the capital'[10] was put in place under the auspices of Captain Viking Tamm, the Swedish officer heading the Military Academy at Holeta, which had been established in 1934 to train Ethiopian officers.[11] Tamm surveyed a possible defensive site at the Termaber Pass, just north of Debre Sina, where the Imperial Road climbed to around 3,000m above sea level along the steep flank of a mountain: the steepest gradient on the entire route from Asmara to Addis Ababa, as well as the highest point.[12] He decided that it would require more resources than could be mustered to defend it properly. He also found that the meagre manpower he did have, equivalent to perhaps two companies, was unreliable: on 27 April about 10 per cent of his command deserted and disappeared.

That the advanced guard of De Meo's Special Group was only some 25km north of the pass, at Shewa Robit, was discovered that same evening; their camp fires, being only some 1,300m above sea level, were clearly visible from Tamm's much loftier vantage point. His small command also began to attract the attention of the *Regia Aeronautica*. There was little option but to withdraw. Before the party retreated, they blew up 30m of the road carved out of the mountainside at one of the steepest hairpin bends.[13] This created a major obstacle, for although the *ascari* could bypass the gap on foot, vehicles couldn't get through. It followed that the main column came to a dead stop when its lead elements reached the area on 29 April. The destruction of the road, plus the efforts required to remedy it, received particular mention in Badoglio's account:

> On a road of this type difficult to travel even with individual vehicles, the enemy, allied to the bad weather, had practised the destruction of some

bridges at various places, a significant example being that at the Tarmaber hill.

The repair of the interruption near the Tarmaber hill alone, carried out in bad weather, with fog and with rain, caused the engineers, national and indigenous, a good thirty-six hours of intense work to rebuild a retaining wall thirty metres high, and as long likewise, and to move about a thousand cubic metres of materials. They worked in very difficult conditions clinging to a steep mountain-side, even suspended in ropes where the ground offered no support.

A single pearl can conveniently represent this among the many efforts made by all: **moving** [*commovente*].[14]

There can be little doubt that such delays greatly exasperated Badoglio himself. Several scholars have remarked on his inclination to view others, and particularly Graziani in the current context, as personal rivals. Giovanni De Luna, for example, opined that the speed of his advance on Addis Ababa was 'a subtle mockery' of his rival who was trying to enter Harar before Badoglio reached the capital.[15] Longo likewise notes that he constantly made attempts to neutralise any competition, whether real or imagined, from potential rivals.[16]

Perhaps the most egregious of these efforts came in a *Radio Nazionale* broadcast on 28 April, when the commander-in-chief was quoted as stating that the recent operations on the southern front had been merely administrative in nature.[17] Graziani responded two days later by telegraphing both Mussolini and Badoglio, telling them that his command had made 'truly titanic efforts' and asking for 'an illustrative communication about the effort they are making' rather than 'a very simplistic formula' reducing them to 'a matter of ordinary administration'. The same message updated both recipients on his current plans and operations, which had received an unexpected, and from his point of view most welcome, boost the previous day.[18]

From 26 to 28 April, whilst the three northern columns advanced on the Ethiopian capital, Graziani had reorganised and rearranged his own forces for action against Ethiopian defences running from Degeh Bur in the west, south-east through Sassabaneh, and then east to Bullaleh. Necessary preparations included constructing bridges over several waterways, with the engineers recorded as having erected a span of 45m across the Jerer river in 19 hours. The original operational plan involved all columns attacking simultaneously, though General Nasi had reported on 26 April that logistical difficulties meant that he could not concentrate the Libyan Division at Daga Medo as projected. The attack on the Ethiopian right would then have to be carried out by the motorised Verne subcolumn alone. The modified order was issued on 28 April, with the assaults on Sassabaneh and Bullaleh still scheduled for 30 April, and the subsequent pursuit pushing towards the line Daga Medo–Degeh Bur. Verne's advance on Degeh Bur, though, would be held back until such time as the situation clarified.

However, as Graziani revealed in his message to Mussolini and Badoglio quoted above, on the afternoon of 29 April a reconnaissance mission flown personally by General Ranza, the air force commander, had revealed a significant change in the situation. His report stated that the enemy were withdrawing from their positions with 'evident signs of a stampede' taking place.[19] According to Steer, whose information must have been received second hand, it was actually on 25 April that Ras Nasibu had ordered the withdrawal, his intention at that time being, as recommended by his Turkish advisers, to fall back and defend Harar.[20] In any event, and immediately upon discovering what had happened, Graziani notified his column commanders and ordered them all to move forward urgently. He was then able to tell Mussolini and Badoglio that he should have Degeh Bur in his possession that day (30 April).[21] He was proved right, and all three target locations were in Italian hands that afternoon. The advance had been unopposed except for sporadic sniping.

The penultimate day of April also saw an event of great significance in Addis Ababa. Steer, who was there, described a great stir when 'A car came down the mountain with black carabineers on either running-board ... It was the Emperor with Ras Kassa, back from the wars ... The cars drove straight to the Great Palace, where a council of Ministers was called.'[22] According to Spencer, the council decided to continue resistance from the capital and then, in the final extremity, withdraw the government to Gore, a far-distant town in south-western Ethiopia. This decision was, he wrote, 'a matter of considerable concern to me, since the results of a combat would be fore-ordained. His Majesty could well be taken hostage for blackmail purposes, should he not first succeed in committing suicide.'[23] Spencer's concerns were allayed the following day, however, when the decision was reversed. Haile Selassie and his entourage would accompany the Empress to Djibouti where, thanks to arrangements made by Sir Sidney Barton, the British Minister at Addis Ababa, preparations had been made for her and her children to be taken to safety.[24] A special train awaited them at the station and, at 23:00 hours on 1 May, according to Spencer, or at 'about' 04:00 hours on 2 May according to Steer, the Imperial party boarded it.[25] With the departure of the Negus and the disappearance of the Abyssinian government, the city descended into a chaos of looting, shooting and rioting.[26] One of those to perish was Dr John Melly of the British Red Cross, who was shot on 3 May and succumbed to his wound a few days later.[27]

Meanwhile, Graziani, still some 150km from Harar in a straight line, and somewhere around 250km away by what passed for a road, was intent on pushing on towards his ultimate target. Having moved his HQ to Degeh Bur, he issued orders for a two-pronged, motorised advance from there on 3 May despite very poor, and worsening, weather. This became so bad in fact that the majority of Nasi's command had perforce to be temporarily disregarded owing to its logistical arrangements being totally disrupted. Thus, on the left General Verne's sub-column would alone head for Farso, some 70km to the north-west, whilst Navarra-Viggiani's 'fast column' was tasked with advancing almost directly north towards Jijiga.[28] Both columns set out on the morning of 4 May, but whilst Verne managed to make progress during a break in the rain, and actually reached Farso later that day, Navarra wasn't so fortunate. Indeed, when the weather worsened again that afternoon, he found the vast majority of his lorries stranded on the wrong side of the Jerer river as it overflowed its banks.[29]

At much the same time as Navarra's 'fast column' found itself static, Haile Selassie was boarding the British cruiser HMS *Enterprise* at Djibouti. From there, he and his party would be conveyed to, firstly, Haifa in the British Mandate of Palestine, and ultimately to the United Kingdom.[30] The vessel's master, Captain Charles Morgan, upon greeting his illustrious passenger, informed him that 'as soon as he stepped over my gangway he would be as safe as the Bank of England'. This, he reported, caused the now ex-Emperor to smile.[31]

It is probably safe to say that there were few smiles at Graziani's HQ some 400km due south of Djibouti. His desire to beat, or at least match, Badoglio by occupying Harar before, or at the same time as, the northern columns entered Addis Ababa was being obviously frustrated. This was compounded by the fact that Harar was completely without any organised defence: Ras Nasibu had fled the scene when it was reported to him that a special train carrying the Emperor had passed through Dire Dawa on the way to Djibouti. Realising that the game was well and truly up, he and Wehib Pasha made sure they were on the next train. The other Turks followed as quickly as they could.[32]

That Graziani felt deeply about the matter is evidenced by a curious message he sent to both Mussolini and Badoglio on 5 May:

> The truck-mounted columns continue to be stuck at Farso and a few kilometres beyond Degeh Bur ... However, the greatest effort ... to achieve the objective [of Harar] is still under way ... If this effort were not though crowned by entry into Harar parallel to that of Addis Ababa, then the cause has to be sought elsewhere than in my will or that of my indomitable troops ... Moreover, any military critic, Italian or foreign, will have to admit that Harar has already been conquered by Somali troops, even if due to *force majeure* they could not proceed beyond Degeh Bur. Nor can it be denied that the absolute victory gained in the Ogaden, and the destruction of Ras Nasibu's army, hastened the flight of the Negus. At any rate my hopes of still reaching Harar, albeit with some delay ... have not yet completely failed and therefore I believe that it is to be considered until the very last moment as an objective to be reached by the Somali troops.[33]

Longo is of the opinion that this was an effort at containing or countering what he terms *badogliano*: 'unnecessary and exhibitionist triumphalism'.[34] Graziani, in particular, as well as Italy and indeed the world more generally, would have to put up with a good deal of *badogliano* over the next few days and weeks, for on the evening of 2 May the lead elements of Brigadier General Sebastiano Gallina's I Eritrean Brigade had come within sight of Addis Ababa. Gallina could undoubtedly have entered the city the following day (and quelled the rioting in doing so) but he was ordered to hold fast outside; it was unthinkable that any forces but those under Badoglio's direct command would enter the capital first.[35] The commander-in-chief reported on 4 May that his advance guard was within 30km of the city, and his main force only 40km behind them. 'Tomorrow,' he informed Mussolini, 'I plan to mass myself a few kilometres outside, in order to set up the columns for the occupation of the various city quarters.'[36]

Badoglio had intended to make a triumphal entry into Addis Ababa on horseback and several mounts, for him and other senior officers, were trucked all the way from Dessie for the purpose. Heavy rain put paid to that idea, however, so instead he rode in a car escorted by motorcyclists, whilst several Ro.37 aircraft circled above.[37]

Dr Spencer had taken refuge in the British Legation which, guarded by a detachment of Sikhs, was safe from the mob. He noted that whilst the British pretty much ignored the Italians, the French gave Badoglio and his staff a 'warm welcome, the secretary of the legation receiving them in full dress uniform'.[38] Steer was at the Legation too, from where he observed the column enter the capital from 16:00 hours onwards:

> Sixteen hundred lorries rolled by, packed with troops. All that afternoon and all night the enormous procession thundered by the gates of the British Legation into Addis Ababa. It was the largest mechanised column thrown out in history... At the Italian Legation... Marshal Badoglio raised again the flag of Italy and saluted King and Duce.[39]

Badoglio's message to *Il Duce*, and also, perhaps tellingly, to Graziani, was sent at 16:15 hours. It was short and to the point: 'Today, 5 May, at 4 pm I entered Addis Ababa at the head of the victorious troops.'[40]

That evening, *Il Duce* addressed a hastily summoned crowd estimated to be 400,000-strong from 'Mussolini's balcony' overlooking the Piazza Venezia in Rome. His speech was broadcast throughout Italy, via both radio and the thousands of loudspeakers installed in the piazzas of Italy's towns and villages for such purposes.[41] To wild cheers he read out the contents of Badoglio's telegram, before proclaiming in his thunderous oratorical style:

> During the thirty centuries of its history, Italy has lived many memorable hours, but today this is certainly one of the most solemn with an announcement to the Italian people and the world that the war is over. I announce to the Italian people and to the world that peace has been restored. It is not without emotion and without pride that, after seven months of bitter hostility, I utter this great word, but it is strictly necessary that I add that it is our peace, the Roman peace which is expressed in this simple, irrevocable, definitive proposition: Ethiopia is Italian. Italian in fact, because it is occupied by our victorious armies; Italian in law, because with the gladiators of Rome, civilization triumphs over barbarity, justice over arbitrary cruelty.[42]

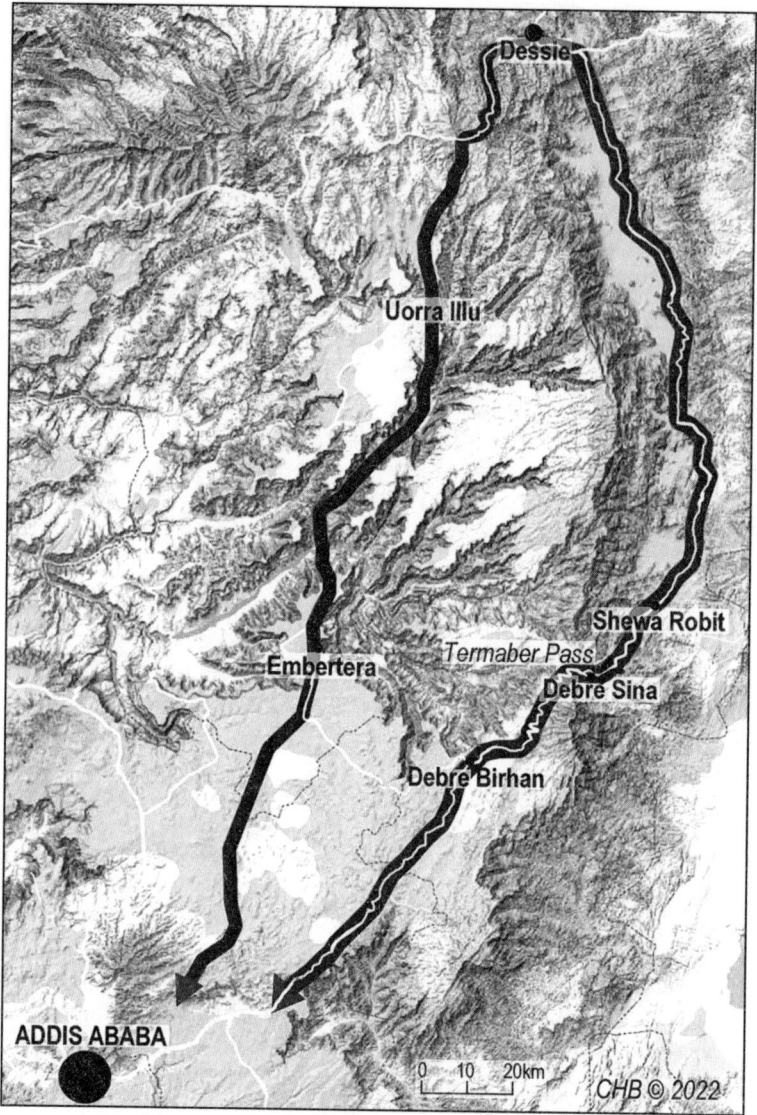

'The March of the Iron Will'. (© *Charles Blackwood*)

There was, of course, more in much the same vein. The crowd went wild with excitement: *Il Duce* had to undertake no fewer than ten curtain calls in response to their acclamation.[43] This sentiment was widespread, and 'a grateful Italy surrendered itself to the most riotous celebration in the annals of Fascism', as the American academic H. Arthur Steiner phrased it.[44] As part of the pageantry, on 7 May King Victor Emmanuel III awarded Mussolini a medal, one usually reserved for those who had accomplished heroic military deeds. The citation read: 'As Minister of the Armed Forces, he prepared, led and won the greatest colonial war in history, a war that he, head of the King's government, sensed and wanted for the prestige, the life, and the greatness of the fascist homeland.'[45]

On 9 May the newly bemedalled Mussolini proclaimed, again from the Piazza Venezia balcony, the 'Founding of the Empire' to another cheering multitude.[46] He announced that 'the fate of Ethiopia is sealed today, 9 May, the fourteenth year of the fascist era ... Italy finally has her empire. A Fascist Empire ...' He went on to state that according to law and from now on:

1. The territories and peoples that belonged to the Empire of Ethiopia are placed under the full and entire sovereignty of the Kingdom of Italy.
2. the King of Italy assumes the title of Emperor of Ethiopia for himself and for his successors.[47]

Victor Emmanuel's newly founded imperial possession would henceforth be governed by a viceroy (*vicerè d'Etiopia*), with Badoglio being proclaimed as the first such.[48] Another glittering prize that came Badoglio's way was the title of Duke of Addis Ababa, awarded on 9 June, although the proposal that the Caesarean motto *Veni, vidi, vici* should appear on his ducal escutcheon was vetoed by Mussolini.[49] Graziani, whose forces had reached Harar on 8 May and Dire Dawa on the day the empire was proclaimed, also received an important accolade, being promoted to the rank of marshal of Italy (*Maresciallo d'Italia*).[50] The newly anointed Emperor of Ethiopia – described by *Time* magazine as 'The first Roman Emperor in 1,460 years'[51] – had a further honour in mind for *Il Duce*. Or at least, according to the recollection of Rachele Guidi, Mussolini's wife. Seemingly Victor Emmanuel asked him to accept, 'for you and your descendants', the title of prince. She relates, however, that the reply had been: 'I have been and I want to remain Mussolini. The Mussolini family through the generations have always been peasants, and I am rather proud of this.'[52]

On a more fundamental level, the question of what Italy would do with respect to governing Ethiopia, and how it would do it in the political sense, had engaged the mind of at least one diplomat. The American *chargé d'affaires* in Rome, Alexander Comstock Kirk, had sent his thoughts on the matter to secretary of state Cordell Hull as early as 6 May, and in doing so raised an intriguing and not entirely academic question concerning international law generally and the League of Nations in particular: 'The theory has been advanced [that] as the League can only function at the request of a member state and as Ethiopia is no longer a state the League can drop the matter without any decision by the Council, Assembly or Secretariat.'[53]

A report in *Time* stated that 'Ethiopia was not even to be considered another Manchukuo, but an out and out Italian colony', and reported that shortly after the occupation:

one of Marshal Badoglio's most dapper staff officers[,] Captain Adolfo Alessandri, dug his Sunday inspection breeches and best white gloves from the bottom of his campaign trunk, [and] visited in turn every foreign legation in Addis Ababa. Clicking his heels he explained politely that each envoy would enjoy 'every diplomatic privilege until the time of your departure'.[54]

In fact, however the politics of it might play out, some of the rudiments of Italian rule were established very early on. Indeed, upon entering Addis Ababa, Badoglio had immediately instituted the death penalty for two crimes: participation in the looting which had gone on since the flight of the Negus, and being discovered in possession of arms. Steer records that eighty-five Ethiopians were tried by a summary court and executed, but that the *Carabinieri* who had the job of policing the city didn't bother with such niceties. 'If things that looked as if they were not his own were found in a tucul, the owner was shot there and then by the search party. French official inquirers calculated that at least fifteen hundred were killed in this way.'[55]

Steer, however, along with several other foreign journalists suspected of 'anti-Italian propaganda and espionage', were expelled from what had become the Viceroyalty of Ethiopia (*Vicereame d'Etiopia*) on 14 May. There was no reason given on the actual order, however: 'I inform you that you have been expelled from all the territory of the Viceroyalty of Ethiopia. You and your family will therefore leave Addis Ababa next Saturday morning, May 16, on the train to Djibouti.'[56] His 'family' consisted of Margarita Herrero, correspondent of the Paris newspaper *Le Journal*, and likewise considered hostile to Italy. They had married at the British Legation on 4 May[57] where, according to one account, 'They spent their honeymoon behind the barbed-wire defences of the legation, awaiting, with some trepidation, the arrival of the Italians.'[58]

Another pair of matrimonially linked war correspondents, the Americans Reynolds and Eleanor Packard, had arrived with Badoglio's column and, as such, were considered non-threatening. After three days under canvas, they were put up at the Greek-owned Imperial Hotel where they noted: 'A number of Blackshirt politicians, including Ciano who had been playing at war, were also lodged ... They came by airplane and stayed only a few days, during which they carefully had themselves photographed on the abandoned throne of the Negus. It was a milestone for them in their Fascist careers.'[59]

Fascists, both Italian and otherwise, were, of course, exultant at the rapid conquest of Ethiopia. But it was Badoglio, a non-Fascist[60] but now a national hero, who coined the most popular phrase used to describe his final advance. Being suitably bombastic and mock-heroic, it was enthusiastically taken up by the Fascist propaganda machine. It was, he affirmed with more than a touch of *badogliano*, a march that would go down in history as 'The March of the Iron Will'.[61]

Chapter Seventeen

'a policy of terror and extermination'

I once again authorise Your Excellency to initiate and systematically carry out a policy of terror and extermination against rebels and accomplice populations. This plague will not be cured in good time without applying the law of tenfold retaliation.[1]

* * *

The Italo-Ethiopian War 1935–1936 was, without question, Mussolini's war. As the citation on the medal awarded him by the King stated: 'As Minister of the Armed Forces, he prepared, led and won the greatest colonial war in history, a war that he, head of the King's government, sensed and wanted for the prestige, the life, and the greatness of the fascist homeland.'[2] Therefore the outcome, considered solely from the immediate political and military point of view, constituted a great personal triumph and vindication. He had confounded his enemies and critics, both domestic and international, and delighted his admirers. Indeed, according to that 'full-blooded' British fascist J.F.C. Fuller: 'He had conquered Abyssinia; but in fact he had done far more than that ... by defying the League of Nations he had defeated the philosophy and the politics of fifty nations.'[3]

This had been achieved in a short time, between 5 October 1935 and 5 May 1936, and in purely military terms at a relatively modest cost. Although exact figures are elusive, the most reliable estimates reckon that 3,981 Italians and about 4,500 African soldiers died during the campaign of various causes, but mostly in combat.[4] This represented about 2 per cent of the total number of personnel – just short of 500,000 officers and men – that were in the theatre of war in May 1936. The scale of materiel supplied to the ground forces was vast: 102,582 pack animals, 18,932 vehicles, 1,542 guns, 492 tanks and armoured cars, 513,276 rifles, 14,570 machine guns, 850 million rounds for small arms and machine guns, and 4,197,936 artillery rounds of various calibres.[5]

If Italy's military costs were moderate, the very opposite was the case financially. Indeed, one fairly recent study concludes that the cost of the war in Ethiopia, and the subsequent pacification and colonisation efforts, proved 'almost unsustainable for Italy'.[6] Although difficult to quantify, the figure arrived at by Angelo Del Boca is generally accepted. He calculated that the 'African adventure' had the 'astronomical cost' of 40 billion lire, which was in the region of 2 billion US dollars at the exchange rate then pertaining.[7] To quote Clark: 'By 1937–8 about

12.5 per cent of the total state budget was being spent in East Africa alone, and the total national debt rose by almost 70 per cent in five years. Ethiopia bled Italy dry, just when all the other powers were rearming.'[8] Indeed so, and, according to Lawrence Pratt, Anthony Eden was wont to remark that possession of Ethiopia 'was the greatest sanction of all'.[9] It was this outpouring of treasure that made the conflict, as Rochat has argued, a modern war in which, on the Italian side, all the power of an industrialized state was brought to bear: 'the only war in our recent history fought with a truly "American" breadth of means'.[10]

This theme was certainly applicable in terms of aviation. By May 1936 the *Regia Aeronautica* had 390 aircraft in the theatre, and between October 1935 and that date had carried out 6,852 sorties totalling 38,418 flight-hours. During these missions 1,529 tonnes of explosives and 705 tonnes of materials had been airdropped, and 346,200 machine-gun rounds discharged in strafing operations. Losses had amounted to seventy-six aircraft over the period of the campaign. Of these sixty-five were due to accidents of one kind or another, whilst eight were downed and three disabled after being hit by enemy fire. In terms of personnel, twenty-six airmen had been killed and eighteen injured in action, whilst twenty-five had died in accidents. Single-engine aircraft accounted for the vast majority, 85 per cent, of accidental losses, most of them occurring on take-off and landing.[11]

Aircraft on the northern front delivered 4,413 C.500.T bombs, containing 935.5 tonnes of mustard gas, over the same period, whilst their southern counterparts dropped 452 C.500.T bombs as well as 175 of their smaller, 21kg bombs, totalling around 100 tonnes of the chemical. In addition to this, some 10.6 tonnes of phosgene were also deployed from the air in the south.[12] The historians of Italy's Chemical Warfare Service (*Servizio Chimica Militare*) wrote that the Ethiopian war represented 'an important test bed' for that branch of the armed forces, which deployed 49 officers, 81 NCOs and 1,583 enlisted men to the East African theatre. Under a Chemical Troop Command, two companies, four platoons and four squads operated with the army, as did thirty-seven flame-thrower sections. The majority, though, were divided amongst seven teams assigned to support the air force at their various bases.[13]

In the 'test bed' context, but pertaining to operational and tactical matters more generally, the campaign was closely scrutinised by commentators and military experts for future portents. Steer had been an eye-witness, and his verdict echoed a point made by a journalist and soldier who witnessed and wrote about an earlier African campaign. Then, on 2 September 1898, the young Winston Churchill had watched the 'White Flags' of the army of Khalifa Abdullah charge the British-Egyptian lines at the Battle of Omdurman. He described their fate thus: 'They were in a dense mass, 2,800 yards from the 32nd Field Battery and the gunboats. The ranges were known. It was a matter of machinery.'[14] Some thirty-eight years later, and in a far larger context, Steer was to record a judgement in much the same vein: 'Modern war is not won by courage: it goes to the man with the most powerful material. Caesars do not trick the enemy, as they did in the

Gallic wars, by stratagem or speed. They are heavier creatures: they roll over him and crush him. They are students of physics, who burn him up.'[15]

It wasn't just that the nature of the 'machinery' had changed and improved and so become more destructive, but rather that the technological advances inherent in this had altered the nature of war itself. As noted in Chapter 7, Major General Fuller saw Fascist operational methods and tactics which utilised these new technologies as heralding an entirely new form of warfare. This he described as 'totalitarian', or the making of war via scientific methods: 'Because the Fascist Government is a scientific political instrument ... it logically follows that the Fascist Army is a scientific military instrument.'[16] His fellow journalist and military historian, Captain Basil Liddell Hart, perceived military development along similar lines, although without the political baggage:

> The Abyssinian Campaign should have given the General Staffs of the world cause for thought. It has shown the fallacy of their argument that machines are not a substitute for men – by which they mean the weight of the many, not the quality, of the essential few. It has shown, more clearly even than the World War, that mass has become a dangerous encumbrance when the attempt is made to concentrate it on the fighting front. Under modern conditions, and especially the growing menace of air attack, the larger the army the weaker a country may prove in war. Technical quality counts, not drilled quantity.[17]

There was, of course, something in these analyses, but neither Fuller nor Liddell Hart could be described as wholly objective. Fuller, as already noted, was a fascist and indeed occupied a senior position in Moseley's British Union of Fascists (BUF), an organisation partly bankrolled by Mussolini.[18] Liddell Hart had nothing in common with Fuller politically, but was engaged in a campaign to modernise and mechanise the British Army and wean it off what he saw as its reliance on mass. Any available evidence in support of this was therefore more than welcome.[19]

An arguably more neutral assessment was supplied by Colonel Xylander, a soldier-scholar serving at Berlin's *Kriegsakademie* (War Academy). He argued that given Italy had been fighting an 'unequal' enemy, it was obvious that the Ethiopian campaign in no way formed a model for any future European war. He cautioned generally, and the Italian armed forces more particularly, that such a notion was to be avoided:

> The history of war has often shown that the incorrect assessment of successes, in battles fought under special conditions, has led to disaster in later clashes. It will be up to the Italian armed forces to guard against such damaging assumptions. It must be their policy to avoid making false calculations on the basis of their current victory.[20]

This was a statement containing an obvious great truth, and one that would have been readily apparent to those in the upper echelons of Italy's armed forces. That 'damaging assumptions' and 'false calculations' exactly along the lines Xylander warned against were indeed being made within the ranks of their political masters was evidenced from an early stage. The Packards, Reynolds and Eleanor, recorded meeting Galeazzo Ciano, Mussolini's son-in-law, at the Imperial Hotel in Addis Ababa a few days after Badoglio's column had arrived:

> Ciano had the room next to ours. Hearing the tinkle of ice against glasses one evening, he came in and joined us for a drink. He was bubbling over with enthusiasm. 'England is through,' he said, 'or she would have taken a stronger stand against us. We have not only won this campaign; we are ready for the future. We have the only experienced army in Europe as a result of our Ethiopian training.'[21]

Ciano was not only a member of *Il Duce*'s family, but also held a ministerial position in his government and was soon (9 May) to be promoted to foreign minister, thus becoming 'the second most important man in Italy'.[22] It was, of course, what *the* most important man in Italy thought that mattered most, and we shall come to that shortly.

Xylander saw the war against Ethiopia as the first modern colonial war of annihilation (*ersten neuzeitlichen Vernichtungskrieg auf kolonialem Boden*) as per the title of his 1937 book.[23] The Swiss historian Aram Mattioli largely agrees with this judgement, as he does with the assessment made by Fuller and others that what had been observed in Ethiopia constituted a new form and indeed level of warfare: 'the Italian attack on the Abyssinian Empire should be interpreted as one of the key events in the history of violence in the twentieth century', and was deserving of scrutiny:

> What at first glance appears to be just another, albeit anachronistic, colonial war in the long history of European expansion turns out, on closer inspection, to be a war of aggression and conquest, waged with sophisticated logistics, immense effort, and the most modern technology, which ... unleashed a new level of violence that had not been seen in earlier colonial campaigns and, in some cases, heralded that seen in the Second World War.[24]

Despite the recorded and indisputable history of ghastly, barbaric treatment, amounting to genocide in some cases, that had been meted out to African peoples previously, Mattioli's thesis is undoubtedly correct. The Italians were able to, and did, kill and injure more Africans more quickly than had ever been done previously. This they achieved via their willingness to use technologies that, even if they had existed previously, were greatly developed during the First World War. The foremost and most visible manifestation of this was the *Regia Aeronautica*, which, in the absence of any effective counter-measures, operated at will, giving the attackers total air supremacy. It was surely the first large-scale international conflict where air power was a decisive factor. Tanks too made an appearance, but there is no evidence that their deployment was of any significant consequence regarding the outcome of the campaign, since Ethiopia was hardly 'tank country'. Indeed, the tanks used by Italy were hardly tanks at all, rather belonging to that class of armoured vehicle which the British termed 'tankettes' or machine-gun carriers.

Nor was Ethiopia a good place for lorries, or indeed vehicles of any kind, yet by dint of devoting massive resources to road-building and related infrastructure, and by importing tens of thousands of vehicles, the Italian commanders had been able to achieve 'totalitarian motorisation of the fighting units'.[25] Graziani, operating across the Ogaden from Somalia with the *treni caterpillar*, had arguably gone furthest in this regard. Liddell Hart penned a piece on the subject of motorisation for *The Times*, shortly after Mussolini had proclaimed Italy's dominion over Ethiopia. He wrote: 'The Lion of Judah has been crushed between the upper and nether jaws of Italy's mechanised forces ... It is a writing on the wall – and the more significant because it is engraved on a remote mountain wall.'[26]

The most controversial weapons were those of the chemical variety, particularly the large-scale employment of mustard gas. Del Boca considers this 'perhaps the worst crime' of the Fascist regime,[27] although most scholars are of the opinion that it was not a decisive factor in the Italian victory. It did, however, provoke the most revulsion. Dr John Melly, head of the British Ambulance Service in Ethiopia, is often quoted in this regard: 'This is not a war – it isn't even a slaughter – it's the torture of tens of thousands of defenceless men, women and children with bombs and poison gas. They're using gas incessantly, and we've treated hundreds of cases, including infants in arms – and the world looks on – and passes by on the other side.'[28]

That the world, the League of Nations, and Britain and France in particular, should continue to emulate those who, in biblical terms, 'passed by on the other side' was the essence of Mussolini's foreign policy. As previously noted, his international political and diplomatic position mirrored, in many ways, that which had applied in an earlier Italian colonial venture: the 1911 invasion of Tripoli (Libya). This had meant war with the Ottoman Empire, whose territory it then was, which in turn threatened to bring to the fore what was termed the 'Eastern Question': what might happen to the Ottoman Balkan territories if and when their Empire disintegrated? Should this occur, then the potential for conflict between, in particular, Austria-Hungary and Russia was extremely high. In 1911 Europe was divided, formally and informally, and with some wriggle room as it would be termed today, into two Great Power blocs: the Triple Alliance of Austria-Hungary, Germany and Italy, and the Triple Entente comprising Britain, France and Russia. Germany and Austria-Hungary disapproved of Italy's Tripoli adventure, but to check it would have been to drive her into the Triple Entente. On the other hand, if the Powers of the Triple Entente wished to secure the goodwill of Italy, they had to acquiesce in her designs on Tripoli. Thus Italy, regarded as the 'Least of the Great Powers' and also thought of, by allies and potential enemies alike, as somewhat lukewarm in its adherence to the Triple Alliance, was able to straddle the Triple Alliance–Triple Entente confrontation.

This meant that neither of the blocs, or their members, would act in such a way as to push her into the arms of the opposing bloc; no power was willing to risk seriously offending Italy.[29]

There were no blocs in the 1930s, just the League of Nations on the one hand and a resurgent Germany under Hitler on the other. The League condemned the Italian attack on Ethiopia and applied sanctions, but the only two member states with the power to back these up with enforcement action were Britain and France. They thus found themselves in much the same kind of bind as had been the case in 1911; if they supported one side, the League, then they pushed the other side, Italy, closer to Germany. If they didn't, then they risked destroying the only collective security system that might constrain Germany, particularly with regards to its designs on Austria. Mussolini was well aware of this dilemma and, through the work of the Military Information Service (*Servizio Informazioni Militari* – SIM), was able to keep abreast of developments on the diplomatic front.

This applied to matters naval as well. Thanks to the Secret Information Service (*Servizio Informazioni Segrete* – SIS), the naval equivalent of the army's SIM, which had cracked British naval ciphers, he was aware that the British fleet deployed in the Mediterranean did not consider itself to be in a strong position. It had, for example, reported a perilous ammunition shortage, particularly of the anti-aircraft variety.[30] He knew then that his bluff was unlikely to be called and that the British feared he might initiate a 'mad dog' act.[31]

Despite the intelligence advantages described, that Mussolini remained to some degree wary of international opinion was demonstrated by his sporadic instructions, revolving around meetings at the League of Nations which he considered significant, to temporarily avoid attacks on Red Cross installations and to cease using *iperite*. Steer was of the opinion that the two were connected: that the hospitals were bombed to drive away foreign witnesses whilst the Italians employed illegal methods of warfare.[32] This may or may not have formed the motivation, or part of it, but it is definitely the case that after the British Red Cross, amongst other foreign organisations and representatives, had left Ethiopia, the use of mustard gas continued on a large and now completely unfettered scale. This was, of course, because the 'Roman peace' proclaimed on 5 May from the balcony overlooking the Piazza Venezia was no peace at all as far as many of those supposedly subject to it were concerned; vast areas of Ethiopia, and the overwhelming majority of its population, remained unconquered. This was so particularly in the west of the 'Viceroyalty', which on 1 June 1936 had been absorbed, along with Italian Somaliland and Eritrea, into a new imperial unit: Italian East Africa (*Africa Orientale Italiana* – AOI). The first governor general of this territory was Graziani, who had been appointed Viceroy of Ethiopia and commander-in-chief of the Italian army in AOI on 21 May 1936 following the newly minted Duke of Addis Ababa's triumphant return to Italy.[33]

The onset of a rule characterised by its imposition of 'Fascist Civilisation' was, unsurprisingly, to prove far from benevolent despite much propaganda to the contrary. Equally unsurprisingly, large numbers of Ethiopians declined their new

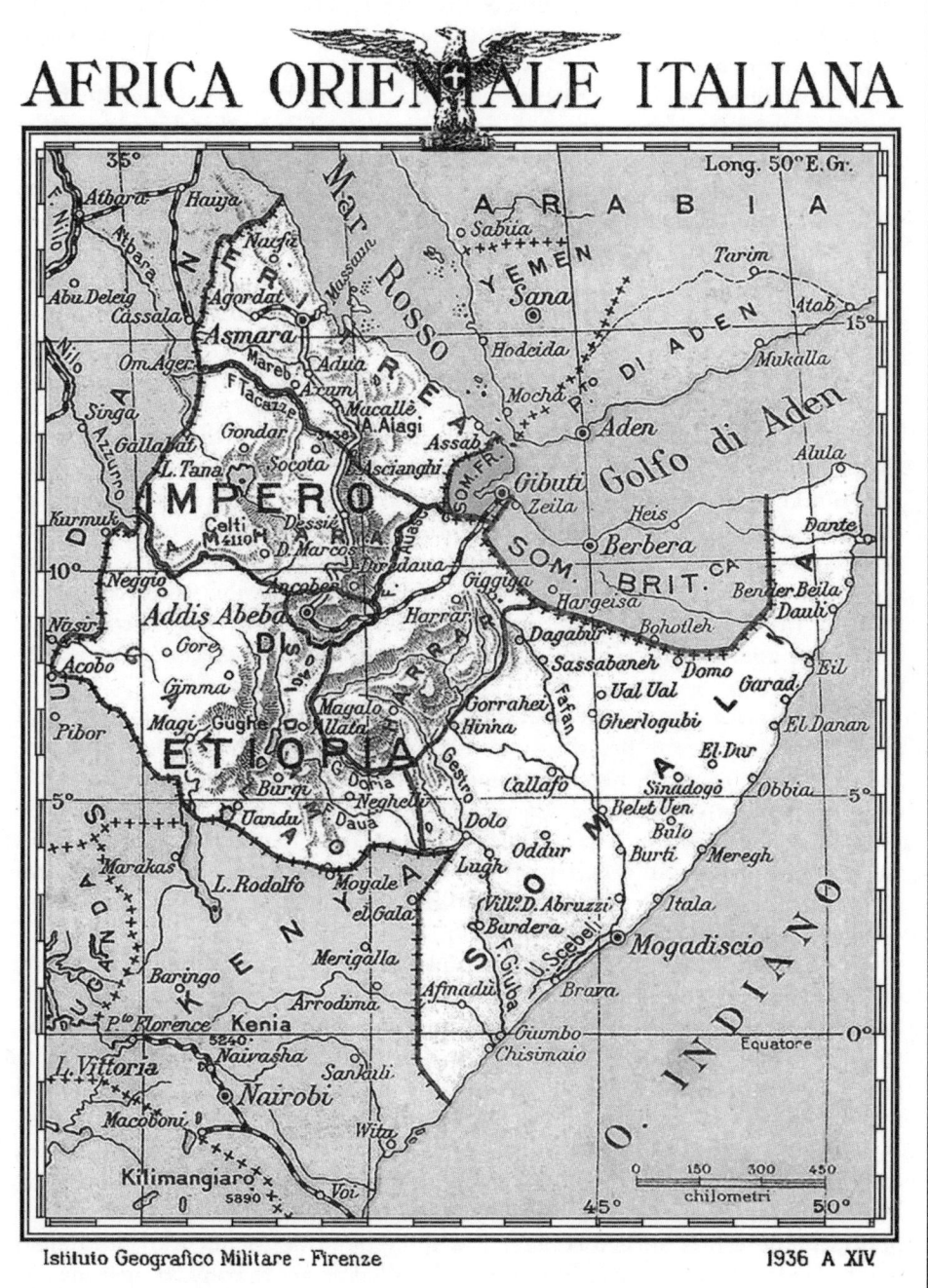

Africa Orientale Italiana, 1936.

status as subjects. This meant, amongst other things, that along with Somalis and Eritreans they were to be targeted by 'the most comprehensive systems of racial segregation in colonial Africa'.[34] Ridiculous lengths were gone to in this regard, and Mussolini 'energetically intervened' if he heard of behaviour which he considered damaging to Italy's prestige. For example, on 5 May 1936 he telegraphed the governor of Eritrea to complain that: 'A foreigner has pointed out to me that he saw in Massawa an NCO playing cards with a native. I most seriously deplore such familiarity. Humanity yes, promiscuity no.'[35]

Predictably, it didn't take long before a violent and very high-profile rebellion occurred when those who had been 'defeated' took to irregular, asymmetric resistance. It came on the night of 26/27 June 1936 with the so-called Massacre of Nekemte (*Eccidio di Lekemti*). This involved the killing of Brigadier General Vincenzo Magliocco and eleven others, including the famous pioneering aviator Antonio Locatelli.[36] They were members of an Italian mission, authorized by Graziani, that had flown – the roads were impassable owing to the rains – in three aircraft to an airfield at Bonaia near Nekemte, about 250km west of Addis Ababa. The object of the exercise was to convince the local leaders to side with the Italians. They didn't get the chance. During the night a number of Ethiopian guerrillas attacked their camp, resulting in the deaths of the entire party, with the exception of the missionary-scholar Father Mario Borello, who managed to hide for three months until the army could travel overland to the area. The resultant retaliation involved aerial attacks on nearby villages: in other words, civilian targets.[37]

Indeed, it soon became clear that Graziani would reprise a role that he had played in Libya, one of brutally suppressing a recalcitrant population with 'fire and sword' to the point of committing genocide.[38] Such measures were explicitly endorsed, indeed commanded, by Mussolini himself, as evidenced by his 8 July message to the Viceroy: 'I once again authorise Your Excellency to initiate and systematically carry out a policy of terror and extermination against rebels and accomplice populations. This plague will not be cured in good time without applying the law of tenfold retaliation.'[39]

That Graziani's programme of 'terror and extermination' would specifically include the use of mustard gas and other chemicals was indicated two days later. That was when *Il Duce* ordered a halt to the demobilisation of the chemical warfare specialists attached to the air force, and instructed that they were to maintain their stocks in East Africa.[40] Rochat calculates that over a three-year period following the declaration of 'peace', about 350 C.500.T *iperite* bombs, and 200 arsine-filled C.IOO.P bombs, were used in an effort to suppress Ethiopian resistance.[41] Around half of these, 177 C.500.T and 103 C.IOO.P, were dropped between May and November 1936.[42]

Whilst the use of such weaponry was thought to be useful from the Italian point of view, many more Ethiopians were killed by more conventional means. There were several major massacres, perhaps the worst being that at Addis Ababa from 19 to 22 February 1937 in which around 20 per cent of the Ethiopian population of the city, some 19,000 people, were brutally killed after an assassination attempt on Graziani.⁴³ Further, believing that they had 'connived' in the attempt, the Viceroy ordered the killing of the monks of Debre Libanos, an ancient monastery some 80km north of the capital with roots that date back to the fifth century. The consequent murders have been dubbed 'the most serious massacre of Christians on the African continent'.⁴⁴ It is thought that about 1,200 monks, priests and pilgrims perished on 21 May 1937, with another 500 shortly afterwards.⁴⁵ Much monastical treasure was also pillaged, leading the historian Paolo Borruso to describe it as 'Italy's most serious war crime'.⁴⁶ There was much more in a similar vein.

It is impossible to arrive at a settled figure for how many Ethiopians perished, whether in combat during the war or afterwards during the 'peace'. A document authored by the Ethiopian government in 1945 put the total number of deaths over the whole period at 760,300, with just over half (56 per cent) of them occurring in combat during 1935–1936.⁴⁷ Subsequent scholarly research has concluded these figures are exaggerated, even if those later arrived at via detailed investigation vary widely. It is now estimated that between 350,000 and 480,000 Ethiopians perished in one way or another between 1935 and 1941.⁴⁸ As Richard Pankhurst put it in 2002: 'Though the fact of Italian fascist war crimes is undeniable, the exact number of victims could, and can, only be rough estimates.'⁴⁹ Of note, however, is that in his memoirs, published in 1949, Graziani pleaded that whatever had occurred he had been, to borrow a phrase, only following orders:

> Intransigent provisions and orders from Rome descended upon me. 'I order you,' said one of them, 'to apply a regime of terror.' 'Without the 100 per cent law of retaliation, it is useless to hope for speedy submission and reconciliation,' suggested another. 'Arrange that all prisoners, however captured, are to be executed' imposed a third. 'I order that all leaders who are captured be shot at once.' Again: 'I repeat to you that it is necessary to establish a regime of absolute terror.' And so on.⁵⁰

This 'defence', which is, of course, no defence at all, is in any case gravely undermined by, to give just one example, his instructional telegram issued on 13 May 1937 to the Italian commanders in Shewa province (the area surrounding Addis Ababa) and copied to Alessandro Lessona in Rome:

> I follow your work with keen attention and passion, which must conclude in the absolute submission of Shewa, including razing to the ground the last house and eliminating all those who do not intend to lay down their arms. I fully rely on your fascist spirit, ability and decision. Above all, remember that any false mercy towards people decidedly hostile to our dominion is a crime … Essential cornerstones [of our policy are]: absolute totalitarian disarmament; elimination of all leaders: impostors, sorcerers, witches, false prophets, etc. Conquest is conquest and when our generosity has been tested

for a whole year, and only answered with bombs, all that remains is the law of retaliation, an eye for an eye, a tooth for a tooth. That moreover is in the spirit of the [Italian] people and constitutes true Roman imperial justice.[51]

Graziani never had to try to formally plead his defence, the so-called 'Nuremburg defence', for the simple reason that he was never called to account for his actions. To understand why, and contextualise this, we need to go back to 1936 and the Italian victory over Ethiopia when Mussolini, who was famously 'always right', seemed to start believing his own propaganda. He had claimed in a ghost-written autobiography dating from 1928 that he wanted to make Italy 'great, respected, and feared'.[52] Whether he had succeeded in these aims eight years later is a moot point but, as Martin Clark argues, the outcome of the Ethiopian war seemed to change him: 'It convinced him that the Italian people really had become disciplined and warlike, and that he himself was a gifted military leader. Self-confidence soon began to shade into megalomania ... Mussolini became convinced of his own infallibility, and that of his magnificent soldiers.'[53]

The aftermath also demonstrated that Britain and France had inherited the worst of all worlds; the post-Versailles order of collective security and the belief in the League of Nations was shattered and Italy was drawing closer to Hitler and his regime. Indeed, when the Spanish Civil War commenced in July 1936, both Germany and Italy supported the Nationalist forces under General Franco with arms and 'volunteer' forces. Italian army and air force assistance was substantial, and there was also significant naval input.[54]

This alignment was duplicated in the diplomatic sphere with the signing of the Italo-German Protocol (*Protocollo italo-tedesco*) of 23 October 1936, and went further when Italy joined the German-Japanese Anti-Comintern Pact (*Patto anti-comintern*) on 6 November 1937. The culmination came with the signing of the military and political alliance known as the Pact of Steel (*Patto d'Acciaio*) or, formally, as the Pact of Friendship and Alliance between Germany and Italy (*Patto di amicizia e di alleanza fra l'Italia e la Germania*) on 22 May 1939.[55]

That Italy could also act unilaterally was demonstrated five days after Franco proclaimed victory in the Spanish Civil War when, on 7 April 1939, the invasion of Albania commenced. This was the brainchild of Ciano rather than Mussolini, and was prompted by German actions in March 1939 against what remained of Czechoslovakia after the Munich Agreement. Given that Italy had dominated Albania economically, militarily and politically for several years the conquest was largely bloodless and was completed within a week. A puppet government was established, and this approved the transformation of the country into an Italian protectorate. This new iteration of the Kingdom of Albania (*Regno albanese*) was constitutionally headed by Victor Emanuele III, who in addition to his other titles became King of the Albanians (*Re degli Albanesi*) on 16 April.[56]

On 10 June 1940, following nine months of non-participation in the war that had broken out in September 1939, Mussolini once again addressed a huge crowd from his balcony on Palazzo Venezia. Convinced that the 'blitzkrieg' which had engulfed France, and led to British forces fleeing the continent via the Dunkirk evacuation, heralded certain victory for his ally in the Pact of Steel, he had decided to join in: 'The declaration of war has already been delivered to the ambassadors of Great Britain and France ... We take the field against the plutocratic and reactionary democracies of the West, which, at all times, have hindered the march, and often undermined the very existence of the Italian people.'[57]

With Britain and France seemingly beaten, here was an opportunity for, amongst other things, seizing whole tracts of their colonial territory. Badoglio, chief of staff of the army since his return from Ethiopia, claimed to have cautioned *Il Duce* that the army was totally unready for any such conflict. He was reassured: 'Everything will be over by September and I only need a few thousand dead in order to get a seat at the negotiating table.'[58]

Dubbed 'the cowardly jackal of Europe' for his actions by one British minister, it is safe to say that Mussolini was not thinking of a September three years hence for it to be 'over'.[59] It was, though, only after some thirty-six months of truly disastrous war, which included the loss of *Africa Orientale Italiana* and the return of Haile Selassie to Addis Ababa five years to the day since Badoglio's entrance, that the war started by *Il Duce* ended for Italy. It did so because, after the deaths of over 200,000 servicemen,[60] the loss of Libya and the invasion of Sicily, amongst other woes, the Italian government was forced to accept terms from its enemies. These terms were embodied in the Armistice of Cassibile, named for the town in Sicily where it was signed on 3 September 1943.[61] Although this ended the Fascist war started by Mussolini, it failed to end the fighting because Italy didn't surrender as such; rather, it changed sides, being granted the status of a co-belligerent by the United Nations,[62] and declared war against its former partner on 13 October 1943.[63]

The chaos that followed the announcement of the armistice on 8 September 'traumatized Italy', according to O'Hara and Cernuschi. They note, though, that whilst the army and air force disintegrated, the *Regia Marina* maintained its discipline, and most of its forces, and stomached the terms that had been agreed.[64] So, despite the fact that the naval command was excluded from the armistice process,[65] most of the navy changed sides, forming the *Regia Marina Cobelligerante* to fight alongside their former foes. It thus became a 'useful ally' and 'the only one of Italy's armed forces to effectively fight the Germans'.[66] So there began another war: the war of liberation from German occupation. Hitler ordered his forces to take control of the northern part of the country, which was completed by 12 September, dividing Italy into two: the south occupied by the Allies and the north by Germany.

Mussolini played no part in the decision to seek an armistice. A vote, effectively of no confidence, in the Fascist Grand Council had gone against him in the early hours of 25 July 1943, and this resulted in his dismissal, and imprisonment, by King Victor Emmanuel later that day. The man chosen to replace him as leader of a new, non-Fascist, government was Marshal Pietro Badoglio.[67]

In addition to concluding the armistice and overseeing the about-face in respect of Germany, plus dissolving the Fascist Party and all of its organs, Badoglio's government had one major policy objective: becoming an ally, and member, of the United Nations.[68] The reasons why, as listed by Kogan, were straightforward:

> If Italy were an ally it would be difficult for the United Nations to deal harshly in terms of boundaries, colonies, and reparations when the peace settlement was made. An ally must be treated with consideration. If Italy were an ally it could get lend-lease and other economic aid needed so badly, and it could expect relaxation of controls over internal affairs.[69]

Kogan might have added that an ally would not be investigated for war crimes, either. The notion was, in any event, politically contentious. The position of the British government, as laid out in a 1944 message to the US State Department, was that granting such status would be 'premature':

> Such a move would not be well received by British public opinion and would almost certainly be opposed by the French, Greeks and Yugoslavs who would bitterly resent Italy being placed on a footing similar to theirs. Immediate grant of allied status might make the situation of Italy at the peace settlement very embarrassing to the allies.[70]

The resentment of the Greeks, Yugoslavs and other Balkan states would indeed have been great: the list of war crimes committed by Italian occupation forces there is long indeed,[71] as it is with regards to Ethiopia.

Although it is not entirely accurate to state that no Italian was ever tried for war crimes,[72] it is the case that questions of *realpolitik* intervened to prevent any large-scale arraignment of those responsible for such crimes outside Italy. In respect of Ethiopia, this was achieved by excluding the country from membership of the United Nations War Crimes Commission (UNWCC), an organisation which had been set up at the behest of the British Foreign Office on 20 October 1943. The UNWCC's main function was to formulate and implement general measures for trial and punishment of alleged Axis war criminals.[73] This exclusion prompted questions which had the potential to embarrass the UK government if they ever had to explain why this was so. The principal reason was laid out in a (confidential) memorandum by Sir Herbert Malkin, principal legal adviser to the Foreign Office, on 11 November 1943:

> The objection to Ethiopian membership which strikes me as important is as follows ... I imagine that their object in being represented would be to bring before the Commission the crimes which the Italians undoubtedly committed during the original conquest of the country. This, however, is surely out of the question for several reasons, one of which is that probably the first name on the Ethiopian list would be Marshal Badoglio.[74]

The British government's support, and indeed protection, of Badoglio can be explained in fairly simple terms: they feared the alternative. Churchill's message to President Roosevelt of 5 August 1943 is evidence of this, and whether what it relates was true or not is irrelevant, since Churchill believed it, as he made plain:

> The following story has been told to British Ambassador Campbell at Lisbon by a newly arrived Italian Counsellor ... I send it to you for what it is worth, which is substantial ... Fascism in Italy is extinct. Every vestige has been swept away. Italy turned Red overnight. In Turin and Milan there were Communist demonstrations which had to be put down by armed force. Twenty years of Fascism has obliterated the middle class. There is nothing between the King, with the Patriots who have rallied round him, who have complete control, and rampant Bolshevism.[75]

The matter had been considered from a slightly different point of view by General Eisenhower, commander-in-chief of the Mediterranean theatre in 1943, who saw only two alternatives: either accept the Badoglio government as legitimate and cobelligerent, or establish an Allied military government. He strongly favoured the first course of action as being best suited to gaining the maximum contribution to the Allied military effort with the minimum expenditure of manpower. Roosevelt and Churchill agreed.[76]

Dismissal of justifiable Ethiopian claims for reasons of expediency was, however, hardly something that could be stated openly. Malkin was aware of this, so went on to phrase the matter in a different way. Ethiopian disqualification from UNWCC could not simply be a matter of time, in the sense that the Italo-Ethiopian War predated the Second World War; the Chinese government, as members of UNWCC, wanted Japanese war crimes that had occurred as far back as 1931 to be investigated. Malkin got around this by arguing that in the case of China the only question revolved around 'how far back to go as regards crimes committed in hostilities which have been continually proceeding since the earliest date which it would be possible to take'. Such continuity was, however, lacking in the case of Ethiopia. There the 'crimes were committed in the course of a quite different war', which had been followed after 1936 by a period when 'Ethiopia did not exist internationally'. Italian actions in Ethiopia whilst they ruled it as a colony could not, in Malkin's judgement, be regarded as 'war crimes'.[77] This was basically the official position taken up by the Foreign Office as per a set of 'Draft Instructions to Theatre Commanders Regarding the Handling of War Crimes' dated 14 November 1944:

> For the purposes of this directive the following dates are established:
> - The war in the Far East began the 7th July, 1937.
> - War between Germany and Czechoslovakia began the 1st September, 1939.
> - The war in Europe began the 1st September, 1939.
> - War crimes do not include offences committed prior to the beginning dates set out ... above.[78]

Badoglio could not then be charged with war crimes in Ethiopia. Further, since he had resigned, or been forced out, of his position as chief of staff in 1940 following *Il Duce*'s ill-fated decision to invade Greece from Albania in October of that year, he hadn't been involved in the Balkans occupation.[79]

Graziani hadn't either, through being dismissed in 1941 following military disasters in North Africa. Nor, although he did eventually find himself in jail, was he punished for anything he had done in Ethiopia. As is well known, Hitler personally ordered the operation that freed Mussolini from captivity on 12 September 1943 before the Badoglio government could hand him over to the British or Americans.[80] On the evening of 15 September a statement was broadcast from Rome which declared that Benito Mussolini had resumed the supreme direction of Fascism. Thus came into being the Italian Social Republic (*Repubblica sociale italiana* – RSI), also known as the Republic of Salo (*La repubblica di Salo*) from the town on the shores of Lake Garda where many ministerial offices were located.[81] So it was that the reborn *Il Duce* exercised nominal authority in those gradually shrinking areas of northern and central Italy that had yet to be taken by the slowly advancing Allied forces. He used such power as he possessed, and which Hitler allowed him, to take revenge on six of those who had 'betrayed' him at the Fascist Grand Council vote of 25 July 1943, and were within his grasp. This number included Emilio De Bono and Galeazzo Ciano, who were executed, alongside four others, by firing squad on 11 January 1944.[82]

Rodolfo Graziani joined Mussolini's new government as minister of national defence.[83] He was then responsible overall for the National Republican Army (*Esercito Nazionale Repubblicano*) which mostly, but not exclusively, contested with the anti-Fascist partisan, and largely communist, movement that had sprung up following the 1943 armistice.[84] There was also an air force that fought alongside the *Luftwaffe*.[85]

The ever-contracting borders of the RSI ultimately disappeared in late April 1945 with the impending surrender of German forces in Italy. This was formalised on 29 April: the very day Graziani was fortunate to escape being shot by partisans into whose hands he had fallen. Instead, he was handed over to a unit of Lieutenant General Willis D. Crittenberger's IV US Army Corps at the town of Ghedi.[86] He spent the next five years in prison or hospital before, on 2 May 1950, being sentenced to nineteen years' incarceration for military collaboration with Germany. However, thirteen years of this sentence were remitted and, since he had already been detained for five years, he was freed on 29 August 1950.[87]

The genesis of this judicial and institutional reluctance to punish Italians charged with war crimes, or to see them extradited to answer such charges in other jurisdictions, can be traced to Badoglio's time in office. In May 1944 he 'vehemently' and successfully opposed legal moves initiated by the Yugoslav government to indict and try General Allesandro Pirzio Biroli, who had commanded the Eritrean Corps in Ethiopia, for war crimes committed during his time as governor of Montenegro, July 1941–July 1943.[88] This policy continued after Badoglio resigned in June 1944, to be replaced by the centre-left Ivanoe

Bonomi. It was, in fact, to endure throughout the tenure of all his successors and can be viewed as forming a part of the construction of the *Italiani brava gente* mythology, and associated amnesia, as discussed in Chapter 1.[89]

This might have been mitigated had Mussolini, the 'head devil' as Roosevelt termed him, been brought to trial in some way. The president had written to Churchill in that regard in July 1943 stating 'I think also that the head devil should be surrendered together with his chief partners in crime.'[90] Churchill professed himself 'indifferent' as to whether these 'criminals' should be shot out of hand or their fate 'decided together with other war criminals' at the end of the war in Europe.[91] Had the latter occurred, then it seems possible, likely even, that Mussolini's fate would have been similar to what befell senior Nazis and, perhaps a more relevant equivalent, Japan's former prime minister Tojo Hideki.[92] Whether events around the invasion and occupation of Ethiopia would have featured in any such tribunal is, of course, impossible to say for sure, although it seems doubtful. However, in the event, Mussolini and his several 'partners in crime' escaped any formal accounting.

They were instead subjected to that type of rougher 'justice' which their regime had frequently meted out in Ethiopia, and indeed in several other locations, especially the Balkans. Captured by communist partisans on 27 April 1945 whilst apparently attempting to flee to Switzerland, Mussolini and sixteen other senior Fascists were shot the next day, as was his mistress Clara Petacci. Their bodies were later taken back to Milan and displayed, hanging upside down, in the Piazzale Loreto. After seeing photographs of this gruesome exhibition, Churchill expressed profound shock and enquired, in respect of Petacci, 'was she on the list of war criminals?' His final comment on the matter was, however, terse: 'But at least the world was spared an Italian Nuremberg.'[93]

This lack of any Italian equivalent of the 1945–1946 trials of German war criminals, or anything resembling the International Military Tribunal for the Far East (Tokyo War Crimes Tribunal) convened in 1946, means no established, official and publicly accessible body of evidence pertaining to such matters was created. Whether or not any such investigation would have included an examination of the campaign of 'terror and extermination', of 'true Roman imperial justice', waged on and in Ethiopia cannot be known. What can be said, though, is that in the absence of any such evidentiary corpus, historians such as Angelo Del Boca and the several others liberally quoted throughout this text, were instead obliged to engage, and fight hard, in *Una lunga battaglia per la verita* (A long battle for the truth).[94]

Notes

Introduction

1. Available at: https://avalon.law.yale.edu/imt/09-30-46.asp#:~:text=To%20initiate%20a%20war%20of,accumulated%20evil%20of%20the%20whole.
2. Menelik II to the governments of Britain, France, Germany, Italy and Russia in 1891. A translated copy of the letter dated 10 April 1891 is in the UK National Archives: Rodd to Sallisbury, No. 15, 4 May 1897. FO 1/32. Special Mission to King Menelik. Mr J. Rennel Rodd Diplomatic. 1897.
3. Document 358, 'Direttive del Capo del Governo e Ministro degli Esteri, Mussolini, Roma, 30 dicembre 1934. Segretissimo', in Ministero degli Affari Esteri, *Documenti diplomatici italiani. Settima Serie: 1922–1935: Volume XVI (28 settembre 1934–14 aprile 1935)* (Roma: Istituto Poligrafico e Zecca dello Stato, MCMXC [1990]), p. 369.
4. David Lloyd George, Hansard, vol. 86, col. 1211, Commons Chamber, Wednesday, 25 July 1900.
5. J.W.S. Macfie, *An Ethiopian Diary: A Record of the British Ambulance Service in Ethiopia* (Liverpool/London: University Press of Liverpool/Hodder & Stoughton, 1936), p. ix.
6. Mussolini a Graziani, 8 luglio 1936. Quoted in: Giorgio Rochat, 'L'impiego dei gas nella guerra d'Etiopia 1935–1936', in Angelo Del Boca (ed.), *I gas di Mussolini: Il fascism e la guerra d'Etiopia* (Roma: Editori Reuniti, 2007), p. 95.
7. There is an abundance of documentary evidence pertaining to the war in Italian, but very little in Amharic. As the journalist George Steer noted of the nobles who commanded the Ethiopian forces: 'most of them were illiterate, ignorant alike of foreign languages and of the Western method of warfare'. G.L. Steer, *Caesar in Abyssinia* (London: Hodder & Stoughton, 1936), p. 310.
8. Longo, Luigi Emilio, *La Campagna Italo-Etiopica (1935–1936): Tomo I* (Roma: Ufficio Storico Stato Maggiore Esercito, 2005); Longo, Luigi Emilio, *La Campagna Italo-Etiopica (1935–1936): Tomo II Allegati* (Roma: Ufficio Storico Stato Maggiore Esercito, 2005).

Chapter 1: Del Boca and the 'Irreducible Montanelli'

1. Angelo Del Boca, 'Una lunga battaglia per la verità', in Angelo Del Boca (ed.), *I gas di Mussolini: Il fascism e la guerra d'Etiopia* (Roma: Editori Reuniti, 2007), p. 173.
2. Martin Evans, 'Statue of slave trader Edward Colston pulled down and thrown into harbour by Bristol protesters', *Daily Telegraph*, 7 June 2020. Marc Wouters en Dirk Hendrikx, 'Leopold II na 147 jaar weg uit Ekeren, allicht definitief: discussie over zijn wandaden laait weer op', *Gazet van Antwerpen*, 10 juni 2020.
3. Alessandra Corica, 'Montanelli e la statua della discordia: a Milano flash mob di Forza Italia e contro manifestazione di "Non una di meno"', *la Repubblica*, 15 Juno 2020.
4. Sandro Gerbi e Raffaele Liucci, *Indro Montanelli: Una biografia (1909–2001)* (Milano: Hoepli, 2014), p. ix. See also the *Comune di Milano* website: https://www.comune.milano.it/aree-tematiche/verde/verde-pubblico/parchi-cittadini/giardini-indro-montanelli.
5. Gerbi e Liucci, *Indro Montanelli*, p. xi. For a less academic, journalistic, treatment of Montanelli see: Riccardo Colao, *Un caffè con Indro Montanelli* (London: Titani Editori, 2015).
6. Giorgio Torelli, *Gli ascari del tenente Indro e altri ascari: i battaglioni indigeni fatti a lor modo e iscritti nella storia d'Italia* (Milano: Edizioni Ares, 2004).
7. Indro Montanelli, «Civilta fascista» n. 1, gennaio 1936. Quoted in: Antonella Randazzo, *L'Africa del Duce: I crimini fascisti in Africa* (Varese: Edizione Arteigere, 2008), p. 266.

8. See: Mario Avagliano e Marco Palmieri, *Di pura razza italiana. L'Italia «ariana» di fronte alle leggi razziali* (Milano: Baldini & Castoldi, 2013). Specifically, it was on 19 April 1937 that *Regio Decreto Legislativo 880* (Royal Legislative Decree 880), which became law on 30 December 1937, was promulgated. It punished, with imprisonment from one to five years, relations 'of a conjugal nature' between Italian citizens and indigenous women. Enzo Collotti, *Il fascismo e gli ebrei: Le leggi razziali in Italia* (Roma-Bari: Editori Laterza, 2003), p. 37.
9. Tommaso Giglio, *Un certo Montanelli* (Milano: Sperling & Kupfer, 1981), p. 171.
10. Enrico Arosio, 'Uno studio svela le bugie di Montanelli: La doppia vita del grande inviato del *Corriere della Sera*.' Available online at: http://forum.laudellulivo.org/index.php?topic=781.0;wap2. See also: Mario Guarino, *Mercanti di parole: storie e nomi del giornalismo asservito al potere* (Bari: Edizioni Dedalo, 2012).
11. «La stanza di Montanelli. Etiopia: colonialismo all'italiana», *Corriere della Sera*, 11 Settembre 1949.
12. Angelo Del Boca, *Italiani, brava gente?: un mito duro a morire* (Vicenza: Neri Pozza Editore, 2005).
13. *La Preparazione*, 1 July 1909.
14. 'UK more nostalgic for empire than other ex-colonial powers', *Guardian*, 11 March 2020. Available at: https://www.theguardian.com/world/2020/mar/11/uk-more-nostalgic-for-empire-than-other-ex-colonial-powers.
15. Gian Luca Mazzini, *Montanelli mi ha detto: Avventure, aneddoti, ricordi del più grande giornalista italiano* (Rimini: Il Cerchio Iniziative Editoriali, 2002), p. 30.
16. Mary Jane Dempsey, 'Finding Postcolonial Figures: Rediscovering Elvira Banotti and her Role in the Italian Feminist Movement', *Women's History Review*, 2018, 27(7):1043–64. See also: Fiori Berhane and Diego Maria Malara, 'The Montanelli Case: Sexuality, Race, and Colonial Forgetting in BLM Italy'. Available at: https://www.academia.edu/44386682/The_Montanelli_Case_Sexuality_Race_and_Colonial_Forgetting_in_BLM_Italy.
17. Desirée Maida, 'Statua di Indro Montanelli imbrattata a Milano. Tutte le volte che la scultura ha creato dissensi', *Artribune*, 14 June 2020.
18. Available at: https://www.lastampa.it/torino/2021/07/06/news/morto-il-giornalista-angelo-del-boca-fu-il-pioniere-degli-studi-sul-colonialismo-italiano-1.40469224/.
19. Particularly following the speech by Haile Selassie to the Assembly of the League of Nations, 30 June 1936. Available at: https://www.mtholyoke.edu/acad/intrel/selassie.htm.
20. For example: Steer, *Caesar in Abyssinia* and Major General J.F.C. Fuller, *The First of the League Wars: Its Lessons and Omens* (London: Eyre & Spottiswoode, 1936). Steer reported the war for *The Times* from the Ethiopian side, whilst Fuller was engaged as a 'special correspondent' by the *Daily Mail* and attached to the Italian Army. Politically, they were polar-opposites. Steer was later 'released' by *The Times* for the anti-Fascist and anti-Nationalist slant of his reporting during the Spanish Civil War of 1936–1939 [Herbert Rutledge Southworth, *Guernica! Guernica! A Study of a Journalism, Diplomacy, Propaganda, and History* (Berkeley, CA: University of California Press, 1977), pp. 331–2]. Fuller, on the other hand, was a convinced Fascist [Mason W. Watson, 'Not Italian or German, but British in Character': J.F.C. Fuller and the Fascist Movement in Britain', Undergraduate Honors Theses. Paper 485. College of William and Mary. Available online at: https://scholarworks.wm.edu/cgi/viewcontent.cgi?article=1494&context=honorstheses].
21. Angelo Del Boca, *La guerra d'Abissinia: 1935–1941* (Milano: Feltrinelli, 1965). English language edition: Angelo Del Boca and P.D. Cummings (trans.), *The Ethiopian War: 1935–1941* (Chicago: University of Chicago Press, 1969).
22. Angelo Del Boca, *Il mio Novecento* (Vicenza: Neri Pozza Editori, 2008), p. 330.
23. Filippo Masina, 'La memoria dei combattenti d'Africa: l'ANRA', in Michela Ponzani (ed.), *Memoria e testimonianza: Deportazione, internamento e Resistenza nell'Italia e nella Francia del dopoguerra* (Roma: Deutsches Historisches Institut in Rom/Istituto Storico Germanico di Roma, 2013), p. 126.
24. Italicus, 'Folle vento antipatria', *Il reduce d'Africa: Mensile dell'Associazione Nazioanle Reduci d'Africa*, settembre 1965, 7.

Notes 185

25. Del Boca, 'Una lunga battaglia', pp. 150–1.
26. After Ypres (*Ipro*), the place where it was first employed in 1917. Mario Sartori and L.W. Morrison (trans.), *The War Gases: Chemistry and Analysis* (New York: D Van Nostrand, 1939), p. 217.
27. Lessona, Alessandro, Dizionario Biografico degli Italiani: https://www.treccani.it/enciclopedia/alessandro-lessona_%28Dizionario-Biografico%29/.
28. Giulio Gigli, *Tito Minniti e Silvio Zannoni: vittime della barbarie etiopica* (Roma: Pinciana Editore, 1936). Most other sources give Zannoni's first name as 'Livio'.
29. Alessandro Lessona, *Un ministro di Mussolini racconta* (Milano: Edizioni Nazionali, 1973), p. 112.
30. Alessandro Lessona, 'Mussolini non voleva la guerra d'Etiopia', *Storia Illustrata*, gennaio 1980, 266:124–5.
31. Del Boca, 'Una lunga battaglia', p. 156.
32. Del Boca, 'Una lunga battaglia', p. 203, n. 38.
33. Formed in 1937 as a successor to the Colonial Ministry following the creation of Italian East Africa. Available at: https://artsandculture.google.com/entity/ministry-of-the-colonies/m05b2dgp?hl=en.
34. The RSI came into being following the German occupation of northern and central Italy. This occurred after the fall of Mussolini in 1943, when the new Italian government announced its defection from the Axis powers to the Allies on 8 September. Having had *Il Duce* rescued from captivity in the Gran Sasso raid, Hitler installed him as leader of the RSI, which existed until it collapsed in April 1945. See: Amedeo Osti Guerrazzi, *Storia della Repubblica sociale italiana* (Roma: Carocci Editore, 2012). For a treatment in English see: Ray Moseley, *Mussolini: The Last 600 Days of Il Duce* (Lanham, MD: Taylor Trade, 2004).
35. Del Boca, 'Una lunga battaglia', pp. 157–8.
36. Del Boca, 'Una lunga battaglia', p. 158. The programme can be viewed here: https://www.youtube.com/watch?v=fvjrlMnWjcA. Use the 'browse' feature to search for *L'impero: un'avventura Africana*. The encounter between Del Boca and Lessona begins at 22.00 minutes in. Del Boca's reading of the telegrams takes place from 25:00–27:00 minutes, which is obviously less than claimed in the book. Nor does Lessona, who is obviously discomfited, raise his arms, although this archive version of the programme may have been edited down to its current length of 40:45.
37. Del Boca, 'Una lunga battaglia', p. 160.
38. Del Boca, 'Una lunga battaglia', p. 160.
39. Angelo Del Boca, *Il Negus: Vita e morte dell'ultimo re dei re* (Roma: Editori Laterza, 1995). Angelo Del Boca and Antony Shugaar (trans.), *The Negus: The Life and Death of the Last King of Kings* (Addis Abeba: Arada Books, 2012).
40. Del Boca, 'Una lunga battaglia', p. 161.
41. Dino Messina, 'Scaffale di storia: Le armi chimiche in Etiopia e l'ammissione di Montanelli', *Corriere della Sera*, 2 aprile 2016. Available online at: https://www.corriere.it/extra-per-voi/2016/04/02/armi-chimiche-etiopia-l-ammissione-montanelli-54d37986-f8fc-11e5-b97f-6d5a0a6f6065.shtml.
42. Del Boca, 'Una lunga battaglia', p. 161.
43. *Corriere della Sera*, 12 agosto 1995. Quoted in: Del Boca, 'Una lunga battaglia', p. 162.
44. Marco Travaglio, on 14 August in *L'Indipendente*, followed the lead of *Reduce d'Africa*, accusing Del Boca not only of being a 'revisionist' but also of founding a new branch of historiography: that of self-harm (*autolesionismo*). Del Boca, 'Una lunga battaglia', pp. 203–4, n. 55.
45. Del Boca, 'Una lunga battaglia', p. 162.
46. *Corriere della Sera*, 13 agosto 1995. Quoted in: Del Boca, *Il mio Novecento*, p. 341. See also: Gianni Riotta, 'Montanelli-Del Boca quel che insegna una polemica civile', *Il Sole 24 Ore*, 18 luglio 2010.
47. Del Boca, *Il mio Novecento*, p. 330.
48. Gianfranco Pasquino, Timothy Cooper (trans.) and Stephen Jewks (trans.), 'The Government of Lamberto Dini', in Mario Cacaiagli and David I. Kertzer (eds), *Italian Politics: The Stalled Transition* (Boulder, CO: Westview Press, 1996), pp. 139–40.

49. Bureaucracies tend towards secrecy. See for example: Marc Parry, 'Uncovering the brutal truth about the British empire', *Guardian*, 18 August 2016. Available at: https://www.theguardian.com/news/2016/aug/18/uncovering-truth-british-empire-caroline-elkins-mau-mau; Caroline Elkins, 'Alchemy of Evidence: Mau Mau, the British Empire, and the High Court of Justice', *Journal of Imperial and Commonwealth History*, 2011, 39(5):731–48; David M. Anderson, 'Mau Mau in the High Court and the "Lost" British Empire Archives: Colonial Conspiracy or Bureaucratic Bungle?', *Journal of Imperial and Commonwealth History*, 2011, 39(5):699–716.
50. A respected historian, his works include: Alberto Rovighi, *Le operazioni in Africa orientale (guigno 1940–novembre 1941): Volume I, Narrazione, Parte Prima* (Roma: Stato Maggiore dell'Esercito Ufficio storico, 1995); Alberto Rovighi, *Le operazioni in Africa orientale (guigno 1940–novembre 1941): Volume I, Narrazione, Parte Secondo* (Roma: Stato Maggiore dell'Esercito Ufficio storico, 1995); Alberto Rovighi, *Le operazioni in Africa orientale (guigno 1940–novembre 1941): Volume II, Documenti* (Roma: Stato Maggiore dell'Esercito Ufficio storico, 1995).
51. Del Boca, 'Una lunga battaglia', pp. 204–5, n. 58.
52. Del Boca, 'Una lunga battaglia', p. 204, n. 58.
53. *Il Messaggero*, 1 novembre 1995.
54. Simonetta Fiori, 'Anche la Difesa ammette: "I gas li abbiamo usati"', *La Repubblica*, 10 novembre 1995. 'Babau' is to Italians what the English-speaking world terms 'the bogeyman'.
55. *Sardegna Nuova*, 12 novembre 1995.
56. Quoted in: Del Boca, 'Una lunga battaglia', p. 166.
57. Del Boca, 'Una lunga battaglia', p. 166.
58. Del Boca, 'Una lunga battaglia', p. 168.
59. Del Boca, *Italiani, brava gente?*, p. 93.
60. Quoted in: Del Boca, 'Una lunga battaglia', p. 206, n. 75.
61. Quoted in: Del Boca, 'Una lunga battaglia', p. 207, n. 75.
62. Del Boca, 'Una lunga battaglia', p. 207, n. 75.
63. *l'Unità*, 9 febbraio 1996.
64. Quoted in: Del Boca, 'Una lunga battaglia', p. 171. See also: 'Lealtà di Indro Montanelli: «Le carte mi danno torto»', *L'Arena*, 23 marzo 2015. Available online at: https://www.larena.it/argomenti/cultura/lealt%C3%A0-di-indro-montanelli-le-carte-mi-danno-torto-1.3170149.
65. Indro Montanelli, 'Gas in Etiopia: i documenti mi danno torto', *Corriere della Sera*, 13 febbraio 1996. Archived at Corriere della Sera, Archivio, 'Gas in Etiopia: i documenti mi danno torto': https://web.archive.org/web/20121107180132/http://archiviostorico.corriere.it/1996/febbraio/13/Gas_Etiopia_documenti_danno_torto_co_0_9602135236.shtml.
66. Quoted in: Del Boca, 'Una lunga battaglia', pp. 172–3. See also: Montanelli, 'Gas in Etiopia'.
67. Del Boca, 'Una lunga battaglia', p. 173.
68. Indro Montanelli, *XX Battaglione Eritreo* (Milano: Editore Panorama, 1936).
69. Angelo Del Boca, 'Introduzione' a Indro Montanelli, *XX Battaglione Eritreo: Il primo romanzo e le lettere inedite dal fronte africano. A cura di Angelo Del Boca* (Milano: Edizione Rizzoli, 2010/Edizione digitale [Kindle], Locs. 168–72).
70. Omar Alfieri, 'A morte Montanelli! Ma Montanelli chi?' ZTL L'information Cambia Rotta, 22 Giugno 2020. Available at: https://ztl.live/cultura/a-morte-montanelli-ma-montanelli-chi.
71. Nicholas Doumanis, 'The Italian Empire and *brava gente*: Oral History and the Dodecanese Islands', in R.J.B. Bosworth and Patrizia Dogliani (eds), *Italian Fascism: History, Memory and Representation* (London: Palgrave Macmillan, 1999), p. 161.
72. Martin Johnes, 'Sometimes Welsh – and British – identities are trapped by their pasts', *Guardian*, 1 March 2022. Available at: https://www.theguardian.com/news/2022/mar/01/roughly-the-size-of-wales-four-reflections-on-welsh-identity-in-the-21st-century.
73. J.F.C. Fuller, 'The Italo-Ethiopian War: A Military Analysis by an Eye-witness Observer', *Army Ordnance*, May–June 1936, 16(96):347.
74. Rudolf Ritter und Edler von Xylander, *Die Eroberung Abessiniens 1935/36: Militärische Erfahrungen und Lehren aus dem ersten neuzeitlichen Vernichtungskrieg auf kolonialem Boden* (Berlin: ES Mittler &

Sohn, 1937). Xylander joined the Royal Bavarian Army in 1890 and fought in the First World War before retiring with the rank of colonel (*Oberst*) in September 1921. After his retirement he undertook military history studies and also wrote several books. From 1935 he was employed at the Berlin War Academy as a teacher of war history. At the beginning of the Second World War he was reactivated as a colonel in the summer of 1939 and later promoted to major general. See: https://www.lexikon-der-wehrmacht.de/Personenregister/X/XylanderRudolfRitterv.htm. His account of the Italian use of mustard gas can be found on pp. 64–5.
75. Thomas Pakenham, *The Scramble for Africa: 1876–1912* (London: Abacus, 1992). The other African state to escape colonisation was Liberia.
76. A translated copy of the letter dated 10 April 1891 is in the UK National Archives: Rodd to Sallisbury, No. 15, 4 May 1897. FO 1/32. Special Mission to King Menelik. Mr J. Rennel Rodd Diplomatic. 1897.
77. Raffaele Ruggeri, '"The Battle of the Lions": Adua, 1896', *Military Illustrated: Past & Present*, April/May 1990, 24:7. See also: Raffaele Girlando, *Marzo 1896 – La Battaglia Di Adua* (Torino: Italia Editrice, 1996).
78. Winston S. Churchill, *The River War: An Historical Account of the Reconquest of The Soudan: Volume I* (London: Longmans, Green & Co., 1899), pp. 170–1.
79. Aristotle A. Kallis, *Fascist Ideology: Territory and Expansionism in Italy and Germany, 1922–1945* (London: Routledge, 2000), p. 32.
80. Benito Mussolini, 'Per l'inaugurazione della lapide a Francesco Crispi, fatta in Roma il 12 gennaio 1924', in Valentino Piccoli (ed.), *Scritti E Discorsi Di Benito Mussolini: Edizione definitiva [Vol.] IV: Il 1924* (Milano: Ulrico Hoepli Editore, 1934-XII), p. 15.
81. Eduardo Ximenes, Marcello Donativi (ed.) and Fabio Cavedagna (ed.), *Sul campo di Adua* (Brindisi: Edizioni Trabant, 2021), pp. 15–16.

Chapter 2: The Sawdust Caesar
1. Noel Malcolm, *Authorihews* (Independently published, 2021), p. 29.
2. Carlo D'Este, 'Not-so-imperial leader'; a review of R.J.B. Bosworth, *Mussolini* (London: Bloomsbury Academic, 2010) in the *Guardian*, 29 August 2002.
3. See, for example: Christian Goeschel, *Mussolini and Hitler: The Forging of the Fascist Alliance* (New Haven, CN: Yale University Press, 2018). R.J.B. Bosworth, *Mussolini* (London: Bloomsbury Academic, 2010).
4. Arnold J. Lien, 'Machiavelli's Prince and Mussolini's Facism' [*sic*], *Social Science*, 1929, 4(4):435–6.
5. 'In 1919 and 1920 fascism was a vague leftist, republican, populist anti-party movement. Then, in 1921, it became a monarchist right-wing party. It believed in laissez-faire economics under Alberto De Stefani from 1922 to 1925, then shifted to policies of state control and cartelisation under subsequent economic ministers. From 1929 to 1934 corporatism was the hallmark of Fascism; in 1935 and 1936, the regime declared a corporative pause and moved to a war footing and autarky. During the late 1930s ... imperialism, colonialism and racism took over as central themes.' Alexander De Grand, 'Mussolini's Follies: Fascism in Its Imperial and Racist Phase, 1935–1940', *Contemporary European History*, May 2004, 13(2):127–8.
6. Office of the Historian, *Papers Relating to the Foreign Relations of the United States, 1925, Volume II*, 'Expulsion from Italy of George Seldes, correspondent of the Chicago Tribune'. Available at: https://history.state.gov/historicaldocuments/frus1925v02/ch38. For the killing of Matteotti and those responsible see: Gigliola Alvisi, *Giacomo Matteotti: Una morte annunciata* (Vicenza: in edibus, 2014). For a brief account in English see: Edward Townley, *Mussolini and Italy* (Oxford: Heinemann Educational, 2002), pp. 53–6.
7. Claire Giordano, Gustavo Piga and Giovanni Trovato, 'Italy's Industrial Great Depression: Fascist Price and Wage Policies', *Macroeconomic Dynamics*, April 2014, 18(3):689–720. Fabrizio Perri, 'The Great Depression in Italy: Trade Restrictions and Real Wage Rigidities', a paper prepared for the conference: Great Depressions of the 20th Century, October 20–21, 2000, at the

Federal Reserve Bank of Minneapolis. Available at: http://faculty.marshall.usc.edu/Vincenzo-Quadrini/papers/deprpap.pdf.
8. George Seldes, *Sawdust Caesar: The Untold History of Mussolini and Fascism* (New York: Harper & Brothers, 1935), p. 364.
9. Benito Mussolini, 'Preludio al Machiavelli (30 aprile 1924)', in *Scritti e Discorsi di Benito Mussolini edizione definitiva IV: Il 1924* (Milano: Ulrico Hoepli, 1934-XII), p. 105.
10. 'Nessuna cosa fa tanto stimare un principe, quanto fanno le grandi imprese eil dare di sesempi rari.' Niccolò Machiavelli and L. Arthur Burd (ed.), *Il Principe* (Oxford: Clarendon Press, 1891), p. 337. As Shakespeare, somewhat later than Machiavelli (c.1597), had King Henry IV put it: 'Be it thy course to busy giddy minds |With foreign quarrels; that action, hence borne out, | May waste the memory of the former days.' *Henry IV, Part 2*: Act 4, Scene 5.
11. Roger Griffin, who has studied and written widely on the subject, defines generic fascism as: 'a term for a singularly protean [the ability to assume different forms] genus of modern politics inspired by the conviction that a process of national rebirth (palingenesis) has become essential to bring to an end a protracted period of social and cultural decadence, and expressing itself ideologically in a revolutionary form of integral nationalism (ultra-nationalism)'. Roger Griffin, 'Fascism', in Roger Griffin (ed.), *International Fascism: Theories, Causes and the New Consensus* (London: Arnold, 1998), pp. 35–6.
12. Kenneth Scott, 'Mussolini and the Roman Empire', *Classical Journal*, June 1932, 27(9):646.
13. There are numerous books in print which explain how Mussolini rose to, and wielded, power in Italy. The best works in English are undoubtedly R.J.B. Bosworth's *Mussolini* and *Mussolini and the Eclipse of Italian Fascism: From Dictatorship to Populism* (New Haven, CT: Yale University Press, 2021).
14. Raffaele Guariglia, *Ricordi: 1922–1946* (Napoli: Scientifiche Italiane, 1950), p. 28.
15. Ruggero Moscati, 'Gli esordi della politica estera fascista. Il periodo Contarini-Corfù', in Augusto Torre et al. (eds), *La politica estera italiana dal 1914 al 1943* (Roma: ERI, 1963), p. 84.
16. James Barros, 'Mussolini's first Aggression: the Corfu Ultimatum', *Balkan Studies*, 1961, 2:257–86.
17. Barros, 'Mussolini's first Aggression', p. 262.
18. Maria Paschalidi, *Constructing Ionian Identities: The Ionian Islands in British Official Discourses; 1815–1864: A Thesis Submitted for the Degree of Doctor of Philosophy* (London: University College London, 2009). Available at: https://discovery.ucl.ac.uk/id/eprint/19415/1/19415.pdf. For Mussolini's claims, see: Max Domarus, *Mussolini und Hitler: Zwei Wege-gleiches Ende* (Würzburg: Domarus, 1977), p. 115. Kallis, *Fascist Ideology*, pp. 50–1.
19. Sami Sarè, *The League of Nations and the Debate on Disarmament (1918–1919)* (Rome: Edizioni Nuova cultura, 2013), p. 151. For the Corfu Incident in particular see: James Barros, *The Corfu Incident of 1923: Mussolini and The League of Nations* (Princeton, NJ: Princeton University Press, 1965).
20. George Scott, *The Rise and Fall of the League of Nations* (London: Hutchinson, 1973), p. 87.
21. H. James Burgwyn, *Italian Foreign Policy in the Interwar Period 1918–1940* (London: Praeger, 1997), p. 24.
22. Angelo Del Boca, *Gli italiani in Libia: Tripoli bel suol d'amore: 1860–1922*, Vol. I (Milan: Mondadori, 1986), vol. 1, p. 261. See also: Mario Isnenghi, *I luoghi della memoria: Simboli e miti dell'Italia unita* (Roma: Laterza, 1996), p. 421.
23. Charles Stephenson, *A Box of Sand: The Italo-Ottoman War 1911–1912: the First Land, Sea and Air War* (Ticehurst: Tattered Flag, 2014).
24. A. James Gregor, *Young Mussolini and the Intellectual Origins of Fascism* (Berkeley, CA: University of California Press, 1979), p. 129.
25. Stefano Marcuzzi, *Britain and Italy in the Era of the Great War: Defending and Forging Empires* (Cambridge: Cambridge University Press, 2020). Gianluigi Bernati, *Fascismo: Nascita, formazione, evoluzione e caduta del Partito Nazionale Fascista* (Torre del Greco: Edizioni Duemme, 2017). Paolo

Soave, *Una vittoria mutilata? L'Italia e la Conferenza di Pace di Parigi* (Soveria Mannelli: Rubbettino Editore, 2020). Giulia Albanese, *La marcia su Roma* (Roma: Editori Laterza, 2006).
26. Quoted in: Mario Bussoni, *La Marcia su Roma* (Fidenza: Mattioli 1885, 2012), p. 31.
27. See: Giorgio Rochat, *Guerre Italiane in Libia e in Etiopia. Studi militari 1921–1939* (Treviso: Pagus Edizione, 1991).
28. See: Ferdinando Pedriali, 'Aerei italiani in Libia (1911–1912)', *Storia Militare*, November 2007, 170:31–40 and Carlo Rinaldi, 'I dirigibili italiani nella campagna di Libia', *Storia Militare*, March 1995, 18:38–49.
29. Sebastiano Licheri, 'Gli ordinamenti dell "aeronautica militare italiana dal 1884 al 1918"', in Ministero per i beni culturali e ambientali Ufficio centrale per i beni archivistici, Le fonti per la storia militare italiana in età contemporanea. *Atti del III seminario, Roma, 16–17 dicembre 1988* (Roma: Ediprint Service, 1993), p. 480.
30. Stephenson, *A Box of Sand*, p. 230.
31. Claudio G. Segrè, *Italo Balbo: A Fascist Life* (Berkeley, CA: University of California Press, 1987), p. 322.
32. Giorgio Rochat, 'La repressione della resistenza in Cirenaica', in Enzo Santarelli et al. (eds), *Omar al-Mukhtar e la riconquista fascista della Libia* (Milano: Marzorati, 1981), pp. 82–3.
33. Angelo Del Boca, *A un passo dalla forca: atrocita? e infamie dell'occupazione italiana della Libia nelle memorie del patriota Mohamed Fekini* (Milano: Baldini Castoldi Dalai, 2007), p. 10.
34. Rochat, 'L'impiego dei gas', p. 73. For a detailed account see: Eric Salerno, *Genocidio in Libia. Le atrocità nascoste dell'avventura coloniale italiana (1911–1931)* (Milano: Sugarco, 1979), pp. 50–61.
35. The four senior Fascist leaders under Mussolini.
36. Italo Balbo, Sottosegretario di Stato per L'aeronautica, *La politica aeronautica dell'Italia fascista: discorso sul bilancio dell'aeronautica pronunciato alla Camera dei deputati nella tornata del 29 marzo 1927* (Roma: Tipografia della camera dei deputati, MCMXXVII-V), p. 23. For an account in English dealing with the life and works of Balbo, see: Segrè, *Italo Balbo*.
37. Captain B.H. Liddell Hart, *Paris or The Future of War* (New York: EP Dutton & Co., 1925), p. 51. The 'Paris' of the title is the son of Priam, King of Troy. As the author has it (p. 22): 'In the Trojan war, after Achilles had slain Hector in direct combat, Paris brought stratagem to bear, and his arrow, guided by Apollo, struck Achilles in his vulnerable heel ... After dashing out the lives of millions in vain assault against the enemy's strength, it might not be amiss now to take a lesson from the objective aimed at by Paris 3,000 years ago.'
38. Colonel T.E. Lawrence, 'France, Britain, and the Arabs', *Observer*, 8 August 1920. Available at: http://www.telstudies.org/writings/works/articles_essays/1920_france_britain_and_the_arabs.shtml.
39. Quoted in: Martin Gilbert, *World in Torment: Winston S Churchill 1917–1922* (London: Minerva, 1990), p. 494. See also: UK National Archives. WO 32/5184. 'GENERAL AND WARLIKE STORES: Gas (Code 45(L)): Policy regarding use of gas bombs by Royal Air Force against hill tribesmen in India and Arabs in Middle East. Design and manufacture of bombs.' 1919.
40. See: R.M. Douglas, 'Did Britain Use Chemical Weapons in Mandatory Iraq?', *Journal of Modern History*, December 2009, 81(4).
41. J.F. Salafranca, *La República del Rif* (Málaga: Algazara, 2004).
42. Sebastian Balfour, *Deadly Embrace: Morocco and the Road to the Spanish Civil War* (Oxford: Oxford University Press, 2002), p. 156. For an account of this 'Secret History of Chemical Warfare Against Moroccans' see Balfour, *Deadly Embrace*, pp. 123–56. See also: UK National Archives. WO 188/765. 'Chemical warfare: Spain'. 1922–1926.
43. B.F. Cheltsov, 'History of the creation and activities of the Air Force headquarters 1912–1945 to the 95th anniversary of the Russian Air Force. *Military Historical Journal*, 2007, 8:3–7.
44. Aeronautica Militare Comando Generale delle Scuole, *Storia dell'Aeronautica Militare Italiana* (Caserta: Divisione Formazione Sottufficiali e Truppa, n.d.), p. 9. Ciro Paoletti, *A Military History of Italy* (Westport, CT: Praeger Security International, 2008), p. 156.
45. Fernando Esposito and Patrick Camiller (trans.), *Fascism, Aviation and Mythical Modernity* (Houndsmills: Palgrave Macmillan, 2015), p. 46.

46. *Anno XI dell'era fascista* (Year 11 of the Fascist Era). The obligation to add, in Roman numerals, the year of the Fascist Era alongside that of the Common Era came into force on 29 October 1927. The Fascist year started on 28 October, the date of Mussolini's accession to power via the March on Rome. Year I of the Fascist Era therefore ran from 28 October 1922 to 27 October 1923. See: *Tabella Cronologica Dell'era Fascista*. Available at: https://www.indire.it/wp-content/uploads/2016/09/Tabella_cronologica_fascista.pdf.
47. For a detailed account see: Italo Balbo, *La Centuria Alata* (Milano: Mondadori, 1934). Guerri points out that had it been possible to organise it a year earlier, the celebration would have been ten years of Fascism. See: Giordano Bruno Guerri, *Italo Balbo. Lo squadrista, il gerarca, l'aviatore, la biografia basata su documenti inediti, del più pericoloso rivale di Mussolini* (Milano: Vallardi, 1984), pp. 349–50.
48. Margherita Grassini Sarfatti and Brian R. Sullivan ('Edited, Annotated, and with Commentary by'), *My Fault: Mussolini As I Knew Him* (New York: Enigma, 2014), pp. 58–9.
49. Regio Decreto Legge 15 ottobre 1925, n. 1911. 'Unificazione del Servizio chimico militare per i Ministeri della guerra, della marina, del l'aeronautica' (*Gazzetta Ufficiale* n. 266 del 16 novembre 1925). Marco Montagnani, Antonino Zarcone e Filippo Cappellano, *Il servizio chimico militare 1923–1945. Storia, ordinamento, equipaggiamento. Tomo I* (Roma: Stato Maggiore dell'Esercito Ufficio storico, 2011), pp. 26, 32–3. For Helbig see: R.M. Corelli, 'Demetrio Helbig', in Gianfranco Scorrano (ed.), *La Chimica Italiana* (Pàdova: Gianfranco Scorrano, 2008), pp. 420–2. Available at: http://wwwdisc.chimica.unipd.it/gianfranco.scorrano/pubblica/la_chimica_italiana.pdf; https://issuu.com/rivista.militare1/docs/il-servizio-chimico-militare-vol-1-testo; https://issuu.com/rivista.militare1/docs/il-servizio-chimico-militare-vol-2-testo.
50. Giorgio Zampetti et al. (eds), *Armi chimiche: un'eredità ancora pericolosa* (Roma: Legambiente e Coordinamento Nazionale Bonifica Armi Chimiche, 2012), p. 5. Contamination of this area, and indeed many others where chemical weapons were produced, stored and indeed disposed of, continues to be a hazard to this day. See: Gianluca Di Feo, *Veleni di Stato* (Milano: BUR Rizzoli, 2009).
51. 'Strategic bombing is an umbrella term referring to the bombing of enemy assets far from the line of battle, usually on the enemy home front (industries, infrastructure, centers of communication, and the general population)', Tami Davis Biddle, *Air Power and Warfare: A Century of Theory and History* (Carlisle, PA: Strategic Studies Institute and US Army War College Press, 2019), p. 5. The American airman Brigadier General William 'Billy' Mitchell formulated similar arguments at the same time as Douhet based on his experiences during the First World War: 'nothing made them [the Germans] cry louder than the bombardment attacks against their centers of production by Allied aircraft. No matter what the propriety of such attacks may have been, it must be taken into consideration that in the World War the Germans adopted and adhered to the theory that with a nation in arms, every man, woman and child of the hostile state is working either on the field of battle, or in factories and fields, to further the object of their armed forces. The Germans having adopted it, the Allies would have suffered a distinct strategical disadvantage had they failed to adopt similar tactics, and on the strength of this precedent of the past war, it is probable that the next war will see the original German theory carried out to a more marked extent.' William Mitchell, *Our Air Force: The Keystone of National Defense* (New York: EP Dutton & Co., 1921), p. 65.
52. Giulio Douhet and Dino Ferrari (trans.), *The Command of the Air* (Maxwell Air Force Base, AL: Air University Press, 2019), p. 18.
53. Richard H. Kohn and Joseph P. Harahan, 'Introduction to the 1983 Edition', in Douhet and Ferrari (trans.), *The Command of the Air*, pp. x–xi.
54. General Henry H. 'Hap' Arnold, commanding general of the United States Army Air Forces during the Second World War, later commented that the USAAF owed something to Douhet: 'As regards strategic bombardment, the doctrines were still Douhet's ideas modified by our own thinking … we felt … that we were doing much to furnish the practical tests for, and proofs of, the Maxwell Field theories. A different attitude from Douhet's toward bomber escort and a very

different view of precision bombing resulted.' H.H. Arnold, *Global Mission* (New York: Harper & Brothers, 1949), p. 149. Maxwell Field, Alabama, was the home of the US Army Air Corps Tactical School from 1931 to 1940, and where the US Army Air Force (USAAF) doctrine of daylight precision bombing was developed. This held that daylight air attacks by defensively armed long-range bombers could defeat an enemy by targeting key parts of its industrial infrastructure. However, it rejected making other civil infrastructure, and civilians as such, a target.

55. But rather, and as applicable to other advocates of strategic bombing, arising via: 'personality, speculation, contention, assumption and in some cases a parochial attempt to ensure an independent role for air forces'. Craig Stockings and Clinton Fernandes, 'Airpower and the Myth of Strategic Bombing as Strategy', in *ISAA* [Independent Scholars Association of Australia] *Review*, December 2006, 5(2):9. 'It is easy to see the seductive charm that Douhet's theories had for airmen ... since he seemed to supply the answers to their problems. His strategy appeared revolutionary, bold and in tune with the new industrial age and the experiences of World War I, when in fact it was none of these. Douhet had borrowed heavily from contemporary prewar sea strategy; his observations about modern industrialism were inaccurate; and his emphasis on strategic bombing was derived from the weakest example of air power during World War I.' Edward Homze, 'The Continental Experience', in Alfred F. Hurley and Robert C. Ehrhart (eds), *Air Power and Warfare: The Proceedings of the 8th Military History Symposium, United States Air Force Academy, 18–20 October 1978* (Washington DC: Office of Air Force History, Headquarters USAF and United States Air Force Academy, 1979), p. 41.

56. Colonel J.F.C. Fuller, *The Reformation of War* (London: Hutchinson & Co., 1923), p. 150. For Fuller, see: Anthony John Trythall, *'Boney' Fuller: Soldier, Strategist, and Writer* (Baltimore: The Nautical & Aviation Publishing Company of America, 1989); Brian Holden Reid, *J.F.C. Fuller: Military Thinker* (New York: St Martin's Press, 1987). See also: Michael Welch, 'The Science of War: A Discussion of J.F.C. Fuller's Shattering of British Continuity', *Journal of the Society for Army Historical Research*, Winter 2001, 79(320), and Brian Holden Reid, 'Major General J.F.C. Fuller and the Revolution in British Military Thought', *Journal of the Society for Army Historical Research*, Spring 1995, 73(293).

57. Hansard, vol. 341, col. 287, 10 November 1938. 'Air-Raid Precautions'. The Lord Privy Seal (Sir John Anderson). Available at: https://hansard.parliament.uk/Commons/1938-11-10/debates/09e9de64-5ff1-4fb3-ad4f-8dd9384efe8b/CommonsChamber.

58. Thomas, Eleventh Earl of Dundonald and H.R. Fox Bourne, *The Life of Thomas, Lord Cochrane, Tenth Earl of Dundonald: Volume II* (London: Richard Bentley, 1869), p. 250. See also: Charles Stephenson, *The Admiral's Secret Weapon: Lord Dundonald and the Origins of Chemical Warfare* (Woodbridge: Boydell Press, 2006).

59. Hansard, vol. 270, col. 632, 10 November 1932. 'Debate on International Affairs'. The Lord President of the Council (Mr Baldwin). Available at: https://api.parliament.uk/historic-hansard/commons/1932/nov/10/international-affairs. Sir Arthur 'Bomber' (also 'Butcher') Harris, then commander-in-chief of RAF's Bomber Command, argued in 1942 that: 'There are a lot of people who say that bombing can never win a war. Well, my answer to that is that it has never been tried yet. Germany ... will make a most interesting initial experiment.' Quoted in: Linda Robertson, 'Dresden (2006): Marketing the Bombing of Dresden in Germany, Great Britain, and the United States', in Douglas A. Cunningham and John C. Nelson (eds), *A Companion to the War Film* (Chichester: Wiley Blackwell, 2016), p. 244.

60. Aeronautica Militare Comando Generale delle Scuole, *Storia dell'Aeronautica Militare Italiana* (Caserta: Divisione Formazione Sottufficiali e Truppa, n.d. [2013]), p. 31.

61. See: Salvatore Minardi, *Alle origini dell'incidente di Ual Ual* (Roma: Salvatore Sciascia Editore, 1990). A concise, English language description of the Italian reaction to the 'incident' can be found in: J. Kenneth Brody, *The Avoidable War Volume 2: Pierre Laval and the Politics of Reality, 1935–1936* (London: Transaction Publishers, 2000), pp. 44–5.

62. 'Regio Decreto-Legge 9 dicembre 1928, n. 3303. Esecuzione del Trattato di amicizia, conciliazione ed arbitrato, fra il Regno d'Italia e l'Impero Etiopico, firmato in Addis Abeba il 2 agosto

1928', *Gazzetta Ufficiale Del Regno D'italia*, Lunedì, 28 gennaio 1929, VII(23):463–4. ['Royal Decree-Law 9 December 1928, n. 3303. Execution of the Treaty of Friendship, Conciliation and Arbitration, between the Kingdom of Italy and the Ethiopian Empire, signed in Addis Ababa on 2 August 1928', *Official Journal of the Kingdom of Italy*, Monday, 28 January 1929, Year VII, 23:463–4].

63. Ian L. Campbell, 'Italian Atrocities in Ethiopia: An Enquiry into the Violence of Fascism's First Military Invasion and Occupation', *Journal of Genocide Research*, 2022, 24(1):119.
64. These were treaties between Italy and the Catholic Church which created the Vatican City State. They also restored the Church to the privileged position it had lost during the unification of Italy. See: David I. Kertzer, *The Pope and Mussolini: The Secret History of Pius XI and the Rise of Fascism in Europe* (Oxford: Oxford University Press, 2014). For the successful military campaign of 1870, which divested the Pope of his temporal holdings see: Stephenson, *A Box of Sand*, pp. 20–1.
65. See: Ian Campbell, *Holy War: The Untold Story of Catholic Italy's Crusade Against the Ethiopian Orthodox Church* (London: Hurst & Co., 2021).
66. Mussolini to Badoglio. Memorandum. 30 December 1934. Quoted in: Giorgio Rochat, *Militari e politici nella preparazione della campagna d'Etiopia: Studio e documenti 1932–1936* (Milano: Franco Angeli Editore, 1971), pp. 377–8. Also: Document 358, 'Direttive del Capo del Governo … Segretissimo', p. 368.
67. Ferdinando Pedriali, *L'aeronautica italiana nelle guerre coloniali: Guerra Etiopica 1935–36* (Roma: Stato Maggiore Aeronautica Ufficio storico, 1997), p. 23.
68. Ferdinando Pedriali, 'Le armi chimiche in Africa Orientale: storia, tecnica, obiettivi, efficacia', in Angelo Del Boca (ed.), *I Gas di Mussolini: Il fascismo e la guerra d'Etopia* (Roma: Editorio Riuniti, 2017), p. 123.
69. 'T' stood for the timed fuse, '500' showed that the external dimensions of the device were equal to those of the 500kg high explosive bomb, whilst 'C' indicated the filling was a chemical. Pedriali, 'Le armi chimiche in Africa Orientale', p. 124.
70. Pedriali, *L'aeronautica italiana*, p. 23.
71. Pedriali, 'Le armi chimiche in Africa Orientale', p. 126.
72. 'The Protocol for the Prohibition of the Use in War of Asphyxiating, Poisonous or other Gases, and of Bacteriological Methods of Warfare'. Signed at Geneva by Italy on 17 June 1925; came into effect 3 April 1928. Available at: https://treaties.unoda.org/t/1925.
73. Document 358, 'Direttive del Capo del Governo … Segretissimo', pp. 366–7.
74. Benito Mussolini, 'Introduction' to Emilio De Bono and Bernard Miall (trans.), *Anno XIIII: the Conquest of an Empire* (London: Cresset Press, 1937), p. xiv. This work is a translation of: Emilio De Bono, *La Preparazione e le Prime Operazioni: La Conquista Dell' Impero* (Roma: Istituto Nazionale Fascista di Cultura, 1937-XV).

Chapter 3: 'A Terrain of Crag and Precipice'

1. Attributed to Omar Bradley. Quoted in: General Sir Richard Shirreff, 'Conducting Joint Operations', in Julian Lindley-French and Yves Boyer (eds), *The Oxford Handbook of War* (Oxford: Oxford University Press, 2012), p. 376.
2. Lieutenant Colonel Charles Andrew Willoughby, *Maneuver in War* (Harrisburg, PA: Military Service Publishing, 1939), p. 239.
3. Mussolini, 'Introduction' [*Anno XIIII*], p. xiv. For De Bono's arrival see p. 58.
4. 'By Royal Decree of 28 March 1935, I was appointed Commander-in-Chief of the troops in East Africa'. De Bono and Miall (trans.), *Anno XIIII: the Conquest of an Empire*, p. 90.
5. Franco Fucci, *Emilio De Bono: il maresciallo fucilato* (Milano: Ugo Mursia Editore, 1989), p. 192. For a history of the MVSN – *Camicia Nera* (singular) or *Camicie Nere* (plural) *aka* CC.NN. – see: Pierluigi Romeo di Colloredo Mels, *Camicia Nera!: Storia militare della Milizia Volontaria per la Sicurezza Nazionale dalle origini al 25 luglio* (ZaniCA: Soldiershop Publishing, 2017).
6. «*Queste Divisioni di CC.NN. saranno la documentazione che l'impresa trova il consenso popolare*». Mussolini to De Bono. 8 March 1935. Quoted in: De Bono, *La Preparazione e le Prime Operazioni*, p. 81.

7. For biographical details see: De Bono, Emilio, di Elvira Valleri Scaffei – Dizionario Biografico degli Italiani vol. 33 (1987). Available at: https://www.treccani.it/enciclopedia/emilio-de-bono_ (Dizionario-Biografico).
8. Longo, *La Campagna Italo-Etiopica, I*, pp. 47–8.
9. Rochat, *Militari e politici nella preparazione della campagna d'Etiopia*, p. 30.
10. Matteo Dominioni, *Lo sfascio dell'impero: Gli italiani in Etiopia 1936–1941* (Roma: Editori Laterza, 2008), p. 8. Giorgio Rochat, *Le guerre italiane 1935–1943: Dall'impero d'Etiopia alla disfatta* (Torino: Giulio Einaudi Editore, 2008), p. 23.
11. De Bono and Miall (trans.), *Anno XIIII: the Conquest of an Empire*, p. 13.
12. This was a process already under way and seemingly popular. For example, at the end of the First World War, and under the Treaty of Versailles, a highly industrialised area of Germany on its border with France, dubbed the Territory of the Saar Basin, had been administered by the League of Nations. France was given control of the coal mines but under the terms of the Treaty after fifteen years a referendum was to be held concerning the Territory's future status. This was held on 13 January 1935, resulting in over 90% of voters opting for reunification with Germany. As one scholar phrased it: 'The verdict of the plebiscite of 1935 demonstrated the power of nationalism over economics and over internationalism ... the overwhelming vote for union with Hitler's Reich was so impressive that only one conclusion could be drawn, namely, that the totalitarian German regime was not distasteful to most of the Saar inhabitants, and that they preferred it even to an efficient, economical, and benevolent international rule.' Frank M. Russell, *The Saar: Battleground and Pawn* (Stanford, CA: Stanford University Press, 1951), pp. 105–6.
13. The Austrian Chancellor, Engelbert Dollfuss, visited Mussolini in April 1933 to seal an alliance between the two states, both being determined to resist the pan-German ideology evinced by Hitler's recently arisen regime in Berlin. Mussolini provided Austria with financial assistance and armaments. In 1934, following Dolfuss' assassination by Austrian Nazis, Italian forces concentrated at the Brenner Pass when it seemed that Germany might take over Austria. See: Alfred D. Low, *The Anschluss Movement, 1931–1938, and the Great Powers* (Boulder, CO: East European Monographs, 1985); Gottfried-Karl Kindermann, Sonia Brough (trans.) and David Taylor (trans.), *Hitler's Defeat in Austria, 1933–1934: Europe's First Containment of Nazi Expansionism* (Boulder, CO: Westview Press, 1988); Jürgen Gehl, *Austria, Germany and the Anschluss 1931–1938* (Oxford: Oxford University Press, 1963).
14. Massimo Mazzetti, *La politica militare italiana fra le due guerre mondiali (1918–1940)* (Salerno: Edizioni Beta, 1974), p. 154.
15. Richard Evans, *The Third Reich in Power 1933–1939* (London: Penguin Books, 2006), p. 33.
16. Longo, *La Campagna Italo-Etiopica, I*, p. 49. De Bono and Miall (trans.), *Anno XIIII: the Conquest of an Empire*, p. 13.
17. De Bono and Miall (trans.), *Anno XIIII: the Conquest of an Empire*, p. 4.
18. John F. Due, *Rail and Road Transport in The Sudan* (Urbana-Champaign, IL: University of Illinois, 1977), p. 3. See also: M.W. Daly and Jane R. Hogan, *Images of Empire: Photographic Sources for the British in the Sudan* (Leiden: Brill 2005); Kenneth J. Perkins, *Port Sudan: The Evolution of a Colonial City* (Abingdon: Routledge, 2019); Richard Hill, *Sudan Transport: A History of Railway, Marine, and River Services in the Republic of the Sudan* (Oxford: Oxford University Press, 1965).
19. The Division of Regional Information from a report by Carlton Hurst, American Consul at Aden, and from Italian official sources, 'Italian Colonial Development 1: Eritrea, Somaliland, and Oltre Giuba', *Commerce Reports: A Weekly Survey Of Foreign Trade Issued by the Bureau of Foreign and Domestic Commerce*, 27 July 1931, 30:200.
20. De Bono and Miall (trans.), *Anno XIIII: the Conquest of an Empire*, p. 84.
21. 'Italian Colonial Development 1: Eritrea, Somaliland, and Oltre Giuba'.
22. De Bono, *La Preparazione e le Prime Operazioni*, p. 12.
23. 'Italian Colonial Development 1: Eritrea, Somaliland, and Oltre Giuba'.
24. De Bono and Miall (trans.), *Anno XIIII: the Conquest of an Empire*, p. 19.

25. Rodolfo Graziani, *Una vita per l'Italia: «Ho difeso la patria»* (Milano: Gruppo Ugo Mursia Editore, 1986), p. 48.
26. Stefano Maggi, *Le ferrovie nell'Africa italiana: aspetti economici, sociali e strategici* [Working Paper n. 18 del Dipartimento di Scienze storiche, giuridiche, politiche e sociali, Università degli Studi di Siena] (Siena: Università degli Studi, 1995), pp. 9–10. Available at: https://www.dispi.unisi.it/sites/st06/files/allegatiparagrafo/22-05-2013/wp18.pdf.
27. Maggi, *Le ferrovie nell'Africa italiana*, pp. 9–10.
28. Graziani, *Una vita per l'Italia*, p. 50.
29. See: Victoria Witkowski, *Remembering Fascism and Empire: The Public Representation and Myth of Rodolfo Graziani in 20th-Century Italy*. A thesis submitted for assessment with a view to obtaining the degree of Doctor of History and Civilisation of the European University Institute, Florence, 24 September 2021. Available online: https://cadmus.eui.eu/handle/1814/72739.
30. The British despatched twenty-four road locomotives to South Africa in 1899, followed by six armoured versions, the latter being equipped with four armoured trailers apiece. They were used to tow heavy guns and their impedimenta, and the British named them 'steam sappers'. However, according to Major General Sir John Headlam of the Royal Artillery, who served with them, they were 'too cumbersome for general use on ordinary roads, and quite unsuited for taking guns into action'. See: Andrew Hills, *Pioneers of Armour: Col REB Crompton* (FWD Publishing, 2019), pp. 44–55. J.F.C. Fuller, *The Conduct of War 1789–1961* (London: Eyre & Spottiswoode, 1961), p. 136. Major General Sir John Headlam, *The History of the Royal Artillery from the Indian Mutiny to the Great War, Volume II 1899–1914* (Woolwich: Royal Artillery Institution, 1937), p. 260. For some splendid photographs see: Richard Willcox, *The Traction Engine Archive* (Stonehouse, UK: The Road Locomotive Society, 2004).
31. Comando delle forze armate della Somalia, *La guerra italo-etiopica fronte sud: Relazione Volume 4* (Addis Ababa: Ufficio superiore topocartografico del Governo generale dell' Africa Orientale, 1937), p. 60.
32. Longo, *La Campagna Italo-Etiopica*, I, p. 81. Rochat, *Le guerre italiane 1935–1943*, p. 71.
33. Comando delle forze armate della Somalia, *La guerra italo-etiopica fronte sud*, 4, p. 42.
34. Faced with the undeveloped state of Somali ports, the Italian Royal Navy (*Regia Marina*) constructed piers and deployed landing rafts to facilitate the unloading of materiel. These were mainly concentrated at Mogadishu and Bosaso (Bender Cassim, Bender Kassin). Ministero della Marina, *Il bilancio di previsione del Ministero della marina per l'esercizio finanziario dal 1° luglio 1934 al 30 giugno 1935* (Roma: Ministero della Marina, 1936), p. 39. The undeveloped state of Mogadishu was described by Edmund Demaitre: 'Ships arriving in Somaliland must anchor in the roadstead of Mogadishu, at a distance of about a mile from the port, which cannot be entered owing to the shallows and sharp rocks which make all navigation impossible along the coast. Passengers and goods are landed in small boats that run to and fro between the ships and the port, a difficult enough business, as the sea is always stormy and the roadstead haunted by the sharks that swarm in all parts of the Indian Ocean.' Edmund Demaitre (War Correspondent to the *Excelsior* (Paris), 'With the Lions of Juba', in Ladislas Farago (ed.), *Abyssinian Stop Press* (London: Robert Hale, MCMXXXVI [1936]), p. 142.
35. Graziani, *Una vita per l'Italia*, p. 50.
36. The Royal Italian Army (*Regio Esercito*) had a tradition, which survives today, of naming its infantry divisions after the regions or cities where they were raised.
37. See: Generale Luigi Frusci, *In Somalia Sul Fronte Meridionale* (Bologna: Licinio Cappelli Editore, 1936).
38. Stato Maggiore Dell'Esercito Ufficio Storico, *L'Esercito Italiano: dal 1° tricolore al 1° centenario* (Roma: Ufficio Storico dello Stato Maggiore Dell'Esercito, 1961), pp. 161, 299. Available at: http://www.regioesercito.it/reparti/fanteria/rediv29.htm; http://www.regioesercito.it/reparti/mvsn/ordmillibia.htm.

39. Comando delle forze armate della Somalia, *La guerra italo-etiopica fronte sud: Relazione Volume 1* (Addis Ababa: Ufficio superiore topocartografico del Governo generale dell' Africa Orientale, 1937), p. 60.
40. Aeronautica Militare Comando Generale delle Scuole, *Storia dell'Aeronautica Militare Italiana* (Caserta: Divisione Formazione Sottufficiali e Truppa, n.d.), p. 31.
41. Rochat, *Le guerre italiane 1935–1943*, p. 35. The British Empire eventually mobilised 365,693 Imperial and 82,742 colonial officers and men during the Second Boer War (1899–1902). Thomas Pakenham, *The Boer War* (London: Futura, 1988), p. 572.
42. The composition of the four Army Corps was as follows: **I Army Corps**: 26th Division *Assietta*, 30th Division *Sabauda*, Alpine Division *Pusteria*, 4th Blackshirt Division *3 Gennaio*. **II Army Corps**: 19th Division *Gaviniana*, 24th Division *Gran Sasso*, 3rd Blackshirt Division *21 Aprile*. **III Army Corps**: 27th Division *Sila*, 1st Blackshirt Division *23 Marzo*. **IV Army Corps**: 5th Division *Cosseria*, 2nd Blackshirt Division *28 Ottobre*, 5th Blackshirt Division *1 Febbraio*.
43. See: 'Tabella n 7 – Unita mobilitate e inviate in AO [*Africa Orientale*] alla data del 2 ottobre 1935 Allegato n. 21' and 'Tabella n 16 – Situazione approssimativa della forza presente in Eritrea al 1 ottobre 1935-XIII', in Longo, *La Campagna Italo-Etiopica, I*, pp. 90, 129–31. See also: 'Annesso n. 9. Ordine di battaglia per la campagna di Etiopia (aprile 1936)', in Stato Maggiore Dell'Esercito Ufficio Storico, *L'Esercito Italiano: dal 1° tricolore al 1° centenario* (Roma: Ufficio Storico dello Stato Maggiore Dell'Esercito, 1961), p. 299.
44. Joseph A. Obieta, *The International Status of the Suez Canal* (The Hague: Martinus Nijhoff, 1970), pp. 2–3.
45. Obieta, *International Status of the Suez Canal*, pp. 2–3, 80. See also: Edward Arthur Whittuck, *International Canals* (London: HMSO, 1920), pp. 77–84.
46. Following Commodore George Dewey's decisive victory at the Battle of Manila Bay on 1 May 1898, Spanish naval power in the Pacific had been utterly destroyed. A relief expedition set off from Cadiz on 16 June, commanded by Rear Admiral Manuel de la Cámara y Libermoore. It reached Port Said on 26 June intent on coaling. The British were extremely concerned that any prolongation of the conflict could lead to it spreading across the Atlantic and so procrastinated to such an extent that it took over a week for the expedition to pass through the canal. However, this transit more or less coincided with the destruction of Spanish naval power in the Atlantic, via the Battle of Santiago de Cuba fought on 3 July 1898. With its last naval reserves on the way to the Philippines, the Spanish government knew that the Americans could now deploy their heavy ships on operations against mainland Spain. Indeed, US propaganda and misinformation techniques made an apparently convincing case that a US naval force would cross the Atlantic and attack the Spanish mainland and other holdings such as the Canary Islands. On 7 July Cámara was ordered to return home. See: Charles Stephenson, *Germany's Asia-Pacific Empire: Colonialism and Naval Policy, 1885–1914* (Woodbridge: Boydell & Brewer, 2009), p. 52. Charles Stephenson, *The Siege of Tsingtau: The German-Japanese War, 1914* (Barnsley: Pen & Sword Military, 2017), p. 25.
47. ARTICLE 16. Should any Member of the League resort to war in disregard of its covenants under Articles 12, 13 or 15, it shall ipso facto be deemed to have committed an act of war against all other Members of the League, which hereby undertake immediately to subject it to the severance of all trade or financial relations, the prohibition of all intercourse between their nationals and the nationals of the covenant-breaking State, and the prevention of all financial, commercial or personal intercourse between the nationals of the covenant-breaking State and the nationals of any other State, whether a Member of the League or not.

It shall be the duty of the Council in such case to recommend to the several Governments concerned what effective military, naval or air force the Members of the League shall severally contribute to the armed forces to be used to protect the covenants of the League.

The Members of the League agree, further, that they will mutually support one another in the financial and economic measures which are taken under this Article, in order to minimise the loss and inconvenience resulting from the above measures, and that they will mutually support one another in resisting any specia l measures aimed at one of their number by the covenant-breaking

State, and that they will take the necessary steps to afford passage through their territory to the forces of any of the Members of the League which are co-operating to protect the covenants of the League.

Any Member of the League which has violated any covenant of the League may be declared to be no longer a Member of the League by a vote of the Council concurred in by the Representatives of all the other Members of the League represented thereon.

[Source: The Avalon Project – Documents in Law, History and Diplomacy (Yale Law School, Lillian Goldman Law Library). Available at: https://avalon.law.yale.edu/20th_century/leagcov.asp#art16.]

48. Arthur Marder, 'The Royal Navy and the Ethiopian Crisis of 1935-36', *American Historical Review*, June 1970, 75(5):1327-8. This article has been reprinted as: Arthur J. Marder, 'The Royal Navy and the Ethiopian Crisis of 1935-1936', in Arthur J. Marder, *From the Dardanelles to Oran: Studies of the Royal Navy in War and Peace 1915-1914* (Barnsley: Seaforth, 2015).
49. De Bono and Miall (trans.), *Anno XIIII: the Conquest of an Empire*, pp. 110-11.
50. Winston S. Churchill, *The Grand Alliance* (Boston, MA: Houghton Mifflin, 1950), p. 71. For a discussion on the matter see: Stephenson, *A Box of Sand*, pp. 59-60.
51. Guariglia, *Ricordi 1922-1946*, p. 234.
52. Marder, 'The Royal Navy and the Ethiopian Crisis of 1935-36', pp. 1328-9. Sir David Kelly, a senior British diplomat in Cairo, remembered how Admiral Sir Charles Forbes, the Mediterranean Fleet's deputy C-in-C, 'confided to me that his ships had enough ammunition to shoot for fifteen minutes and that, as he could take no war-time precautions to protect the Fleet crowded into Alexandria Harbour, he sighed with relief each time dawn arrived'. Quoted in: Lord Vansittart, *The Mist Procession: The Autobiography of Lord Vansittart* (London: Hutchinson & Co., 1958), p. 544. As Sir Robert Vansittart, the author had been Permanent Under-Secretary of State for Foreign Affairs. The Fleet had moved from Malta to Egypt in late August and early September 1935.
53. A.J. Barker, *The Civilizing Mission: A History of the Italo-Ethiopian War of 1935-1936* (New York: Dial Press, 1968), p. 131.
54. Alberto Sbacchi, *Legacy of Bitterness: Ethiopia and Fascist Italy, 1935-1941* (Asmara: Red Sea Press, 1997), p. 44.
55. Alberto Sbacchi, 'The Italians and the Italo-Ethiopian War, 1935-1936', *Transafrican Journal of History*, 1976, 5(2):125.
56. Sbacchi, 'The Italians and the Italo-Ethiopian War', p. 125. According to an account by a former head of the organisation, OVRA (or Ovra) was not an acronym and didn't stand for anything. Rather it originated in Mussolini wanting them 'to have serious control – reaching like octopus tentacles (*tentacolare come una piovra*) – throughout the country'. Probably through typographical error, *piovra* became OVRA. See: Guido Leto, *OVRA: Fascismo Antifascismo* (Bologna: Cappelli Editori, 1952), p. 52. There are other opinions. The German diplomat and SS colonel Eugen Dollmann considered OVRA to be highly efficient. See: Giandomenico Cosmo, 'I servizi di polizia politica durante il fascismo', in *Il movimento di liberazione in Italia rassegna bimestrale di studi e documenti a cura dell'Istituto nazionale per la storia del movimento di Liberazione in Italia*, Gennaio 1952, n 16, p. 46. For a modern treatment see: Mimmo Franzinelli, *I tentacoli dell'Ovra: Agenti, collaboratori e vittime della polizia politica fascista* (Torino: Bollati Boringhieri Editore, 1999).
57. Sbacchi, 'The Italians and the Italo-Ethiopian War', pp. 126, 135, nn. 22, 25, 27.
58. «*in quanto ai trasporti ti lascio non carta bianca ma bianchissima*». De Bono, *La Preparazione e le Prime Operazioni*, p. 52. As translated by Bernard Miall: 'As for the transport, I give you not *carta bianca* (carte blanche) but *carta bianchissima*.' Quoted in: De Bono and Miall (trans.), *Anno XIIII: the Conquest of an Empire*, p. 78.
59. «*è sempre stato cretino ed ora è anche invecchiato*». Galeazzo Ciano and Renzo De Felice (ed.), *Diario 1937-1943* (Milano: Rizzoli, 1980), p. 272.
60. De Bono, *La Preparazione e le Prime Operazioni*, p. 84.

61. As he put it: 'the climate of the lowlands, and especially that of the eastern lowlands, has all the drawbacks of a tropical climate, and not all white men can adapt themselves to it'. De Bono and Miall (trans.), *Anno XIIII: the Conquest of an Empire*, p. 41. A modern study concurs: 'The climate of Eritrea is shaped by its diverse topographical features and its location within the tropics ... The highlands have temperate climate throughout the year, while the lowlands are scorched by blazing heat ... The temperature of various locations ... is usually determined by variations in altitude rather than latitude.' Mussie Tesfagiorgis G., *Eritrea* (Santa Barbara, CA: ABC-CLIO, 2011), p. 10.
62. For details see: Longo, *La Campagna Italo-Etiopica*, I, pp. 81–3, 90–5.
63. Longo, *La Campagna Italo-Etiopica*, I, p. 95.
64. The transformation of Italy under, and by, Fascism is a recurring theme in his account. For example, see: De Bono and Miall (trans.), *Anno XIIII: the Conquest of an Empire*, pp. 38, 78, 126, 148, 185, 200.
65. J.L. Maffey et al., 'The Maffey Report: Report of an Inter-Departmental Committee on British Interests in Ethiopia', 18 June 1935. Appendix II of W.N. Medlicott, Douglas Dakin and M.E. Lambert (eds), *Documents on British Foreign Policy 1919–1939, Second Series, Volume XIV: The Italo-Ethiopian Dispute March 1934–October 1935* (London: HMSO, 1976), p. 761.
66. Mortimer Durand, *Crazy Campaign: A Personal Narrative of the Italo-Abyssinian War* (London: George Routledge, 1936), p. 197. See also: Mortimer Durand (War-Correspondent to the *Daily Telegraph*), 'The Crazy War', in Farago (ed.), *Abyssinian Stop Press*, p. 109.
67. J.A. Rogers, *The Real Facts about Ethiopia* (Baltimore, MD: Black Classic Press, 1982 [Reprint of 1936 Edition]), pp. 22, 33.
68. Fuller, 'The Italo-Ethiopian War', p. 341.
69. Hubert-Pierre Dubois, *Cheminot de Djibouti a? Addis-Abeba; le chemin de fer franco-éthiopien* (Paris: Librairie académique Perrin, 1959). Rosanna Van Gelder de Pineda, *Le chemin de fer de Djibouti à Addis-Abeba* (Paris: Editions L'Harmattan, 1995). For the time taken to make the journey in 1935 see: Steer, *Caesar in Abyssinia*, p. 21.

Chapter 4: 'Fascism believes neither in the possibility nor ...'

1. James Barros, 'The Greek-Bulgarian Incident of 1925: The League of Nations and the Great Powers', *Proceedings of the American Philosophical Society*, August 1964, 108(4):377–8.
2. Fuller, 'The Italo-Ethiopian War', p. 340.
3. 'On November 2 [1930] Ras Tafari Makonnen was crowned King of Kings, Lion of Judah, Emperor Haile Selassie I at Addis Ababa. Delegations from the entire civilised world were present to wish him, in the name of their countries, a long and prosperous reign and to assure him of their friendly intentions.' Evelyn Waugh, *Waugh in Abyssinia* (London: Longmans, Green and Co., 1936), p. 7.
4. Waugh, *Waugh in Abyssinia*, pp. 9–10.
5. UK National Archives. FO 371/8409. Abyssinia. Code 1 Files 2318–5097 (to paper 5513). Memorandum by Sir Rennell Rodd on the Abyssinian Request for Admission to the League of Nations, 26 August 1923. A 5209/5097/1.
6. Stuart Emeny (War Correspondent to the *News Chronicle*), 'Under Fire with the Emperor', in Farago (ed.), *Abyssinian Stop Press*, pp. 177–8.
7. Angelo Del Boca, *Gli italiani in Africa Orientale Volume 2: La conquista dell'Impero* (Milano: Mondadori Editore, 2009), pp. 351–7. Ladislas Farago, 'The Busu Tshiki Tshik', in Farago (ed.), *Abyssinian Stop Press*, p. 220.
8. Thomas E. Simmons, *The Man Called Brown Condor: The Forgotten History of an African American Fighter Pilot* (New York: Skyhorse Publishing, 2013), p. 128.
9. Phillip Tucker, *John C Robinson: Father of the Tuskegee Airmen* (Dulles, VA: Potomac Books, 2012), p. 103.

10. For details see: Jacques Jadoul, 'Les missions militaires belges en Ethiopie, Janvier 1930–Octobre 1935: La collaboration officielle: Aspects techniques, economiques et diplomatiques', *Revue belge d'histoire militaire*, 1987, 27(1):23–50.
11. See: David Scheere, 'Léopold Reul in Ethiopië: van officiële naar officieuze militaire samenwerking: Konden huurlingen de formele coöperatie voortzetten?' A paper produced under the auspices of Vrije Universsteit Brussel Faculteit Letteren En Wijsbegeerte. Available online at: https://www.academia.edu/12209035/L%C3%A9opold_Reul_in_Ethiopi%C3%AB_van_offici%C3%ABle_naar_officieuze_militaire_samenwerking.
12. João Bertonha, 'Paranoie fasciste? Il volontariato in favore dell'Etiopia durante la guerra del 1935–1936', *Diacronie: Studi di storia contemporanea*, 2013, 14(2). Available at: https://journals.openedition.org/diacronie/282.
13. De Bono and Miall (trans.), *Anno XIIII: the Conquest of an Empire*, p. 185.
14. Del Boca, *Gli italiani in Africa Orientale*, 2, pp. 362–3. Dominioni, *Lo sfascio dell'impero*, pp. 14–15. See also: Christopher Othen, *Lost Lions of Judah: Haile Selassie's Mongrel Foreign Legion 1935–41* (Stroud: Amberley Publishing, 2017).
15. Yuksel İzamoglu, 'Mehmet Vehib Kacı: Hayati ve Askeri Faaliyetleri', basılmamış Doktora Tezi, İstanbul Üniversitesi Sosyal Bilimler Enstitüsü, Tarih Anabilim Dali, 2010, pp. 414, 417, 419. This thesis is available at: https://www.academia.edu/37615180/VEH%C4%B0P_PA%C5%9EA_KA%C3%87I_NIN_HAYATI_VE_ASKER%C4%B0_FAAL%C4%B0YETLER%C4%B0. See also: Yuksel Nizamoglu, *Vehip Pasa: Kahramanlıktan Surgune* (Istanbul: Yitik Hazine Yayınları, 2013).
16. Emeny, 'Under Fire with the Emperor', p. 170.
17. Treaty of Versailles, 28 June 1919 (Germany); Treaty of Saint-Germain, 10 September 1919 (Austria); Treaty of Neuilly, 27 November 1919 (Bulgaria); Treaty of Trianon, 4 June 1920 (Hungary); and the Treaty of Sevres, 10 August 1920 (Ottoman Empire).
18. Richard M. Watt, *The Kings Depart: The Tragedy of Germany: Versailles and the German Revolution* (London: Literary Guild, 1969), p. 59.
19. The Avalon Project.
20. See: John Milton Cooper, *Breaking the Heart of the World: Woodrow Wilson and the Fight for the League of Nations* (Cambridge: Cambridge University Press, 2001).
21. Australia, Canada, India, New Zealand, South Africa and the United Kingdom.
22. Antoinette Iadarola, 'Ethiopia's Admission into the League of Nations: An Assessment of Motives', *International Journal of African Historical Studies*, 1975, 8(4):616, 620. The other state was Liberia, which, having sent a delegation to the Peace Conference at the end of the First World War, was an original member. This was despite Britain and France seeking to have it placed under a United States mandate. Michael D. Callahan, *A Sacred Trust: The League of Nations and Africa, 1929–1946* (Brighton: Sussex Academic Press, 2004), p. 55.
23. Hansard, vol. 305, col. 365, 24 October 1935. House of Commons Debates. Available at: https://api.parliament.uk/historic-hansard/commons/1935/oct/24/international-situation.
24. Patrick J. Buchanan, *Churchill, Hitler, and the Unnecessary War: How Britain Lost Its Empire and the West Lost the World* (New York: Three Rivers Press, 2008), pp. 159–62.
25. Robert Pearce and Graham Goodlad, *British Prime Ministers from Balfour to Brown* (Abingdon: Routledge, 2013), p. 78.
26. See Chapter 3.
27. For a brief description of the creation of Manchukuo see: Charles Stephenson, *Stalin's War on Japan: The Red Army's Manchurian Strategic Offensive Operation, 1945* (Barnsley: Pen & Sword Military, 2021), p. 16. For an in-depth account see: Thomas W. Burkman, *Japan and the League of Nations: Empire and World Order, 1914–1938* (Honolulu, HI: University of Hawai'i Press, 2008), pp. 165–93. A copy of the report is in the UK National Archives. FO 262/1802. Lytton Commission Report. 1932.
28. Barros, 'The Greek-Bulgarian Incident of 1925'.

29. An excellent primer on the war can be found in: Alejandro de Quesada with P. Jowett, *The Chaco War 1932–35: South America's Greatest Modern Conflict* (Oxford: Osprey Publishing, 2011). Another short, but interesting, account is: Antonio Sapienza, *The Chaco Air War 1932–35: The First Modern Air War in Latin America* (Solihull: Helion, 2018).
30. Bruce W. Farcau, *The Chaco War: Bolivia and Paraguay, 1932–1935* (Westport, CT: Praeger, 1996), p. 94.
31. Pierre-Etienne Bourneuf, '"We Have Been Making History": The League of Nations and the Leticia Dispute (1932–1934)', *International History Review*, 2017, 39(4):592–614. United States Department of State, *Foreign Relations of the United States: Diplomatic Papers 1933 Volume IV: The American Republics* (Washington DC: US Government Printing Office, 1950), pp. 144–5.
32. P.J. Beck, 'From the Geneva Protocol to the Greco-Bulgarian Dispute: The Development of the Baldwin Government's Policy Towards the Peacekeeping Role of the League of Nations, 1924–1925', *British Journal of International Studies*, April 1980, 6(1):64. For a thorough account of the affair see: Barros, 'The Greek-Bulgarian Incident of 1925', pp. 354–85.
33. H.A.L. Fisher, *A History of Europe: Complete Edition in One Volume* (London: Edward Arnold & Co., 1936), p. 1175.
34. Andrew Blick and Peter Hennessey, *Good Chaps No More: Safeguarding the Constitution in Stressful Times* (London: Constitution Society, 2019), p. 3.
35. Though Mussolini was the only named author, the first half of the text had been written by Giovanni Gentile, the so-called *Philosopher of Fascism*. See: A. James Gregor, *Giovanni Gentile: Philosopher of Fascism* (Abingdon: Routledge, 2017), p. 63.
36. Benito Mussolini and Jane Soames (trans.), *The Political and Social Doctrine of Fascism* (London: Hogarth Press, 1933), p. 11.
37. For an analysis of the League's successes and failures see: F.H. Hinsley, *Power and the Pursuit of Peace: Theory and Practice in the History of Relations Between States* (Cambridge: Cambridge University Press, 1967), p. 315.
38. Germany applied to join the League and did so in 1926, being granted a permanent seat on the Council. It then left, although there was supposed to be a two-year notice period, in October 1933 following Hitler's accession to power. The Soviet Union joined in September 1934, occupying the permanent seat which Germany had vacated. See: Konstantin D. Magliveras, 'The Withdrawal From the League of Nations Revisited', *Penn State International Law Review*, September 1991, 10(1):34, 52. Anique H.M. van Ginneken, *Historical Dictionary of the League of Nations* (Lanham, MD: Scarecrow Press, 2006), p. 175.
39. At least according to Britain's Foreign Secretary, Anthony Eden, writing on 24 July 1937. The Earl of Avon, *The Eden Memoirs: Facing the Dictators* (London: Cassell, 1962), p. 451.
40. Steer, *Caesar in Abyssinia*, p. 26.
41. League of Nations, *Treaty Series: Publication of Treaties and International Engagements registered with the Secretariat of the League of Nations, Volume XCIV, Numbers 1, 2, 3 and 4* (Lausanne: League of Nations, 1929), pp. 419–21.
42. Full title: 'The Protocol for the Prohibition of the Use in War of Asphyxiating, Poisonous or other Gases, and of Bacteriological Methods of Warfare'. League of Nations, *Treaty Series*, p. 73. See also: Drazan Djukic and Niccolo Pons (eds), *The Companion to International Humanitarian Law* (Leiden: Brill Nijhoff, 2018), p. 355.
43. '0.515.105. Protocollo concernente la proibizione di usare in guerra gas asfissianti, tossici o simili e mezzi batteriologici', p. 3. Fedlex: La piattaforma di pubblicazione del diritto federale. Available at: https://fedlex.data.admin.ch/filestore/fedlex.data.admin.ch/eli/cc/48/375_387_405/20040910/it/pdf-a/fedlex-data-admin-ch-eli-cc-48-375_387_405-20040910-it-pdf-a.pdf.
44. As per the Treaty of Versailles, the United States refused to ratify the Protocol. Arguments against doing so included: the comparative humanity of chemical warfare; the need to be prepared for future wars; and that the League of Nations might acquire control of the US chemical industry. Daniel P. Jones, 'American Chemists and the Geneva Protocol', *Isis: the Journal of The History of Science Society*, September 1980, 71(3):432.

45. Cristiano Andrea Ristuccia, 'The 1935 Sanctions against Italy: Would Coal and Oil have made a Difference?', *European Review of Economic History*, 2000, 4(1):87.

Chapter 5: War in the 'Old-Style'
1. Fuller, *The First of the League Wars*, p. 15.
2. 'During the 1930s the defence debate in Britain was dominated by Captain Basil Liddell Hart. The most prolific defence journalist, strategic analyst, and military historian of his day, he exerted great influence not only through his publications but also through private connections with leading politicians, particularly Leslie Hore-Belisha, Secretary of State for War 1937–1940.' Robert O'Neill, 'Liddell Hart Unveiled', *Twentieth Century British History*, 1990, 1(1):101. He was the military correspondent of *The Times* from 1935 to 1939. For a biographical account see: Alex Danchev, *Alchemist of War: The Life of Basil Liddell Hart* (London: Weidenfield & Nicolson, 1998).
3. Captain Liddell Hart, 'The Armies of Europe: IV. Italy', *Spectator*, 25 December 1936, 157(5661):1115. The same piece, or essentially so, was recycled and appeared in other journals. For example: Liddell Hart, 'The Armies of Europe', *Foreign Affairs*, January 1937, 15(2):250–3.
4. De Bono and Miall (trans.), *Anno XIIII: the Conquest of an Empire*, p. 220.
5. Longo, *La Campagna Italo-Etiopica*, I, p. 149. Unless otherwise stated, Longo '*Capitolo V: Le operazioni iniziali al fronte nord (3.X–15.X. 1935)*', pp. 149–66, is the source for this section.
6. De Bono and Miall (trans.), *Anno XIIII: the Conquest of an Empire*, p. 224.
7. De Bono and Miall (trans.), *Anno XIIII: the Conquest of an Empire*, p. 227.
8. Longo, *La Campagna Italo-Etiopica*, I, p. 157.
9. Quoted in: De Bono, *La Preparazione e le Prime Operazioni*, pp. 166–7.
10. Short for *Dajjazmac* (*Dejenazmach*), a noble rank below that of Ras. Reidulf Knut Molvaer, *Tradition and Change in Ethiopia: Social and Cultural Life as Reflected in Amharic Fictional Literature, ca 1930–1974* (Leiden: E.J. Brill, 1980), p. 40.
11. 'Deserter Pledges Help to Italians; Gugsa Says His 15,000 Men Also Will Fight Relative, Ruler of Ethiopia', *New York Times*, 13 October 1935.
12. Del Boca, *Gli italiani in Africa Orientale*, 2, pp. 408–9.
13. Longo, *La Campagna Italo-Etiopica*, I, p. 158.
14. De Bono and Miall (trans.), *Anno XIIII: the Conquest of an Empire*, p. 227.
15. David H. Shinn and Thomas P. Ofcansky, *Historical Dictionary of Ethiopia* (Lanham, MD: Scarecrow Press, 2013), pp. 50, 271.
16. Longo, *La Campagna Italo-Etiopica*, I, p. 158.
17. Del Boca, *Gli italiani in Africa Orientale*, 2, pp. 406–7.
18. De Bono and Miall (trans.), *Anno XIIII: the Conquest of an Empire*, pp. 260–1.
19. Fuller, 'The Italo-Ethiopian War', p. 341.
20. Longo, *La Campagna Italo-Etiopica*, I, p. 159.
21. Mussolini to De Bono. 17 October 1935. Quoted in: De Bono and Miall (trans.), *Anno XIIII: the Conquest of an Empire*, p. 270.
22. United Press (News Agency) report: Geneva, 5 October 1935. Available online at: https://www.upi.com/Archives/1935/10/05/Ethiopia-asks-League-of-Nations-to-act-against-Italy/9298410341771/.
23. For in-depth analysis see: George W. Baer, *Test Case: Italy, Ethiopia, and the League of Nations* (Stanford, CA: Hoover Institution Press, 1976), pp. 20–42. See also: R.A.C. Parker, 'Great Britain, France and the Ethiopian Crisis 1935–1936', *English Historical Review*, April 1974, LXXXIX(CCCLI):293–332.
24. Parker, 'Great Britain, France and the Ethiopian Crisis', p. 293.
25. Anthony L. Cardoza, *Benito Mussolini: The First Fascist* (New York: Pearson Longman, 2006), pp. 198–9.
26. Christopher Duggan, *A Concise History of Italy* (Cambridge: Cambridge University Press, 1969), p. 238.

27. Oberst Rudolf Ritter und Edler von Xylander, *Die kriegswirtschaftliche Verfassung Italiens: Stoff und Geist im modernen Krieg* (Hamburg: Hanseatische Verlagsanstalt, 1935), p. 18.
28. Watson, 'J.F.C. Fuller and the Fascist Movement in Britain', p. 38.
29. Martin Clark, *Mussolini* (Abingdon: Routledge, 2014), p. 203.
30. Quoted in: Graham Macklin, *Failed Führers: A History of Britain's Extreme Right* (Abingdon: Routledge, 2020), p. 96.
31. Watson, 'J.F.C. Fuller and the Fascist Movement in Britain', p. 41.
32. Fuller, *The First of the League Wars*, p. 12.
33. The seventh of the 'Ten Axioms' in: Leo Longanesi, *Vade-mecum del perfetto fascista: seguito da Dieci assiomi per il milite ovvero Avvisi ideali* (Firenze: Vallecchi Editore, 1926), p. 53.
34. Mussolini to De Bono 20 October 1935. Quoted in: Longo, *La Campagna Italo-Etiopica*, I, pp. 165–6. Also quoted, in part, in: De Bono and Miall (trans.), *Anno XIIII: the Conquest of an Empire*, pp. 276–7.
35. Fuller, *The First of the League Wars*, p. 15.
36. Fuller, *The First of the League Wars*, p. 15.
37. Fuller, *The First of the League Wars*, p. 15.
38. Fuller, *The First of the League Wars*, pp. 16–17.
39. Fuller, *The First of the League Wars*, p. 17.
40. Liddell Hart, *Europe in Arms* (London: Faber & Faber, 1937), p. 254.
41. De Bono to Mussolini. 21 October 1935. Quoted in: De Bono and Miall (trans.), *Anno XIIII: the Conquest of an Empire*, pp. 277–8.
42. Longo, *La Campagna Italo-Etiopica*, I, pp. 174–5.
43. Mussolini to De Bono. 25 October 1935. Quoted in: De Bono and Miall (trans.), *Anno XIIII: the Conquest of an Empire*, p. 279.
44. Mussolini to De Bono and De Bono to Mussolini. 29 October 1935. Quoted in: De Bono and Miall (trans.), *Anno XIIII: the Conquest of an Empire*, p. 283.
45. Longo, *La Campagna Italo-Etiopica*, I, p. 176.
46. De Bono and Miall (trans.), *Anno XIIII: the Conquest of an Empire*, p. 292.
47. Longo, *La Campagna Italo-Etiopica*, I, pp. 173–4.
48. Fuller, *The First of the League Wars*, p. 18.
49. Fuller, 'The Italo-Ethiopian War', p. 342.
50. Fuller, *The First of the League Wars*, p. 19.
51. De Bono and Miall (trans.), *Anno XIIII: the Conquest of an Empire*, p. 300. Amba Alagi (Imba Alaje) is a mountain (*amba*), some 70km from Makalle. It was a vital strategic point owing to its dominance of the Alagi Pass, through which wound the road south. Lake Ascianghi (Hashenge) is about 90km further south along that road.
52. Mussolini to De Bono. 11 November 1935. Quoted in: De Bono and Miall (trans.), *Anno XIIII: the Conquest of an Empire*, p. 305.
53. Fuller, *The First of the League Wars*, pp. 58–62.
54. De Bono to Mussolini. 11 November 1935. Quoted in: De Bono and Miall (trans.), *Anno XIIII: the Conquest of an Empire*, p. 307.
55. Mussolini to De Bono. 11 November 1935. Quoted in: De Bono and Miall (trans.), *Anno XIIII: the Conquest of an Empire*, p. 307.
56. Longo, *La Campagna Italo-Etiopica*, I, pp. 179–80.
57. Franco Fucci, *Emilio De Bono: il maresciallo fucilato* (Milano: Ugo Mursia Editore, 1989), p. 212. 'Various hypotheses have been made and can be made about the reasons that led Mussolini to replace De Bono with Badoglio, but the most convincing is probably the simplest: given the difficulty of the international situation ... and the complexity of the military operations from an organisational and logistical point of view, Mussolini wanted to entrust the command to a general who was undoubtedly more experienced and energetic than De Bono.' Giorgio Candeloro, *Storia dell'Italia moderna IX: Il fascismo e le sue guerre 1922–1939* (Milano: Feltrinelli Editore, 1981), p. 388.

58. Mussolini to De Bono. 17 November 1935. Quoted in: Del Boca, *Gli italiani in Africa Orientale*, 2, p. 438.

Chapter 6: Graziani

1. Steer, *Caesar in Abyssinia*, p. 170.
2. Longo, *La Campagna Italo-Etiopica*, I, p. 198.
3. Fuller, *The First of the League Wars*, pp. 23, 25.
4. Fuller, *The First of the League Wars*, p. 13.
5. Mussolini to De Bono. 28 September 1935. Quoted in: De Bono and Miall (trans.), *Anno XIIII: the Conquest of an Empire*, p. 219.
6. De Bono and Miall (trans.), *Anno XIIII: the Conquest of an Empire*, p. 218.
7. Steer, *Caesar in Abyssinia*, p. 169.
8. Longo, *La Campagna Italo-Etiopica*, I, p. 183.
9. Steer, *Caesar in Abyssinia*, p. 170.
10. Norman E. Fiske, Major, Cavalry, USA. Military Observer, *Report of Military Observer with Italian Armies in East Africa: Report No 5* (Washington, DC: Military Intelligence Division General Staff, 1936), p. 218.
11. Longo, *La Campagna Italo-Etiopica*, I, p. 188.
12. Steer, *Caesar in Abyssinia*, p. 170.
13. Steer, *Caesar in Abyssinia*, p. 172.
14. Maurizio Parri, *Tracce di cingolo: compendio generale di storia dei carristi 1917–2009* (Verona: Associazione Carristi veronese, 2016), p. 33.
15. An obsolete French rifle.
16. Steer, *Caesar in Abyssinia*, pp. 176–7.
17. Longo, *La Campagna Italo-Etiopica*, I, p. 190.
18. Parri, *Tracce di cingolo*, pp. 33–8.
19. US Army General Staff Military Intelligence Division, *Certain Studies On and Deductions from Operations of Italian Army in East Africa, October 1935–May 1936* (Washington, DC: US Army General Staff Military Intelligence Division, 1937), p. 56.
20. Parri, *Tracce di cingolo*, p. 43. For information on the L3 see: Andrea Tallillo, Antonio Tallillo and Daniele Guglielmi, *Carro L3: Carri veloci, carri leggeri, derivati* (Trento: Gruppo Modellistico Trentino, 2004). For an English language work see: Nicola Pignato, *Italian Armored Vehicles of World War Two* (Carrollton, TX: Squadron-Signal Publications, 2004).
21. Fiske, *Report of Military Observer, Report No. 5*, p. 220.
22. Longo, *La Campagna Italo-Etiopica*, I, p. 215.
23. Anthony Mockler, *Haile Selassie's War* (London: Grafton Books, 1987), p. 70.
24. Demaitre, 'With the Lions of Juba', pp. 132–3. Demaitre was the correspondent of the French journal *Excelsior*.
25. Demaitre, 'With the Lions of Juba', p. 141.
26. Rochat, *Le guerre italiane 1935–1943*, p. 41.
27. Steer, *Caesar in Abyssinia*, p. 177.
28. An interesting account of Italian propaganda around the theme can be found in: Francis O. Wilcox, 'The Use of Atrocity Stories in War', *American Political Science Review*, December 1940, 34(6):1167–78.
29. 'During my period of attendance at the Hospital of Asmara (Abyssinia) I found two groups of wounded soldiers, somewhat at variance with the usual type of gunshot and cold steel wounds familiar to European military surgeons. The first group, a large one, was constituted by the Ascari, black soldiers in the Italian service, who, having been made prisoners by the forces of the Negus, had the right hand and left foot cut off; the second, a much smaller number of cases, was formed chiefly of Italian soldiers who had survived the complete removal of their genital organs.' Thomas Fiaschi MD, 'A Report on the Mutilated and Evirated of the Battle of Adowa' (Part One), *British Medical Journal*, 29 August 1896, 2(1861):505–6. Also: Thomas Fiaschi MD, 'A Report on the

Mutilated and Evirated of the Battle of Adowa' (Part Two), *British Medical Journal*, 12 September 1896, 2(1863):649–50.
30. Communication from the Italian Government, Official No. C.123.M.62, Geneva, 19 March 1936. 'Abyssinian Atrocities Committed against Italian Workmen: Protest by the Italian Government to the League of Nations'. Available online at: https://upload.wikimedia.org/wikipedia/commons/e/e4/C-123-M-62-1936-VII_EN.pdf.
31. Unless otherwise stated, this section is based on: Longo, *La Campagna Italo-Etiopica*, I, pp. 215–19.
32. Franco Astuto and Adriano Scheggi (eds), *Le Trasmissioni dell'Esercito nel Tempo* (Roma: Rivista Militare, 1995), p. 58. Claudio Ciaralli, '"Hostes Per Aethera Eruo": La Guerra Elettronica dell'Esercito Italiano', in *i Quaderni della SCSM: Societa di Cultura e Storia Militare*, dicembre 2015, 2(XVI):14. See also: Cosmo Colavito, 'Violatori di cifrari: I crittografi del Regio Esercito (1915–1943)', in *Nuova Antologia Militare: Rivista interdisciplinare della Società Italiana di Storia Militare: Fascicolo Speciale 2021: Intelligence militare, guerra clandestina e Operazioni Speciali*, pp. 137–92. Silvio Hénin, *Non solo enigma: Storia delle guerre nascoste* (Milano: Editore Ulrico Hoepli, 2017). For a treatment of the subject in English see: David Alvarez, 'Left in the Dust: Italian Signals Intelligence, 1915–1943', *International Journal of Intelligence and CounterIntelligence*, 2001, 14(3):388–408.
33. Maria Gabriella Pasqualini, *Breve storia dell'organizzazione dei Servizi d'Informazione della Regia Marina e Regia Aeronautica 1919–1945* (Roma: Ministero della Difesa CISM – Commissione Italiana di Storia Militare, 2013), pp. 231–2. See also: Stato Maggiore della Difesa, *Il servizio informazioni militare italiano dalla sua constituzione alla fine della seconda guerra mondiale* (Roma: Stato Maggiore della Difesa, 1957), pp. 56–7.
34. Rochat, *Le guerre italiane 1935–1943*, pp. 33–4.
35. Vanda Wilcox, *The Italian Empire and the Great War* (Oxford: Oxford University Press, 2021), p. 238. For a detailed account see: George L. Simpson Jr, 'The 1925 Cession of Jubaland: A View from Great Britain's Imperial Periphery', *Journal of Global South Studies*, Spring 2020, 37(1):1–30.
36. Generale Michele Molinari, *Agli ordini di Graziani in Somalia: L'opera del Genio Militare* (Milano: Società Anonima Edizioni Scientifiche e Letterarie, 1940), p. 164.
37. Longo, *La Campagna Italo-Etiopica*, I, p. 217, n. 238.
38. Steer, *Caesar in Abyssinia*, p. 238.
39. Baer, *Test Case*, p. 64.

Chapter 7: 'a small masterpiece'

1. Telegramma del 2 gennaio 1936. Quoted in: Angelo Del Boca, 'Le fonti etiopiche e straniere sull'impiego dei gas', in Angelo Del Boca (ed.), *I gas di Mussolini: Il fascism e la guerra d'Etiopia* (Roma: Editori Reuniti, 2007), p. 55.
2. Longo, *La Campagna Italo-Etiopica*, I, p. 220. Rosaria Quartararo, 'Imperial Defence in the Mediterranean on the Eve of the Ethiopian Crisis (July–October 1935)', *Historical Journal*, March 1977, 20(1):186.
3. Francesco Rossi, *Mussolini e lo stato maggiore: avvenimenti del 1940* (Roma: Tipografia regionale, 1951), pp. 24–6.
4. Whilst all Blackshirt formations were of strictly limited military value, this one was even more so given it was composed of the over-aged, amputees (*mutilate*), foreign-resident Italians and university students. Despite their 'high fighting spirit', and supposedly because Graziani lacked sufficient transport to move them, they got no further than the 'entrenched camp of Mogadishu'. Longo, *La Campagna Italo-Etiopica*, I, p. 220. Rochat, *Le guerre italiane 1935–1943*, p. 72, n. 30.
5. Stanley Baldwin, J. Ramsay MacDonald and Sir John Simon, 'A Call to the Nation: The Joint Manifesto of the leaders. National Government', in Iain Dale (ed.), *Conservative Party General Election Manifestos 1900–1997* (Abingdon: Routledge, 2000), pp. 53–4.
6. For a thorough analysis see: James C. Robertson, 'The British General Election of 1935', *Journal of Contemporary History*, January 1974, 9(1):163.

7. Martin Ceadel, 'The First British Referendum: The Peace Ballot, 1934–5', *English Historical Review*, October 1980, 95(377):810.
8. Harold Nicolson, 'British Public Opinion and Foreign Policy', *Public Opinion Quarterly*, January 1937, 1(1):57–8.
9. Baldwin, Ramsay MacDonald and Simon, 'A Call to the Nation', p. 53.
10. Hansard, vol. 289, col. 2139, Friday, 18 May 1934. 'The Lord President of the Council (Mr [Stanley] Baldwin)'.
11. *Il Solco Fascista*, Numero 223, 18 settembre anno VIII 1935.
12. Sir Robert Vansittart, Permanent Under-Secretary at the Foreign Office, to Sir Percy Loraine, British Ambassador to Turkey. 24 July 1935. Quoted in: Michael L. Roi, *Alternative to Appeasement: Sir Robert Vansittart and Alliance Diplomacy, 1934–1937* (Westport, CT: Praeger Publishers, 1997), p. 95.
13. Fuller, 'The Italo-Ethiopian War', p. 342.
14. Burgwyn, *Italian Foreign Policy*, p. 126.
15. Steer, *Caesar in Abyssinia*, p. 240.
16. Longo, *La Campagna Italo-Etiopica*, I, p. 236.
17. Graziani to Badoglio and Lessona. 15 December 1935. Telegram reproduced in: Longo, *La Campagna Italo-Etiopica*, II, p. 418.
18. Graziani to Bernasconi. 17 December 1935. Telegram reproduced in: Longo, *La Campagna Italo-Etiopica*, II, p. 417.
19. Telegramma del 2 gennaio 1936. Quoted in: Del Boca, 'Le fonti etiopiche', p. 55.
20. Longo, *La Campagna Italo-Etiopica*, I, p. 236.
21. A detailed account of the hospital and the destruction of it can be found in: Rainer Baudendistel, *Between Bombs and Good Intentions: The Red Cross and the Italo-Ethiopian War, 1935–1936* (New York: Berghahn Books, 2006), pp. 126–39.
22. Bernasconi to Graziani. 30 December 1935. Quoted in: Alessandro Cova, *Graziani: Un generale per il regime: la prima biografia documentata di uno dei personaggi più violenti e controversi della nostra storia, che ha incarnato miti, ferocie e contraddizioni del periodo fascista* (Roma: Newton Compton Editore, 1987), p. 147.
23. Vincenzo Lioy, *L'Italia in Africa, Serie Storico-Militare, Volume Terzo: L'opera dell'Aeronautica, Tomo II, Eritrea – Somalia – Etiopia (1919–1937)* (Roma: Istituto Poligrafico dello Stato, MCMLXV [1965]), p. 238.
24. Pedriali, *L'aeronautica italiana*, p. 60.
25. Baudendistel, *Between Bombs and Good Intentions*, p. 239.
26. See Chapter 1.
27. *League of Nations Official Journal*, February 1936, 17(2):649.
28. Baudendistel, *Between Bombs and Good Intentions*, p. 127.
29. Steer, *Caesar in Abyssinia*, p. 243.
30. Aline Zuber, 'The cross in the crosshairs. A photographic record of the bombing of Red Cross field hospitals during the Second Italo-Ethiopian war: 4 January 2022, Article/Audiovisual/Photo'. Available at: https://blogs.icrc.org/cross-files/the-cross-in-the-crosshairs-a-photographic-record-of-the-bombing-of-red-cross-field-hospitals-during-the-second-italo-ethiopian-war/#_ftnref10.
31. Longo, *La Campagna Italo-Etiopica*, I, p. 237, n. 218.
32. Mussolini to Badoglio. 1 January 1936. Telegram reproduced in: Longo, *La Campagna Italo-Etiopica*, II, p. 419.
33. Rochat, *Le guerre italiane 1935–1943*, pp. 72–3.
34. Rochat, *Le guerre italiane 1935–1943*, p. 73.
35. Rochat, *Le guerre italiane 1935–1943*, p. 74, n. 32.
36. Graziani to Lessona and Badoglio. 6 gennaio 1936-XIV. Telegram reproduced in: Longo, *La Campagna Italo-Etiopica*, II, pp. 396–7.
37. Longo, *La Campagna Italo-Etiopica*, I, p. 237.

38. Longo, *La Campagna Italo-Etiopica*, I, pp. 237–8. Rochat, *Le guerre italiane 1935–1943*, p. 73.
39. Margherita Sarfatti and Brian Sullivan (ed.), *My Fault: Mussolini as I Knew Him* (New York: Enigma Books, 2014), p. 138.
40. Vittorio Mussolini, *Voli sulle ambe* (Firenze: GC Sansoni Editore, 1937-XV), p. 28.
41. King Victor Emmanuel III made Graziani Marquis of Neghelli on 6 December 1937. Cova, *Graziani: Un generale per il regime*, p. 49.
42. Fuller, 'The Italo-Ethiopian War', p. 343.
43. He later noted that 'Apparently 5,000 stood for: "Unknown, but very many".' Fuller, *The First of the League Wars*, p. 35.
44. Fuller, 'The Italo-Ethiopian War', p. 346.
45. Longo, *La Campagna Italo-Etiopica*, I, p. 238.
46. Del Boca, *Gli italiani in Africa Orientale*, 2, p. 515.
47. Rochat, *Le guerre italiane 1935–1943*, pp. 73–4.
48. Longo, *La Campagna Italo-Etiopica*, I, p. 238.
49. Longo, *La Campagna Italo-Etiopica*, I, p. 240.
50. Rochat, *Le guerre italiane 1935–1943*, p. 41.
51. J.F.C. Fuller, 'Lessons of the Italian Drive', *Daily Mail*, 20 April 1936. Quoted in: Watson, 'J.F.C. Fuller and the Fascist Movement in Britain', p. 57.

Chapter 8: 'The Awful Warning'

1. Longo, *La Campagna Italo-Etiopica*, I, p. 343.
2. Rochat, *Le guerre italiane 1935–1943*, p. 55.
3. Longo, *La Campagna Italo-Etiopica*, I, p. 244.
4. Waugh, *Waugh in Abyssinia*, p. 209.
5. Linton Wells, *Blood on the Moon: The Autobiography of Linton Wells* (New York: Houghton Mifflin Co., 1937), p. 345.
6. Linton Wells, 'The Rape of Ethiopia', in Eugene Lyons (ed.), *We Cover the World: by Fifteen Foreign Correspondents* (New York: Harcourt, Brace & Co., 1937), p. 118.
7. Wells, 'The Rape of Ethiopia', p. 119.
8. Wells, 'The Rape of Ethiopia', p. 119.
9. Wells, 'The Rape of Ethiopia', p. 120.
10. Wells, 'The Rape of Ethiopia', p. 117. Wells, *Blood on the Moon*, p. 387.
11. Roberto Gentilli, *Guerra aerea sull'Etiopia 1935–1939* (Firenze: EDAI-Edizioni Aeronautiche Italiane, 1992), pp. 42–3, 113.
12. To put it in some sort of context, the daylight bombing of London on 13 June 1917, carried out by seventeen Gotha G.IV bombers of the *Luftstreitkräfte*, the air arm of the German Army, had dropped 4,000kg of explosives and incendiaries. The human cost amounted to 162 dead and 432 injured. The political fallout, particularly after a second raid on 7 July, was out of all proportion and, goaded by vitriolic attacks in the press, and signs of panic amongst the population, the War Cabinet decided to set up a committee to examine what could be done. The result was pithily expressed by the author of the British official history: 'Hauptmann Brandenburg's No. 3 Bombing Squadron may lay claim to an important share in the foundation of the Royal Air Force.' H.A. Jones, *The War In The Air: Being the Story of the part played in the Great War by the Royal Air Force*, Vol. V [History of the Great War based on Official Documents by Direction of The Historical Section of the Committee of Imperial Defence] (Oxford: Clarendon, 1935), p. 42.
13. Arnold J. Toynbee assisted by V.M. Boulter, *Survey of International Affairs 1935: Volume II Abyssinia and Italy* (London: Oxford University Press, 1936), p. 276, n. 2.
14. Toynbee assisted by V.M. Boulter, *Survey of International Affairs 1935*, p. 276.
15. Toynbee assisted by V.M. Boulter, *Survey of International Affairs 1935*, p. 243.
16. Cristiano Andrea Ristuccia, 'The 1935 Sanctions against Italy: Would coal and oil have made a difference?', *European Review of Economic History*, 2000, 4(1):98.

17. Renzo De Felice, *Mussolini il duce Volume III Part 1: Gli anni del consenso 1929–1936* (Torino: Giulio Einaudi editore, 1974), p. 713. See also: Eugenio Di Rienzo, *Il 'Gioco degli Imperi': La Guerra d'Etiopia e le origini del secondo conflitto Mondiale* (Roma: Società Editrice Dante Alighieri, 2016), p. 98. Anand Toprani, *Oil and the Great Powers: Britain and Germany, 1914 to 1945* (Oxford: Oxford University Press, 2019), p. 98.
18. For details on Long, see: David McKean, *Watching Darkness Fall: FDR, His Ambassadors, and the Rise of Adolf Hitler* (New York: St Martin's Press, 2021).
19. Long to Roosevelt. 29 November 1935. Quoted in: Fred L. Israel, 'Introduction' to Breckinridge Long and Fred L. Israel (ed.), *The War Diary of Breckinridge Long: Selections from the Years 1939–1944* (Lincoln, NE: University of Nebraska Press, 1966), p. xxiii.
20. Wallace Murray, 'Memorandum by the Chief of the Division of Near Eastern Affairs to the Secretary of State, December 12, 1935', in Rogers P. Churchill et al. (eds), *Foreign Relations of the United States Diplomatic Papers, 1935: General, The Near East and Africa, Volume I* (Washington DC: United States Government Printing Office, 1953), p. 905.
21. Toynbee assisted by V.M. Boulter, *Survey of International Affairs 1935*, p. 279.
22. Longo, *La Campagna Italo-Etiopica*, I, p. 212.
23. Longo, *La Campagna Italo-Etiopica*, I, p. 212, n. 225.
24. Longo, *La Campagna Italo-Etiopica*, I, pp. 212–13.
25. Henderson B. Braddick, 'The Hoare-Laval Plan: A Study in International Politics', *Review of Politics*, July 1962, 24(3):361.
26. Quoted in: Jo-Anne Pemberton, *The Story of International Relations, Part Three: Cold-Blooded Idealists* (Cham: Springer Nature, 2020), p. 14.
27. Viscount Templewood (The Rt Hon Sir Samuel Hoare), *Nine Troubled Years* (London: Collins, 1954), p. 168.
28. Neville Chamberlain to Florence 'Ida' Chamberlain, 5 October 1935. Robert Self (ed.), *The Neville Chamberlain Diary Letters: Volume 4: The Downing Street Years, 1934–1940* (Aldershot: Ashgate, 2005), p. 154.
29. Winston S. Churchill, *The Second World War Volume I: The Gathering Storm* (London: Reprint Society, 1950), p. 153.
30. Hoare, Conservative MP for Chelsea, was the only serving MP to become an MI5 officer. Christopher Andrew, *The Defence of the Realm: The Authorised History of MI5* (London: Allen Lane, 2009), pp. 104–5.
31. Toynbee assisted by V.M. Boulter, *Survey of International Affairs 1935*, p. 281.
32. Peter Neville, *Hitler and Appeasement: The British Attempt to Prevent the Second World War* (London: Hambledon Continuum, 2006), p. 55.
33. Sir Robert Vansittart. Memorandum on: 'The Future of Anglo-Italian Relations and the League of Nations', 21 May 1936. Quoted in part in: Ian Colvin, *None so Blind: A British Diplomatic View of the Origins of World War II* (New York: Harcourt, Brace & World, 1965), p. 106.
34. Braddick, 'The Hoare-Laval Plan', p. 361.
35. Templewood (Hoare), *Nine Troubled Years*, p. 181.
36. Neville, *Hitler and Appeasement*, p. 52.
37. Robert Crowcroft, *The End is Nigh: British Politics, Power, and the Road to the Second World War* (Oxford: Oxford University Press, 2019), p. 57.
38. Genevieve Tabouis, *They Called Me Cassandra* (New York: Charles Scribner's Sons, 1942), pp. 267–8.
39. 'In the Thirties, the *Daily Telegraph* correspondent in Paris was André Géraud, writing under the name of Pertinax. He was famous for the accuracy of his political information, and when asked about it he replied: "It is all due to my cook, who every morning shops in the market where he has a little gossip with the Prime Minister's cook ... et voilà!"' Gil Dowdall-Brown. Letter to the *Daily Telegraph*, 26 September 2010.
40. Harold Macmillan, *Winds of Change 1914–1939* (New York: Harper & Row, 1966), p. 401.

41. Entry for 14 December in Ivan Maisky and Gabriel Gorodetsky (ed.), translated by Tatiana Sorokina and Oliver Ready, *The Complete Maisky Diaries Volume I: The Rise of Hitler and the Gathering Clouds of War 1932–1938* (New Haven, CT: Yale University Press, 2017), pp. 144–5. For a review of the diaries and a short biography of their author see: https://www.theguardian.com/books/2016/jan/20/the-miasky-diaries-review.
42. Letter dated 15 December 1935. Self (ed.), *The Neville Chamberlain Diary Letters*, p. 166.
43. Robert Boothby, *I Fight to Live* (London: Victor Gollancz, 1947), p. 135.
44. He returned to Government as First Lord of the Admiralty in June 1936. Templewood (Hoare), *Nine Troubled Years*, p. 203.
45. Claude Croubois, *Pierre Laval* (La Creche: Geste editions, 2010), p. 36.
46. Vansittart to Sir Percy Loraine. 24 July 1935. Quoted in: Roi, *Alternative to Appeasement*, p. 95.
47. 'The real death of the League was in December 1935 … One day it was a powerful body imposing sanctions, seemingly more effective than ever before; the next day it was an empty sham, everyone scuttling from it as quickly as possible. What killed the League was the publication of the Hoare-Laval plan.' A.J.P. Taylor, *The Origins of the Second World War* (New York: Simon & Schuster, 2005), p. 96.
48. George Martelli, *Italy Against the World* (London: Chatto & Windus, 1937), pp. 223–4.
49. Churchill, *The Gathering Storm*, p. 153.
50. Toynbee assisted by V.M. Boulter, *Survey of International Affairs 1935*, p. 307.
51. 'Declaration addressed by the Government at Addis Ababa to the President of the Assembly, the President of the Council and all the Members of the League'. 12 December 1935. Quoted in: Toynbee assisted by V.M. Boulter, *Survey of International Affairs 1935*, p. 309.
52. Renzo De Felice, *Mussolini il duce Volume III Part 1: Gli anni del consenso 1929–1936* (Torino: Giulio Einaudi editore, 1974), p. 719. Eugenio Di Rienzo, *Il 'Gioco degli Imperi': La Guerra d'Etiopia e le origini del secondo conflitto Mondiale* (Roma: Società Editrice Dante Alighieri, 2016), pp. 100–1.
53. David Alvarez, 'Left in the Dust: Italian Signals Intelligence, 1915–1943', *International Journal of Intelligence and Counter Intelligence*, 2001, 14(3):392. See also: Angelo Acampora, *Senza licenza di uccidere: operazioni segrete militari italiane 1935–1943* (Bologna: Casa editrice Odoya, 2017).
54. Brian R. Sullivan, 'Soviet penetration of the Italian intelligence services in the 1930s', in Tomaso Vialardi di Sandigliano e Virgilio Ilari, *Storia dello spionaggio: l'intelligence militari italiana, l'intelligence elettronica, l'intelligence cinese* (Sandigliano: Associazione Europea degli Amici degli Archivi Storici, 2006), pp. 83, 88–9.
55. J.L. Maffey et al., 'The Maffey Report: Report of an Inter-Departmental Committee on British Interests in Ethiopia', 18 June 1935. Appendix II of W.N. Medlicott, Douglas Dakin and M.E. Lambert (eds), *Documents on British Foreign Policy 1919–1939, Second Series, Volume XIV: The Italo-Ethiopian Dispute March 1934–October 1935* (London: HMSO, 1976), p. 761.
56. Guariglia, *Ricordi 1922–1946*, p. 302. A.W. Brian Simpson, 'The Invention of Trials *in camera* in Security Cases', in R.A. Melikan (ed.), *Domestic and International Trials, 1700–2000: The Trial in History Volume II* (Manchester: Manchester University Press, 2003), pp. 94–5. D. Cameron Watt, 'Francis Herbert King: A Soviet Source in the Foreign Office', *Intelligence and National Security*, 1988, 3(4):62–82.
57. Diary entry, 8 December 1935. Self (ed.), *The Neville Chamberlain Diary Letters*, p. 165.
58. Longo, *La Campagna Italo-Etiopica*, I, p. 196.
59. Longo, *La Campagna Italo-Etiopica*, I, p. 213.
60. Pedriali, 'Le armi chimiche in Africa Orientale', p. 128.

Chapter 9: Keeping Mussolini awake at night

1. 'Testimonianza all'Autore di ras Immiru Haile Sellase, raccolta a Addis Abeba il 13 aprile 1965', in Del Boca, *Gli italiani in Africa Orientale*, 2, p. 490.
2. Pietro Badoglio, Maresciallo d'Italia Duca di Addis Abeba, *La Guerra D' Etiopia* (Milano: Arnoldo Mondadori Editore, 1936-XIV), p. 18.

3. Longo, *La Campagna Italo-Etiopica*, I, p. 198.
4. Badoglio to Mussolini. 8 December 1935. Quoted in: Piero Pieri and Giorgio Rochat, *Pietro Badoglio: maresciallo d'Italia* (Torino: Unione tipografico-editrice torinese, 1974), p. 687.
5. Del Boca, *Gli italiani in Africa Orientale*, 2, p. 447.
6. Unless otherwise stated, this section is derived from the following works: Rochat, *Le guerre italiane 1935–1943*, pp. 54–5. Longo, *La Campagna Italo-Etiopica*, I, pp. 203–5. Del Boca, *Gli italiani in Africa Orientale*, 2, pp. 472–82.
7. Unless otherwise stated, this section is derived from the following: Tenente Adolfo Van Axel-Castelli, 'Rapporto: sul combattimento del giorno 15 dicembre 1935. XIV di Dembeguina', undated. Reproduced in: Longo, *La Campagna Italo-Etiopica*, II, pp. 351–3.
8. The son of Alessandro Martelli, a former government minister.
9. Although really a tankette – a designation normally used for a vehicle smaller than a light tank – it remained Italy's main battle tank until mid-1941. John Sweet, *Iron Arm: The Mechanization of Mussolini's Army, 1920–1940* (Mechanicsburg, PA: Stackpole Books, 2007), p. 84. Filippo Cappellano and Pier Paolo Battistelli, *Italian Light Tanks 1919–45* (Oxford: Osprey Publishing, 2012), p. 12.
10. Sergeant Major Giuseppe Bruno does not appear on the casualty list.
11. Longo, *La Campagna Italo-Etiopica*, I, p. 206, n. 215.
12. Fuller, 'The Italo-Ethiopian War', p. 343.
13. Fuller, *The First of the League Wars*, p. 26.
14. Longo, *La Campagna Italo-Etiopica*, I, pp. 207–8.
15. Rochat, *Le guerre italiane 1935–1943*, p. 56.
16. *Norme per L'Impiego delle Unità Carriste*. 1 gennaio 1936/XIV. Reproduced in: Longo, *La Campagna Italo-Etiopica*, II, p. 801.
17. Pedriali, *L'aeronautica italiana*, p. 50.
18. Rochat, *Le guerre italiane 1935–1943*, p. 55.
19. Pedriali, *L'aeronautica italiana*, p. 51.
20. Rochat, *Le guerre italiane 1935–1943*, p. 56.
21. Giulio Douhet, *Il dominio dell'aria saggio sull'arte della guerra aerea con una appendice contenente nozioni elementari di aeronautica* (Roma: L'Amministrazione Della Guerra, 1921).
22. Melvin G. Deaile, 'Foreword' to Giulio Douhet and Dino Ferrari (trans.), *The Command of the Air* (Maxwell Air Force Base, AL: Air University Press, 2019), p. v.
23. For Douhet and Douhetism see: Azar Gat, *Fascist and Liberal Visions of War: Fuller, Liddell Hart, Douhet, and Other Modernists* (Oxford: Clarendon Press, 1998), pp. 43–79.
24. Mario Ajmone Cat, 'prefazione', in Antonio Monti (documenti raccolti e ordinati), *Giulio Douhet: scritti inediti* (Firenze: Tipo-litografia scuola di guerra aerea, 1951), p. v.
25. Roberti Gentilli, 'L'aeronautica in Libia e in Etiopia', in Paolo Ferrari (ed.), *L'aeronautica italiana: una storia del Novecento* (Milano: Franco Angeli Storia, 2005), p. 311.
26. Ajmone Cat, in 1937, summarised the main roles of the air force in the Ethiopian conflict as follows: long-range reconnaissance, carried out by multi-engined bombers; reconnaissance on the fronts and flanks of advancing columns; liaison between the troops and the commands and between the commands; bombing and low-altitude machine-gun strafing; transport of men, materials and food. Scuola di Guerra Aerea, 'L'aeronautica nella guerra in Africa orientale: conferenza del generale DA Mario Ajmone Cat, Ministero dell'aeronautica, 1937-XV'. Quoted in: l'Ufficio storico dello Stato maggiore dell'Aeronautica, *Fondo 'Africa orientale italiana 1935–1938': Inventario*, p. 11, n. 7. Available at: https://www.aeronautica.difesa.it/storia/ufficiostorico/archiviofondi/Lists/DocumentiArchivioFondi/Africa_orientale.pdf.
27. Gentilli, 'L'aeronautica in Libia e in Etiopia', p. 314. Pedriali, *L'aeronautica italiana*, p. 26.
28. Giorgio Rochat, *Militari e politici nella preparazione della campagna d'Etiopia: Studio e documenti 1932–1936* (Milano: Franco Angeli Editore, 1971), pp. 379–81.
29. Rochat, *Le guerre italiane 1935–1943*, p. 46.
30. Longo, *La Campagna Italo-Etiopica*, I, pp. 290–1.

31. Rochat, *Le guerre italiane 1935–1943*, p. 67, n. 18.
32. Pedriali, 'Le armi chimiche in Africa Orientale', p. 128.
33. 'Testimonianza all'Autore di ras Immiru Haile Sellase, raccolta a Addis Abeba il 13 aprile 1965', in Del Boca, *Gli italiani in Africa Orientale*, 2, p. 490.
34. Anthony Howard, *RAB: The Life of R A Butler* (London: Jonathan Cape, 1986), p. xiv.
35. Pedriali, *L'aeronautica italiana*, p. 57.
36. Pedriali, *L'aeronautica italiana*, p. 57.
37. Angelo Del Boca, *L'Africa nella coscienza degli italiani: miti, memorie, errori, sconfitte* (Roma: Editori Laterza, 1992), p. 61.
38. Badoglio, *La guerra d'Etiopia*, p. 47.
39. Pedriali, *L'aeronautica italiana*, p. 55.
40. Longo, *La Campagna Italo-Etiopica*, I, p. 211.
41. Vincent Patriarca, 'Two Wars in One Year', *American Cavalcade*, May 1937, 1(1):11.
42. For the life (and death) of Pavolini, see: Arrigo Petacco, *Il superfascista: vita e morte di Alessandro Pavolini* ((Milano: Mondadori Editore, 1998).
43. Alessandro Pavolini, *Disperata* (Firenze: Vallecchi Editore, 1937-XV), pp. 131–2.
44. Joseph Vincent Patriarca, *Un americano a Gorizia, Diario di un pilota del 4 Stormo Prima parte: 1931–1937* (Milano: Vittorelli Edizioni per conto dell' Associazione Culturale 4 Stormo Gorizia, 2007). Online edition: https://www.associazione4stormo.it/un-americano-a-gorizia-1931-1937/ and http://www.asso4stormo.it/arc_01/Pubblicazioni/Patriarca1.htm.
45. Patriarca, *Un americano a Gorizia*. Pedriali also details this incident, as does Lioy. See: Pedriali, *L'aeronautica italiana*, p. 56; Lioy, *L'Italia in Africa*, p. 56.
46. Pedriali, *L'aeronautica italiana*, p. 56. In any case, ten days after leaving Axum the column returned there having suffered around 150 personnel, mostly Eritrean, killed between times. Longo, *La Campagna Italo-Etiopica*, I, p. 211. Pedriali, *L'aeronautica italiana*, p. 56. The fate of Allavena in particular, echoing as it did the earlier example of Minniti and Zannoni, also served to demonstrate that the tactic of low-level strafing with fighter aircraft had its dangers.
47. Longo, *La Campagna Italo-Etiopica*, I, p. 211.
48. Rochat, *Le guerre italiane 1935–1943*, pp. 56–7. Manoeuvring large-scale forces to threatened areas was a fraught business owing to the undeveloped roads; Longo states that to move a single division from Adua to Makalle took about fifteen days. Longo, *La Campagna Italo-Etiopica*, I, p. 208.
49. Longo, *La Campagna Italo-Etiopica*, I, p. 210.
50. 'Discorso pronunciato alla Radio il 10 dicembre 1936-XV dal generale Filippo Diamanti', appendice in Reginaldo Giuliani, *Per Cristo e per la patria: (ultimi scritti dall'Africa)* (Firenze: casa editrice Adriano Salani, 1937-XV), p. 298. Available at: https://www.lacabalesta.it/biblioteca/Giuliani/CristoPatria/CristoPatria_04_Appendice.html.
51. Badoglio, *La Guerra D' Etiopia*, p. 55.
52. For example, see: Del Boca, *Gli italiani in Africa Orientale*, 2, p. 485. Longo, *La Campagna Italo-Etiopica*, I, pp. 210–11. Longo argues that 'in the light of what had really happened', Badoglio's assertion was 'unreliable as well as ungenerous'.
53. Arrigo Petacco, *Faccetta nera: L'illusione coloniale italiana* (Milano: DeA Planeta Libri, 2018), p. 115.
54. Rochat, *Le guerre italiane 1935–1943*, p. 56.
55. Pedriali, *L'aeronautica italiana*, p. 87.
56. Roberto Gentilli, 'Elenco completo dei bombardmento a gas sul fronte Nord: La storiografia aeronautica e il problema dei gas', in Angelo Del Boca (ed.), *I gas di Mussolini: Il fascism e la guerra d'Etiopia* (Roma: Editori Reuniti, 2007), p. 141.
57. Fuller, 'The Italo-Ethiopian War', p. 238.

Chapter 10: An 'African Thermopylae'

1. Pavolini, *Disperata*, p. 159.
2. Badoglio to the Minister of the Colonies, 30 December 1935; Badoglio to the Head of Government, 30 December 1935. Reproduced in: Longo, *La Campagna Italo-Etiopica*, II, pp. 356–60.

3. Roughly half-way between Adigrat and Makalle.
4. Badoglio, *La Guerra D' Etiopia*, p. 47.
5. Mussolini to Badoglio and Graziani. 5 January 1936. Quoted in: Longo, *La Campagna Italo-Etiopica*, I, p. 243.
6. Gentilli, 'Elenco completo dei bombardmento a gas sul fronte Nord', p. 141.
7. Rochat, *Le guerre italiane 1935–1943*, p. 46.
8. Robert Gale Woolbert, 'Italy in Abyssinia', *Foreign Affairs*, April 1935, 13(3):501.
9. Badoglio to Army Corps Commanders. 7 January 1936. Reproduced in: Longo, *La Campagna Italo-Etiopica*, II, p. 432.
10. Longo, *La Campagna Italo-Etiopica*, I, p. 244. Del Boca, *Gli italiani in Africa Orientale*, 2, pp. 521–2.
11. Longo, *La Campagna Italo-Etiopica*, I, p. 247.
12. The title of Chapter V of Badoglio, *La Guerra D' Etiopia*, pp. 59–71.
13. Rochat, *Le guerre italiane 1935–1943*, p. 57.
14. Longo, *La Campagna Italo-Etiopica*, I, p. 248. This section is based on Longo unless otherwise stated.
15. A Blackshirt rank corresponding to brigadier general.
16. For a precise breakdown of the composition of this column see: Ettore Lucas and Giorgio De Vecchi, *Storia delle Unita? combattenti della Milizia volontaria per la sicurezza nazionale, 1923–1943* (Roma: Edizioni Volpe, 1976), pp. 73–4.
17. Rochat, *Le guerre italiane 1935–1943*, p. 58.
18. Longo, *La Campagna Italo-Etiopica*, I, p. 254.
19. 'resista mio Somma; oggi le Camicie Nere si copriranno di gloria'. Vari autori, *La Formazione De l'Impero Coloniale Italiano Volume Secondo: L'Impero (Dai Precedenti del Conflitto Etiopico alla Battaglia dell'Ascianghi)* (Milano: SA Fratelli Treves Editori, 1938), p. 386.
20. Pavolini, *Disperata*, p. 159.
21. Longo, *La Campagna Italo-Etiopica*, I, p. 258, n. 256.
22. Gentilli, 'Elenco completo dei bombardmento a gas sul fronte Nord', p. 141.
23. Rochat, *Le guerre italiane 1935–1943*, p. 58.
24. Pedriali, *L'aeronautica italiana*, p. 87.
25. Gentilli, *Guerra aerea sull'Etiopia*, p. 64. Pedriali, *L'aeronautica italiana*, pp. 83–4.
26. United States Adjutant-General's Office, *Machine-gun Drill Regulations (Provisional) 1917* (Washington DC: Government Printing Office, 1918), p. 84.
27. H.B. (Hilaire Belloc) and B.T.B. (Basil Temple Blackwood), *The Modern Traveller* (London: Edward Arnold, 1898), p. 41.
28. Rochat, *Le guerre italiane 1935–1943*, p. 58.
29. Rochat, *Le guerre italiane 1935–1943*, p. 58. For accounts of the battle also see: Edoardo Scala, *Storia delle fanterie italiane Volume 4: Le fanterie italiane nelle conquiste coloniali* (Roma: Stato Maggiore Esercito, 1952), pp. 441–3. Longo, *La Campagna Italo-Etiopica*, I, pp. 254–8. Ferdinando Pedriali, 'Passo Uarieu', *Storia Militare*, febbraio 2008-XVI, 173:15–21.
30. Ernest Ialongo, 'Filippo Tommaso Marinetti: The Futurist as Fascist, 1929–37', *Journal of Modern Italian Studies*, 2013, 18(4):410.
31. F.T. Marinetti, *Il poema africano della divisione «28 ottobre»* (Milano: Casa Editrice A Mondadori, 1937-XV).
32. 'Termopoli d'Africa, Passo Uarieu nella eloquenza di Marinetti', 13 June 1936. Ernest Ialongo, *Filippo Tommaso Marinetti: The Artist and His Politics* (Madison, NJ/Lanham, MD: Fairleigh Dickinson University Press/Rowman & Littlefield Publishing Group, 2015), p. 238, n. 113.
33. A title also utilised for another good account of the battle: Pierluigi Romeo di Colloredo, *Passo Uarieu: Le Termopili delle camicie nere in Etiopia* (Genova: L'Associazione Culturale 'ITALIA Storica', 2008).
34. General Alessandro Pirzio Biroli, commander of the Eritrean Corps, *Relazione sulle operazioni nel Tembien dal 19 al 24 gennaio 1936-XIV 1 battaglia del Tembien*. p. 7. This document can be found in: Longo, *La Campagna Italo-Etiopica*, II, pp. 454–60.

35. Del Boca, *Gli italiani in Africa Orientale*, 2, p. 537. Among the many honours heaped on him was the naming of a 'Liuzzi-Class' submarine in his memory. The *Reginaldo Giuliani* was later named *Aquila II* and used to transport supplies to the Indian Ocean. It was seized by the Japanese after the Italian surrender in 1943, and then transferred to the Germans to become UIT-23 (UIT = *Untersee/Unterwasser Italien Transport*). The boat was sunk off the entrance to the Malacca Strait in February 1944. Charles Stephenson, *The Eastern Fleet and the Indian Ocean 1942–1944: The Fleet that Had to Hide* (Barnsley: Pen & Sword, 2020), pp. 155, 159.
36. Lucia Ceci and Peter Spring (trans.), *The Vatican and Mussolini's Italy* (Leiden: Brill, 2017), p. 53.
37. https://italianiinguerra.wordpress.com/2019/01/21/padre-reginaldo-giuliani-cappellano-delle-camicie-nere/.
38. *Cantate di legionari*. Testo: Auro D'Alba. Musica: Francesco Pellegrino. Verse two (of eight): 'I morti che lasciammo a Passo Uarieu | sono i pilastri del romano imperi | Gronda di sangue il gagliardetto nero | che contro l'Amba il barbaro inchiodò | Sui morti che lasciammo a Passo Uarieu | la Croce di Giuliani sfolgorò. | Per il Duce e per l'impero | Eia Eia Alala! Alala! Alala.' ['The dead we left at Passo Uarieu | are the pillars of the Roman empire | The black pennant is dripping with blood | which the barbarian nailed against the Amba | on the dead that we left at Passo Uarieu | the Cross of Giuliani dazzled. | For the Duce and for the empire]. Available at: http://www.aclorien.it/archiviocantipatriottici/song.php?id=4625.
39. Longo, *La Campagna Italo-Etiopica*, I, p. 260.
40. Diary entry for 2 February 1936 in: Giuseppe Bottai, *Quaderno Affricano* (Firenze: GC Sansoni Editore, XVIII-1938), pp. 45–6. For an analysis of this particular work and its author, see: Loredana Polezzi, '"Mal d'Africa" and its Memory: Heroes and Anti-Heroes in Pre-and Postwar Readings of the Italian Presence in Africa', in Danielle Hipkins and Gill Plain (eds), *War-torn Tales: Literature, Film and Gender in the Aftermath of World War II* (Oxford: Peter Lang, 2007), pp. 46–9. For Bottai more generally see: Giordano Bruno Guerri, *Giuseppe Bottai, un fascista critico: ideologia e azione del gerarca che avrebbe voluto portare l'intelligenza nel fascismo e il fascismo alla liberalizzazione* (Milano: Feltrinelli Editore, 1976).
41. 'Promemoria per sua Eccellenza il capo del Governo. 28 gennaio 1936-XIV.' Reproduced in: Longo, *La Campagna Italo-Etiopica*, II, p. 464. Emphases in the original.
42. Pino Rauti (Umberto Giusti), *Storia d'Italia nei discorsi di Mussolini 1915–1945: Volume II* (Roma: Centro Editoriale Nazionale, 1966), p. 850.
43. Badoglio, *La Guerra D' Etiopia*, p. 70.
44. Badoglio, *La Guerra D' Etiopia*, p. 77.
45. Pedriali, *L'aeronautica italiana*, pp. 83–4.
46. Estimates, and they are no more than that, vary wildly between 5,000 and 20,000 killed. There is no consensus. According to Steer: 'The Ethiopians never counted the dead, their own or the enemy's.' Steer, *Caesar in Abyssinia*, p. 255. Longo quotes an estimate of 8,000. Longo, *La Campagna Italo-Etiopica*, I, p. 259, n. 258.
47. Steer, *Caesar in Abyssinia*, p. 255.
48. Fuller, 'The Italo-Ethiopian War', p. 345.
49. Steer, *Caesar in Abyssinia*, p. 256.
50. Del Boca, *Gli italiani in Africa Orientale*, 2, pp. 543–4.
51. Longo, *La Campagna Italo-Etiopica*, I, p. 265.
52. Gentilli, 'L'aeronautica in Libia e in Etiopia', p. 314.
53. Rochat, *Le guerre italiane 1935–1943*, p. 59.
54. Fuller, 'The Italo-Ethiopian War', p. 346.

Chapter 11: Amba Aradam

1. 'A 50 anni dalla più sciagurata avventura del regime, stasera la Rai propone una sconvolgente inchiesta su come andarono davvero le cose Guerra d'Etiopia Vietnam italiano', *l'Unita*, giovedi 3 ottobre 1985, p. 9.
2. *30ª Divisione di fanteria 'Sabauda'*; *4ª Divisione CC.NN. '3 Gennaio'*; *5ª Divisione alpina 'Pusteria'*.

3. 27ª *Divisione di fanteria 'Sila'*; 1ª *Divisione CC.NN. '23 Marzo'*.
4. Rochat, *Le guerre italiane 1935–1943*, p. 59. The Italian Order of Battle is tabulated in: Longo, *La Campagna Italo-Etiopica*, I, p. 270.
5. Steer, *Caesar in Abyssinia*, pp. 259–60.
6. Longo, *La Campagna Italo-Etiopica*, I, p. 268.
7. 'A colorless gas with a distinct, disagreeable garlicky odor ... Exposure induces vomiting and arsine can be classed as a vomiting agent.' Benjamin C. Garrett, *Historical Dictionary of Nuclear, Biological, and Chemical Warfare* (Lanham, MD: Rowman & Littlefield Publishers, 2017), pp. 27–8.
8. Gentilli, 'Elenco completo dei bombardmento a gas sul fronte Nord', pp. 141–2.
9. Angelo Del Boca, 'Le fonti etiopiche e straniere sull'impiego dei gas', in Angelo Del Boca (ed.), *I gas di Mussolini: Il fascism e la guerra d'Etiopia* (Roma: Editori Reuniti, 2007), p. 62.
10. Steer, *Caesar in Abyssinia*, p. 250.
11. Richard Pankhurst, 'Le memoria del capitano Alejandro Del Vallemy Suero: due lettere sul'invasione fascista dell'Etiopia', *Studi Piacentini: Rivista Dell'istituto Storico Della Resistenza Di Piacenza*, 1994, 15:245–7. Also quoted in: Del Boca, 'Le fonti etiopiche e straniere sull'impiego dei gas', pp. 62–3.
12. Four per cent fell on non-classifiable targets. Pedriali, 'Le armi chimiche in Africa Orientale', pp. 128–9.
13. A pamphlet distributed in 1936 by the *Servizio chimico militare del Regio Esercito* specified that: 'In the tactical field it [mustard gas] can be used defensively to create an obstacle and, offensively, to make areas where one does not want to advance intolerable. This chemical obstacle, however, is not insurmountable; it can be inadvertently overcome by those who do not detect it, allowing them to fight for a few hours before suffering the consequences, just as it can be overcome by those who know it well, employing simple makeshift means ...' Quoted in: Pedriali, 'Le armi chimiche in Africa Orientale', p. 127.
14. Augustin M. Prentiss, *Chemicals in War: A Treatise on Chemical Warfare* (New York: McGraw Hill, 1937), p. 19.
15. 'A walker on the South Downs was recently burned when he touched a gate post used for mustard gas experiments in the last war.' Paul Brown, 'Mustard gas dump danger to M-way workers', *Guardian*, 9 February 1982.
16. Pedriali, 'Le armi chimiche in Africa Orientale', p. 127.
17. Rochat, *Le guerre italiane 1935–1943*, p. 59.
18. Longo, *La Campagna Italo-Etiopica*, I, p. 267. This section is based on Longo unless otherwise stated.
19. Steer, *Caesar in Abyssinia*, p. 250.
20. Rochat, *Le guerre italiane 1935–1943*, pp. 58–9.
21. Longo, *La Campagna Italo-Etiopica*, I, p. 273.
22. Norman E. Fiske, Major, Cavalry, USA. Military Observer, *Report of Military Observer with Italian Armies in East Africa: Report No. 9* (Washington, DC: Military Intelligence Division General Staff, 1936), pp. 313–15.
23. Il Maresciallo d'Italia Badoglio, 'Direttive impartite dall'osservatorio di amba Ghedem il giorno 13 febbraio, per la prosecuzione dell'azione (battaglia dell'Enderta) 13 febbraio 1936-XIV'. Reproduced in: Longo, *La Campagna Italo-Etiopica*, II, p. 486.
24. Longo, *La Campagna Italo-Etiopica*, I, p. 275.
25. Del Boca, 'Le fonti etiopiche e straniere sull'impiego dei gas', p. 63.
26. Pavolini, *Disperata*, pp. 254–5.
27. Rochat, *Le guerre italiane 1935–1943*, p. 59, n. 11.
28. Gentilli, 'Elenco completo dei bombardmento a gas sul fronte Nord', pp. 141–2.
29. John H. Spencer, *Ethiopia at Bay: A Personal Account of the Haile Selassie Years* (Hollywood, CA: Tsehai Publishers, 2006), p. 50.
30. Steer, *Caesar in Abyssinia*, p. 165.

31. Longo, *La Campagna Italo-Etiopica*, I, p. 276.
32. Steer, *Caesar in Abyssinia*, p. 266.
33. Gentilli, *Guerra aerea sull'Etiopia*, p. 70.
34. Peter Thompson, *Anzac Fury: The Battle of Crete 1941* (Sydney: Random House Australia, 2011), p. 34.
35. Fiske, *Report of Military Observer: Report No. 9*, pp. 313–15.
36. Angelo Del Boca, 'Italo Pietra, tredici anni in divisa', *Studi Piacentini*, 1991, 10(2).
37. 'A 50 anni dalla più sciagurata avventura del regime', p. 9.
38. Badoglio to Mussolini. 15 February 36 at 18:30. Reproduced in: Longo, *La Campagna Italo-Etiopica*, II, p. 498.
39. Longo, *La Campagna Italo-Etiopica*, I, p. 275, n. 268.
40. Pedriali, *L'aeronautica italiana*, p. 56.
41. Angelo Del Boca, 'La verità sul massacro della Gondrand', *Storia Illustrata*, 4 ottobre 1983, 311:68–74. Unless otherwise stated, this section is based Del Boca's article and Alberto Caminiti, *L'eccidio dei cantieri Gondrand AOI 1936* (Genova: Libri Liberodiscrivere Edizioni, 2014). The latter work uses the same sources as Del Boca, but accuses him of giving a 'pro-Ethiopian' version of events.
42. Barbara Sòrgoni, 'The Scripts of Alberto Pollera, an Italian officer in Colonial Eritrea: Administration, Ethnography and Gender', in Helen Tilley with Robert J. Gordon (eds), *Ordering Africa: Anthropology, European Imperialism, and the Politics of Knowledge* (Manchester: Manchester University Press, 2010), pp. 285–308.
43. Del Boca, *Gli italiani in Africa Orientale*, 2, p. 585.
44. Fulvio Suvich (Undersecretary of Foreign Affairs), 'Abyssinian Atrocities Committed against Italian Workmen, Communication from the Italian Government to the League of Nations (Translation from the Italian)'. Official No: C. 123. M. 62. 1936. VII.' 19 March 1936. Available online at: https://upload.wikimedia.org/wikipedia/commons/e/e4/C-123-M-62-1936-VII_EN.pdf.
45. Ignazio Scurto, *Il cantico di Lydia: in memoria di Lydia Maffioli Rocca caduta nel Mareb a fianco dello sposo* (Novara: Delegazione Provinciale dei Fasci Femminili, 1937).
46. Federico Martinelli, 'Ignazio Scurto: manifesti, poesie e articoli dell'ardente poeta della radio', *Verona Sette*, 15 settembre 2020, 21(12):11.
47. Luciano Marrocu, 'Flaiano in Africa: A Rare Example of Lucidity', in Paolo Bertella and Cecilia Dau Novelli (eds), *Colonialism and National Identity* (Newcastle upon Tyne: Cambridge Scholars Publishing, 2015), p. 95. See also: Marisa S. Trubiano, *Ennio Flaiano and His Italy: Postcards from a Changing World* (Madison, NJ: Fairleigh Dickinson University Press, 2010), p. 37.
48. It was Italian practice to cremate Ethiopian corpses via the use of flamethrowers.
49. Ennio Flaiano, 'Aethiopia: Appunti per una canzonetta (1935–1936)' Appendice a Ennio Flaiano, *Tempo di uccidere* (Milano: Rizzoli, 1973), p. 299.
50. Flaiano, 'Aethiopia: Appunti per una canzonetta (1935–1936)', pp. 112–13. Del Boca made a similar point: 'The Libyans took no prisoners in order to avenge the violence perpetrated by *ascari* and *dubats* against them during the reconquest of their country over the years 1923–1932. Like other colonial powers, Fascist Italy exploited intra-African rivalries and old conflicts in its colonial ventures.' See: Del Boca, *Gli italiani in Africa Orientale*, 2, p. 497. See also: Nir Arielli, 'Colonial Soldiers in Italian Counter-Insurgency Operations in Libya, 1922–32', *British Journal for Military History*, February 2015, 1(2):47–56.

Chapter 12: The Second Battle of Tembien and the Battle of Shire

1. Badoglio to Minstero Della Colonie, 27 febbraio 1936-XIV. Reproduced in: Longo, *La Campagna Italo-Etiopica*, II, p. 523.
2. Steer, *Caesar in Abyssinia*, p. 274.
3. Longo, *La Campagna Italo-Etiopica*, I, pp. 279–80.

4. Badoglio Marescialle d'italia, 'Oggetto - norme per prossine operazione - diramazione estera fino ai comandi di battaglioni o equivelanti, 21 febbraio 1936/XIV'. Reproduced in: Longo, *La Campagna Italo-Etiopica*, II, p. 515.
5. Badoglio, *La Guerra D' Etiopia*, p. 121.
6. Badoglio's orders in respect of the Second Battle of Tembien, which included the campaign against Ras Imru, were issued on 24 February: Badoglio Marescialle d'italia, 'Direttive impartite da Macalle il 24 febbraio, per le operazioni nel Tembien (seconda battaglia del Tembien). 24 febbraio 1936-XIV.' Reproduced in: Longo, *La Campagna Italo-Etiopica*, II, pp. 518–19.
7. Badoglio to Ministere Colonie, 23 febbraio 1936. ' Reproduced in: Longo, *La Campagna Italo-Etiopica*, II, pp. 516–17.
8. Pavolini, *Disperata*, p. 79 and between pp. 256–7.
9. 30^a Divisione di fanteria 'Sabauda'; 4^a Divisione CC.NN. '3 Gennaio'; 5^a Divisione alpina 'Pusteria'; 27^a Divisione di fanteria 'Sila'.
10. 1^a Divisione CC.NN. '23 Marzo'.
11. 2^a Divisione eritrea and 2^a Divisione CC.NN. '28 Ottobre'.
12. 19^a Divisione fanteria 'Gavinana'; 24^a Divisione fanteria 'Gran Sasso'; 3^a Divisione CC.NN. '21 Aprile'.
13. 5^a Divisione fanteria 'Cosseria'; 5^a Divisione CC.NN. '1 Febbraio'.
14. 'The Italian occupation army in Abyssinia, outnumbered, poorly trained and equipped, firstly lost the Battle of Amba Alagi of 7 December 1895 and then suffered a great defeat at Adwa ... on 1 March 1896.' Gabriele Abbondanza, *Italy as a Regional Power: The African Context from National Unification to the Present Day* (Rome: Aracne Editrice, 2016), p. 39.
15. Longo, *La Campagna Italo-Etiopica*, I, p. 285, n. 277.
16. Pierluigi Romeo Di Colloredo, *I pilastri del romano impero: le camicie nere in Africa Orientale, 1935–1936* (Genova: L'Associazione Culturale 'ITALIA Storica', 2009), p. 173.
17. Badoglio, *La Guerra D' Etiopia*, p. 105.
18. Steer, *Caesar in Abyssinia*, p. 268.
19. Longo, *La Campagna Italo-Etiopica*, I, p. 288.
20. Badoglio to Minstero Della Colonie, 27 febbraio 1936-XIV. Reproduced in: Longo, *La Campagna Italo-Etiopica*, II, p. 523.
21. Steer, *Caesar in Abyssinia*, p. 269.
22. Longo, *La Campagna Italo-Etiopica*, I, p. 288.
23. Lioy, *L'Italia in Africa*, p. 67.
24. It was, though, utilised strategically; Gentilli tabulates sixty-two T.500.C being dropped between 26 and 27 February, mostly on the area around Korem and Lake Hashenge some 130km southeast of Abiy Addi. Italian intelligence had suggested the Negus had moved to that area, but this was later found to be false. Gentilli, 'Elenco completo dei bombardmento a gas sul fronte Nord', p. 142.
25. Steer, *Caesar in Abyssinia*, pp. 268–9.
26. Steer, *Caesar in Abyssinia*, p. 270.
27. Longo, *La Campagna Italo-Etiopica*, I, p. 289.
28. Longo, *La Campagna Italo-Etiopica*, I, p. 289.
29. Badoglio to Ministero Colonie. 1 marzo 1936-XIV. Reproduced in: Longo, *La Campagna Italo-Etiopica*, II, p. 525.
30. Gentilli, 'Elenco completo dei bombardmento a gas sul fronte Nord', p. 142.
31. Longo, *La Campagna Italo-Etiopica*, I, p. 289.
32. Longo, *La Campagna Italo-Etiopica*, I, p. 294.
33. Comando Superiore AO Stato Maggiore, *Occupazione di Amba Alagi Battaglie del Tembien e dello Scire: Ordine del Giorno* (1° sezione topocartografica, 1936-XIV) Reproduced in: Longo, *La Campagna Italo-Etiopica*, II, pp. 542–57. This section is based on this report unless otherwise stated.

34. Norman E. Fiske, Major, Cavalry, USA. Military Observer, *Report of Military Observer with Italian Armies in East Africa: Report No 6* (Washington, DC: Military Intelligence Division General Staff, 1936), p. 244.
35. Longo, *La Campagna Italo-Etiopica*, I, pp. 293–4.
36. Steer, *Caesar in Abyssinia*, p. 274.
37. 19ª Divisione fanteria 'Gavinana'.
38. 3ª Divisione CC.NN. '21 Aprile'.
39. 24ª Divisione fanteria 'Gran Sasso'.
40. Longo, *La Campagna Italo-Etiopica*, I, p. 295.
41. Steer, *Caesar in Abyssinia*, p. 275. Del Boca, *Gli italiani in Africa Orientale*, 2, p. 591.
42. Angelo Del Boca, *La guerra d'Etiopia: l'ultima impresa del colonialismo* (Longanesi, 2010), p. 195.
43. 'Dalla Relazione riassuntiva dell'occupazione dell'Amba Alagi e delle battaglie del Tembien e dello Scirè di Pietro Badoglio'. Reproduced in: Longo, *La Campagna Italo-Etiopica*, II, p. 557.
44. Gentilli, 'Elenco completo dei bombardmento a gas sul fronte Nord', p. 142.
45. Longo, *La Campagna Italo-Etiopica*, I, p. 298.

Chapter 13: Serdo and Gondar

1. Paul Gentizon, *La conquête de l'Éthiopie* (Paris: Editions Berger-Levrault, 1936), p. 243.
2. Longo, *La Campagna Italo-Etiopica*, I, p. 302.
3. Baer, *Test Case*, p. 226.
4. A detailed account of the matter can be found in: Rainer Baudendistel, *Between Bombs and Good Intentions: The Red Cross and the Italo-Ethiopian War, 1935–1936* (New York: Berghahn Books, 2006), pp. 145–53.
5. Macfie, *An Ethiopian Diary*, pp. 81–2.
6. Macfie, *An Ethiopian Diary*, p. 89.
7. Kathleen Nelson and Alan Sullivan (eds), *John Melly of Ethiopia* (London: Faber & Faber, 1937), p. 218.
8. 'Copia di telegramma in arrivo. Ministero delle Colonie. Asmara. 4/3/1936-XIV ore 22.35. Massima precedenza assoluta'. Reproduced in: Longo, *La Campagna Italo-Etiopica*, II, p. 527.
9. Steer, *Caesar in Abyssinia*, p. 279. One British journalist, writing in 1943, gave his impression: 'Some years ago I read a copy of Vittorio Mussolini's book ... and found in it surprisingly lyrical descriptions of the amusement that could be derived from dropping tons of high explosives upon Abyssinians. For Il Duce's son it seems to have been great fun.' Denis Weaver, *Front Page Europe* (London: Cresset Press, 1943), p. 128.
10. Longo, *La Campagna Italo-Etiopica*, I, p. 292.
11. Hansard, vol. 309, col. 1781, 9 March 1936. 'British Red Cross (Italian Bombing)'.
12. Baudendistel, *Between Bombs and Good Intentions*, p. 152.
13. Churchill, *The Gathering Storm*, pp. 165–6.
14. R.A.C. Parker, 'The First Capitulation: France and the Rhineland Crisis of 1936', *World Politics*, April 1956, 8(3):355–73.
15. Franklin D. Laurens, *France and the Italo-Ethiopian Crisis 1935–1936* (The Hague: Mouton, 1967), p. 343.
16. 'Memorandum by Mr Eden on Germany and the Locarno Treaty', 8 March 1936. In W.N. Medlicott, Douglas Dakin, and M.E. Lambert (eds), *Documents on British Foreign Policy 1919–1939: Second Series, Volume XVI* (London: HMSO, 1977), p. 60.
17. Giorgio Rochat, *Italo Balbo: La vita sociale della nuova Italia* (Torino: UTET-Unione Tipografico-Editrice Torinese, 1986), p. 138. Baudendistel, *Between Bombs and Good Intentions*, p. 153.
18. *Journal of the League of Nations*, 91st Session of the Council, Annex 1952, April 1936. Quoted in: Nicola Perugini and Neve Gordon, 'Between Sovereignty and Race: The Bombardment of Hospitals in the Italo-Ethiopian War and the Colonial Imprint of International Law', *State Crime Journal*, 2019, 8(1):116.
19. Longo, *La Campagna Italo-Etiopica*, I, p. 304.

20. De Bono, *La Preparazione e le Prime Operazioni*, p. 65.
21. Capitano Giovanni Braca e Capitano Renzo Comolli, 'La dancalia meridionale', *Gli annali dell'Africa italiana*, marzo MCMXXXIX anno XVII, II(I):216.
22. Del Boca, *Gli italiani in Africa Orientale*, 2, p. 237.
23. Longo, *La Campagna Italo-Etiopica*, I, p. 308.
24. Emilio Salgari, 'Master of Adventure'. Available at: https://www.rohpress.com/en_salgari.html.
25. V. Beonio-Brocchieri, *Cieli d'Etiopia: Avventure di un pilota di guerra* (Milano: A Mondadori, 1936), pp. 118, 121.
26. Fidenzio Dall'Ora, *Intendenza in AO* (Roma: Istituto nazionale fascista di cultura, 1937-IV), p. 71.
27. L.M. Nesbitt, who explored the area in the late 1920s, recorded what he considered to be 'true Danakil philosophy' as outlined by one of the inhabitants: 'men must think of blood ... for it is better to die than to live without killing'. L.M. Nesbitt, *Hell-Hole of Creation: The Exploration of Abyssinian Danakil* (New York: Alfred A. Knopf, 1935), p. 106. According to Ladislas Farago: 'A Danakil warrior may not marry until he has killed an enemy and has brought home his severed genitals as a trophy of his valour.' Farago, 'The Busu Tshiki Tshik', p. 238. See also: Wilfred Thesiger, *The Danakil Diary: Journeys through Abyssinia 1930–34* (London: Harper Collins, 1996).
28. Longo, *La Campagna Italo-Etiopica*, I, p. 310.
29. Gentizon, *La conquête de l'Éthiopie*, p. 243.
30. Generale di Divisione Aerea Mario Aimone Cat, 'L'aviazione in AO: Da Adua a Addis Abeba', *L'Ala d'Italia: Periodico Nazionale dell'Aviazione Fascista*, maggio 1937-XV. p. 14.
31. Raffaele Di Lauro, 'I bollettini di guerra del Negus ed altri documenti di fonte etiopica', *Gli annali dell'Africa italiana*, marzo MCMXXXIX, anno XVII, II(I):173.
32. Del Boca, *Gli italiani in Africa Orientale*, 2, p. 601.
33. Beonio-Brocchieri, *Cieli d'Etiopia*, p. 122.
34. V. Beonio-Brocchieri, 'La marcia della colonna che conquistò L'aussa. Forte di Sardo, 11 marzo', in Rosario Mascia, *I giornalisti alla conquista dell'impero: corrispondenze di guerra dall'Africa Orientale 1935–1936* (Milano: ASEFI, 2003), p. 247.
35. Gentilli, *Guerra aerea sull'Etiopia*, p. 117.
36. Rochat, *Le guerre italiane 1935–1943*, p. 60, n. 12.
37. Chris Prouty Rosenfeld, *A Chronology of Menilek II of Ethiopia 1844–1913, Emperor of Ethiopia, 1889–1913* (East Lansing, MI: Michigan State University, 1976), p. 21.
38. Longo, *La Campagna Italo-Etiopica*, I, p. 313.
39. Attilio Teruzzi, *La Milizia delle Camicie Nere e le sue specialità* (Milano: A Mondadori, Anno XVII-1939), p. 100. Longo, *La Campagna Italo-Etiopica*, I, p. 315.
40. Badoglio al Ministero delle Colonie. 1 aprile 1936-XIV. Reproduced in: Longo, *La Campagna Italo-Etiopica*, II, p. 364.
41. Antonio Spinosa, *Starace: l'uomo che inventò lo stile fascista* (Milano: Casa Editrice Rizzoli, 1988), p. 147.
42. Edoardo Scala, *Storia delle fanterie italiane: Volume VIII, Tomo 1, I Bersaglieri* (Roma: Stato Maggiore dell'Esercito Ufficio storico, 2020), pp. 256–7.
43. Del Boca, *Gli italiani in Africa Orientale*, 2, p. 611. Spinosa, *Starace*, p. 144.
44. Achille Starace, *La marcia su Gondar: della colonna celere AO e le successive operazioni nella Etiopia Occidentale* (Milano: A Mondadori, XIV-1936), p. 67. Del Boca, *Gli italiani in Africa Orientale*, 2, p. 611.
45. Scala, *Storia delle fanterie italiane*, p. 255.
46. Literally 'To the Very End' or 'fight on until death'.
47. Quoted in: Starace, *La marcia su Gondar*, p. 78. See also: Spinosa, *Starace*, p. 155.
48. Angelo Del Boca, *La guerra d'Etiopia: l'ultima impresa del colonialismo* (Milano: Casa Editrice Longanesi, 2010), p. 281, n. 3. There is evidence that Starace attempted to impose the compulsory purchase of this 'grandiloquent and highly unreliable account' on members of *Opera Nazionale Dopolavoro* (the National Afterwork Club), the Fascist recreational organisation. Bosworth, *Mussolini*, p. 410, n. 122.

49. Attilio Teruzzi, *La Milizia delle Camicie Nere e le sue specialità* (Milano: A. Mondadori, Anno XVII-1939), p. 100. See also: Giuseppe Capponcini, *Con l'82° Battaglione CCNN 'Benito Mussolini', in Africa Orientale: Dall'Amba Alagi alle sorgenti del Nilo Azzurro* (Forli: Stabilimento tipografico Valbonesi, 1937-XV).
50. Longo, *La Campagna Italo-Etiopica*, I, p. 316.
51. A contemporaneous piece in the *New York Times* explains why: 'The one interest of Great Britain in Ethiopia is Lake Tana, a sheet about an eighth as large as Lake Erie, source of the Blue Nile, a stream which supplies not only 70 per cent of the water that flows into the Nile at Khartum, center of the irrigated cotton-growing region of the Sudan and Egypt, but also most of the silt, without which there would be no cotton', see 'Italy, Britain and Tana', *New York Times*, 5 April 1936. For a concise account of the matter see: Mats Harsmar, Emil Sandstrom and Atakilte Beyene, 'Lake Tana: Source of Disputes or Collaboration over the Blue Nile?', in Emil Sandstrom, Anders Jagerskog and Terje Oestigaard (eds), *Land and Hydropolitics in the Nile River Basin: Challenges and New Investments* (Abingdon: Routledge, 2016), pp. 191–2.
52. Longo, *La Campagna Italo-Etiopica*, I, p. 316.
53. Rochat, *Le guerre italiane 1935–1943*, p. 60.
54. See: David Evans, *War: A Matter of Principles* (Houndsmills: Macmillan Press, 1997), p. 12.
55. Emphasis in the original: '*Ricevo vostro saluto dopo la magnifica marcia su Gondar, che è stata VERAMENTE DI STILE FASCISTA. Tributo il mio elogio agli Ufficiali e alle truppe.*' As quoted in: Starace, *La marcia su Gondar*, p. 79.

Chapter 14: 'Fascism believes neither in the possibility nor ...'

1. Steer, *Caesar in Abyssinia*, p. 314.
2. Longo, *La Campagna Italo-Etiopica*, I, p. 316, n. 307.
3. Longo, *La Campagna Italo-Etiopica*, I, p. 318. See also: Del Boca, *Gli italiani in Africa Orientale*, 2, p. 616.
4. Longo, *La Campagna Italo-Etiopica*, I, p. 316.
5. Badoglio a Ministero Colonie – 'Urgente per SE Mussolini' - 18 March 1936. Reproduced in: Longo, *La Campagna Italo-Etiopica*, II, pp. 568–9.
6. Steer, *Caesar in Abyssinia*, p. 281.
7. Gentilli, 'Elenco completo dei bombardmento a gas sul fronte Nord', p. 142.
8. Hansard, vol. 100, col. 340, 30 March 1936. House of Lords Debates. 'Italo-Abyssinian Dispute: Methods of Warfare', Viscount Cecil of Chelwood. Coryne Hall, *Princesses on the Wards: Royal Women in Nursing Through Wars and Revolutions* (Cheltenham: History Press, 2022), p. 49.
9. Steven Morewood, *The British Defence of Egypt, 1935–40: Conflict and Crisis in the Eastern Mediterranean* (Abingdon: Frank Cass, 2005), p. 79.
10. Steer, *Caesar in Abyssinia*, p. 298.
11. J. Calvitt Clarke III, 'Feodor Konovalov and the Italo-Ethiopian War (Part I)', *World War II Quarterly*, Winter 2008, 5(1):4. Del Boca, *Gli italiani in Africa Orientale*, 2, p. 379.
12. Steer, *Caesar in Abyssinia*, p. 404.
13. This chapter deals with the Battle of Maychew. Steer, *Caesar in Abyssinia*, pp. 298–338.
14. Clarke, 'Feodor Konovalov and the Italo-Ethiopian War (Part I)', p. 5.
15. Col. T.H. Konovaloff, *Con le armate del Negus (un bianco fra i neri)* (Bologna: Nicola Zanichelli Editore, 1937-XV).
16. See: Clarke, 'Feodor Konovalov and the Italo-Ethiopian War (Part I)', pp. 10–11; Boris Gorelik, 'Colonel Konovaloff: A friend of Ethiopia or an Apologist of Fascism?' A paper read at the 11th Conference of Africanists held at Moscow, May 2008. Available online at: https://www.researchgate.net/publication/361276404. For a thorough account of the 'different versions of Colonel Konovaloff's testimony', see: Richard Pankhurst, 'Le diverse versioni della testimonianza del colonnello Konovaloff sull'invasione fascista dell'Etiopia', *Studi Piacentini*, 2003, 34(2):137–78. See also: J. Calvitt Clarke III and Boris Gorelik, 'Konovalov, Fjodor Evgenjevič',

in Alessandro Bausi and Siegbert Uhlig (eds), *Encyclopaedia Aethiopica: Volume 5* (Wiesbaden: Harrassowitz Verlag, 2014), pp. 379–80.
17. Steer, *Caesar in Abyssinia*, p. 298.
18. Steer, *Caesar in Abyssinia*, p. 302.
19. Longo, *La Campagna Italo-Etiopica*, I, p. 319.
20. Longo, *La Campagna Italo-Etiopica*, I, p. 319.
21. Renzo Dalmazzo, generale di divisione, 'Il terreno della battaglia dell'Ascianghi (31 marzo– 5 aprile 1936-XIV)', *Rivista di fanteria: Rassegna mensile di studi militari*, giugno 1937-XV, IV(6):902. Col. Emilio Battisti, *Il 7° Alpini in AO: 'Feltre' Pieve di Teco' 'Exilles'* (Roma: 10° Reggimento Alpini Editore, 1937-XV), p. 109.
22. Dalmazzo, 'Il terreno della battaglia dell'Ascianghi', p. 903.
23. Longo, *La Campagna Italo-Etiopica*, I, p. 321. The complete Italian order of battle can be found in: 'Battaglia del lago asciangi 31 marzo–4 Aprile 1936', in Longo, *La Campagna Italo-Etiopica*, II, p. 579.
24. Steer, *Caesar in Abyssinia*, p. 309.
25. Badoglio, 'Oggette: Avansata su Quoram'. 28 marzo 1936-XIV. Reproduced in: Longo, *La Campagna Italo-Etiopica*, II, pp. 574–8.
26. Longo, *La Campagna Italo-Etiopica*, I, p. 319.
27. Longo, *La Campagna Italo-Etiopica*, I, p. 320.
28. Rochat, *Le guerre italiane 1935–1943*, p. 61.
29. Pedriali, *L'aeronautica italiana*, p. 112.
30. Del Boca, *Gli italiani in Africa Orientale*, 2, p. 630.
31. Francesco 'Cesco' Tomaselli, special correspondent for the *Corriere della Sera*, quoted in: Longo, *La Campagna Italo-Etiopica*, I, p. 322.
32. Longo, *La Campagna Italo-Etiopica*, I, p. 322.
33. Steer, *Caesar in Abyssinia*, pp. 313–14.
34. Badoglio, *La Guerra D' Etiopia*, p. 180. Longo, *La Campagna Italo-Etiopica*, I, p. 323.
35. Pedriali, *L'aeronautica italiana*, p. 113.
36. Gustavo Pesenti, generale di divisione, *Storia della Prima divisione eritrea (8 aprile 1935-XIII – 1° maggio XIV)* (Milano: Casa Editrice L'Eroica, 1937-XV), p. 131.
37. Pedriali, *L'aeronautica italiana*, pp. 114–15.
38. Longo, *La Campagna Italo-Etiopica*, I, p. 325.
39. Steer, *Caesar in Abyssinia*, p. 315.
40. Quoted in: Rochat, *Le guerre italiane 1935–1943*, p. 61; Longo, *La Campagna Italo-Etiopica*, I, p. 325.
41. 'One would have expected that these Ethiopian masses thrown into an offensive against the drastic fire developed by modern military technique would suffer severely, but their casualties as a matter of fact were relatively small.' Steer, *Caesar in Abyssinia*, p. 314.
42. Gustavo Pesenti generale di divisione, *Storia della Prima divisione eritrea (8 aprile 1935-XIII – 1° maggio XIV)* (Milano: Casa Editrice L'Eroica, 1937-XV), p. 139. Badoglio, *La Guerra D' Etiopia*, p. 184.
43. Longo, *La Campagna Italo-Etiopica*, I, p. 325.
44. Gentilli, *Guerra aerea sull'Etiopia*, p. 89. Pedriali, *L'aeronautica italiana*, p. 115.
45. The last deployment was on 28 March. Gentilli, 'Elenco completo dei bombardmento a gas sul fronte Nord', p. 142.
46. Steer, *Caesar in Abyssinia*, p. 314.
47. Pedriali, *L'aeronautica italiana*, p. 115.
48. Longo, *La Campagna Italo-Etiopica*, I, p. 325.
49. Peter Garretson, *A Victorian Gentleman & Ethiopian Nationalist: The Life and Times of Hakim Warqenah, Dr Charles Martin* (Woodbridge: James Currey, 2012).
50. 'Telegramma intercettato e decrittato: 2 aprile 1936 – da Ministero Esteri Etiopico a Legazione Etiopia – Parigi.' Reproduced in: Longo, *La Campagna Italo-Etiopica*, II, p. 589.

51. See Chapter 4.
52. Steer, *Caesar in Abyssinia*, p. 321.
53. Gentilli, *Guerra aerea sull'Etiopia*, p. 91.
54. Pedriali, *L'aeronautica italiana*, p. 115.
55. Rochat, *Le guerre italiane 1935–1943*, p. 59.
56. Steer, *Caesar in Abyssinia*, p. 324.
57. Steer, *Caesar in Abyssinia*, p. 330.
58. Longo, *La Campagna Italo-Etiopica*, I, p. 326, n. 329.
59. Badoglio, *La Guerra D' Etiopia*, p. 183.
60. 'Badoglio a Ministero Colonie. 4 aprile 1936-XIV.' Reproduced in: Longo, *La Campagna Italo-Etiopica*, II, p. 596.
61. Quoted in: Aldo Cabiati, *La conquista dell'impero: cronaca ragionata della guerra italo-abissina 1935–1936* (Milan: Casa Editrice Sonsogno, 1936), p. 163.
62. Pedriali, *L'aeronautica italiana*, p. 116.
63. Longo, *La Campagna Italo-Etiopica*, I, pp. 327–9.
64. Pedriali, *L'aeronautica italiana*, p. 115.

Chapter 15: Totalitarian Motorisation

1. Giuseppe Carlo Mosconi, maggiore d'artiglieria, 'Il servizio automobilistico militare in Somalia', *Rivista di fanteria: Rassegna mensile di studi militari*, giugno 1937-XV, IV(6):929.
2. Longo, *La Campagna Italo-Etiopica*, I, p. 332.
3. Longo, *La Campagna Italo-Etiopica*, I, p. 332.
4. Longo, *La Campagna Italo-Etiopica*, I, p. 345.
5. Longo, *La Campagna Italo-Etiopica*, I, p. 341.
6. Longo, *La Campagna Italo-Etiopica*, I, p. 342. Del Boca, *La guerra d'Abissinia*, p. 80.
7. Two former Ottoman officers: Farouk Bey, a Turk, and Tarik Bey, a Sudanese. Spencer, *Ethiopia at Bay*, p. 45. Steer, *Caesar in Abyssinia*, pp. 189–90.
8. Longo, *La Campagna Italo-Etiopica*, I, p. 342. According to Steer, Nasibu was 'a civilised man of some administrative capacity' but no commander. Nor was he amenable to taking 'foreign advice'. Steer, *Caesar in Abyssinia*, p. 352.
9. Mussolini to De Bono. 28 September 1935. Quoted in: De Bono and Miall (trans.), *Anno XIIII: the Conquest of an Empire*, p. 219.
10. Pino Rauti e Rutilio Sermonti, *Storia del fascismo volume 5: L'espansione e l'asse* (Roma: Centro Editoriale Nazionale, 1976), p. 130. Pino Rauti (Umberto Giusti), *Storia d'Italia nei discorsi di Mussolini 1915–1945: Volume II* (Roma: Centro Editoriale Nazionale, 1966), p. 850.
11. Badoglio a Graziani. 3 marzo 1936-XIV. Reproduced in: Longo, *La Campagna Italo-Etiopica*, II, p. 608.
12. Graziani a Badoglio. 4 marzo 1936-XIV. Reproduced in: Longo, *La Campagna Italo-Etiopica*, II, p. 608.
13. Varo Varanini, *La formazione de L'Impero Coloniale Italiano Volume terzo: L'Impero (Dall'occupazione di Dessié all'assetto definitivo dell'Impero)* (Milano: Aldo Garzanti Editore, 1939), p. 128.
14. 270 Italian officers, 600 Italian soldiers and 8,000 Libyan *ascari*. Comando divisione di fanteria coloniale «Libia» Stato Maggiore, Harar. 20 maggio 1936-XIV, 'Relazione sulle operazioni effettuate per l'occupazione di Harar (14 aprile–8 maggio 1936-XIV)'. Reproduced in: Longo, *La Campagna Italo-Etiopica*, II, p. 639. Mussolini had delayed the transfer of this unit as mentioned in Chapter 7. See also: Longo, *La Campagna Italo-Etiopica*, I, p. 338.
15. Longo, *La Campagna Italo-Etiopica*, I, p. 220. Rosaria Quartararo, 'Imperial Defence in the Mediterranean on the Eve of the Ethiopian Crisis (July–October 1935)', *Historical Journal*, March 1977, 20(1):186.
16. Raffaello Micaletti, tenente colonnello di fanteria, 'Nell'Ogaden con gli Ascari Libici', *Rivista di fanteria: Rassegna mensile di studi militari*, maggio 1937-XV, IV(5):744.

17. *Carabinieri* (Roma: Edizione dell'Istituto di Divulgazione Storica, 1956), pp. 155–6. See also: Alberto Galazzetti, *Le bande autocarrate dei Carabinieri reali in Africa Orientale italiana: Immagini e storia* (febbraio–luglio 1936) (Voghera: Marvia editione, 2013). Domenico Capecelatro Gaudioso, *Una fucina d'eroi: l'arma dei carabinieri* (Napoli: Adriano Gallina editore, 1978), pp. 45–6.
18. Such as the Italo-Ottoman War of 1911–1912 and the First World War. See: *Carabinieri* (Roma: Edizione dell'Istituto di Divulgazione Storica, 1956), pp. 235, 391–2.
19. Fuller, *The First of the League Wars*, p. 57.
20. Longo, *La Campagna Italo-Etiopica*, I, p. 343. For a brief account of the militia see: http://rivistanuovastoria.com/2017/10/16/la-guardia-forestale-suo-passato-glorioso-dimenticato-politicamente-corretto/.
21. Longo, *La Campagna Italo-Etiopica*, I, p. 339. Pedriali, *L'aeronautica italiana*, p. 118.
22. Pedriali, *L'aeronautica italiana*, p. 119.
23. Pedriali, *L'aeronautica italiana*, p. 119.
24. Magalo and Ghigner are today known as Megalo and Ginir.
25. Federigo Valli, 'Bombardamenti sul Gestro: Magalo e Ghigner', *L'Ala d'Italia: Periodico Nazionale dell'Aviazione Fascista*, aprile 1936-XIV, 14–15.
26. Rochat, 'L'impiego dei gas', p. 88.
27. Gentilli, 'Elenco completo dei bombardmento a gas sul fronte Sud: La storiografia aeronautica e il problema dei gas', in Angelo Del Boca (ed.), *I gas di Mussolini: Il fascism e la guerra d'Etiopia* (Roma: Editori Reuniti, 2007), p. 143.
28. Pedriali, *L'aeronautica italiana*, p. 120.
29. Mussolini e Graziani, 11 marzo 1936. Quoted in: Pedriali, *L'aeronautica italiana*, p. 120.
30. Gentilli, 'Elenco completo dei bombardmento a gas sul fronte Sud', p. 143.
31. Gentilli, 'Elenco completo dei bombardmento a gas sul fronte Sud', p. 143.
32. Gentilli, 'Elenco completo dei bombardmento a gas sul fronte Sud', p. 143. Pedriali, *L'aeronautica italiana*, p. 121.
33. Badoglio e Graziani. 2 aprile 1936-XIV. Reproduced in: Longo, *La Campagna Italo-Etiopica*, II, p. 611.
34. Mussolini e Graziani. 3 aprile 1936-XIV. Quoted in: Del Boca, *Gli italiani in Africa Orientale*, 2, p. 661.
35. Del Boca, *Gli italiani in Africa Orientale*, 2, p. 661. Rodolfo Graziani, Maresciallo d'Italia, Marchese di Neghelli, *Il fronte sud* (Milano: A Mondadori Editore, 1938), p. 303.
36. Mussolini a Graziani, 14 aprile 1936-XIV. Reproduced in: Longo, *La Campagna Italo-Etiopica*, II, p. 636.
37. Longo, *La Campagna Italo-Etiopica*, I, p. 343.
38. Longo, *La Campagna Italo-Etiopica*, I, p. 343. Micaletti, 'Nell'Ogaden con gli Ascari Libici', p. 749.
39. Pedriali, *L'aeronautica italiana*, p. 122.
40. Left column: 510; central column: 515; right column: 519. Micaletti, 'Nell'Ogaden con gli Ascari Libici', pp. 939–40.
41. Longo, *La Campagna Italo-Etiopica*, I, p. 339.
42. Micaletti, 'Nell'Ogaden con gli Ascari Libici', pp. 750–1. General Nasi reported an estimate of 10,000, but how accurate this might be is impossible to say. Comando divisione di fanteria coloniale «Libia» Stato Maggiore, Harar. 20 maggio 1936-XIV, 'Relazione sulle operazioni effettuate per l'occupazione di Harar (14 aprile–8 maggio 1936-XIV)'. Reproduced in: Longo, *La Campagna Italo-Etiopica*, II, p. 639. Del Boca wrote that this force had missed an opportunity by not attacking Danan before the Libyan Division got there. Doing so 'could have put Graziani in difficulty'. Del Boca, *Gli italiani in Africa Orientale*, 2, p. 665.
43. 'That area had been chosen by the enemy, for the numerous existing caves, and for the suitable wooded vegetation, which could easily hide it from aerial observation as well as, in part, from terrestrial observation.' Comando divisione di fanteria coloniale «Libia» Stato Maggiore, Harar. 20 maggio 1936-XIV, 'Relazione sulle operazioni effettuate per l'occupazione di Harar (14 aprile–8 maggio 1936-XIV)'. Reproduced in: Longo, *La Campagna Italo-Etiopica*, II, p. 640.

44. Longo, *La Campagna Italo-Etiopica*, I, p. 347.
45. Rochat, *Le guerre italiane 1935–1943*, p. 73.
46. Pedriali, *L'aeronautica italiana*, p. 123.
47. Longo, *La Campagna Italo-Etiopica*, I, p. 347. For an account in English of these battles see: Mark Thompson, *The White War: Life and Death on the Italian Front 1915–1919* (London: Faber & Faber, 2009).
48. Longo, *La Campagna Italo-Etiopica*, I, p. 347.
49. Pedriali, *L'aeronautica italiana*, p. 123.
50. Postscriptal note to: Federigo Valli, 'Ricognizioni sull'Uebi', *L'Ala d'Italia: Periodico Nazionale dell'Aviazione Fascista*, maggio 1936-XIV, 17.
51. Micaletti, 'Nell'Ogaden con gli Ascari Libici', p. 753.
52. 'Graziani a Mussolini e Badoglio, 17 aprile 1936-XIV'. Reproduced in: Longo, *La Campagna Italo-Etiopica*, II, pp. 666–7.
53. Micaletti, 'Nell'Ogaden con gli Ascari Libici', p. 754. Del Boca later calculated the Italian losses at about 740 dead and wounded in total. Del Boca, *Gli italiani in Africa Orientale*, 2, p. 669.
54. Comitato per la «Storia dell'Artiglieria italiana», *Storia dell'Artiglieria italiana, parte V (dal 1920 al 1945), Vol. XVI (l'artiglieria nelle operazioni belliche dal 1920 al 1945)* (Roma: Biblioteca d'Artiglieria e Genio, 1955), pp. 117, 973. A single 65mm calibre *Cannone da 65/17 modello 13* was easily broken down into five loads for transport by pack animals.
55. Pedriali, *L'aeronautica italiana*, p. 124. Longo, *La Campagna Italo-Etiopica*, I, p. 349.
56. Longo, *La Campagna Italo-Etiopica*, I, p. 349.
57. Comando delle forze armate della Somalia, *La guerra italo-etiopica fronte sud*, 4, p. 289.
58. Longo, *La Campagna Italo-Etiopica*, I, p. 349.
59. Carlo Boidi, *Legionari universitari sul fronte somalo* (Milano: Sperling & Kupfer, 1937-XV).
60. Unless otherwise stated, this section of the work is based on: Longo, *La Campagna Italo-Etiopica*, I, pp. 350–7.
61. Micaletti, 'Nell'Ogaden con gli Ascari Libici', p. 746.
62. Gentilli, 'Elenco completo dei bombardmenti a gas sul fronte Sud', p. 143.
63. Mario Bassi, 'Quadro d'insieme della battaglia dell'Ogaden', in Emilio Ceretti (ed.), *Con l'Esercito Italiano in AO Volume II: Dalla battaglia dello Scirè all'Impero* (Milano: A Mondadori, 1937), p. 589.
64. Pedriali, *L'aeronautica italiana*, p. 124.
65. Vittorio Verne, *Alla battaglia dell'Ogaden con la colonna Verne* (Milano: Societa Nazionale Editrice Propaganda, 1937), pp. 349–54.
66. Steer, *Caesar in Abyssinia*, p. 350.
67. Messages quoted in: Comando delle forze armate della Somalia, *La guerra italo-etiopica fronte sud*, 4, p. 193.
68. Achille Benedetti, *La Guerra Equatoriale: Con L'Armata del Maresciallo Graziani* (Milano: Casa Editrice Oberdan Zucchi via Cesare Battisti, 1937), p. 213. Benedetti was special correspondent for the *Corriere della Sera*. See also: Longo, *La Campagna Italo-Etiopica*, I, p. 356.
69. Longo, *La Campagna Italo-Etiopica*, I, p. 356. Steer, *Caesar in Abyssinia*, p. 351.
70. Frusci, *In Somalia sul fronte meridionale*, p. 104.
71. Longo, *La Campagna Italo-Etiopica*, I, p. 357.
72. Generale di brigata Luigi Frusci, 'Relazione sulla battaglia di Birgot: Riferisco con la presente sull'attività della colonna centrale nel periodo compreso dall'11 al 25 aprile c.a.e, in particolare, sulla battaglia di Birgot e sui successivi scontri nella zona a sud di Hamanlei', in Comando delle forze armate della Somalia, *La guerra italo-etiopica fronte sud*, 4, pp. 196–208. The same report can also be found in: Longo, *La Campagna Italo-Etiopica*, II, pp. 668–76.
73. Longo, *La Campagna Italo-Etiopica*, I, p. 356. Steer, *Caesar in Abyssinia*, p. 351.
74. Giorgio De Vecchi di Val Cismon, *Dubat: Gli arditi neri* (Milano: A Mondadori Editore, 1936-XIV), p. 173.
75. Graziani, *Il fronte sud*, p. 326.
76. Vadala, *Fiamme d'argento in Abissinia*, p. 106.

77. Telegramma. Graziani a Mussolini e Badoglio, 25 aprile 1936-XIV. Reproduced in: Longo, *La Campagna Italo-Etiopica*, II, p. 678.
78. Vadala, *Fiamme d'argento in Abissinia*, p. 121.
79. Carlo Fettarappa Sandri, *La Unità e i Capi* (Roma: Unione Editoriale d'Italia, 1938), p. 292.
80. Telegramma. Graziani a Mussolini e Badoglio, 25 aprile 1936-XIV. Reproduced in: Longo, *La Campagna Italo-Etiopica*, II, p. 678.
81. Longo, *La Campagna Italo-Etiopica*, I, p. 358.
82. Vadala, *Fiamme d'argento in Abissinia*, p. 165.
83. Graziani a Lessona e Badoglio, 25 aprile 1936-XIV. Quoted in: Longo, *La Campagna Italo-Etiopica*, I, p. 359.
84. Telegramma. Graziani a Mussolini e Badoglio, 25 aprile 1936-XIV. Reproduced in: Longo, *La Campagna Italo-Etiopica*, II, p. 678.
85. Comando delle forze armate della Somalia, *La guerra italo-etiopica fronte sud*, 4, p. 339.
86. Mosconi, 'Il servizio automobilistico militare in Somalia', p. 929.
87. Graziani a Lessona e Badoglio, 25 aprile 1936-XIV. Quoted in: Longo, *La Campagna Italo-Etiopica*, I, p. 359.

Chapter 16: 'The March of the Iron Will'

1. Quoted in: *Graphicus: Notiziario Grafico, Rivista mensile delle arti della stampa*, agosto 1936, XXVI(8):II.
2. See: Maresciallo Pietro Badoglio, 'Relazione riassuntiva relativa alla marcia su Addis Abeba', in Varanini, *La formazione de L'Impero Coloniale Italiano*, pp. 59–61.
3. Longo, *La Campagna Italo-Etiopica*, I, pp. 371–2.
4. Badoglio. *Graphicus*, XXVI(8):II.
5. 'Marcia da Dessie ad Addis Abeba (24 aprile–5 maggio)'. Reproduced in: Longo, *La Campagna Italo-Etiopica*, II, p. 714.
6. Badoglio. *Graphicus*, XXVI(8):III. The British journalist Stuart Emeny, who had made the journey earlier, was of a similar impression: 'I jolted off in the lorry along the Great North Road which runs for 200 miles from Addis [Ababa] to Dessie. The road at its best is a flattened mud track which switchbacks like a giant racer up and down the mountains, frequently running on the top of precipices. At one moment the road is 11,000 feet above sea level and within half an hour by car it has plunged down a matter of 6,000 feet into baking hot valleys. It is a remarkable engineering feat considering that most of it has been carved out of sheer mountain-side by native workmen, using curved sticks with a small iron point as their principal tool.' Emeny, 'Under Fire with the Emperor', p. 180.
7. Aimone Cat, 'L'aviazione in AO: Da Adua a Addis Abeba', p. 13.
8. The Negus was still travelling south from Maychew using circuitous routes and travelling at night so as to avoid attention, particularly of the aerial variety. In this he was successful, but he would not reach Addis Ababa until 30 April. Steer, *Caesar in Abyssinia*, p. 356.
9. Spencer, *Ethiopia at Bay*, p. 61. *Ishshi naga* = 'I understand, perhaps tomorrow'.
10. Del Boca, *La guerra d'Abissinia*, p. 81.
11. Spencer, *Ethiopia at Bay*, p. 6.
12. Del ministero dell'AI (ed.), 'Le opere stradali, la costruzione dell'impero: l'opera dell'italia in AOI dopo la conquista dell'etiopia', in *Gli annali dell'Africa italiana*, MCMXXXIX-anno XVIII, II(IV):340.
13. Del Boca, *Gli italiani in Africa Orientale*, 2, p. 684. Viking Tamm, *I tjänst hos Negus: aderton månader som krigskolechef i Etiopien* (Stockholm: Wahlström & Widstrand, 1936), pp. 278–99.
14. Comando Superiore AO Stato Maggiore, *La marcia su Addis Abeba: Ordine del Giorno* (Asmara: 7ª Sezione Topocartografica, 1936-XIV), pp. 12–13. Emphasis in the original. The term *commovente* connotes touching or stirring in the emotional sense.
15. Giovanni De Luna, *Badoglio: un militare al potere* (Milano: Casa Editrice Valentino Bompiani, 1974), p. 154.

16. Longo, *La Campagna Italo-Etiopica*, I, p. 331.
17. Longo, *La Campagna Italo-Etiopica*, I, p. 360.
18. Graziani a Mussolini e Badoglio, 30 aprile 1936-XIV. Reproduced in: Longo, *La Campagna Italo-Etiopica*, II, p. 682.
19. Longo, *La Campagna Italo-Etiopica*, I, p. 359.
20. Steer, *Caesar in Abyssinia*, p. 352.
21. Graziani a Mussolini e Badoglio, 30 aprile 1936-XIV. Reproduced in: Longo, *La Campagna Italo-Etiopica*, II, p. 682.
22. Steer, *Caesar in Abyssinia*, p. 356.
23. Spencer, *Ethiopia at Bay*, pp. 61–2.
24. See: Paul G. Halpern (ed.), 'Chapter VIII: Conveying the Emperor Haile Selassie into Exile', in Brian Vale (ed.), The Naval Miscellany: Vol. VIII (Abingdon: Routledge for the Navy Records Society, 2017), pp. 347–87.
25. Spencer, *Ethiopia at Bay*, pp. 63–4. Steer, *Caesar in Abyssinia*, p. 371.
26. Steer gives a thorough account: Steer, *Caesar in Abyssinia*, pp. 370–99.
27. Kathleen Nelson and Alan Sullivan (eds), *John Melly of Ethiopia* (London: Faber & Faber, 1937), pp. 260–5.
28. Graziani, *Il fronte sud*, p. 334.
29. Longo, *La Campagna Italo-Etiopica*, I, p. 381.
30. See: Lutz Haber, 'The Emperor Haile Selassie I in Bath 1936–1940'. Available at: http://anglo-ethiopian.org/publications/articles.php?type=O&reference=publications/occasionalpapers/papers/haileselassiebath.php.
31. Halpern, 'Conveying the Emperor Haile Selassie into Exile', pp. 367–8.
32. Steer, *Caesar in Abyssinia*, p. 353.
33. Graziani a Mussolini e Badoglio, 5 maggio 1936-XIV. Reproduced in: Longo, *La Campagna Italo-Etiopica*, II, p. 723.
34. Longo, *La Campagna Italo-Etiopica*, I, p. 381.
35. Longo, *La Campagna Italo-Etiopica*, I, p. 377.
36. Badoglio a Mussolini, 4 aprile 1936-XIV. Reproduced in: Longo, *La Campagna Italo-Etiopica*, II, p. 719.
37. Longo, *La Campagna Italo-Etiopica*, I, p. 377.
38. Spencer, *Ethiopia at Bay*, p. 68.
39. Steer, *Caesar in Abyssinia*, p. 401.
40. Badoglio e Mussolini a Graziani, 5 maggio XIV. Reproduced in: Longo, *La Campagna Italo-Etiopica*, II, p. 720.
41. Piero Melograni, 'The Cult of the Duce in Mussolini's Italy', *Journal of Contemporary History*, October 1976, 11(4):231.
42. Benito Mussolini, 'L'Etiopia è italiana, 6 maggio 1936', in Edoardo e Duilio Susmel (eds), *Opera omnia di Benito Mussolini [Volume] XXVII: Dall'Inaugurazione della provincia di Littoria alla proclamazione dell'Impero (19 Dicembre 1934–9 Maggio 1936)* (Firenze: La Fenice, 1959), pp. 265–6. It can be viewed/heard at: https://www.youtube.com/watch?v=w1TInA93WEo&ab_channel=-TEMPOLESSMUSIC.
43. Indro Montanelli e Mario Cervi, *Storia d'Italia Volume 41: L'impero* (Milano: Biblioteca universale Rizzoli, 1981), p. 326.
44. H. Arthur Steiner, 'The Government of Italian East Africa', *American Political Science Review*, October 1936, 30(5):884.
45. 'Rome, May 7, 1936-XIV – His Majesty the King awarded the Duce the insignia of Knight of the Grand Cross of the Military Order of Savoy'. *Graphicus*, XXVI(8):II.
46. On 19 May the British ambassador, Sir Eric Drummond, wrote of how 'the boasting, the posturing, the rampant nationalism, the gross misrepresentation of the British attitude, the absurd egotism and the conceit have been enough to turn the least Anglo-Saxon stomachs'. Quoted in: Donald Theodore Rotunda, 'The Rome Embassy of Sir Eric Drummond, 16th Earl of Perth,

1933–1939'. A thesis submitted to the University of London in fulfilment of the requirement for the degree Doctor of Philosophy, Department of International History, London School of Economics and Political Science, University of London, June 1972, p. 193, n. 85. Available online at: https://ethos.bl.uk/OrderDetails.do?uin=uk.bl.ethos.297019.
47. Benito Mussolini, 'La proclamazione dell'Impero, 9 maggio 1936', in Susmel and Susmel (eds), *Opera omnia di Benito Mussolini*, pp. 268–9.
48. Steiner, 'The Government of Italian East Africa', 30(5):884.
49. Alberto Consiglio, *Badoglio re di complemento* (Milano: Cino Del Duca Le Edizioni Mondiali, 1964), p. 227. Del Boca, *Gli italiani in Africa Orientale*, 2, p. 736, n. 123. Mussolini, according to his own words, as taken down in 1932, was a great fan of the Roman dictator: 'I love [Julius] Caesar. He was unique in that he combined the will of the warrior with the genius of the sage.' Quoted in: Emil Ludwig (translated from German by Eden and Cedar Paul), *Talks with Mussolini* (Boston: Little, Brown & Co., 1933), p. 62.
50. 'Regio decreto – legge 4 giugno 1936-XIV, n. 1235. Conferimento del grado di Maresciallo d'Italia al generale di corpo d'armata , comandante designato d'armata, Rodolfo Graziani', in Romolo Astraldi (Redattore capo), *La legislazione fascista nella XXIX legislatura, 1934–1939 (XII–XVII): Volume Primo* (Roma: Pubblicazione a cura del Senato del regno e della Camera dei fasci e delle corporazioni, 1939-XVII), p. 286.
51. 'Italy: *Re ed Imperatore*', *Time Magazine*, 18 May 1936, XXVII(20):23.
52. Giorgio Pini a Duilio Susmel, *Mussolini: l'uomo e l'opera III: Dalla dittatura all'impero (1925–1938)* (Firenze: La Fenice, 1955), p. 352.
53. The *chargé d'affaires* in Italy (Kirk) to the Secretary of State, Rome, 6 May 1936. Reproduced in: Department of State, *Foreign Relations of the United States, Diplomatic Papers 1936: Volume III, The Near East and Africa* (Washington DC: Government Printing Office, 1953), p. 220.
54. 'Foreign News: Occupation', *Time Magazine*, 18 May 1936, XXVII(20):23.
55. Steer, *Caesar in Abyssinia*, p. 402.
56. Quoted in: Nicholas Rankin, *Telegram from Guernica: The Extraordinary Life of George Steer: Reporter, Adventurer and Soldier* (London: Faber & Faber, 2013), p. 14. See also: Steer, *Caesar in Abyssinia*, p. 403.
57. Also known as Marguerite de Herrero. Rankin, *Telegram from Guernica*, p. 12.
58. Phillip Knightley, *From the Crimea to Vietnam: The War Correspondent as Hero, Propagandist, and Myth Maker* (New York: Harcourt Brace Jovanovich, 1975), p. 171.
59. Reynolds & Eleanor Packard, *Balcony Empire: Fascist Italy at War* (London: Chatto & Windus, 1943), p. 24.
60. Officers and soldiers swore an oath of obedience to the King, not to the regime; the symbols of their uniforms and flags were those of the country, not of Fascism. Piero Melograni, 'The Cult of the Duce in Mussolini's Italy', *Journal of Contemporary History*, October 1976, 11(4):235.
61. Comando Superiore AO Stato Maggiore, *La marcia su Addis Abeba: Ordine del Giorno* (Asmara: 7ª Sezione Topocartografica, 1936-XIV), p. 14. For an example of how this name stuck, see also: Varo Varanini, *La Marcia Della Ferrea Volonta* (Milano: Istituto Editoriale Cisalpino, 1938-XVI).

Chapter 17: 'a policy of terror and extermination'

1. Mussolini a Graziani, 8 luglio 1936. Quoted in: Rochat, 'L'impiego dei gas', p. 95.
2. Quoted in: *Graphicus*, XXVI(8):II.
3. Fuller, *The First of the League Wars*, p. 49.
4. Del Boca, *Gli italiani in Africa Orientale*, 2, pp. 717–20. Paolo Caccia Dominion, *Ascari K7* (Milano: Ugo Mursia Editore, 1995), p. 608.
5. Highly detailed Order of Battle statistics can be found in: Longo, *La Campagna Italo-Etiopica, I*, pp. 402–28.
6. Alessandro Secciani, *L'impero: le colonie italiane in Africa* (Milano: Editoriale Nuova, 2005), p. 166.
7. Angelo Del Boca, 'Il fascismo e la "fatalita" dell'impresa di Etiopia', in Patrizia Caccia e Mirella Mingardo (eds), *Ti saluto e vado in Abissinia: Propaganda, consenso, vita quotidiana, attraverso la stampa*

periodica, le pubblicazioni e i documenti della Biblioteca Nazionale Braidense (Milano: Viennepierre, 1998), p. 11. 'In 1927, the lira was pegged to the US dollar at a rate of 1 dollar = 19 lire. This rate lasted until 1934, with a separate "tourist" rate of US$ 1 = 24.89 lire being established in 1936. In 1939, the "official" rate was 19.8 lire.' See: http://www.exchangerate.com/currency-information/italian-lira.html.
8. Martin Clark, *Mussolini* (Abingdon: Routledge, 2014), pp. 199–200. See also: Anthony L. Cardoza, *Benito Mussolini: The First Fascist* (New York, NY: Pearson Longman, 2006), pp. 198–9.
9. Lawrence R. Pratt, *East of Malta West of Suez: Britain's Mediterranean Crisis 1936–1939* (Cambridge: Cambridge University Press, 1975), p. 29.
10. Rochat, *Guerre Italiane in Libia e in Etiopia*, p. 106.
11. Pedriali, *L'aeronautica italiana*, pp. 129–30.
12. Gentilli, 'Elenco completo dei bombardmento a gas sul fronte Nord' and Gentilli, 'Elenco completo dei bombardmento a gas sul fronte Sud', pp. 141–3.
13. Marco Montagnani, Antonino Zarcone e Filippo Cappellano, *Il servizio chimico militare 1923–1945. Storia, ordinamento, equipaggiamento. Tomo I* (Roma: Stato Maggiore dell'Esercito Ufficio storico, 2011), p. 45.
14. Churchill, *The River War*, pp. 114–15.
15. Steer, *Caesar in Abyssinia*, p. 51.
16. Watson, 'J.F.C. Fuller and the Fascist Movement in Britain', p. 58.
17. Liddell Hart, 'The Armies of Europe: IV. Italy', p. 1115.
18. Christopher Andrew, *The Defence of the Realm: The Authorised History of MI5* (London: Allen Lane, 2009), pp. 191, 193. It is also the case that what Fuller wrote for public consumption was different from what he kept private. What he observed in Eritrea and Ethiopia disillusioned him in respect of Italian Fascism. Thus, the British version, he concluded, was basing itself on a flawed model. Moseley evidently agreed. A new name, the British Union of Fascists and National Socialists, was announced on 20 June 1936, which indicated the origins of the new model. Watson, 'J.F.C. Fuller and the Fascist Movement in Britain', p. 55. Thomas Linehan, *British Fascism 1918–39: Parties, Ideology and Culture* (Manchester: Manchester University Press, 2000), p. 120, n. 104.
19. See: B.H. Liddell Hart, *The Memoirs of Captain Liddell Hart: Volume 1* (London: Cassell, 1965), pp. 260–79.
20. Von Oberst a D. Rudolf Ritter von Xylander, 'Vom Krieg in Abessinien (Fortsetzung)', *Allgemeine schweizerische Militärzeitung – Journal militaire suisse – Gazetta militare svizzer*, 1936, 82(7):450.
21. Reynolds and Eleanor Packard, *Balcony Empire: Fascist Italy at War* (London: Chatto & Windus, 1943), p. 25.
22. Tobias Hof, *Galeazzo Ciano: The Fascist Pretender* (Toronto: University of Toronto Press, 2021), p. 219.
23. The articles he had published during the conflict were later released in book form: Ritter und Xylander, *Die Eroberung Abessiniens 1935/36*.
24. Aram Mattioli, 'Entgrenzte Kriegsgewalt: Der italienische Giftgaseinsatz in Abessinien 1935–1936', *Vierteljahrshefte für Zeitgeschichte*, Juli 2003, 51(3):312–13.
25. Mosconi, 'Il servizio automobilistico militare in Somalia', p. 929.
26. Liddell Hart, *Memoirs*, p. 277.
27. Del Boca, *Gli italiani in Africa Orientale*, 2, p. 497.
28. Letter from John Melly, at the British Legation in Addis Ababa, to 'KN' [his sister Kathleen Nelson], 12 April 1936. In: Kathleen Nelson and Alan Sullivan (eds), *John Melly of Ethiopia* (London: Faber & Faber, 1937), p. 240.
29. See: Stephenson, *A Box of Sand*, pp. vi, 145–9.
30. David Alvarez, 'Left in the Dust: Italian Signals Intelligence, 1915–1943', *International Journal of Intelligence and CounterIntelligence*, 2001, 14(3):393. It was estimated that each long-range AA gun had only 22 minutes' worth of ammunition, whilst the short-range weapons could only fire for 13 minutes. Arthur Marder, 'The Royal Navy and the Ethiopian Crisis of 1935–36', *American Historical Review*, June 1970, 75(5):1344–5.

31. Marder, 'The Royal Navy and the Ethiopian Crisis of 1935–36', p. 1335.
32. Steer, *Caesar in Abyssinia*, pp. 243, 280.
33. Vari autori, *La Formazione De l'Impero Coloniale Italiano Volume Terzo: L'impero (dall'occupazione di Dessiè all'assetto definitivo dell'impero)* (Milano: SA Fratelli Treves Editori, 1939), p. 389. The Viceroy of Ethiopia automatically became governor general of AOI.
34. Giulia Barrera, 'Mussolini's Colonial Race Laws and State–Settler Relations in *Africa Orientale Italiana* (1935–41)', *Journal of Modern Italian Studies*, 2003, 8(3):426. For example, a law enacted on 19 April 1937 stated: 'An Italian citizen who in the territory of the Kingdom or of the Colonies maintains a conjugal relationship with a subject of Italian East Africa, or a foreigner belonging to a population that has traditions, customs and juridical and social concepts analogous to those of Italian East African subjects, is punished with imprisonment from one to five years.' Gianluca Gabrielli, 'Colpevole di leso razzismo: Una sentenza per il reato di unione di indole coniugale tra cittadini e sudditi', *Anuac*, giugno 2012, I(1):9.
35. Quoted in: Barrera, 'Mussolini's Colonial Race Laws', p. 428.
36. Locatelli had taken part in the famous 'Flight over Vienna' as part of Gabriele D'Annunzio's mission on 9 August 1918, and the following year crossed the Andes: a flight of 370km at an altitude of 6,500m. See: Vittorio Polli, *Antonio Locatelli: vita e documenti* (Bergamo: Edizioni Bolis, 1986).
37. Guido Mattioli, *L'aviazione fascista e la conquista dell'impero* (Roma: Editrice L'Aviazione, XVII-1939), p. 112. Ovidio Ferrante, 'Lekemti: la Kindu della Regia Aeronautica', *Rivista Militare*, febbraio-marzo 2006, 5(6):80–7. Lioy, *L'Italia in Africa*, p. 162. Newspaper reports on the massacre, and the 'aerial reprisals', are quoted in: Pompeo Volpe, *Auasc, Etiopia, 18 maggio 1937: quattro volti senza nome e la memoria coloniale nell'Italia repubblicana* (Padova: Padova University Press, 2021), p. 83, n. 74.
38. Bosworth, *Mussolini and the Eclipse of Italian Fascism*, p. 61. See also: Angelo Del Boca, *Gli italiani in Libia: dal fascismo al Gheddafi* (Milano: Mondadori Editore, 1994); Salerno, *Genocidio in Libia*; Angelo Del Boca and Antony Shugaar (trans.), *Mohamed Fekini and the Fight to Free Libya* (Houndsmills: Palgrave Macmillan, 2011).
39. Mussolini a Graziani, 8 luglio 1936. Quoted in: Rochat, 'L'impiego dei gas', p. 95.
40. 'the head of the government wishes to suspend, for the moment, the reshipment of specially loaded bombs sent to East Africa and the repatriation of the chemical teams, placed at the disposal of this ministry, for the needs of East Africa.' Telegram from the Air Ministry to General Aurelio Ricchetti, head of the Military Chemical Service (*servizio chimico militare*). 10 July 1936. Quoted in: Rochat, 'L'impiego dei gas', pp. 94–5.
41. Rochat, 'L'impiego dei gas', pp. 94–6. For an excellent treatment of the subject in English see: Alberto Sbacchi, 'Poison Gas and Atrocities in the Italo-Ethiopian War (1935–1936)', in Ruth Ben-Ghiat and Mia Fuller (eds), *Italian Colonialism* (Houndsmills: Palgrave Macmillan, 2005), pp. 47–56.
42. Roberto Gentilli, 'Azione con aggressivi chimici dopo la proclamazione dell'Impero riportate nei Diari storici dei reparti dell'aeronautica AOI: La storiografia aeronautica e il problema dei gas', in Angelo Del Boca (ed.), *I gas di Mussolini: Il fascism e la guerra d'Etiopia* (Roma: Editori Reuniti, 2007), pp. 144–5.
43. Ian Campbell, *The Addis Ababa Massacre: Italy's National Shame* (Oxford: Oxford University Press, 2017), pp. 324–8.
44. Paolo Borruso, *Debre Libanos 1937: Il più grave crimine di guerra dell'Italia* (Roma: Editori Laterza, 2020). Kindle edition. Loc. 400.
45. Ian Campbell, 'Reconstructing the Fascist Occupation of Ethiopia: The Italian Telegrammes as Historical Sources', *International Journal of Ethiopian Studies*, Winter-Spring 2004, 1(2):123–4.
46. Borruso, *Debre Libanos 1937*. For a full-length treatment of the massacre in English, see: Ian Campbell, *The Massacre of Debre Libanos Ethiopia 1937: The Story of One of Fascism's most Shocking Atrocities* (Addis Ababa: Addis Ababa University Press, 2014).

47. '275,000 persons killed in action during the war. 78,500 patriots killed in battle during the five years struggle. 17,800 children, women, old and infirm killed by bombing during five years struggle. 30,000 persons killed during the massacre of February, 1937. 24,000 patriots condemned by Italian Courts Martial and executed. 35,000 persons of both sexes and all ages who died in concentration camps. 300,000 persons who, due to destruction of their villages perished from hunger and deprivations during the five years of occupation.' Ethiopia, Ministry of Foreign Affairs, *Digest of Memoranda Presented by the Imperial Ethiopian Government to the Council of Foreign Ministers in London September 1945* (revised edition, April 1946) (Addis Ababa: Ministry of Foreign Affairs, 1946), p. 21.
48. Mattioli, 'Entgrenzte Kriegsgewalt', p. 311, n. 2.
49. Written communication from Richard Pankhurst to Aram Mattioli, 24 May 2002. Quoted in: Mattioli, 'Entgrenzte Kriegsgewalt', p. 312, n. 3.
50. Graziani, *Una vita per l'Italia*, p. 65.
51. Graziani a Lessona, 13 maggio 1937. Quoted in: Giorgio Rochat, 'L'attentato a Graziani e la repressione italiana in Etiopia nel 1936–1937', *Italia Contemporanea*, gennaio-marzo 1975, 118:38.
52. 'I was the leader of the revolution and chief of the government at thirty-nine. Not only have I not finished my job, but I often feel that I have not even begun it . . . My objective is simple: I want to make Italy great, respected, and feared.' Benito Mussolini, *My Autobiography* (New York: Charles Scribner's Sons, 1928), pp. 308–9.
53. Martin Clark, *Mussolini* (Abingdon: Routledge, 2014), p. 204.
54. Alberto Rovighi e Filippo Stefani, *La partecipazione italiana alla guerra civile Spagnola: Volume I: Documenti e Allegati. Volume II: Testo* (Roma: Stato Maggiore dell'Esercito, 1992). For a recent work in English see: Javier Rodrigo, *Fascist Italy in the Spanish Civil War, 1936–1939* (Abingdon: Routledge, 2021).
55. See: Goeschel, *Mussolini and Hitler*.
56. Bernd Jurgen Fischer, *Albania at War 1939–45* (London: C. Hurst & Co., 1999), pp. 5–32. Massimo Borgogni, *Tra continuità e incertezza. Italia e Albania (1914–1939): la strategia politico-militare dell'Italia in Albania fino all'operazione 'Oltre mare Tirana'* (Milano: FrancoAngeli, 2007), pp. 348–79.
57. Available at: http://www.polyarchy.org/basta/documenti/guerra.1940.html.
58. Pietro Badoglio, *L'Italia nella seconda guerra mondiale (memorie e documenti)* (Milano: Arnoldo Mondadori Editore, 1946), p. 37.
59. The 'cowardly jackal' reference is in: Sir Archibald Sinclair, Secretary of State for Air, 'We Must Rely on Ourselves', *The Listener*, 29 August 1940, XXIV(607):297.
60. Dana A. Glei, Silvia Bruzzone and Graziella Caselli, 'Effects of War Losses on Mortality Estimates for Italy: A First Attempt', *Demographic Research*, 17 November 2005, 13(15):379 – 'Table 5: Military deaths by sex and year, Italy, World War II'.
61. Elena Agarossi and Harvey Ferguson II (trans.), *A Nation Collapses: The Italian Surrender of September 1943* (Cambridge: Cambridge University Press, 2006).
62. The official term for the Allies.
63. Richard Carrier, 'The *Regio Esercito* in Co-Belligerency, October 1943–April 1945', in Emanuele Sica and Richard Carrier (eds), *Italy and the Second World War: Alternative Perspectives* (Leiden: Brill, 2018), p. 96.
64. Vincent O'Hara and Enrico Cernuschi, *Dark Navy: The Italian Regia Marina and the Armistice of 8 September 1943* (Ann Arbor, MI: Nimble Books, 2009), p. 3.
65. Alberto Santoni, 'Intelligence navale italiano dalle rivelazioni di ufficiali della Regia Marina cobelligerante', *Bollettino d'archivio dell'Ufficio Storico della Marina Militare*, dicembre 2003, XVII:77–98.
66. O'Hara and Cernuschi, *Dark Navy*, p. 3.
67. For 'The First Fall of Mussolini, July 1943', see: Philip Morgan, *The Fall of Mussolini: Italy, the Italians, and the Second World War* (Oxford: Oxford University Press, 2007), pp. 11–33.

68. A policy continued by his successors. On 15 July 1945 Italy declared war on Japan, and even before that serious consideration had been given to a proposal for sending an Italian fleet based around the fast, modern battleships *Vittorio Veneto* and *Italia* to fight in the Indian Ocean and Pacific. See: Massimo Gusso, *Italia e Giappone: dal Patto Anticomintern alla dichiarazione di guerra del luglio 1945: Inquiete convergenze, geopolitica, diplomazia, conflitti globali e drammi individuali (1934–1952)* (Venezia: Edizioni Ca' Foscari – Venice University Press, 2022). Stephenson, *The Eastern Fleet*, p. 289, n. 27.
69. Norman Kogan, *Italy and the Allies* (Cambridge MA: Harvard University Press, 1956), p. 66.
70. The British Embassy to the State Department, aide-memoire, 25 May 1944. In: US Department of State, *Foreign Relations of the United States: Diplomatic Papers 1944: Volume III: The British Commonwealth and Europe* (Washington DC: US Government Printing Office, 1965), p. 1,117.
71. See: Davide Conti, *L'occupazione italiana dei Balcani: Crimini di guerra e mito della «brava gente» (1940–1943)* (Roma: Odradek Edizioni, 2008).
72. Between July 1945 and May 1947 there were forty British trials conducted in Italy of Italians suspected of war crimes committed during the Second World War. These, though, were limited to offences against British or Commonwealth prisoners of war. The most high-profile case was that against General Nicola Bellomo, who was found guilty of shooting two PoWs. He was tried in July 1945 and subsequently executed by firing squad in September that year. Jane L. Garwood-Cutler, 'The British War Crimes Trials of Suspected Italian War Criminals, 1945–1947', in John Carey, William V. Dunlap, and R. John Pritchard (eds), *International Humanitarian Law: Origins* (Ardsley, NY: Transnational Publishers, 2003), pp. 89–90.
73. Sabina Ferhadbegovic, Kerstin von Lingen and Julia Eichenberg, 'The United Nations War Crimes Commission (UNWCC), 1943–1948, and the Codification of International Criminal Law: An Introduction to the Special Issue', *Journal of the History of International Law/Revue d'histoire du droit international*, 2022, 24(3):305.
74. Quoted in: Richard Pankhurst, 'Italian Fascist War Crimes in Ethiopia: A History of Their Discussion, from the League of Nations to the United Nations (1936–1949)', *Northeast African Studies*, 1999, 6(1/2):101.
75. Former Naval Person to President Roosevelt, 5 August 1943. Quoted in: Winston S. Churchill, *The Second World War Volume Five: Closing the Ring* (London: Reprint Society, 1961), p. 92.
76. Harry L. Coles and Albert K. Weinberg, *United States Army in World War II: Special Studies: Civil Affairs: Soldiers Become Governors* (Washington DC: Office of the Chief of Military History: Department of the Army, 1964), p. 426.
77. Pankhurst, 'Italian Fascist War Crimes in Ethiopia', p. 101.
78. Memorandum by the Secretary of State for Foreign Affairs [Anthony Eden] and Lord Chancellor [John Simon, 1st Viscount Simon]: 'War Crimes'. 14 November 1944. UK National Archives CAB 66/57/48, p. 3.
79. Adalberto Baldoni, *Fascisti: 1943–1945* (Roma: Editore Settimo Sigillo, 1993), p. 21, n. 8.
80. Oscar Gonzalez, *Freeing Mussolini: Dismantling the Skorzeny Myth in the Gran Sasso Raid* (Barnsley: Pen & Sword Military, 2018).
81. Diego Meldi, *La repubblica di Salò* (Roma: Gherardo Casini Editore, 2015), Kindle edition, Loc. 685.
82. Gian Franco Vene, *Il processo di Verona: La storia, le cronache, i documenti, le testimonianze* (Milano: Arnoldo Mondadori Editore, 1967).
83. Meldi, *La repubblica di Salò*, Loc. 750.
84. Luca Stefano Cristini, *Le forze armate della RSI 1943–1945* (ZaniCA: Soldiershop Publishing, 2016), Kindle edition, Loc. 158.
85. Nino Arena, *L'Aeronautica Nazionale Repubblicana: la guerra aerea in Italia: 1943–1945* (Parma: Ermanno Albertelli Editore, 1995).
86. Claudia Cernigoi, 'Le serpi in seno. L'infiltrazione e la provocazione nei movimenti comunisti', *La Nuova Alabarda e la Coda del Diavolo*, 3 dicembre 2021, 416:13. Moseley, *Mussolini: The Last 600 Days*, p. 319.

87. Antonino Repaci, 'Il processo Graziani', *Il Movimento di Liberazione in Italia: Rassegna Bimestrale di Studi e Documenti*, marzo-maggio 1952, 17–18:20–49. Moseley, *Mussolini: The Last 600 Days*, p. 365.
88. Effie G.H. Pedaliu, 'Britain and the "Hand-over" of Italian War Criminals to Yugoslavia, 1945–48', *Journal of Contemporary History*, October 2004, 39(4):514. Filippo Focardi and Lutz Klinkhammer, 'La questione dei "criminali di guerra" italiani e una Commissione di inchiesta dimenticata', *Contemporanea*, luglio 2001, IV(3):497–528.
89. For a thorough treatment of the issue, see: Pedaliu, 'Britain and the 'Hand-over' of Italian War Criminals to Yugoslavia', pp. 503–29.
90. 'From the President for the Former Naval Person Personal and Secret'. 25 July 1943. Quoted in: Warren F. Kimball, *Churchill and Roosevelt, The Complete Correspondence: Volume 2, Alliance Forged November 1942–February 1944* (Princeton NJ: Princeton University Press, 1984), p. 347.
91. Former Naval Person to President Roosevelt, 26 July 1943. 'Thoughts on the Fall of Mussolini'. Quoted in: Churchill, *Closing the Ring*, p. 63.
92. Viviane E. Dittrich, Kerstin von Lingen, Philipp Osten and Jolana Makraiova (eds), *The Tokyo Tribunal: Perspectives on Law, History and Memory* (Brussels: Torkel Opsahl Academic EPublisher, 2020).
93. Winston S. Churchill, *The Second World War Volume Six: Triumph and Tragedy* (London: Reprint Society, 1956), p. 425.
94. The title of Chapter 6: Angelo Del Boca (ed.), *I gas di Mussolini: Il fascism e la guerra d'Etiopia* (Roma: Editori Reuniti, 2007), pp. 147–77.

Bibliography

Newspapers

L'Arena
Artribune
Corriere della Sera
Daily Mail
Daily Telegraph
Gazet van Antwerpen

Gazzetta Ufficiale Del Regno D'italia
L'Indipendente
Guardian
League of Nations – Official Journal
Il Messaggero
La Preparazione

Reduce d'Africa
la Repubblica
Sardegna Nuova
Il Solco Fascista
Time
l'Unita

Books, Articles and Documents

Abbondanza, Gabriele. *Italy as a Regional Power: The African Context from National Unification to the Present Day* (Rome: Aracne Editrice, 2016).

Acampora, Angelo. *Senza licenza di uccidere: operazioni segrete militari italiane 1935–1943* (Bologna: Casa editrice Odoya, 2017).

Aeronautica Militare Comando Generale delle Scuole. *Storia dell'Aeronautica Militare Italiana* (Caserta: Divisione Formazione Sottufficiali e Truppa, n.d.).

Agarossi, Elena and Ferguson II, Harvey (trans.). *A Nation Collapses: The Italian Surrender of September 1943* (Cambridge: University Press, 2006).

Aimone Cat, Generale di Divisione Aerea Mario. 'L'aviazione in AO: Da Adua a Addis Abeba', *L'Ala d'Italia: Periodico Nazionale dell'Aviazione Fascista*, maggio 1937-XV.

Albanese, Giulia. *La marcia su Roma* (Roma: Editori Laterza, 2006).

Alvarez, David. 'Left in the Dust: Italian Signals Intelligence, 1915–1943', *International Journal of Intelligence and CounterIntelligence*, Volume 14, Issue 3, 2001.

Alvisi, Gigliola. *Giacomo Matteotti: Una morte annunciata* (Vicenza: Casa editrice Edibus, 2014).

Anderson, David M. 'Mau Mau in the High Court and the 'Lost' British Empire Archives: Colonial Conspiracy or Bureaucratic Bungle?', *Journal of Imperial and Commonwealth History*, Volume 39, Issue 5, 2011.

Andrew, Christopher. *The Defence of the Realm: The Authorised History of MI5* (London: Allen Lane, 2009).

Arena, Nino. *L'Aeronautica Nazionale Repubblicana: la guerra aerea in Italia: 1943–1945* (Parma: Ermanno Albertelli Editore, 1995).

Arielli, Nir. 'Colonial Soldiers in Italian Counter-Insurgency Operations in Libya, 1922–32', *British Journal for Military History*, Volume 1, Issue 2, February 2015.

Astraldi, Romolo (Redattore capo). *La legislazione fascista nella XXIX legislatura, 1934–1939 (XII–XVII): Volume Primo* (Roma: Pubblicazione a cura del Senato del regno e della Camera dei fasci e delle corporazioni, 1939-XVII).

Astuto, Franco and Scheggi, Adriano (eds). *Le Trasmissioni dell'Esercito nel Tempo* (Roma: Rivista Militare, 1995).

Avagliano, Mario e Palmieri, Marco. *Di pura razza italiana. L'Italia «ariana» di fronte alle leggi razziali* (Milano: Baldini & Castoldi, 2013).

Avon, The Earl of. *The Eden Memoirs: Facing the Dictators* (London: Cassell, 1962).

Baer, George W. *Test Case: Italy, Ethiopia, and the League of Nations* (Stanford, CA: Hoover Institution Press, 1976).

Badoglio, Pietro, Maresciallo d'Italia, Duca di Addis Abeba. *La Guerra D'Etiopia* (Milano: Arnoldo Mondadori Editore, 1936-XIV).
Badoglio, Pietro. *L'Italia nella seconda guerra mondiale (memorie e documenti)* (Milano: Arnoldo Mondadori Editore, 1946).
Balbo, Italo. *La Centuria Alata* (Milano: Mondadori, 1934).
Balbo, Italo. Sottosegretario di Stato per L'aeronautica, *La politica aeronautica dell'Italia fascista: discorso sul bilancio dell'aeronautica pronunciato alla Camera dei deputati nella tornata del 29 marzo 1927* (Roma: Tipografia della camera dei deputati, MCMXXVII-V).
Baldoni, Adalberto. *Fascisti: 1943–1945* (Roma: Editore Settimo Sigillo, 1993).
Baldwin, Stanley, MacDonald, J. Ramsay, and Simon, Sir John. 'A Call to the Nation: The Joint Manifesto of the leaders National Government', Iain Dale (ed.), *Conservative Party General Election Manifestos 1900–1997* (Abingdon: Routledge, 2000).
Balfour, Sebastian. *Deadly Embrace: Morocco and the Road to the Spanish Civil War* (Oxford: Oxford University Press, 2002).
Barker, A.J. *The Civilizing Mission: A History of the Italo-Ethiopian War of 1935–1936* (New York: Dial Press, 1968).
Barrera, Giulia. 'Mussolini's Colonial Race Laws and State–Settler Relations in *Africa Orientale Italiana* (1935–41)', *Journal of Modern Italian Studies*, Volume 8, Issue 3, 2003.
Barros, James. 'Mussolini's first Aggression: the Corfu Ultimatum', *Balkan Studies*, Volume 2, 1961.
Barros, James. 'The Greek-Bulgarian Incident of 1925: The League of Nations and the Great Powers', *Proceedings of the American Philosophical Society*, Volume 108, No. 4, 27 August 1964.
Bassi, Mario. 'Quadro d'insieme della battaglia dell'Ogaden', Emilio Ceretti (ed.), *Con l'Esercito Italiano in AO Volume II: Dalla battaglia dello Scirè all'Impero* (Milano: A Mondadori, 1937).
Battisti, Col. Emilio. *Il 7° Alpini in AO: 'Feltre' Pieve di Teco' 'Exilles'* (Roma: 10° Reggimento Alpini Editore, 1937-XV).
Baudendistel, Rainer. *Between Bombs and Good Intentions: The Red Cross and the Italo-Ethiopian War, 1935–1936* (New York: Berghahn Books, 2006).
Beck, P.J. 'From the Geneva Protocol to the Greco-Bulgarian Dispute: The Development of the Baldwin Government's Policy Towards the Peacekeeping Role of the League of Nations, 1924–1925', *British Journal of International Studies*, Volume 6, No. 1, April 1980.
Belloc, Hilaire and Blackwood, Basil Temple (writing as 'HB' and 'BTB'). *The Modern Traveller* (London: Edward Arnold, 1898).
Benedetti, Achille. *La Guerra Equatoriale: Con L'Armata del Maresciallo Graziani* (Milano, Casa Editrice Oberdan Zucchi via Cesare Battisti, 1937-XV).
Beonio-Brocchieri, V. *Cieli d'Etiopia: Avventure di un pilota di guerra* (Milano: A Mondadori, 1936-XIII).
Beonio-Brocchieri, Vittorio. 'La marcia della colonna che conquistò L'aussa. Forte di Sardo, 11 marzo', Rosario Mascia, *I giornalisti alla conquista dell'impero: corrispondenze di guerra dall'Africa Orientale 1935–1936* (Milano: ASEFI, 2003).
Bernati, Gianluigi. *Fascismo: Nascita, formazione, evoluzione e caduta del Partito Nazionale Fascista* (Torre del Greco: Edizioni Duemme, 2017).
Biddle, Tami Davis. *Air Power and Warfare: A Century of Theory and History* (Carlisle, PA: Strategic Studies Institute and US Army War College Press, 2019).
Blick, Andrew and Hennessey, Peter. *Good Chaps No More: Safeguarding the Constitution in Stressful Times* (London: Constitution Society, 2019).
Boidi, Carlo. *Legionari universitari sul fronte somalo* (Milano: Sperling & Kupfer, 1937-XV).
Boothby, Robert. *I Fight to Live* (London: Victor Gollancz, 1947).
Borgogni, Massimo. *Tra continuità e incertezza. Italia e Albania (1914–1939): la strategia politico-militare dell'Italia in Albania fino all'operazione 'Oltre mare Tirana'* (Milano: FrancoAngeli, 2007).
Borruso, Paolo. *Debre Libanos 1937: Il più grave crimine di guerra dell'Italia* (Roma: Editori Laterza, 2020).
Bosworth, R.J.B. *Mussolini* (London: Bloomsbury Academic, 2010).

Bosworth, Richard J.B. *Mussolini* (London: Bloomsbury Academic, 2010).
Bosworth, R.J.B. *Mussolini and the Eclipse of Italian Fascism: From Dictatorship to Populism* (New Haven, CT: Yale University Press, 2021).
Bosworth, R.J.B. *Mussolini and the Eclipse of Italian Fascism: From Dictatorship to Populism* (New Haven, CT: Yale University Press, 2021).
Bottai, Giuseppe. *Quaderno Affricano* (Firenze: GC Sansoni Editore, XVIII-1938).
Bourneuf, Pierre-Etienne. "We Have Been Making History': The League of Nations and the Leticia Dispute (1932–1934)', *International History Review*, Volume 39, Issue 4, 2017.
Braca, Capitano Giovanni e Comolli, Capitano Renzo. 'La dancalia meridionale', *Gli annali dell'Africa italiana*, anno II, volume I, marzo MCMXXXIX anno XVII.
Braddick, Henderson B. 'The Hoare-Laval Plan: A Study in International Politics', *Review of Politics*, Volume 24, No. 3, July, 1962.
Brody, J Kenneth. *The Avoidable War Volume 2: Pierre Laval and the Politics of Reality, 1935–1936* (London: Transaction Publishers, 2000).
Buchanan, Patrick J. *Churchill, Hitler, and the Unnecessary War: How Britain Lost Its Empire and the West Lost the World* (New York: Three Rivers Press, 2008).
Burgwyn, H. James. *Italian Foreign Policy in the Interwar Period 1918–1940* (London: Praeger, 1997).
Burkman, Thomas W. *Japan and the League of Nations: Empire and World Order, 1914–1938* (Honolulu, HI: University of Hawai'i Press, 2008).
Cabiati, Aldo. *La conquista dell'impero: cronaca ragionata della guerra italo-abissina 1935–1936* (Milan: Casa Editrice Sonsogno, 1936).
Callahan, Michael D. *A Sacred Trust: The League of Nations and Africa, 1929-1946* (Brighton: Sussex Academic Press, 2004).
Calvitt Clarke III, J. 'Feodor Konovalov and the Italo-Ethiopian War (Part I)', *World War II Quarterly*, Volume 5, No. 1, Winter 2008.
Calvitt Clarke III, J, and Gorelik, Boris. 'Konovalov, Fjodor Evgenjevic', Alessandro Bausi and Siegbert Uhlig (eds), *Encyclopaedia Aethiopica: Volume 5* (Wiesbaden: Harrassowitz Verlag, 2014).
Caminiti, Alberto. *L'eccidio dei cantieri Gondrand AOI 1936* (Genova: Libri Liberodiscrivere Edizioni, 2014).
Campbell, Ian. 'Reconstructing the Fascist Occupation of Ethiopia: The Italian Telegrammes as Historical Sources', *International Journal of Ethiopian Studies*, Volume 1, No. 2, Winter-Spring 2004.
Campbell, Ian. *The Massacre of Debre Libanos Ethiopia 1937: The Story of One of Fascism's most Shocking Atrocities* (Addis Ababa: Addis Ababa University Press, 2014).
Campbell, Ian. *The Addis Ababa Massacre: Italy's National Shame* (Oxford: Oxford University Press, 2017).
Campbell, Ian. *Holy War: The Untold Story of Catholic Italy's Crusade Against the Ethiopian Orthodox Church* (London: Hurst & Company, 2021).
Campbell, Ian L. 'Italian Atrocities in Ethiopia: An Enquiry into the Violence of Fascism's First Military Invasion and Occupation', *Journal of Genocide Research*, Volume 24, Issue 1, 2022.
Candeloro, Giorgio. *Storia dell'Italia moderna IX: Il fascismo e le sue guerre 1922–1939* (Milano: Feltrinelli Editore, 1981).
Cappellano, Filippo and Battistelli, Pier Paolo. *Italian Light Tanks 1919–45* (Oxford: Osprey Publishing, 2012).
Capponcini, Giuseppe. *Con l'82° Battaglione CCNN 'Benito Mussolini', Africa Orientale: Dall'Amba Alagi alle sorgenti del Nilo Azzurro* (Forli: Stabilimento tipografico Valbonesi, 1937-XV).
Cardoza, Anthony L. *Benito Mussolini: The First Fascist* (New York: Pearson Longman, 2006).
Carrier, Richard. 'The *Regio Esercito* in Co-Belligerency, October 1943–April 1945', Emanuele Sica and Richard Carrier (eds), *Italy and the Second World War: Alternative Perspectives* (Leiden: Brill, 2018).
Ceadel, Martin. 'The First British Referendum: The Peace Ballot, 1934–5', *English Historical Review*, Volume 95, No. 377, October, 1980.
Ceci, Lucia and Spring, Peter (trans.). *The Vatican and Mussolini's Italy* (Leiden: Brill, 2017).

Cernigoi, Claudia. 'Le serpi in seno. L'infiltrazione e la provocazione nei movimenti comunisti', *La Nuova Alabarda e la Coda del Diavolo*, Supplemento al No. 416, 3 dicembre 2021.

Cheltsov, B.F. 'History of the creation and activities of the Air Force headquarters 1912–1945 to the 95th anniversary of the Russian Air Force. *Military Historical Journal*, 2007, Volume 8, p. 3–7.

Ciaralli, Claudio. '"Hostes Per Aethera Eruo": La Guerra Elettronica dell'Esercito Italiano', *i Quaderni della SCSM: Societa di Cultura e Storia Militare*, no 2, dicembre 2015, anno XVI.

Churchill, Rogers P., Axton, Matilda F., Landau, Shirley F., and Prescott, Francis C. (eds). *Foreign Relations of the United States Diplomatic Papers, 1935: General, The Near East and Africa, Volume I* (Washington DC: United States Government Printing Office, 1953).

Churchill, Winston Spencer. *The River War: An Historical Account of the Reconquest of The Soudan: Volume I* (London: Longmans, Green & Co., 1899). Also Volume II, same publisher same year.

Churchill, Winston S. *The Second World War Volume I: The Gathering Storm* (London: Reprint Society, 1950).

Churchill, Winston S. *The Second World War Volume III: The Grand Alliance* (Boston, MA: Houghton Mifflin, 1950).

Churchill, Winston S. *The Second World War Volume V: Closing the Ring* (London: Reprint Society, 1961).

Churchill, Winston S. *The Second World War Volume VI: Triumph and Tragedy* (London: Reprint Society, 1956).

Clark, Martin. *Mussolini* (Abingdon: Routledge, 2014).

Coles, Harry L and Weinberg, Albert K. *United States Army in World War II: Special Studies: Civil Affairs: Soldiers Become Governors* (Washington DC: Office of the Chief of Military History: Department of the Army, 1964).

Colloredo, Pierluigi Romeo di. *Passo Uarieu: Le Termopili delle camicie nere in Etiopia* (Genova: L'Associazione Culturale 'ITALIA Storica', 2008).

Colloredo, Pierluigi Romeo di. *I pilastri del romano impero: le camicie nere in Africa Orientale, 1935–1936* (Genova: L'Associazione Culturale 'ITALIA Storica', 2009).

Colloredo Mels, Pierluigi Romeo di. *Camicia Nera!: Storia militare della Milizia Volontaria per la Sicurezza Nazionale dalle origini al 25 luglio* (Zanica: Soldiershop Publishing, 2017).

Collotti, Enzo. *Il fascismo e gli ebrei: Le leggi razziali in Italia* (Roma-Bari: Editori Laterza, 2003).

Colvin, Ian. *None so Blind: A British Diplomatic View of the Origins of World War II* (New York: Harcourt, Brace & World, 1965).

Comando delle forze armate della Somalia, *La guerra italo-etiopica fronte sud: Relazione Volume 4* (Addis Ababa: Ufficio superiore topocartografico del Governo generale dell'Africa Orientale, 1937).

Comando Superiore AO Stato Maggiore, *La marcia su Addis Abeba: Ordine del Giorno* (Asmara: 7a Sezione Topocartografica, 1936-XIV).

Comitato per la «Storia dell'Artiglieria italiana», *Storia dell'Artiglieria italiana, parte V (dal 1920 al 1945), Vol. XVI (l'artiglieria nelle operazioni belliche dal 1920 al 1945)* (Roma: Biblioteca d'Artiglieria e Genio, 1955).

Consiglio, Alberto. *Badoglio re di complemento* (Milano: Cino Del Duca Le Edizioni Mondiali, 1964).

Conti, Davide. *L'occupazione italiana dei Balcani: Crimini di guerra e mito della «brava gente» (1940–1943)* (Roma: Odradek Edizioni, 2008).

Cooper, John Milton *Breaking the Heart of the World: Woodrow Wilson and the Fight for the League of Nations* (Cambridge: Cambridge University Press, 2001).

Cosmo, Giandomenico. 'I servizi di polizia politica durante il fascismo', *Il movimento di liberazione in Italia rassegna bimestrale di studi e documenti a cura dell'Istituto nazionale per la storia del movimento di Liberazione in Italia*, Gennaio 1952, N 16.

Cova, Alessandro. *Graziani: Un generale per il regime: la prima biografia documentata di uno dei personaggi più violenti e controversi della nostra storia, che ha incarnato miti, ferocie e contraddizioni del periodo fascista* (Roma: Newton Compton Editore, 1987).

Cristini, Luca Stefano. *Le forze armate della RSI 1943–1945* (Zanica: Soldiershop Publishing, 2016), Kindle edition.

Croubois, Claude. *Pierre Laval* (La Creche: Geste editions, 2010).
Crowcroft, Robert. *The End is Nigh: British Politics, Power, and the Road to the Second World War* (Oxford: Oxford University Press, 2019).
Dalmazzo, Renzo, generale di divisione. 'Il terreno della battaglia dell'Ascianghi (31 marzo–5 aprile 1936-XIV)', *Rivista di fanteria: Rassegna mensile di studi militari*, anno IV, N 6 giugno 1937-XV.
Dall'Ora, Fidenzio. *Intendenza in AO* (Roma: Istituto nazionale fascista di cultura, 1937-IV).
Daly, M.W. and Hogan, Jane R. *Images of Empire: Photographic Sources for the British in the Sudan* (Leiden: Brill 2005).
Danchev, Alex. *Alchemist of War: The Life of Basil Liddell Hart* (London: Weidenfield & Nicolson, 1998).
De Bono, Emilio. *La Preparazione e le Prime Operazioni: La Conquista Dell' Impero* (Roma: Istituto Nazionale Fascista di Cultura, 1937-XV).
De Bono, Emilio and Miall, Bernard (trans.). *Anno XIIII: the Conquest of an Empire* (London: Cresset Press, 1937).
De Felice, Renzo. *Mussolini il duce Volume III Part 1: Gli anni del consenso 1929–1936* (Torino: Giulio Einaudi editore, 1974).
Del Boca, Angelo. *La guerra d'Abissinia: 1935–1941* (Milano: Feltrinelli, 1965).
Del Boca, Angelo and Cummings, P.D. (trans.). *The Ethiopian War: 1935–1941* (Chicago: University of Chicago Press, 1969).
Del Boca, Angelo. 'La verità sul massacro della Gondrand', *Storia Illustrata*, No. 311, 4 ottobre 1983.
Del Boca, Angelo. *Gli Italiani in Libia*: Tripoli bel suol d'amore: 1860–1922, Vol. I (Milan: Mondadori, 1986).
Del Boca, Angelo. *L'Africa nella coscienza degli italiani: miti, memorie, errori, sconfitte* (Roma: Editori Laterza, 1992).
Del Boca, Angelo. *Il Negus: Vita e morte dell'ultimo re dei re* (Roma: Editori Laterza, 1995).
Del Boca, Angelo. 'Il fascismo e la 'fatalita' dell'impresa di Etiopia', Patrizia Caccia e Mirella Mingardo (eds), *Ti saluto e vado in Abissinia: Propaganda, consenso, vita quotidiana, attraverso la stampa periodica, le pubblicazioni e i documenti della Biblioteca Nazionale Braidense* (Milano: Viennepierre, 1998).
Del Boca, Angelo. *Italiani, brava gente?: un mito duro a morire* (Vicenza: Neri Pozza Editore, 2005).
Del Boca, Angelo (ed.). *I gas di Mussolini: Il fascism e la guerra d'Etiopia* (Roma: Editori, Reuniti, 2007).
Del Boca, Angelo. *A un passo dalla forca: atrocita? e infamie dell'occupazione italiana della Libia nelle memorie del patriota Mohamed Fekini* (Milano: Baldini Castoldi Dalai, 2007).
Del Boca, Angelo. *Il mio Novecento* (Vicenza: Neri Pozza Editori, 2008).
Del Boca, Angelo. *Gli italiani in Africa Orientale Volume 2: La conquista dell'Impero* (Milano: Mondadori Editore, 2009).
Del Boca, Angelo and Shugaar, Antony (trans.). *The Negus: The Life and Death of the Last King of Kings* (Addis Abeba: Arada Books, 2012).
Del Boca, Angelo and Shugaar, Antony (trans.). *Mohamed Fekini and the Fight to Free Libya* (Houndmills: Palgrave Macmillan, 2011).
De Luna, Giovanni. *Badoglio: un militare al potere* (Milano: Casa Editrice Valentino Bompiani, 1974).
Demaitre, Edmund. (War Correspondent to the *Excelsior* (Paris), 'With the Lions of Juba', Ladislas Farago (ed.), *Abyssinian Stop Press* (London: Robert Hale, MCMXXXVI-1936).
Dempsey, Mary Jane. 'Finding Postcolonial Figures: Rediscovering Elvira Banotti and her Role in the Italian Feminist Movement', *Women's History Review*, Volume 27, Issue 7, 2018.
De Vecchi di Val Cismon, Giorgio. *Dubat: Gli arditi neri* (Milano: A Mondadori Editore, 1936-XIV).
Di Feo, Gianluca. *Veleni di Stato* (Milano: BUR Rizzoli, 2009).
Di Lauro, Raffaele. 'I bollettini di guerra del Negus ed altri documenti di fonte etiopica', *Gli annali dell'Africa italiana*, anno II, volume I, marzo MCMXXXIX anno XVII.
Di Rienzo, Eugenio. *Il 'Gioco degli Imperi': La Guerra d'Etiopia e le origini del secondo conflitto Mondiale* (Roma: Società Editrice Dante Alighieri, 2016).

Dittrich, Viviane E., Lingen, Kerstin von, Osten, Philipp and Makraiova, Jolana (eds). *The Tokyo Tribunal: Perspectives on Law, History and Memory* (Brussels: Torkel Opsahl Academic EPublisher, 2020).
Djukic, Drazan and Pons, Niccolo (eds). *The Companion to International Humanitarian Law* (Leiden: Brill Nijhoff, 2018).
Domarus, Max. *Mussolini und Hitler: Zwei Wege-gleiches Ende* (Würzburg, Domarus, 1977).
Dominioni, Matteo. *Lo sfascio dell'impero: Gli italiani in Etiopia 1936–1941* (Roma: Editori Laterza, 2008).
Douglas, R.M. 'Did Britain Use Chemical Weapons in Mandatory Iraq?', *Journal of Modern History*, Volume 81, No. 4, December, 2009.
Douhet, Giulio. *Il dominio dell'aria saggio sull'arte della guerra aerea con una appendice contenente nozioni elementari di aeronautica* (Roma: L'Amministrazione Della Guerra, 1921).
Douhet, Giulio and Ferrari, Dino (trans.). *The Command of the Air* (Maxwell Air Force Base, AL: Air University Press, 2019).
Doumanis, Nicholas. 'The Italian Empire and *brava gente*: Oral History and the Dodecanese Islands', R.J.B. Bosworth and Patrizia Dogliani (eds), *Italian Fascism: History, Memory and Representation* (London: Palgrave Macmillan, 1999).
Dubois, Hubert-Pierre. *Cheminot, de Djibouti a? Addis-Abeba; le chemin de fer franco-éthiopien* (Paris: Librairie académique Perrin, 1959).
Due, John F. *Rail and Road Transport in The Sudan* (Urbana-Champaign, IL: University of Illinois, 1977).
Duggan, Christopher. *A Concise History of Italy* (Cambridge: Cambridge University Press, 1969).
Dundonald, Thomas, Eleventh Earl of and Fox Bourne, HR. *The Life of Thomas, Lord Cochrane, Tenth Earl of Dundonald: Volume II* (London: Richard Bentley, 1869).
Durand, Mortimer. *Crazy Campaign: A Personal Narrative of the Italo-Abyssinian War* (London: George Routledge, 1936).
Durand, Mortimer (War-Correspondent to the *Daily Telegraph*). 'The Crazy War', Ladislas Farago (ed.), *Abyssinian Stop Press* (London: Robert Hale, MCMXXXVI-1936).
Elkins, Caroline. 'Alchemy of Evidence: Mau Mau, the British Empire, and the High Court of Justice', *Journal of Imperial and Commonwealth History*, Volume 39, Issue 5, 2011.
Emeny, Stuart (War-Correspondent to the *News Chronicle*). 'Under Fire with the Emperor', Ladislas Farago (ed.), *Abyssinian Stop Press* (London: Robert Hale, MCMXXXVI-1936).
Esposito, Fernando and Camiller, Patrick (trans.). *Fascism, Aviation and Mythical Modernity* (Houndsmills: Palgrave Macmillan, 2015).
Ethiopia, Ministry of Foreign Affairs, *Digest of Memoranda Presented by the Imperial Ethiopian Government to the Council of Foreign Ministers in London September 1945* (Revised Edition, April 1946) (Addis Ababa: Ministry of Foreign Affairs, 1946).
Evans, David. *War: A Matter of Principles* (Houndsmills: Macmillan Press, 1997).
Evans, Richard. *The Third Reich in Power 1933–1939* (London: Penguin Books, 2006).
Farago, Ladislas. 'The Busu Tshiki Tshik', Ladislas Farago (ed.), *Abyssinian Stop Press* (London: Robert Hale, MCMXXXVI-1936).
Farago, Ladislas (ed.). *Abyssinian Stop Press* (London: Robert Hale, MCMXXXVI-1936).
Farcau, Bruce W. *The Chaco War: Bolivia and Paraguay, 1932–1935* (Westport, CT: Praeger, 1996).
Ferhadbegovic, Sabina, Lingen, Kerstin von, and Eichenberg, Julia. 'The United Nations War Crimes Commission (UNWCC), 1943–1948, and the Codification of International Criminal Law: An Introduction to the Special Issue', *Journal of the History of International Law/Revue d'histoire du droit international*, Volume 24, Issue 3, 2022.
Ferrante, Ovidio. 'Lekemti: la Kindu della Regia Aeronautica', *Rivista Militare*, No. 5/6, febbraio-marzo 2006.
Fiaschi, Thomas M.D. 'A Report on the Mutilated and Evirated of the Battle of Adowa' (Part One), *British Medical Journal*, Volume 2, No. 1861, 29 August 1896, pp. 505–6. Also: Thomas Fiaschi,

MD, 'A Report on the Mutilated and Evirated of the Battle of Adowa' (Part Two), *British Medical Journal*, Volume 2, No. 1863, 12 September 1896.
Fischer, Bernd Jurgen. *Albania at War 1939–45* (London: C. Hurst & Co., 1999).
Fisher, H.A.L. *A History of Europe: Complete Edition in One Volume* (London: Edward Arnold & Co., 1936).
Fiske, Norman E. Major, Cavalry, USA. Military Observer, *Report of Military Observer with Italian Armies in East Africa: Report No. 5* (Washington, DC: Military Intelligence Division General Staff, 1936).
Flaiano, Ennio. *Tempo di uccidere* (Milano: Rizzoli, 1973).
Focardi, Filippo and Klinkhammer, Lutz. 'La questione dei "criminali di guerra" italiani e una Commissione di inchiesta dimenticata', *Contemporanea*, Volume IV, No. 3, luglio 2001.
Franzinelli, Mimmo. *I tentacoli dell'Ovra: Agenti, collaboratori e vittime della polizia politica fascista* (Torino: Bollati Boringhieri Editore, 1999).
Frusci, Generale Luigi. *In Somalia Sul Fronte Meridionale* (Bologna: Licinio Cappelli Editore, 1936).
Fucci, Franco. *Emilio De Bono: il maresciallo fucilato* (Milano: Ugo Mursia Editore, 1989).
Fuller, Colonel J.F.C. *The Reformation of War* (London: Hutchinson & Co., 1923).
Fuller, J.F.C. 'The Italo-Ethiopian War: A Military Analysis by an Eye-witness Observer', *Army Ordnance*, Volume 16, No. 96, May-June, 1936.
Fuller, Major General J.F.C. *The First of the League Wars: Its Lessons and Omens* (London: Eyre & Spottiswoode, 1936).
Fuller, J.F.C. *The Conduct of War 1789–1961* (London: Eyre & Spottiswoode, 1961).
Gabrielli, Gianluca. 'Colpevole di leso razzismo: Una sentenza per il reato di unione di indole coniugale tra cittadini e sudditi', *Anuac*, Anno I, Numero 1, giugno 2012.
Galazzetti, Alberto. *Le bande autocarrate dei Carabinieri reali in Africa Orientale italiana: Immagini e storia* (febbraio-luglio 1936) (Voghera: Marvia editione, 2013).
Garretson, Peter. *A Victorian Gentleman & Ethiopian Nationalist: The Life and Times of Hakim Warqenah, Dr Charles Martin* (Woodbridge: James Currey, 2012).
Garrett, Benjamin C. *Historical Dictionary of Nuclear, Biological, and Chemical Warfare* (Lanham, MD: Rowman & Littlefield Publishers, 2017).
Garwood-Cutler, Jane L. 'The British War Crimes Trials of Suspected Italian War Criminals, 1945–1947', John Carey, William V. Dunlap, and R. John Pritchard (eds), *International Humanitarian Law: Origins* (Ardsley, NY: Transnational Publishers, 2003).
Gat, Azar. *Fascist and Liberal Visions of War: Fuller, Liddell Hart, Douhet, and Other Modernists* (Oxford: Clarendon Press, 1998).
Gaudioso, Domenico Capecelatro. *Una fucina d'eroi: l'arma dei carabinieri* (Napoli: Adriano Gallina editore, 1978).
Gehl, Jurgen. *Austria, Germany and the Anschluss 1931–1938* (Oxford: Oxford University Press, 1963).
Gentilli, Roberto. *Guerra aerea sull'Etiopia 1935–1939* (Firenze: EDAI-Edizioni Aeronautiche Italiane, 1992).
Gentilli, Roberto. 'L'aeronautica in Libia e in Etiopia', Paolo Ferrari (ed.), *L'aeronautica italiana: una storia del Novecento* (Milano: Franco Angeli Storia, 2005).
Gentizon, Paul. *La conquête de l'Éthiopie* (Paris: Editions Berger-Levrault, 1936).
Gerbi, Sandro e Liucci, Raffaele. *Indro Montanelli: Una biografia (1909–2001)* (Milano: Hoepli, 2014).
Gigli, Giulio. *Tito Minniti e Silvio Zannoni: vittime della barbarie etiopica* (Roma: Pinciana Editore, 1936).
Gilbert, Martin. *World in Torment: Winston S Churchill 1917–1922* (London: Minerva, 1990).
Ginneken, Anique H.M. van. *Historical Dictionary of the League of Nations* (Lanham, MD: Scarecrow Press, 2006).
Giordano, Claire, Piga, Gustavo and Trovato, Giovanni. 'Italy's Industrial Great Depression: Fascist Price and Wage Policies', in *Macroeconomic Dynamics*, Volume 18, Issue 3, April, 2014.
Girlando, Raffaele. *Marzo 1896 – La Battaglia Di Adua* (Torino: Italia Editrice, 1996).

Giuliani, Reginaldo. *Per Cristo e per la patria: (ultimi scritti dall'Africa)* (Firenze: casa editrice Adriano Salani, 1937-XV).

Glei, Dana A, Bruzzone, Silvia and Caselli, Graziella. 'Effects of War Losses on Mortality Estimates for Italy: A First Attempt', *Demographic Research*, Volume 13, Article 15, 17 November 2005.

Goeschel, Christian. *Mussolini and Hitler: The Forging of the Fascist Alliance* (New Haven, CN: Yale University Press, 2018).

Gonzalez, Oscar. *Freeing Mussolini: Dismantling the Skorzeny Myth in the Gran Sasso Raid* (Barnsley: Pen & Sword Military, 2018).

Grand, Alexander De. 'Mussolini's Follies: Fascism in Its Imperial and Racist Phase, 1935–1940', *Contemporary European History*, Volume 13, No. 2, May, 2004.

Graziani, Rodolfo. Maresciallo d'Italia – Marchese di Neghelli, *Il fronte sud* (Milano: A. Mondadori Editore, 1938-XIV).

Graziani, Rodolfo. *Una vita per l'Italia: «Ho difeso la patria»* (Milano: Gruppo Ugo Mursia Editore, 1986).

Gregor, A. James. *Young Mussolini and the Intellectual Origins of Fascism* (Berkeley, CA: University of California Press, 1979).

Gregor, A. James. *Giovanni Gentile: Philosopher of Fascism* (Abingdon: Routledge, 2017).

Griffin, Roger (ed.). *International Fascism: Theories, Causes and the New Consensus* (London: Arnold, 1998).

Guariglia, Raffaele. *Ricordi: 1922–1946* (Napoli: Scientifiche Italiane, 1950).

Guarino, Mario. *Mercanti di parole: storie e nomi del giornalismo asservito al potere* (Bari: Edizioni Dedalo, 2012).

Guerrazzi, Amedeo Osti. *Storia della Repubblica sociale italiana* (Roma: Carocci Editore, 2012).

Guerri, Giordano Bruno. *Giuseppe Bottai, un fascista critico: ideologia e azione del gerarca che avrebbe voluto portare l'intelligenza nel fascismo e il fascismo alla liberalizzazione* (Milano: Feltrinelli Editore, 1976).

Guerri, Giordano Bruno. *Italo Balbo. Lo squadrista, il gerarca, l'aviatore, la biografia basata su documenti inediti, del più pericoloso rivale di Mussolini* (Milano: Vallardi, 1984).

Gusso, Massimo. *Italia e Giappone: dal Patto Anticomintern alla dichiarazione di guerra del luglio 1945: Inquiete convergenze, geopolitica, diplomazia, conflitti globali e drammi individuali (1934–1952)* (Venezia: Edizioni Ca' Foscari – Venice University Press, 2022).

Hall, Coryne. *Princesses on the Wards: Royal Women in Nursing Through Wars and Revolutions* (Cheltenham: History Press, 2022).

Halpern, Paul G. (ed.). 'Conveying the Emperor Haile Selassie into Exile', Brian Vale (ed.), *The Naval Miscellany: Volume VIII* (Abingdon: Routledge for the Navy Records Society, 2017).

Harsmar, Mats, Sandstrom, Emil, and Beyene, Atakilte. 'Lake Tana: Source of Disputes or Collaboration over the Blue Nile?', Emil Sandstrom, Anders Jagerskog and Terje Oestigaard (eds), *Land and Hydropolitics in the Nile River Basin: Challenges and New Investments* (Abingdon: Routledge, 2016).

Headlam, Major General Sir John. *The History of the Royal Artillery from the Indian Mutiny to the Great War, Volume II 1899–1914* (Woolwich: Royal Artillery Institution, 1937).

Hénin, Silvio. *Non solo enigma: Storia delle guerre nascoste* (Milano: Editore Ulrico Hoepli, 2017).

Hill, Richard. *Sudan Transport: A History of Railway, Marine, and River Services in the Republic of the Sudan* (Oxford: Oxford University Press, 1965).

Homze, Edward. 'The Continental Experience', in Alfred F. Hurley and Robert C. Ehrhart (eds), *Air Power and Warfare: The Proceedings of the 8th Military History Symposium, United States Air Force Academy, 18–20 October 1978* (Washington DC: Office of Air Force History, Headquarters USAF and United States Air Force Academy, 1979).

Hills, Andrew. *Pioneers of Armour: Col REB Crompton* (No place: FWD Publishing, 2019).

Hinsley, F.H. *Power and the Pursuit of Peace: Theory and Practice in the History of Relations Between States* (Cambridge: Cambridge University Press, 1967).

Hof, Tobias. *Galeazzo Ciano: The Fascist Pretender* (Toronto: University of Toronto Press, 2021).

Howard, Anthony. *RAB: The Life of R A Butler* (London: Jonathan Cape, 1986).

Hurst, Carlton. 'Italian Colonial Development 1: Eritrea, Somaliland, and Oltre Giuba', *Commerce Reports: A Weekly Survey of Foreign Trade Issued by the Bureau of Foreign and Domestic Commerce*, No. 30, 27 July 1931.
Iadarola, Antoinette. 'Ethiopia's Admission into the League of Nations: An Assessment of Motives', *International Journal of African Historical Studies*, Volume 8, No. 4, 1975.
Ialongo, Ernest. 'Filippo Tommaso Marinetti: The Futurist as Fascist, 1929–37', *Journal of Modern Italian Studies*, Volume 18, No. 4, 2013.
Ialongo, Ernest. *Filippo Tommaso Marinetti: The Artist and His Politics* (Madison, NJ/Lanham, MD: Fairleigh Dickinson University Press/Rowman & Littlefield Publishing Group, 2015).
Italicus, 'Folle vento antipatria', *Il reduce d'Africa: Mensile dell'Associazione Nazioanle Reduci d'Africa*, Anno V, No. 7, settembre 1965.
Isnenghi, Mario. *I luoghi della memoria: Simboli e miti dell'Italia unita* (Roma: Laterza, 1996).
Jadoul, Jacques. 'Les missions militaires belges en Ethiopie, Janvier 1930–Octobre 1935: La collaboration officielle: Aspects techniques, économiques et diplomatiques', *Revue belge d'histoire militaire*, Volume 27, No. 1.
Jones, Daniel P. 'American Chemists and the Geneva Protocol', *Isis: The Journal of The History of Science Society*, Volume 71, No. 3, September 1980.
Jones, H.A. *The War In The Air: Being the Story of The part played in the Great War by the Royal Air Force*, Vol. V [History of the Great War based on Official Documents by Direction of The Historical Section of the Committee of Imperial Defence] (Oxford: Clarendon, 1935).
Kallis, Aristotle A. *Fascist Ideology: Territory and Expansionism in Italy and Germany, 1922–1945* (London: Routledge, 2000).
Kertzer, David I. *The Pope and Mussolini: The Secret History of Pius XI and the Rise of Fascism in Europe* (Oxford: Oxford University Press, 2014).
Kimball, Warren F. *Churchill and Roosevelt, The Complete Correspondence: Volume 2, Alliance Forged November 1942–February 1944* (Princeton NJ: Princeton University Press, 1984).
Kindermann, Gottfried-Karl, Brough, Sonia (trans.) and Taylor, David (trans.). *Hitler's Defeat in Austria, 1933–1934: Europe's First Containment of Nazi Expansionism* (Boulder, CO: Westview Press, 1988).
Knightley, Phillip. *From the Crimea to Vietnam: The War Correspondent as Hero, Propagandist, and Myth Maker* (New York: Harcourt Brace Jovanovich, 1975).
Kogan, Norman. *Italy and the Allies* (Cambridge MA: Harvard University Press, 1956).
Konovaloff, Col T.H. *Con le armate del Negus (un bianco fra i neri)* (Bologna: Nicola Zanichelli Editore, 1937-XV).
Laurens, Franklin D. *France and the Italo-Ethiopian Crisis 1935–1936* (The Hague: Mouton, 1967).
League of Nations, *Treaty Series: Publication of Treaties and International Engagements registered with the Secretariat of the League of Nations, Volume XCIV, Numbers 1, 2, 3 and 4* (Lausanne: League of Nations, 1929).
Lessona, Alessandro. *Un ministro di Mussolini racconta* (Milano: Edizioni Nazionali, 1973).
Lessona, Alessandro. 'Mussolini non voleva la guerra d'Etiopia', *Storia Illustrata*, numero 266, gennaio 1980.
Licheri, Sebastiano. 'Gli ordinamenti dell aeronautica militare italiana dal 1884 al 1918', *Ministero per i beni culturali e ambientali Ufficio centrale per i beni archivistici, Le fonti per la storia militare italiana in età contemporanea*. Atti del III seminario, Roma, 16–17 dicembre 1988 (Roma: Ediprint Service, 1993).
Liddell Hart, Captain B.H. *Paris or The Future of War* (New York: E.P. Dutton & Co., 1925).
Liddell Hart, Captain. 'The Armies of Europe: IV. Italy', *Spectator*, Volume 157, No. 5661, 25 December 1936.
Liddell Hart, 'The Armies of Europe', *Foreign Affairs*, Volume 15, No. 2, January 1937.
Liddell Hart, *Europe in Arms* (London: Faber & Faber, 1937).
Liddell Hart, B.H. *The Memoirs of Captain Liddell Hart: Volume 1* (London: Cassell, 1965).

Lien, Arnold J. 'Machiavelli's Prince and Mussolini's Facism' [sic], in *Social Science*, Volume 4, No. 4, August, September and October, 1929.
Linehan, Thomas. *British Fascism 1918–39: Parties, Ideology and Culture* (Manchester: Manchester University Press, 2000).
Lioy, Vincenzo. *L'Italia in Africa, Serie Storico-Militare, Volume Terzo: L'opera dell'Aeronautica, Tomo II, Eritrea–Somalia–Etiopia (1919–1937)* (Roma: Istituto Poligrafico dello Stato, MCMLXV [1965]).
Long, Breckinridge and Israel, Fred L. (ed.). *The War Diary of Breckinridge Long: Selections from the Years 1939–1944* (Lincoln, NE: University of Nebraska Press, 1966).
Longanesi, Leo. *Vade-mecum del perfetto fascista: seguito da Dieci assiomi per il milite ovvero Avvisi ideali* (Firenze: Vallecchi Editore, 1926).
Longo, Luigi Emilio. *La Campagna Italo-Etiopica (1935–1936): Tomo I* (Roma: Ufficio Storico Stato Maggiore Esercito, 2005).
Longo, Luigi Emilio. *La Campagna Italo-Etiopica (1935–1936): Tomo II Allegati* (Roma: Ufficio Storico Stato Maggiore Esercito, 2005).
Low, Alfred D. *The Anschluss Movement, 1931–1938, and the Great Powers* (Boulder, CO: East European Monographs, 1985).
Lucas, Ettore and De Vecchi, Giorgio. *Storia delle Unita? combattenti della Milizia volontaria per la sicurezza nazionale, 1923–1943* (Roma: Edizioni Volpe, 1976).
Ludwig, Emil (translated from German by Eden and Cedar Paul), *Talks with Mussolini* (Boston: Little, Brown & Co., 1933).
McKean, David. *Watching Darkness Fall: FDR, His Ambassadors, and the Rise of Adolf Hitler* (New York: St. Martin's Press, 2021).
Macfie, J.W.S. *An Ethiopian Diary: A Record of the British Ambulance Service in Ethiopia* (Liverpool/London: University Press of Liverpool/Hodder & Stoughton, 1936).
Machiavelli, Niccolo and Burd, L. Arthur (ed.). *Il Principe* (Oxford: Clarendon Press, 1891).
Macklin, Graham. *Failed Führers: A History of Britain's Extreme Right* (Abingdon: Routledge, 2020).
Macmillan, Harold. *Winds of Change 1914–1939* (New York: Harper & Row, 1966).
Maffey, J.L. et al. 'The Maffey Report: Report of an Inter-Departmental Committee on British Interests in Ethiopia', 18 June 1935. Appendix II of W.N. Medlicott, Douglas Dakin, and M.E. Lambert (eds), *Documents on British Foreign Policy 1919–1939, Second Series, Volume XIV: The Italo-Ethiopian Dispute March 1934–October 1935* (London: HMSO, 1976).
Magliveras, Konstantin D. 'The Withdrawal From the League of Nations Revisited', *Penn State International Law Review*, Volume 10, Number 1, September 1991.
Maisky, Ivan and Gorodetsky, Gabriel (ed.), translated by Tatiana Sorokina and Oliver Ready. *The Complete Maisky Diaries Volume I: The Rise of Hitler and the Gathering Clouds of War 1932–1938* (New Haven, CT: Yale University Press, 2017).
Malcolm, Noel. *Authoribews* (No place: Noel Malcolm, 2021).
Marcuzzi, Stefano. *Britain and Italy in the Era of the Great War: Defending and Forging Empires* (Cambridge: Cambridge University Press, 2020).
Marder, Arthur. 'The Royal Navy and the Ethiopian Crisis of 1935–36', *American Historical Review*, Volume 75, No. 5, June 1970.
Marder, Arthur J. 'The Royal Navy and the Ethiopian Crisis of 1935–1936', Arthur J. Marder, *From the Dardanelles to Oran: Studies of the Royal Navy in War and Peace 1915–1914* (Barnsley: Seaforth, 2015).
Marinetti, F.T. *Il poema africano della divisione «28 ottobre»* (Milano: Casa Editrice A Mondadori, 1937-XV).
Marrocu, Luciano. 'Flaiano in Africa: A Rare Example of Lucidity', in Paolo Bertella and Cecilia Dau Novelli (eds), *Colonialism and National Identity* (Newcastle upon Tyne: Cambridge Scholars Publishing, 2015).
Martelli, George. *Italy Against the World* (London: Chatto & Windus, 1937).
Martinelli, Federico. 'Ignazio Scurto: manifesti, poesie e articoli dell'ardente poeta della radio', *Verona Sette*, Anno 21, No. 12, 15 settembre 2020.

Masina, Filippo. 'La memoria dei combattenti d'Africa: l'ANRA', Michela Ponzani (ed.), *Memoria e testimonianza: Deportazione, internamento e Resistenza nell'Italia e nella Francia del dopoguerra* (Roma: Deutsches Historisches Institut in Rom/Istituto Storico Germanico di Roma, 2013).

Mattioli, Aram. 'Entgrenzte Kriegsgewalt: Der italienische Giftgaseinsatz in Abessinien 1935–1936', *Vierteljahrshefte für Zeitgeschichte*, Jahrgang 51, Heft 3, Juli, 2003.

Mattioli, Guido. *L'aviazione fascista e la conquista dell'impero* (Roma: Editrice L'Aviazione, XVII [1939]).

Mazzetti, Massimo. *La politica militare italiana fra le due guerre mondiali (1918–1940)* (Salerno: Edizioni Beta, 1974).

Mazzini, Gian Luca. *Montanelli mi ha detto: Avventure, aneddoti, ricordi del più grande giornalista italiano* (?Rimini: Il Cerchio Iniziative Editoriali, 2002)

Medlicott, W.N., Dakin, Douglas, and Lambert M.E. (eds). *Documents on British Foreign Policy 1919–1939: Second Series, Volume XVI* (London: HMSO, 1977).

Minardi, Salvatore. *Alle origini dell'incidente di Ual Ual* (Roma: Salvatore Sciascia Editore, 1990).

Meldi, Diego. *La repubblica di Salò* (Roma: Gherardo Casini Editore, 2015), Kindle edition.

Melograni, Piero. 'The Cult of the Duce in Mussolini's Italy', *Journal of Contemporary History*, Volume 11, No. 4, October, 1976).

Micaletti, Raffaello tenente colonnello di fanteria. 'Nell'Ogaden con gli Ascari Libici', *Rivista di fanteria: Rassegna mensile di studi militari*, anno IV, N 5, maggio 1937-XV.

Ministero degli Affari Esteri, *Documenti diplomatici italiani. Settima Serie: 1922–1935: Volume XVI (28 settembre 1934–14 aprile 1935)* (Roma: Istituto Poligrafico e Zecca dello Stato, MCMXC [1990]).

Ministero dell'AI (ed.), 'Le opere stradali, la costruzione dell'impero: l'opera dell'italia in AOI dopo la conquista dell'etiopia', *Gli annali dell'Africa italiana*, anno II, volume IV, MCMXXXIX – anno XVIII.

Ministero della Marina, *Il bilancio di previsione del Ministero della marina per l'esercizio finanziario dal 1° luglio 1934 al 30 giugno 1935* (Roma: Ministero della Marina, 1936-XIII).

Mitchell, William. *Our Air Force: The Keystone of National Defense* (New York: E.P. Dutton & Co., 1921).

Mockler, Anthony. *Haile Selassie's War* (London: Grafton Books, 1987).

Molinari, Generale Michele. *Agli ordini di Graziani in Somalia: L'opera del Genio Militare* (Milano: Società Anonima Edizioni Scientifiche e Letterarie, 1940).

Molvaer, Reidulf Knut. *Tradition and Change in Ethiopia: Social and Cultural Life as Reflected in Amharic Fictional Literature, ca 1930–1974* (Leiden: E.J. Brill, 1980).

Montagnani, Marco, Zarcone, Antonino e Cappellano, Filippo. *Il servizio chimico militare 1923–1945. Storia, ordinamento, equipaggiamento. Tomo I* (Roma: Stato Maggiore dell'Esercito Ufficio Storico, 2011).

Montanelli, Indro. *XX Battaglione Eritreo* (Milano: Editore Panorama, 1936).

Montanelli, Indro e Cervi, Mario. *Storia d'Italia Volume 41: L'impero* (Milano: Biblioteca universale Rizzoli, 1981).

Montanelli, Indro. *XX Battaglione Eritreo: Il primo romanzo e le lettere inedite dal fronte africano. A cura di Angelo Del Boca* (Milano: Edizione Rizzoli, 2010).

Monti, Antonio. *Giulio Douhet: scritti inediti (documenti raccolti e ordinati)* (Firenze: Tipo-litografia scuola di guerra aerea, 1951).

Morewood, Steven. *The British Defence of Egypt, 1935–40: Conflict and Crisis in the Eastern Mediterranean* (Abingdon: Frank Cass, 2005).

Morgan, Philip. *The Fall of Mussolini: Italy, the Italians, and the Second World War* (Oxford: Oxford University Press, 2007).

Moscati, Ruggero. 'Gli esordi della politica estera fascista. Il periodo Contarini-Corfù', Augusto Torre, Rudolfo Mosca, Ruggero Moscati, Renato Crispo, Renato Mori, Masio Toscano, Gian Luca Andre, and Pietro Pastorelli, *La politica estera italiana dal 1914 al 1943* (Roma: ERI, 1963).

Mosconi, Giuseppe Carlo maggiore d'artiglieria. 'Il servizio automobilistico militare in Somalia', *Rivista di fanteria: Rassegna mensile di studi militari*, anno IV, N 6, giugno 1937-XV.
Moseley, Ray. *Mussolini: The Last 600 Days of Il Duce* (Lanham, MD: Taylor Trade, 2004).
Mussolini, Benito. *My Autobiography* (New York: Charles Scribner's Sons, 1928).
Mussolini, Benito and Soames, Jane (trans.). *The Political and Social Doctrine of Fascism* (London: Hogarth Press, 1933).
Mussolini, Benito. 'Preludio al Machiavelli (30 aprile 1924)', *Scritti e Discorsi di Benito Mussolini edizione definitiva IV: Il 1924* (Milano: Ulrico Hoepli, 1934-XII).
Mussolini, Benito. 'L'Etiopia è italiana, 6 maggio 1936', Edoardo e Duilio Susmel (eds), *Opera omnia di Benito Mussolini [Volume] XXVII: Dall'Inaugurazione della provincia di Littoria alla proclamazione dell'Impero (19 Dicembre 1934–9 Maggio 1936)* (Firenze: La Fenice, 1959).
Mussolini, Vittorio. *Voli sulle ambe* (Firenze: GC Sansoni Editore, 1937-XV).
Nelson, Kathleen and Sullivan, Alan (eds). *John Melly of Ethiopia* (London: Faber & Faber, 1937).
Nesbitt, L.M. *Hell-Hole of Creation: The Exploration of Abyssinian Danakil* (New York: Alfred A. Knopf, 1935).
Nessun Autore, *Carabinieri* (Roma: Edizione dell'Istituto di Divulgazione Storica, 1956).
Neville, Peter. *Hitler and Appeasement: The British Attempt to Prevent the Second World War* (London: Hambledon Continuum, 2006).
Nicolson, Harold. 'British Public Opinion and Foreign Policy', *Public Opinion Quarterly*, Volume 1, No. 1, January, 1937.
Nizamoglu, Yuksel *Vehip Pasa: Kahramanlıktan Surgune* (Istanbul: Yitik Hazine Yayınları, 2013).
Obieta, Joseph A. *The International Status of the Suez Canal* (The Hague: Martinus Nijhoff, 1970).
O'Hara, Vincent and Cernuschi, Enrico. *Dark Navy: The Italian Regia Marina and the Armistice of 8 September 1943* (Ann Arbor, MI: Nimble Books, 2009).
O'Neill, Robert. 'Liddell Hart Unveiled', *Twentieth Century British History*, Volume 1, Issue 1, 1990.
Othen, Christopher. *Lost Lions of Judah: Haile Selassie's Mongrel Foreign Legion 1935–41* (Stroud: Amberley Publishing, 2017).
Packard, Reynolds & Eleanor. *Balcony Empire: Fascist Italy at War* (London: Chatto & Windus, 1943).
Pakenham, Thomas. *The Scramble for Africa: 1876–1912* (London: Abacus, 1992).
Pankhurst, Richard. 'Le memoria del capitano Alejandro Del Vallemy Suero: due lettere sull'invasione fascista dell'Etiopia', *Studi Piacentini: Rivista Dell'istituto Storico Della Resistenza Di Piacenza*, 15, 1994.
Pankhurst, Richard. 'Italian Fascist War Crimes in Ethiopia: A History of Their Discussion, from the League of Nations to the United Nations (1936–1949)', *Northeast African Studies*, Volume 6, No. 1/2, 1999.
Pankhurst, Richard. 'Le diverse versioni della testimonianza del colonnello Konovaloff sull'invasione fascista dell'Etiopia', *Studi Piacentini*, Volume 34, Issue 2, 2003.
Paoletti, Ciro. *A Military History of Italy* (Westport, CT: Praeger Security International, 2008).
Parker, R.A.C. 'The First Capitulation: France and the Rhineland Crisis of 1936', *World Politics*, Volume 8, No. 3, April 1956.
Parker, R.A.C. 'Great Britain, France and the Ethiopian Crisis 1935–1936', *English Historical Review*, Volume LXXXIX, Issue CCCLI, April 1974.
Parri, Maurizio. *Tracce di cingolo: compendio generale di storia dei carristi 1917–2009* (Verona: Associazione Carristi veronese, 2016).
Pasqualini, Maria Gabriella. *Breve storia dell'organizzazione dei Servizi d'Informazione della Regia Marina e Regia Aeronautica 1919–1945* (Roma: Ministero della Difesa CISM – Commissione Italiana di Storia Militare, 2013).
Pasquino, Gianfranco, Cooper, Timothy (trans.) and Jewks, Stephen (trans.). 'The Government of Lamberto Dini', Mario Cacaiagli and David I. Kertzer (eds), *Italian Politics: The Stalled Transition* (Boulder, CO: Westview Press, 1996).
Patriarca, Vincent. 'Two Wars in One Year', *American Cavalcade*, Volume 1, No. 1, May 1937.
Pavolini, Alessandro. *Disperata* (Firenze: Vallecchi Editore, 1937-XV).

Pearce, Robert and Goodlad, Graham. *British Prime Ministers from Balfour to Brown* (Abingdon: Routledge, 2013).
Pedaliu, Effie G.H. 'Britain and the "Hand-over" of Italian War Criminals to Yugoslavia, 1945–48', *Journal of Contemporary History*, Volume 39, No. 4, October 2004.
Pedriali, Ferdinando. *L'aeronautica italiana nelle guerre coloniali: Guerra Etiopica 1935–36* (Roma: Stato Maggiore Aeronautica Ufficio Storico, 1997).
Pedriali, Ferdinando. 'Aerei italiani in Libia (1911–1912)', *Storia Militare* N° 170 – novembre 2007.
Pedriali, Ferdinando. 'Le armi chimiche in Africa Orientale: storia, tecnica, obiettivi, efficacia', Angelo Del Boca (ed.), *I Gas di Mussolini: Il fascismo e la guerra d'Etopia* (Roma: Editorio Riuniti, 2017).
Pemberton, Jo-Anne. *The Story of International Relations, Part Three: Cold-Blooded Idealists* (Cham: Springer Nature, 2020).
Perkins, Kenneth J. *Port Sudan: The Evolution of a Colonial City* (Abingdon: Routledge, 2019).
Perugini, Nicola and Gordon, Neve. 'Between Sovereignty and Race: The Bombardment of Hospitals in the Italo-Ethiopian War and the Colonial Imprint of International Law', *State Crime Journal*, Volume 8, Issue 1, 2019.
Pesenti, Gustavo generale di divisione. *Storia della Prima divisione eritrea (8 aprile 1935-XIII – 1° maggio XIV)* (Milano: Casa Editrice L'Eroica, 1937-XV).
Petacco, Arrigo. *Il superfascista: vita e morte di Alessandro Pavolini* (Milano: Mondadori Editore, 1998).
Petacco, Arrigo. *Faccetta nera: L'illusione coloniale italiana* (Milano: DeA Planeta Libri, 2018).
Piccoli, Valentino (ed.). *Scritti E Discorsi Di Benito Mussolini: Edizione Definitiva [Volume] IV: Il 1924* (Milano: Ulrico Hoepli Editore, 1934-XII).
Pignato, Nicola. *Italian Armored Vehicles of World War Two* (Carrollton, TX: Squadron-Signal Publications, 2004).
Pini, Giorgio a Susmel, Duilio. *Mussolini: l'uomo e l'opera III: Dalla dittatura all'impero (1925–1938)* (Firenze: La Fenice, 1955).
Polezzi, Loredana. '"Mal d'Africa" and its Memory: Heroes and Anti-Heroes in Pre-and Postwar Readings of the Italian Presence in Africa', Danielle Hipkins and Gill Plain (eds), *War-torn Tales: Literature, Film and Gender in the Aftermath of World War II* (Oxford: Peter Lang, 2007).
Polli, Vittorio. *Antonio Locatelli: vita e documenti* (Bergamo: Edizioni Bolis, 1986).
Pratt, Lawrence R. *East of Malta West of Suez: Britain's Mediterranean Crisis 1936–1939* (Cambridge: Cambridge University Press, 1975).
Prentiss, Augustin M. *Chemicals in War: A Treatise on Chemical Warfare* (New York: McGraw Hill, 1937).
Quartararo, Rosaria. 'Imperial Defence in the Mediterranean on the Eve of the Ethiopian Crisis (July–October 1935)', *Historical Journal*, Volume 20, No. 1, March, 1977.
Quesada, Alejandro de with Jowett, P. *The Chaco War 1932–35: South America's Greatest Modern Conflict* (Oxford: Osprey Publishing, 2011).
Randazzo, Antonella. *L'Africa del Duce: I crimini fascisti in Africa* (Varese: Edizione Arteigere, 2008).
Rankin, Nicholas. *Telegram from Guernica: The Extraordinary Life of George Steer: Reporter, Adventurer and Soldier* (London: Faber & Faber, 2013).
Rauti, Pino (*aka* Umberto Giusti), *Storia d'Italia nei discorsi di Mussolini 1915–1945: Volume II* (Roma: Centro Editoriale Nazionale, 1966).
Rauti, Pino e Sermonti, Rutilio. *Storia del fascismo volume 5: L'espansione e l'asse* (Roma: Centro Editoriale Nazionale, 1976).
Reid, Brian Holden. *J.F.C. Fuller: Military Thinker* (New York: St. Martin's Press, 1987).
Reid, Brian Holden. 'Major General J.F.C. Fuller and the Revolution in British Military Thought', *Journal of the Society for Army Historical Research*, Volume 73, No. 293, Spring 1995.
Repaci, Antonino. 'Il processo Graziani', *Il Movimento di Liberazione in Italia: Rassegna Bimestrale di Studi e Documenti*, marzo–maggio 1952, No. 17–18.
Rinaldi, Carlo. 'I dirigibili italiani nella campagna di Libia', *Storia Militare* No. 18 – marzo 1995.
Ristuccia, Cristiano Andrea. 'The 1935 Sanctions against Italy: Would Coal and Oil have made a Difference?', *European Review of Economic History*, Volume 4, No. 1, 2000.

Robertson, James C. 'The British General Election of 1935', *Journal of Contemporary History*, Volume 9, No. 1, January, 1974.
Robertson, Linda. 'Dresden (2006): Marketing the Bombing of Dresden in Germany, Great Britain, and the United States', Douglas A. Cunningham and John C. Nelson (eds), *A Companion to the War Film* (Chichester: Wiley Blackwell, 2016).
Rochat, Giorgio. *Militari e politici nella preparazione della campagna d'Etiopia: Studio e documenti 1932–1936* (Milano: Franco Angeli Editore, 1971).
Rochat, Giorgio. 'L'attentato a Graziani e la repressione italiana in Etiopia nel 1936–1937', *Italia Contemporanea*, No. 118, gennaio-marzo 1975.
Rochat, Giorgio. 'La repressione della resistenza in Cirenaica', Enzo Santarelli, Giorgio Rochat, Romain H. Rainero and Luigi Goglia, *Omar al-Mukhtar e la riconquista fascista della Libia* (Milano: Marzorati, 1981).
Rochat, Giorgio. *Italo Balbo: La vita sociale della nuova Italia* (Torino: UTET-Unione Tipografico-Editrice Torinese, 1986).
Rochat, Giorgio. *Guerre Italiane in Libia e in Etiopia. Studi militari 1921–1939* (Treviso: Pagus Edizione, 1991).
Rochat, Giorgio. *Le guerre italiane 1935–1943: Dall'impero d'Etiopia alla disfatta* (Torino: Giulio Einaudi Editore, 2008).
Rochat, Giorgio. *Le guerre italiane in Libia e in Etiopia dal 1896 al 1939* (Udine: Gaspari Editore, 2009).
Rochat, Giorgio. 'L'impiego dei gas nella guerra d'Etopia 1935–1936', Angelo Del Boca (ed.), *I Gas di Mussolini: Il fascismo e la guerra d'Etopia* (Roma: Editorio Riuniti, 2017).
Rodrigo, Javier. *Fascist Italy in the Spanish Civil War, 1936–1939* (Abingdon: Routledge, 2021).
Rogers, J.A. *The Real Facts about Ethiopia* (Baltimore, MD: Black Classic Press, 1982 [Reprint of 1936 Edition]).
Roi, Michael L. *Alternative to Appeasement: Sir Robert Vansittart and Alliance Diplomacy, 1934–1937* (Westport, CT: Praeger Publishers, 1997).
Rosenfeld, Chris Prouty. *A Chronology of Menilek II of Ethiopia 1844–1913, Emperor of Ethiopia, 1889–1913* (East Lansing, MI: Michigan State University, 1976).
Rossi, Francesco. *Mussolini e lo stato maggiore: avvenimenti del 1940* (Roma: Tipografia regionale, 1951).
Rovighi, Alberto e Stefani, Filippo. *La partecipazione italiana alla guerra civile Spagnola: Volume I: Documenti e Allegati. Volume II: Testo* (Roma: Stato Maggiore dell'Esercito, 1992).
Ruggeri, Raffaele. '"The Battle of the Lions": Adua, 1896', *Military Illustrated: Past & Present*, No. 24, April/May 1990.
Russell, Frank M. *The Saar: Battleground and Pawn* (Stanford, CA: Stanford University Press, 1951).
Salafranca, J.F. *La República del Rif* (Málaga: Algazara, 2004).
Salerno, Eric. *Genocidio in Libia. Le atrocità nascoste dell'avventura coloniale italiana (1911–1931)* (Milano: Sugarco, 1979).
Santoni, Alberto. 'Intelligence navale italiano dalle rivelazioni di ufficiali della Regia Marina cobelligerante', *Bollettino d'archivio dell'Ufficio Storico della Marina Militare*, XVII, dicembre 2003.
Sapienza, Antonio. *The Chaco Air War 1932–35: The First Modern Air War in Latin America* (Solihull: Helion, 2018).
Sare, Sami. *The League of Nations and the Debate on Disarmament (1918–1919)* (Rome: Edizioni Nuova cultura, 2013).
Sarfatti, Margherita Grassini, and Sullivan, Brian R. ('Edited, Annotated, and with Commentary by'), *My Fault: Mussolini As I Knew Him* (New York: Enigma, 2014).
Sartori, Mario and Morrison, L.W. (trans.). *The War Gases: Chemistry and Analysis* (New York: D. Van Nostrand, 1939).
Sbacchi, Alberto. 'The Italians and the Italo-Ethiopian War, 1935–1936', *Transafrican Journal of History*, Volume 5, No. 2, 1976.
Sbacchi, Alberto. *Legacy of Bitterness: Ethiopia and Fascist Italy, 1935–1941* (Asmara: Red Sea Press, 1997).

Sbacchi, Alberto. 'Poison Gas and Atrocities in the Italo-Ethiopian War (1935–1936)', Ruth Ben-Ghiat and Mia Fuller (eds), *Italian Colonialism* (Houndmills: Palgrave Macmillan, 2005).
Scala, Edoardo. *Storia delle fanterie italiane Volume IV: Le fanterie italiane nelle conquiste coloniali* (Roma: Stato Maggiore Esercito, 1952).
Scala, Edoardo. *Storia delle fanterie italiane: Volume VIII, Tomo 1, I Bersaglieri* (Roma: Stato maggiore dell'Esercito ufficio storico, 2020).
Scurto, Ignazio. *Il cantico di Lydia: in memoria di Lydia Maffioli Rocca caduta nel Mareb a fianco dello sposo* (Novara: Delegazione Provinciale dei Fasci Femminili, 1937).
Scott, George. *The Rise and Fall of the League of Nations* (London: Hutchinson, 1973).
Scott, Kenneth. 'Mussolini and the Roman Empire', *Classical Journal*, Volume 27, No. 9, June, 1932.
Secciani, Alessandro. *L'impero: le colonie italiane in Africa* (Milano: Editoriale Nuova, 2005).
Segre, Claudio G. *Italo Balbo: A Fascist Life* (Berkeley, CA: University of California Press, 1987).
Seldes, George. *Sawdust Caesar: The Untold History of Mussolini and Fascism* (New York: Harper & Brothers, 1935).
Self, Robert (ed.). *The Neville Chamberlain Diary Letters: Volume 4: The Downing Street Years, 1934–1940* (Aldershot: Ashgate, 2005).
Shinn, David H. and Ofcansky, Thomas P. *Historical Dictionary of Ethiopia* (Lanham, MD: Scarecrow Press, 2013).
Shirreff, General Sir Richard. 'Conducting Joint Operations', Julian Lindley-French and Yves Boyer (eds), *The Oxford Handbook of War* (Oxford: Oxford University Press, 2012).
Simmons, Thomas E. *The Man Called Brown Condor: The Forgotten History of an African American Fighter Pilot* (New York: Skyhorse Publishing, 2013).
Simpson, A.W. Brian. 'The Invention of Trials *in camera* in Security Cases', in R.A. Melikan (ed.), *Domestic and International Trials, 1700–2000: The Trial in History Volume II* (Manchester: Manchester University Press, 2003).
Simpson, George L. Jr. 'The 1925 Cession of Jubaland: A View from Great Britain's Imperial Periphery', *Journal of Global South Studies*, Volume 37, Issue 1, Spring 2020.
Sinclair, Sir Archibald Secretary of State for Air. 'We Must Rely on Ourselves', *The Listener*, Volume XXIV, No. 607, 29 August 1940.
Soave, Paolo. *Una vittoria mutilata? L'Italia e la Conferenza di Pace di Parigi* (Soveria Mannelli: Rubbettino Editore, 2020).
Sorgoni, Barbara. 'The Scripts of Alberto Pollera, an Italian officer in Colonial Eritrea: Administration, Ethnography and Gender', Helen Tilley with Robert J. Gordon (eds), *Ordering Africa: Anthropology, European Imperialism, and the Politics of Knowledge* (Manchester: Manchester University Press, 2010).
Southworth, Herbert Rutledge. *Guernica! Guernica! A Study of a Journalism, Diplomacy, Propaganda, and History* (Berkeley, CA: University of California Press, 1977).
Spencer, John H. *Ethiopia at Bay: A Personal Account of the Haile Selassie Years* (Hollywood, CA: Tsehai Publishers, 2006).
Spinosa, Antonio. *Starace: l'uomo che inventò lo stile fascista* (Milano: Casa editrice Rizzoli, 1988).
Starace, Achille. *La marcia su Gondar: della colonna celere AO e le successive operazioni nella Etiopia Occidentale* (Milano: A Mondadori, XIV-1936).
Stato Maggiore della Difesa, *Il servizio informazioni militare italiano dalla sua constituzione alla fine della seconda guerra mondiale* (Roma: Stato Maggiore della Difesa, 1957).
Stato Maggiore Dell'Esercito Ufficio Storico, *L'Esercito Italiano: dal 1° tricolore al 1° centenario* (Roma: Ufficio Storico dello Stato Maggiore Dell'Esercito, 1961).
Steer, G.L. *Caesar in Abyssinia* (London: Hodder & Stoughton, 1936).
Steiner, H. Arthur. 'The Government of Italian East Africa', *American Political Science Review*, Volume 30, No. 5, October 1936.
Stephenson, Charles. *The Admiral's Secret Weapon: Lord Dundonald and the Origins of Chemical Warfare* (Woodbridge: Boydell Press, 2006).

Stephenson, Charles. *Germany's Asia-Pacific Empire: Colonialism and Naval Policy, 1885–1914* (Woodbridge: Boydell & Brewer, 2009).
Stephenson, Charles. *A Box of Sand: The Italo-Ottoman War 1911–1912: the First Land, Sea and Air War* (Ticehurst: Tattered Flag, 2014).
Stephenson, Charles. *The Siege of Tsingtau: The German-Japanese War, 1914* (Barnsley: Pen & Sword Military, 2017).
Stephenson, Charles. *The Eastern Fleet and the Indian Ocean 1942–1944: The Fleet that Had to Hide* (Barnsley: Pen & Sword, 2020).
Stephenson, Charles. *Stalin's War on Japan: The Red Army's Manchurian Strategic Offensive Operation, 1945* (Barnsley: Pen & Sword Military, 2021).
Stockings, Craig and Fernandes, Clinton. 'Airpower and the Myth of Strategic Bombing as Strategy', *ISAA* [Independent Scholars Association of Australia] *Review*, Volume 5, Issue 2, December 2006.
Sullivan, Brian R. 'Soviet penetration of the Italian intelligence services in the 1930s', Tomaso Vialardi di Sandigliano e Virgilio Ilari, *Storia dello spionaggio: l'intelligence militare italiana, l'intelligence elettronica, l'intelligence cinese* (Sandigliano: Associazione Europea degli Amici degli Archivi Storici, 2006).
Sweet, John Joseph Timothy. *Iron Arm: The Mechanization of Mussolini's Army, 1920–1940* (Mechanicsburg, PA: Stackpole Books, 2007).
Tabouis, Genevieve. *They Called Me Cassandra* (New York: Charles Scribner's Sons, 1942).
Tallillo, Andrea, Tallillo, Antonio and Guglielmi, Daniele. *Carro L3: Carri veloci, carri leggeri, derivati* (Trento: Gruppo Modellistico Trentino, 2004).
Tamm, Viking. *I tjänst hos Negus: aderton månader som krigsskolechef i Etiopien* (Stockholm: Wahlström & Widstrand, 1936).
Taylor, A.J.P. *The Origins of The Second World War* (New York: Simon & Schuster, 2005).
Templewood, Viscount (The Rt Hon Sir Samuel Hoare). *Nine Troubled Years* (London: Collins, 1954).
Teruzzi, Attilio. *La Milizia delle Camicie Nere e le sue specialità* (Milano: A Mondadori, Anno XVII-1939).
Tesfagiorgis G., Mussie. *Eritrea* (Santa Barbara, CA: ABC-CLIO, 2011).
Thesiger, Wilfred. *The Danakil Diary: Journeys through Abyssinia 1930–34* (London: Harper Collins, 1996).
Thompson, Peter. *Anzac Fury: The Battle of Crete 1941* (Sydney: Random House Australia, 2011).
Toprani, Anand. *Oil and the Great Powers: Britain and Germany, 1914 to 1945* (Oxford: Oxford University Press, 2019).
Torelli, Giorgio. *Gli ascari del tenente Indro e altri ascari: i battaglioni indigeni fatti a lor modo e iscritti nella storia d'Italia* (Milano: Edizioni Ares, 2004).
Townley, Edward. *Mussolini and Italy* (Oxford: Heinemann Educational, 2002).
Toynbee, Arnold J. assisted by Boulter, V.M. *Survey of International Affairs 1935: Volume II Abyssinia and Italy* (London: Oxford University Press, 1936).
Trubiano, Marisa S. *Ennio Flaiano and His Italy: Postcards from a Changing World* (Madison, NJ: Fairleigh Dickinson University Press, 2010).
Trythall, Anthony John. *'Boney' Fuller: Soldier, Strategist, and Writer* (Baltimore: Nautical & Aviation Publishing Company of America, 1989).
Tucker, Phillip Thomas. *John C. Robinson: Father of the Tuskegee Airmen* (Dulles, VA: Potomac Books, 2012).
UK National Archives. WO 32/5184. 'GENERAL AND WARLIKE STORES: Gas (Code 45(L)): Policy regarding use of gas bombs by Royal Air Force against hill tribesmen in India and Arabs in Middle East. Design and manufacture of bombs.' 1919.
UK National Archives. WO 188/765. 'Chemical warfare: Spain'. 1922–1926.
UK National Archives. FO 371/8409. Abyssinia. Code 1 Files 2318–5097 (to paper 5513). Memorandum by Sir Rennell Rodd on the Abyssinian Request for Admission to the League of Nations, 26 August 1923. A 5209/5097/1.

UK National Archives. FO 262/1802. Lytton Commission Report. 1932.
UK National Archives CAB 66/57/48. Memorandum by the Secretary of State for Foreign Affairs [Anthony Eden] and Lord Chancellor [John Simon, 1st Viscount Simon]: 'War Crimes'. 14 November 1944.
United States Adjutant-General's Office, *Machine-gun Drill Regulations (Provisional) 1917* (Washington DC: Government Printing Office, 1918).
US Army General Staff Military Intelligence Division, *Certain Studies on and Deductions from Operations of Italian Army in East Africa, October 1935–May 1936* (Washington, DC: US Army General Staff Military Intelligence Division, 1937).
US Department of State, *Foreign Relations of the United States: Diplomatic Papers 1933 Volume IV: The American Republics* (Washington DC: US Government Printing Office, 1950).
US Department of State, *Foreign Relations of the United States, Diplomatic Papers 1936: Volume III The Near East and Africa* (Washington DC: Government Printing Office, 1953).
US Department of State, *Foreign Relations of the United States: Diplomatic Papers 1944: Volume III: The British Commonwealth and Europe* (Washington DC: US Government Printing Office, 1965).
Vadala, Rocco. *Fiamme d'argento in Abissinia: le bande dei Carabinieri Reali alla battaglia di Gunu Gadu* (Roma: Unione editoriale d'Italia, Anno XV [1937]).
Valli, Federigo. 'Bombardamenti sul Gestro: Magalo e Ghigner', *L'Ala d'Italia: Periodico Nazionale dell'Aviazione Fascista*, aprile 1936-XIV.
Valli, Federigo. 'Ricognizioni sull'Uebi', *L'Ala d'Italia: Periodico Nazionale dell'Aviazione Fascista*, maggio 1936-XIV.
Van Gelder de Pineda, Rosanna. *Le chemin de fer de Djibouti à Addis-Abeba* (Paris: Editions L'Harmattan, 1995).
Vansittart, Lord. *The Mist Procession: The Autobiography of Lord Vansittart* (London: Hutchinson & Co., 1958).
Varanini, Varo. *La Marcia Della Ferrea Volonta* (Milano: Istituto Editoriale Cisalpino, 1938-XVI).
Varanini, Varo. *La formazione de L'Impero Coloniale Italiano Volume terzo: L'Impero (Dall'occupazione di Dessié all'assetto definitivo dell'Impero)* (Milano: Aldo Garzanti Editore, 1939).
Vari autori. *Graphicus: Notiziario Grafico, Rivista mensile delle arti della stampa*, agosto 1936, No. 8, anno XXVI.
Vari autori. *La Formazione De l'Impero Coloniale Italiano Volume Secondo: L'Impero (Dai Precedenti del Conflitto Etiopico alla Battaglia dell'Ascianghi)* (Milano: SA Fratelli Treves Editori, 1938).
Vene, Gian Franco. *Il processo di Verona: La storia, le cronache, i documenti, le testimonianze* (Milano: Arnoldo Mondadori Editore, 1967).
Verne, Vittorio. *Alla battaglia dell'Ogaden con la colonna Verne* (Milano: Societa Nazionale Editrice Propaganda, 1937-XV).
Volpe, Pompeo. *Auasc, Etiopia, 18 maggio 1937: quattro volti senza nome e la memoria coloniale nell'Italia repubblicana* (Padova: Padova University Press, 2021).
Watt, D. Cameron. 'Francis Herbert King: A Soviet Source in the Foreign Office', *Intelligence and National Security*, Volume 3, Issue 4, 1988.
Watt, Richard M. *The Kings Depart: The Tragedy of Germany: Versailles and the German Revolution* (London: Literary Guild, 1969).
Waugh, Evelyn. *Waugh in Abyssinia* (London: Longmans, Green & Co., 1936).
Weaver, Denis. *Front Page Europe* (London: Cresset Press, 1943).
Welch, Michael. 'The Science of War: A Discussion of J.F.C. Fuller's Shattering of British Continuity', *Journal of the Society for Army Historical Research*, Volume 79, No. 320, Winter 2001.
Wells, Linton. 'The Rape of Ethiopia', in Eugene Lyons (ed.), *We Cover the World: by Fifteen Foreign Correspondents* (New York: Harcourt, Brace & Co., 1937).
Wells, Linton. *Blood on the Moon: The Autobiography of Linton Wells* (New York: Houghton Mifflin Company, 1937).
Whittuck, Edward Arthur. *International Canals* (London: HMSO, 1920).

Wilcox, Francis O. 'The Use of Atrocity Stories in War', *American Political Science Review*, Volume 34, No. 6, December 1940.
Wilcox, Vanda. *The Italian Empire and the Great War* (Oxford: Oxford University Press, 2021).
Willcox, Richard. *The Traction Engine Archive* (Stonehouse, UK: Road Locomotive Society, 2004).
Willoughby, Lieutenant Colonel Charles Andrew. *Maneuver in War* (Harrisburg, PA: Military Service Publishing, 1939).
Woolbert, Robert Gale. 'Italy in Abyssinia', *Foreign Affairs*, Volume 13, No. 3, April, 1935.
Ximenes, Eduardo, Donativi, Marcello (ed.) and Cavedagna Fabio (ed.), *Sul campo di Adua* (Brindisi: Edizioni Trabant, 2021).
Xylander, Von Oberst und Rudolf Ritter von. 'Vom Krieg in Abessinien (Fortsetzung)', *Allgemeine schweizerische Militärzeitung – Journal militaire suisse – Gazetta militare svizzer*, Band 82, Heft 7, 1936.
Xylander, Rudolf Ritter und Edler von. *Die Eroberung Abessiniens 1935/36: Militärische Erfahrungen und Lehren aus dem ersten neuzeitlichen Vernichtungskrieg auf kolonialem Boden* (Berlin: E.S. Mittler & Sohn, 1937).
Zampetti, Giorgio, Ciafani, Stefano, Giometti, Fabrizio e Lelli, Alessandro (eds). *Armi chimiche: un'eredità ancora pericolosa* (Roma: Legambiente e Coordinamento Nazionale Bonifica Armi Chimiche, 2012).

Online Sources

Arosio, Enrico. 'Uno studio svela le bugie di Montanelli: La doppia vita del grande inviato del *Corriere della Sera*.' Available at: http://forum.laudellulivo.org/index.php?topic=781.0;wap2.
Avalon Project. Documents in Law, History and Diplomacy. Yale Law School, Lillian Goldman Law Library. Available at: https://avalon.law.yale.edu/20th_century/leagcov.asp#art16.
Berhane, Fiori and Malara, Diego Maria. 'The Montanelli Case: Sexuality, Race, and Colonial Forgetting in BLM Italy'. Available at: https://www.academia.edu/44386682/The_Montanelli_Case_Sexuality_Race_and_Colonial_Forgetting_in_BLM_Italy.
Bertonha, João Fábio. 'Paranoie fasciste? Il volontariato in favore dell'Etiopia durante la guerra del 1935–1936', *Diacronie: Studi di storia contemporanea*, No. 14, 2, 2013. Available at: https://journals.openedition.org/diacronie/282.
Cantate dei legionari. Available at: http://www.aclorien.it/archiviocantipatriottici/song.php?id=4625.
Colavito, Cosmo. 'Violatori di cifrari: I crittografi del Regio Esercito (1915–1943)', *Nuova Antologia Militare: Rivista interdisciplinare della Società Italiana di Storia Militare: Fascicolo Speciale 2021: Intelligence militare, guerra clandestina e Operazioni Speciali*. Available at: https://www.nam-sism.org/Articoli/2.%20GRAWE%20An%20Unimportant%20Obstacle%20The%20Prusso-German%20General%20Staff.pdf.
Communication from the Italian Government, Official No. C.123.M.62, Geneva, 19 March 1936. 'Abyssinian Atrocities Committed against Italian Workmen: Protest by the Italian Government to the League of Nations'. Available at: https://upload.wikimedia.org/wikipedia/commons/e/e4/C-123-M-62-1936-VII_EN.pdf.
Comune di Milano website. Available at: https://www.comune.milano.it/aree-tematiche/verde/verde-pubblico/parchi-cittadini/giardini-indro-montanelli.
LESSONA, Alessandro, Dizionario Biografico degli Italiani. Available at: https://www.treccani.it/enciclopedia/alessandro-lessona_%28Dizionario-Biografico%29/.
Corelli, R.M. 'Demetrio Helbig', Gianfranco Scorrano (ed.), *La Chimica Italiana* (Pàdova: Gianfranco Scorrano, 2008). Available at: http://wwwdisc.chimica.unipd.it/gianfranco.scorrano/pubblica/la_chimica_italiana.pdf; https://issuu.com/rivista.militare1/docs/il-servizio-chimico-militare-vol-2-testo.
Currency Information: Italian Lira: http://www.exchangerate.com/currency-information/italian-lira.html.
De Bono, Emilio, di Elvira Valleri Scaffei – Dizionario Biografico degli Italiani – Volume 33 (1987). Available at: https://www.treccani.it/enciclopedia/emilio-de-bono_(Dizionario-Biografico).

Forest Militia: http://rivistanuovastoria.com/2017/10/16/la-guardia-forestale-suo-passato-glorioso-dimenticato-politicamente-corretto/.

Giuliani, Padre Reginaldo, cappellano delle Camicie Nere: https://italianiinguerra.wordpress.com/2019/01/21/padre-reginaldo-giuliani-cappellano-delle-camicie-nere/.

Gorelik, Boris. 'Colonel Konovaloff: A friend of Ethiopia or an Apologist of Fascism?' A paper read at the 11th Conference of Africanists held at Moscow, May 2008. Available at: https://www.researchgate.net/publication/361276404.

Haber, Lutz. 'The Emperor Haile Selassie I in Bath 1936–1940'. Available at: http://anglo-ethiopian.org/publications/articles.php?type=O&reference=publications/occasionalpapers/papers/haileselassiebath.php.

Hansard, vol. 341, col. 287, 10 November 1938. 'Air-Raid Precautions'. The Lord Privy Seal (Sir John Anderson). Available at: https://hansard.parliament.uk/Commons/1938-11-10/debates/09e9de64-5ff1-4fb3-ad4f-8dd9384efe8b/CommonsChamber.

Hansard, vol. 270, col. 632, 10 November 1932. Debate on International Affairs. The Lord President of the Council (Mr Baldwin). Available at: https://api.parliament.uk/historic-hansard/commons/1932/nov/10/international-affairs.

Hansard, vol. 305, col. 365, 24 October 1935. House of Commons Debates. Available at: https://api.parliament.uk/historic-hansard/commons/1935/oct/24/international-situation.

Lawrence, Colonel T.E. 'France, Britain, and the Arabs', *Observer*, 8 August 1920. Available at: http://www.telstudies.org/writings/works/articles_essays/1920_france_britain_and_the_arabs.shtml.

Maggi, Stefano. *Le ferrovie nell'Africa italiana: aspetti economici, sociali e strategici* [Working Paper n. 18 del Dipartimento di Scienze storiche, giuridiche, politiche e sociali, Università degli Studi di Siena] (Siena: Università degli Studi, 1995) pp. 9–10. Available at: https://www.dispi.unisi.it/sites/st06/files/allegatiparagrafo/22-05-2013/wp18.pdf.

Messina, Dino. 'Scaffale di storia: Le armi chimiche in Etiopia e l'ammissione di Montanelli', *Corriere della Sera*, 2 aprile 2016. Available at: https://www.corriere.it/extra-per-voi/2016/04/02/armi-chimiche-etiopia-l-ammissione-montanelli-54d37986-f8fc-11e5-b97f-6d5a0a6f6065.shtml.

Mussolini, Benito. Discorso Del 5 Maggio 1936. Available at: https://www.youtube.com/watch?v=w1TInA93WEo&ab_channel=TEMPOLESSMUSIC.

Nizamoglu, Yuksel. 'Mehmet Vehib Kacı: Hayatı ve Askeri Faaliyetleri', basılmamış Doktora Tezi, İstanbul Üniversitesi Sosyal Bilimler Enstitüsü, Tarih Anabilim Dali. 2010. pp. 414, 417, 419. This thesis is available at: https://www.academia.edu/37615180/VEH%C4%B0P_PA%C5%9EA_KA%C3%87I_NIN_HAYATI_VE_ASKER%C4%B0_FAAL%C4%B0YETLER%C4%B0.

Paschalidi, Maria. *Constructing Ionian Identities: The Ionian Islands in British Official Discourses; 1815–1864: A Thesis Submitted for the Degree of Doctor of Philosophy* (London: University College London, 2009). Available at: https://discovery.ucl.ac.uk/id/eprint/19415/1/19415.pdf.

Patriarca, Joseph Vincent. *Un americano a Gorizia, Diario di un pilota del 4 Stormo Prima parte: 1931–1937* (Milano: Vittorelli Edizioni per conto dell' Associazione Culturale 4 Stormo Gorizia, 2007). Available at: https://www.associazione4stormo.it/un-americano-a-gorizia-1931-1937/ and http://www.asso4stormo.it/arc_01/Pubblicazioni/Patriarca1.htm.

Perri, Fabrizio. 'The Great Depression in Italy: Trade Restrictions and Real Wage Rigidities', a paper prepared for the conference: Great Depressions of the 20th Century, October 20–21, 2000, at the Federal Reserve Bank of Minneapolis. Available at: http://faculty.marshall.usc.edu/Vincenzo-Quadrini/papers/deprpap.pdf.

The Protocol for the Prohibition of the Use in War of Asphyxiating, Poisonous or other Gases, and of Bacteriological Methods of Warfare': https://treaties.unoda.org/t/1925. See also: 'Protocollo concernente la proibizione di usare in guerra gas asfissianti, tossici o simili e mezzi batteriologici', p. 3. Available from: Fedlex: La piattaforma di pubblicazione del diritto federale: https://www.fedlex.admin.ch/eli/cc/48/375_387_405/it; https://fedlex.data.admin.ch/filestore/fedlex.data.admin.ch/eli/cc/48/375_387_405/20040910/it/pdf-a/fedlex-data-admin-ch-eli-cc-48-375_387_405-20040910-it-pdf-a.pdf.

Rotunda, Donald Theodore. 'The Rome Embassy of Sir Eric Drummond, 16th Earl of Perth, 1933–1939'. A thesis submitted to the University of London in fulfilment of the requirement for the degree Doctor of Philosophy; Department of International History. The London School of Economics and Political Science. The University of London. June 1972. Available at: https://ethos.bl.uk/OrderDetails.do?uin=uk.bl.ethos.297019.

Salgari, Emilio. Master of Adventure. Available at: https://www.rohpress.com/en_salgari.html.

Scheere, David. 'Léopold Reul in Ethiopië: van officiële naar officieuze militaire samenwerking: Konden huurlingen de formele coöperatie voortzetten?' A paper produced under the auspices of Vrije Universsteit Brussel Faculteit Letteren En Wijsbegeerte. Available at: https://www.academia.edu/12209035/L%C3%A9opold_Reul_in_Ethiopi%C3%AB_van_offici%C3%ABle_naar_officieuze_militaire_samenwerking.

Stato Maggiore Dell'Esercito Ufficio Storico, *L'Esercito Italiano: dal 1° tricolore al 1° centenario* (Roma: Ufficio Storico dello Stato Maggiore Dell'Esercito, 1961). Available at: http://www.regioesercito.it/reparti/fanteria/rediv29.htm; http://www.regioesercito.it/reparti/mvsn/ordmillibia.htm.

Suvich, Fulvio (Undersecretary of Foreign Affairs). 'Abyssinian Atrocities Committed against Italian Workmen, Communication from the Italian Government to the League of Nations (Translation from the Italian)'. Official No: C. 123. M. 62. 1936. VII.' 19 March 1936. Available at: https://upload.wikimedia.org/wikipedia/commons/e/e4/C-123-M-62-1936-VII_EN.pdf.

l'Ufficio storico dello Stato maggiore dell'Aeronautica, *Fondo 'Africa orientale italiana 1935–1938': Inventario*. Available at: https://www.aeronautica.difesa.it/storia/ufficiostorico/archiviofondi/Lists/DocumentiArchivioFondi/Africa_orientale.pdf.

United Press (News Agency) report: Geneva, 5 October 1935. Available at: https://www.upi.com/Archives/1935/10/05/Ethiopia-asks-League-of-Nations-to-act-against-Italy/9298410341771/.

Watson, Mason W. *'Not Italian or German, but British in Character': J.F.C. Fuller and the Fascist Movement in Britain*, Undergraduate Honors Theses. Paper 485. College of William and Mary. Available at: https://scholarworks.wm.edu/cgi/viewcontent.cgi?article=1494&context=honorstheses.

Witkowski, Victoria. *Remembering Fascism and Empire: The Public Representation and Myth of Rodolfo Graziani in 20th-Century Italy*. A thesis submitted for assessment with a view to obtaining the degree of Doctor of History and Civilisation of the European University Institute, Florence, 24 September 2021. Available at: https://cadmus.eui.eu/handle/1814/72739.

Zuber, Aline. 'The cross in the crosshairs. A photographic record of the bombing of Red Cross field hospitals during the Second Italo–Ethiopian war: 4 January 2022, Article/Audiovisual/Photo'. Available at: https://blogs.icrc.org/cross-files/the-cross-in-the-crosshairs-a-photographic-record-of-the-bombing-of-red-cross-field-hospitals-during-the-second-italo-ethiopian-war/#_ftnref10.

Index

Adua (Adwa, Adowa) Battle of (1896), 11, 21, 115
  Baratieri, Major General Oreste, and, 11
  Mussolini, shame of and, 11, 22
Air Force, Italian (*Regia Aeronautica*),
  Ajmone Cat, Air Brigadier General Mario
    Air Force, Eritrean chief of staff and theatre commander, 82, 87
    Douhet's theories, and, 87–8
    Logistical support, on, 127
    Mustard gas, ordered to use, 82, 88
  Army (tactical) cooperation with, and, 58, 100, 146
  Deficiencies rectified, 68
  Douhetism (strategic bombing), abandoned for, 87–8
    Logistical support, 97, 126, 127, 140
  Balbo, Italo, the 'father' of Italy's independent air force, 17, 18, 19, 23
  Bernasconi, Air Brigadier General Mario, First Somalia theatre commander, 65, 66, 144
  Chemical Warfare Service (*Servizio Chimica Militare*) and, 168
  Douhet, General Giulio, Air-power theorist, 19, 87
  Establishment of, 18
  Hospitals, bombing of (see separate entry)
  Mustard gas (see separate entry)
  Performance and losses, 168
  Ranza, Brigadier General Ferruccio, Second Somalia theatre commander, 144, 161
  Valle, General Giuseppe, Chief of Staff, Rome, and Eritrean command, 87
Amba Aradam (Enderta), battle of, 100–1, 103–9
Army, Italian (*Regio Esercito*),
  Air Force, and
    Logistical support from, 97, 126, 127, 140
    Tactical cooperation with, 58, 100, 146
  Corps formed with Blackshirt divisions, 195, n. 42

Divisions:
  Ascari (Eritrean)
    1ª Divisione eritrea: I Brigata Eritrea, Addis Ababa, march on, 158; Amba Aradam, Battle of, 103, 105; Maychew, Battle of, 131, 135, 136, 138; Tembien, Second Battle of, 114, 115
    2ª Divisione eritrea: Maychew, Battle of, 134, 135, 136, 138; Tembien, First Battle of, 90, 94, 97, Uarieu Pass, 96
  Ascari (Libyan)
    Divisione indigena Libia I: Caterpillar trains (*mastodontici autotreni*), 151; Egypt, ordered to frontier of, 63; Ogaden, battles of, 146, 148, 150, 160; Prisoners, and 'custom' towards taking, 150; Somalia, arrives in, 143
  Spahis (zaptie), 115; unable to distinguish between Eritreans and Ethiopians, 111
  Dubats – Corpo indigeni somali (Somali Native Corps), 28; Ogaden, battles of, 56, 143; Birgot, Battle of, 152–3, *coraggiatori* ('encouragers') utilized, 153; Gunu Gadu, Battle of, 153; Motorized (truck-mounted) infantry, as, 148, Verne, Lieutenant General Vittorio, column commanded by, 148, 151, 152, 160, 162; 'Lions of Juba', characteristics as described by Edmund Demaitre, 59
  Metropolitan
    5ª Divisione alpina '*Pusteria*'; Amba Uork, taking of, 115, 117; Amba Aradam, Battle of, 105, 107, 108, 109; replaces Blackshirt division during, 106; Maychew, Battle of, 131, 133, 134, 135, 138
    5ª Divisione fanteria '*Cosseria*', 109
    19ª Divisione fanteria '*Gavinana*', 120, 121

24ª Divisione fanteria '*Gran Sasso*', 86, 120
27ª Divisione fanteria '*Sila*', 106, 107, 108, 114
29ª Divisione fanteria '*Peloritana*', 28
30ª Divisione fanteria '*Sabauda*', 105, 106, 107, 129; 3° Reggimento Bersaglieri, detached for duty with Starace's 'fast column', 129; 'March of the Iron Will', 158
Tactical instructions, issued by Badoglio, 114
Tanks, L3/35 (or Carro Veloce CV-35) light tank,
   10° Squadrone carri veloci «*Esploratori del Nilo*» (the 'Explorer of the Nile' Fast Tank Squadron), 84
   Ogaden, valueless in, 58
   'Affair of the three tanks', 59
   Inda Aba Guna, battle (*Battaglia al Passo Dembeguina*), demonstrates vulnerability, 84–5, 86–7

Badoglio, Marshal Pietro, Theatre Commander-in-Chief,
   Abiy Addi, fighting around, and, 90–1
   Addis Ababa, advance on, and, 125, 131, 140–1
      Enters and takes possession of, 163
      Institutes death penalty for looting and possession of arms, 166
      'March of the Iron Will', 157–60, 166
   Airpower, and, 87, 88, 121
   Amba Aradam, battle of, and, 100–1, 103–9
   Appointed, 51
   Censorship policy of, 53, 110
   Chemical warfare, and, 4, 8, 93
   Chief of Staff of the Italian Army, 177
   De Bono, and, 24, 47, 48, 49, 51
   Duke of, title awarded, 165
   Graziani, and, 65, 142, 145–6, 155, 160, 162
   Hospitals, bombing of, and, 67, 124
   Inda Aba Guna, battle of, and, 86, 87
      Eritrea, worries over incursions into, 89, 109
   'March on Rome' (1922), and, 16
   Maychew, Battle of, and, 128, 131, 133–4, 138, 139–40
      Operational command delegated, 136
      Orders to senior commanders in respect of, 135
   Operations, and, 70, 71, 72, 82, 83
   Prime Minister of Italy, replaces Mussolini as, 177
   Government of, legitimate and cobelligerent, 179
   Potential for being charged with war crimes, 178, 180
      Opposes war crimes trial for Italians, 180
   Resigns, 180
   Shire, Battle of, and, 120–1
   Starace's 'fast column', and, 128, 129, 130
   Tembien, First Battle of, and, 94–100
      Criticism of, 98–9
      Uarieu [Worsege] Pass, and, 91, 96–7
   Tembien, Second Battle of, and, 113–18
      Amba Uork, taking of, 115–17
      Tactical instructions regarding, 114
   Viceroy of Ethiopia, proclaimed, 165
Baldwin, Stanley, British prime minister, 20
   Elected on pro League of Nations ticket, 63
   Hoare-Laval Plan, and, 79
   League of Nations sanctions, and, 29, 64
Blackshirts (*Camice Nere* or CC,NN) – *Milizia Volontaria per la Sicurezza Nazionale* or MVSN (Voluntary Militia for National Security),
   1ª Divisione CC,NN, '23 Marzo',
      Amba Aradam, attack on, 106; Capture of summit, 108–9; shown to be a propaganda sham, 109
   2ª Divisione CC,NN, '28 Ottobre',
      Tembien, First Battle of, 94–8
      Uarieu Pass, Battle of, 96–8
      Diamanti, Consul-General Filippo, precipitates crisis at, 94–6
      Giuliani, Father Reginaldo, 98
      Propaganda extols, 98
      Somma, Major General Umberto, 94, 97
   3ª Divisione CC,NN, '21 Aprile', 120
      Amba Uork, and, 115, 116–17
      Polo, *capomanipolo* (Lieutenant) Tito, and, 116
   4ª Divisione CC,NN, '3 Gennaio',
      Relieved and relegated to road construction, 106
   5ª Divisione CC,NN, '1 Febbraio',
      Shire, Battle of, and, 109
   6ª Divisione CC,NN, 'Tevere', 28, 63, 148, 151
      Navarra-Viggiani, Consul-General Franco, 'Navarra's fast column' (*Colonna Celere Navarra*), 146, 161, 162

'Forestry Militia Cohort' (*Coorte milizia forestale*), 144, 153
Military value, or lack thereof, of Blackshirt formations,
  Fiske, Norman E., 106
  Fuller, J.F.C., 50
  Starace, Achille, Fascist Party secretary, Gondor, 'fast column' (*colonna celere*) to, 128–30
    82° Battaglione CC,NN, 'Benito Mussolini', 129

Carabinieri,
  Addis Ababa, policing of, and, 166
  Bande autocarrate (truck-mounted bands) 143–4, 146
    Gunu Gadu, Battle of, and, 153, 154
  Talamo, Major Manfredi, Head of the Military Information Service's 'Extraction Section', 81
Caterpillar trains, 27–8, 31, 70, 144, 147, 151, 155, 171
Chamberlain, Neville, British senior politician, 77, 79, 82
Chemical warfare,
  Arsine, 8, 103, 174
  Balbo, Italo, Aircraft and chemical weapons a 'natural union', 17
  Douhet, General Giulio, and, 19
  Geneva Protocol (1925), prohibition of, 22, 38, 70, 132
    British Chiefs of Staff, opinion on Italian contravention, 132
  Lawrence, Colonel T.E., *aka* 'Lawrence of Arabia', advocates use of in Mesopotamia, 17
  Liddell Hart, Captain Basil, and, 17
  Mustard gas (see separate entry)
  Phosgene, 17, 18, 19, 68, 145
Churchill, Winston,
  Chemical warfare in Mesopotamia, on, 17
  Ethiopian admittance to the League of Nations, opinion, 36
  Italy, and
    Mussolini and his regime, admirer of, 36
    Perceived danger of communist takeover, 179
    War criminals, fate of, 181
  Omdurman, Battle of, 168
  Rhineland, Hitler's reoccupation of, and, 125

Sanctions against Italy, British dilemma, 77, 80
Ciano, Galeazzo,
  Addis Ababa, visits, 166
    Packard, Reynolds and Eleanor, conversation with, 170
  Albania, invasion the brainchild of (as foreign minister), 176
  De Bono, Mussolini's opinion of, reports, 30–1
  'Disperata' bomber squadron (*squadriglia aerea 'Disperata'*), commander of, 89
  Executed, 180
Corcione, General Domenico, defence minister, 6, 8, 9

Dall'Ora, Brigadier General Fidenzio, Head of logistics, northern front,
  De Bono's assessment of abilities, 126
  Del Boca's assessment of abilities, 126
  Makalle, Badoglio orders to assemble over a thousand lorries around, 125–6, 131
De Bono, Emilio, Theatre Commander-in-Chief,
  Adowa, captures, 43
  Appointed, 23
  Badoglio and Lessona report on, 49
  British, perceived problems with, 29
  Eritrea, and communications in, 25–6
  Invasion force, largest ever assembled for an African war, 28
    Crosses the frontier at 05:00 hours on 3 October 1935, 41
  Mussolini, relations with, and, 30–1
    Executes for 'betrayal', 180
    Loses faith in, 47
    Relieves of command, 51
    Urges capture of Makalle, 44
  Operational plans (1932 and 1935), 24
Del Boca, Angelo
  Amba Aradam, truth about the battle of, and, 109
  Chemical warfare
    long battle for the truth' over, 2, 4–11
    'The worst crime' of the Fascist regime, 171
  Cost of the war (financial) calculated, 167
  Ganale Doria, analysis of battle of, 69
  Haile Selassie, biography of published, 5
  Montanelli, dispute with, 2, 4–5, 9–10

Ras Imru Haile Selassie, publishes testimony
    of, 88, 109
Desta Damtew, Ras
  Army based around Neghelli (southern
      front), 60
    Advance along the Ganale Doria and
        Dawa rivers, 60
      Precautions to avoid aerial detection, 61;
          Failure of, 65
      Graziani attacks – 'Battle of Ganale Doria'
          – and defeats, 68–9
Djibouti–Addis Ababa railway, 32, 58, 93, 100,
    126, 145, 159

Fiske, Major Norman E., Official American
    Military Observer,
  Air transport and supply, 119
  Blackshirts at Amba Aradam, on, 106, 108
  Tanks, valueless in Ogaden, 58
  Volatile meteorological conditions of
      Ogaden, 54
Fuller, Major General J.F.C.,
  Future war, on, 20
  Mustard gas, on, 10
  War correspondent, as
    Arrives in theatre, 45
    Badoglio, and, 47, 53
      Censorship regime and, 86
      Operational methods, and, 91
    De Bono, assessment of, 47–8
    Operational plan, analysis of, 53
    Ganale Doria, Opinion on battle of, 68–9,
        70
    Inaugurates 'totalitarian warfare', 70
    Italian expeditionary force, analysis of, 50,
        51, 84, 144
    League of Nations, effect of sanctions, 64
    Italian victory, and, 167
    Makkale, significance of capturing, 49
    Mussolini, interview with, 46
    'Totalitarian warfare', and, 70, 169, 170

Getachew Abate, Ras,
  Maychew, battle of, commands left hand
      column, 135, 137
Graziani, General Rodolfo,
  Badoglio, and
    Relations with, strained, 160, 162
    Slated to replace, 99, 142

Caterpillar trains, and, 27–8, 31, 70, 144,
    147, 151, 155, 171
Marshal, promoted to, 165
Minister of Defence of Italian Social
    Republic, appointed, 180
Prison sentence for military collaboration
    with Germany, 180
Somalia, appointed governor general and
    commander-in-chief of, 26
  Chemical warfare, initiates, 65–6
  Ganale Doria, battle of, 60–1, 65, 68–70
  Harar, advance on, 141–55
  Hospital (Swedish Red Cross), bombing
      of, 66–7
  Operation No. 1, and, 54–60
  Passive role, ordered to assume, 53
  Totalitarian warfare, initiates, 70
Viceroy of Ethiopia, and governor general of
    Italian East Africa, promoted to, 172
  Assassination attempt on, 175
  'Terror and extermination', policy of, 174
  Debre Libanos, massacre, 175

Haile Selassie, Negus (King of Kings or
    Emperor of Ethiopia),
  Exile, return from, 177
  Head of state, head of government and the
      ultimate holder of executive, judicial
      and legislative power, 33
    Addis Ababa, returns to after defeat at
        Maychew, 161; Flees to Djibouti and
        exile, 161, 162
    Command difficulties, 134
    Communications, compromised, 60, 72,
        113
    Dessie, relocates to, 72; Moves north from,
        113, 131
    Imperial Guard, responsible directly to the
        Negus, 34, 113, 134, 135, 136
    Kassa, Ras, disagreements with, 113
    Logistical difficulties, 100
    Maychew, Battle of, 131–8; Retreats south
        from, 139
  League of Nations, and,
    Faith in, 38
    Italian invasion, orders forces to pull back
        to demonstrate aggression of, 43
    Prime mover behind Ethiopian
        membership, 36
  Solomonic Dynasty, and, 44
  Wehib Pasha, and, 35

Index   255

Haile Selassie Gugsa, 43–4
Hitler, Adolf,
  Austria, designs on and Mussolini's resistance to, 24
  Germany resurgent under, 172
  Mussolini, and
    Draws closer to, 176
    Italian Social Republic (*Repubblica sociale italiana*), and, 180
    Orders rescue of following imprisonment, 180
    Orders occupation of northern Italy, 177
  Rhineland, reoccupation of, 125
  Vansittart characterises as 'Dictator Major', in comparison to Mussolini as 'Dictator Minor,' 78
Hoare, Samuel (UK foreign secretary),
  Address to the League, 77
  Hoare-Laval Plan (Pact), 78–9, 80
  Resigns over, 79
Hoare-Laval Plan (Pact), 78–9, 80

Imru Haile Selassie, Ras, [1] Army of the Left (northern front), 72
  Af Gaga pass, battle of, 89–90
  Communications, or lack thereof, 113
  Guerrilla strategy adopted after defeat at, 109; Gondrand Worksite Massacre, 110–11
  Inda Aba Guna, battle (*Battaglia al Passo Dembeguina*), 83–6
    Ethiopian advance towards Eritrean border, 89; Mussolini, 'kept awake at night' by, 89; Renounced, 90
    Italian front broken, 86
    Tanks, problems with, 84–5, 86–7
  Shire, Battle of, defeated at, 114, 118–21
  [2] Mustard gas, testimony to Del Boca concerning, 88–9
Intelligence, Italian,
  Fails to detect advance, 93
  Strength, estimates of, 33, 60, 120, 153
  Haile Selassie,
    Kassa, Ras, communications with read, 113
    Movement, discovered, 113
    Radio communications and ciphers, compromised, 60
    Strategy, discerned, 72
  Maffey Report, and, 81
  Military Information Service (*Servizio Informazioni Militari* – SIM),

Deciphers British and French diplomatic traffic, 80, 138–9, 172
Gamba, General Vittorio, Head of, 80
Section P (*Sezione P*)-Extraction Section (*Sezione Prevelamento*),
  Acquisition of British Embassy documents, 81
Talamo, Major Manfredi (of the Carabinieri), Head of, 81
Secret Information Service (*Servizio Informazioni Segrete* – SIS)
  British naval ciphers, cracked, 172
Italian East Africa (*Africa Orientale Italiana* – AOI),
  Founding of the empire, proclaimed by Mussolini, 165
  Racial segregation in, 174
  Terror and extermination, policy towards 'rebels', 174

Journalists, correspondents, and writers (contemporary),
  Beonio-Brocchieri, Vittorio, 126, 127
  Bottai, Major Giuseppe, 98
  Demaitre, Edmund (Demeter Ödön), 59
  Emeny, Stuart, 34, 35
  Flaiano, Ennio, 111
  Fuller, J.F.C., see separate entry
  Gentizon, Paul, 127, 140
  Géraud André (*Pertinax*), 79
  Herrero, Margarita, 166
  Liddell Hart, Captain Basil, 17, 41, 169, 171
  Marinetti, Filippo Tommaso, 98
  Packard, Eleanor, 166, 170
  Packard, Reynolds, 166, 170
  Pavolini, Alessandro, 89, 97, 115
  Pietra, Italo, 109
  Steer, George, see separate entry
  Tabouis, Genevieve, 78
  Waugh, Evelyn, 33
  Wells, Fay Gillis, 72–5
  Wells, Linton, 72–5
  Xylander, Oberst Rudolf Ritter und Edler von, 11, 169–70

Kassa Hailu, Ras, [1] Army of the Centre (northern front), 72, 90
  Abiy Addi, advance on, 90
  Victory considered to have been achieved, 100

Army destroyed, 118
Promoted above Ras Seyoum, 113
Radio communications intercepted, 113
Tembien, Second Battle of, 113, 114, 115–18
  Amba Uork, taking of, 115–17
  Konovalov, Colonel Feodor, advises retreat, 118
  Uarieu [Worsege] Pass, and, 97
[2] Maychew, battle of, 134
  Addis Ababa, arrives at with Haile Selassie following defeat, 161
  Centre column, commands, 135

Laval, Pierre, 47
  Hoare-Laval Plan (Pact), 78–9, 80
League of Nations,
  Britain, committed to, formally, 36, 64
    'National Declaration on the League of Nations and Armaments', 63
  Dilemma regarding Italy, 38–9, 45, 64, 172, 176
  Hoare, Samuel (foreign secretary), address to the League, 77
    Hoare-Laval Plan (Pact), 78
    Resigns, 79
  Chaco War (Bolivia-Paraguay), and, 37
  Ethiopia, and,
    Faith in, 35, 38
    Italy, League demands punishment of, 45
    Joins, 36
      Churchill, Winston, opinion of, 36
  Fuller, J.F.C., on Mussolini's defiance of, 167
  Greek-Bulgarian Incident ('War of the Stray Dog', 'Incident at Petrich', 'Demir-Kapu Incident'), 37
  Italo-Ethiopian arbitration commission, and, 29
  Italy, and,
    Complaints concerning the 'Gondrand Worksite Massacre', 110
    Corfu Incident (occupation), 14
    Sanctions imposed on, 62
      Churchill, Winston, opinion concerning, 80
    Oil sanctions, considered, 75, 123
  Leticia War (Colombia-Peru), 37
  Manchukuo, and, 36
  Origins, 35
  Tsehai Haile Selassie, Princess, addresses concerning Italy's use of chemical weapons, 132

USA, and, 75–6, 165
Lessona, Alessandro,
  De Bono, reports on, 47, 48, 49, 51
  Del Boca, TV appearance with, 3–4
  Graziani, and,
    Asks for permission to use chemical weaponry, 65
    Copied message to regarding ruthlessness, 175–6
Libya,
  Badoglio, as Governor, 24
  De Bono, as Governor, 23
  Graziani, and, 174
  Italo-Ottoman War, and, 29–30, 35, 171–2
  Reconquest of, 16–17, 21, 174
  Troops (Spahis, zaptie) in Ethiopia, 111, 115
    1st Libyan Division (*Divisione indigena Libia I*) 28, 63, 70
      Mobilised to Somalia, 142–3
      Ogaden-Harar operations, and, 146, 148–50, 160

Maisky Ivan, 79
Maychew, Battle of, 131–8
  Addis Ababa, leaflets announcing the Italian victory dropped on, 140
  Ethiopia, fate of, decided at, 138, 140
  Haile Selassie, decides to attack Italian positions, 133
  Imperial Guard, at, 136
Menelik II, emperor of Ethiopia, 11
Military advisers to Ethiopia ('mercenaries' to the Italians), 34–5
  Belgian Military Mission, 34, 159
  Del Valle, Alejandro (Alejandro Ramón Narciso del Valle y Suero), 103
  Konovalov (Konovaloff), Colonel Feodor Evgenievich,
    Amba Uork, on, 117
    Biographical details, 133
    Kassa, Ras, advised to retreat (Second Battle of Tembien), 118
    Maychew, Battle of, and, 134, 136, 137, 138, 139
    Steer, George, and, 133
  Robinson, John, 34
  Tamm, Captain Viking, 159
  Wehib Pasha (Vehip Pasha, Weib (or Wehib) pascia) Mehmed Vehib, 35, 141, 162

Index 257

Montanelli, Indro,
  Civiltà fascista (Fascist Civilization) journal,
    Correspondent for, 1
  Colonialism, views on, 1, 2
  Dispute with Angelo Del Boca over use of
    chemical weapons, 2, 4–5, 9–10
  Elvira Banotti, and, 2
  Statue defaced, 1, 2
Mulugeta Yeggazu, Ras, Army of the Right
    (northern front), 72, 94, 101
  Amba Alagi, occupied by, 83
  Amba Aradam, centrepiece of his defence,
    105
    Abandons, 107
    Battle of, and, 100–1, 103–9
    Killed on retreat from, 108
Mussolini, Benito,
  Adua (Adwa, Adowa) Battle of (1896), shame
    and, 11, 22
  Army, relations with Fascism, and, 24
  Balbo, Italo, sidelining of, 18
  Britain and France, and
    Egypt, sabre rattling at Libyan border, 63
    French government, determined to avoid
      estranging Italy, 77
    Intelligence on intentions of, and, 81–2
    Non-intervention of, gambles on, 30
    Reluctance to intervene, 45–6
    'Sanctions mean war' with, 64
  Characterisations of, 13
  Churchill, Winston, admiration of, 36
  Djibouti-Addis Ababa railway, forbids attacks
    on, 126, 145
  'Doctrine of Fascism' (La dottrina del
    fascismo), and, 13, 38
  Ethiopia, invasion of
    Adua, capture of, and, 43
    A Fascist war above all, 23, 128
    Badoglio, and
      Addis Ababa, sends victory report after
        entry into, 163; Addis Ababa, elevates
        to Duke of, but vetoes ducal motto,
        165
      Amba Aradam, sends victory telegram
        to, 109
      Appointed in succession to De Bono, 51
      Criticism of, received and rejected, 99
      Hospital, bombing of British Ambulance
        Service in Ethiopia (BASE)
        installation, reports on, 123
      Maychew, Battle of: Reports imminence
        of, 132; Reports victory at, 139–40

  Military situation, appreciation of, 83
  Mustard gas (see also separate entry):
    Authorises use of, 88; Suspends use
      of, 93, 172
    Reinforcements sent to, 90
    Reports summary of his command to,
      114
    Tembien, Battle of, victory report sent
      to, 118
    Uork Amba, telegraphs report on taking
      of, 117
  De Bono, and
    Appoints to Ethiopian theatre
      command, 23, 24
    Disparagement of, 31
    Relieves of command, 51
    Resources, promises of, 30
    Speed, presses for (largely in vain), 44,
      45, 47, 48, 49, 51
  Decrees all and every means to be used in
    conquest of, 21, 22
  Graziani, and
    Defensive strategy, ordered, 53
    Gianagobo, Battle of, reports to, 150
    Hospital bombing, orders Red Cross to
      be respected, 67
    Impatience with, 145, 146
    Justifies campaign, and delays thereof,
      to, 160, 161; Badogliano, countering
      of, 162
    Support for, 28
  'Place in the sun' card plays, 20
  'Populist bombast', and, 21
  Foreign policy, attitude towards
    Corfu Incident (occupation), and, 14–15
    Fuller, J.F.C., interview with, 46
    Hitler, opposition to Austrian policy of, 24
    Hoare, Samuel, and, 77
    Hoare-Laval Plan (Pact), and, 78, 80
  Imru, Ras, campaign of, 'keeps awake at
    night', 89
  Italian East Africa (Africa Orientale Italiana –
    AOI), and
    Founding of, proclaims, 165
    Racial segregation in, endorses, 174
    Terror and extermination, policy of
      towards 'rebels', 174
  Italo-Ottoman War, opposition to, 15
  League of Nations, and, see separate entry
  Never wrong (Benito Mussolini ha sempre
    ragione), 46
  Propaganda, starts to believe his own, 176

Second World War, and
  Badoglio, replaces, 177
  Britain and France, declares war on, 177
  Dismissal, and imprisonment of, 177;
    Freed by order of Hitler, 180
  Italian Social Republic (*Repubblica sociale italiana* – RSI), and, 180
  Shot by communist partisans, 181
  Starace's 'fast column', and, 129, 130
  Vansittart, characterises as 'Dictator Minor' in comparison to Hitler as 'Dictator Major', 78
  Victor Emmanuel III, King, and
    Dismisses and imprisons, 177
    Emperor of Ethiopia, becomes, 165
    Medal, awards, 163–5
    Prime Minister, appoints, 16
    Prince, offers title of to, 165
Mussolini, Bruno, 136
Mussolini, Vito, 89
Mussolini, Vittorio, 68, 124
Mustard gas (*Iprite*)
  Britain, proposed use of in Mesopotamia, 17–18
  British Chiefs of Staff, opinion on Italian use, 132
  C.500.T bomb,
    Deployment, 88, 91, 92, 93, 97, 103, 107, 108, 132, 145, 152
      Post war, 172, 174
      Statistics, northern and southern fronts, 168
        Tekeze river fords, used on, 88; Imru, Ras, describes effects, 88–9
  Development, 21–2
  Doctrine regarding usage, 104
  Field tested, 82, 88
  Graphic of, 22
  Characteristics, 104
  Chemical City (*Città della Chimica*) near Rome, and, 19
  Fuller, J.F.C.,
    Ethiopia, on usage in, 10
    Future war, potential usage, 20
  Graziani, initiates use against enemy targets, 65–6
  Ganale Doria, battle, and, 68, 69
  Italian government belatedly (1995) admit use of in Ethiopia, 6–9
  Libya, use in by Italy, 17
  Minniti, Lieutenant Tito, grim fate as excuse for use of, 66
  Mussolini, orders suspension of use, 93
  Spain, use in Morocco, 18
  Spraying of, proposal, 21
  Zannoni, Sergeant Livio, grim fate as excuse for use of, 66

Nasibu Zeamanuel, Ras, Army based around Degeh Bur and Jijiga (southern front), 141
  Badoglio, concerns about withdrawal to cover Addis Ababa, 141
  Flees the scene with Haile Selassie, 162
  Graziani, advance on Harar against, 141–55
    On success of, 162
  Wehib Pasha, chief of staff to, 141
    Advice to, 142, 153, 161

OVRA, Fascist secret police, 30

Rodd, Sir Rennell, describes Ethiopian system of government, 33
Rovighi, General Alberto, 6, 7

Seldes, George, on Mussolini and Fascism, 13
Serdo, column across the Danakil to, 126–7
  Air supply of, 127
    'first case of transporting live animals to supply units on the march', 127
    Mattei, Lieutenant Colonel Simon Pietro, brainchild of, 127
  Litta Modignani, Lieutenant Gianfranco, Commander, 126, 127
  Mercenaries, used instead of regular troops, 126
  Strategic result of, 127
Seyoum Mengesha, Ras, Army of the Centre (northern front), 72, 90
  Abiy Addi, advance on, 90
    Victory considered to have been achieved, 100
  Kassa, Ras, subordinated to, 113
  Shire, Battle of, 114, 118–21
  Spencer Dr John H., legal adviser to Haile Selassie,
    Addis Ababa, panic as Italian forces approach, 159
    Takes refuge in the British Legation, 163
  Chemical warfare, effect of, 108
  Haile Selassie, decision to flee rather than resist, 161

Steer, George, war correspondent,
  Abiy Addi, Ethiopian 'victory' at, 100
  Air power, decisive factor in the war, 118
  Amba Aradam, on battle of, 103, 105, 108
  Amba Uork, on the taking of, 117
  Badoglio, entry into Addis Ababa, described, 163
    Shooting of looters etc., 166
  Bir-qod and Hamanle, Ethiopian defenders and, 152
  Chemical warfare, on, 132–3
  Ethiopian troops, locust-like nature of, 108
  Expelled from Ethiopia by the new regime, 166
  Gorrahei, defences of, 56
  Haile Selassie, on, 38
    Return to Addis Ababa and journey into exile, 161
  Hospitals, bombing of, 66, 172
    Mussolini, Vittorio, and, 124
  Konovalov, Colonel Feodor, and, 118
    Account forms basis for Chapter XVIII of Steer's post-war book, 133
  Modern war, as waged by Italy, verdict on, 168–9
  Nasibu, Ras, withdrawal of, 161
  Ogaden, climatic conditions pertaining, 54
  Shire, battle of, on, 120
  Three tanks, affair of, 56–7
    Aftermath, 59

Tembien, First Battle of, 94–100
Tembien, Second Battle of, 113, 114, 115–18
  Amba Uork, taking of, 115–17

Vansittart, Sir Robert, British permanent Foreign Office under-secretary, 78, 80
Victor Emmanuel III, King of Italy,
  Mussolini, and
    Bemedals as Knight of the Grand Cross of the Military Order of Savoy, 164–5

Dismissal and imprisonment of, 177
Emperor of Ethiopia, proclaimed by, 165
Prime Minister, appoints as, 16
Prince, offers to raise to rank of, 165
Opposition (supposed) to Ethiopian invasion, 30

War crimes (atrocities), actual and alleged,
  'Affair of the three tanks', 59
  Allavena, Attilio, 90
  Gondrand Worksite Massacre, 110–11
    Italian reprisals for, 111
  Hospitals, Italian attacks on,
    British Ambulance Service in Ethiopia (BASE) hospital bombed, 123–4
    House of Commons, questions asked, 124
    Macfie, Dr John, describes, 123–4
    Melly, Dr John, and, 123, 124, 171
    Red Cross symbols, alleged exploitation of by Ethiopians, 66, 124
    Swedish Red Cross field hospital, bombed, 65–6
    Hylander, Dr Fride, warns of dangers of mustard gas, 65
    Mussolini's concerns regarding, 67
    Retaliation for deaths of Minniti and Zannoni, 66
    Tafari Makonnen (American) Hospital, bombed
    Reports lead to curtailment of similar actions, 76–7
    US Government reaction to, 76
    Wells, Linton (US war correspondent), experiences, 72–5
  Minniti, Lieutenant Tito, 66
  Nuremberg, Italian, 'the world spared', 181
  Patriarca, Vincent, account of in US journal, 89
  Vaschi, Luigi, 89
  Zannoni, Sergeant Livio, 66